The PGA MANUAL OF GOLF

The PGA

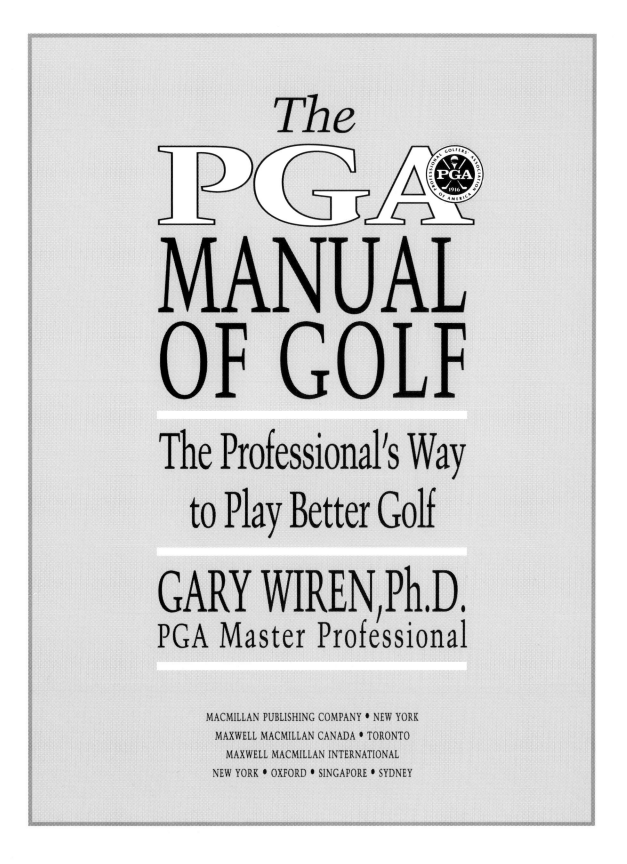

MANUAL OF GOLF

The Professional's Way to Play Better Golf

GARY WIREN, Ph.D.
PGA Master Professional

MACMILLAN PUBLISHING COMPANY • NEW YORK

MAXWELL MACMILLAN CANADA • TORONTO

MAXWELL MACMILLAN INTERNATIONAL

NEW YORK • OXFORD • SINGAPORE • SYDNEY

Macmillan Publishing Company   Maxwell Macmillan Canada, Inc.
866 Third Avenue   1200 Eglinton Avenue East
New York, NY 10022   Suite 200
                                    Don Mills, Ontario M3C 3N1

Macmillan Publishing Company is part of the Maxwell Communication
Group of Companies.

Library of Congress Cataloging-in-Publication Data

Wiren, Gary.
    The PGA manual of golf: the professional way to play better golf /
by Gary Wiren.
        p.   cm.
    Includes bibliographical references and index.
    ISBN 0–02–599291–0
    1. Golf.   2. Golf—United States.   I. Title.   II. Title:
Professional Golfers' Association of America manual of golf.
GV965.W725 1991   91–13642 CIP
796.352—dc20

10 9 8 7 6 5 4 3 2 1

Printed in the United States of America
Design by Robert Bull Design

Contents

ACKNOWLEDGMENTS

A great deal of appreciation is offered to the following people for their help and assistance: to the PGA members who served on the Teaching Manual Committee (see Introduction for listing), plus Tom Addis III, Frank Sluciak, Jerry Mowlds, Mike Hebron, Dr. Jim Suttie, Fred Griffin, Dick Harmon, Tony Morosco, George Lewis, Jerry Tucker, John Schlee, Jim McLean, Jon Reese, Peter Donahue and Jim Surber. Thanks for your contributions goes to Dr. Stan Plagenhoef, Dr. Richard Coop, Dr. Bob Rotella, Dr. Rolla Campbell, Dr. Ralph Mann, Dr. Ken Blanchard, Dr. De De Owens, Dr. David Miller, Dr. Orrin Hunt, Herb Boehm, Mark Wilson, Lloyd Kahn, Anders Janson, Dave Pelz, Frank Thomas, Don Krog, Swing Meyer, Joe Murdoch, Bill Holden, Janet Seagle and Joanne Winter.

Appreciation is expressed for the help from the USGA and National Golf Foundation, also to Acushnet, True Temper, Wilson, The Golf Works, The Chicago Golfer, Ohio Golfer, Svensk Golf and Shelter Publications.

Special recognition and thanks goes to the staff at Golf Digest and Golf World and former publishers Howard Gill and Bill Davis for their invaluable assistance on photographs. I'd also like to thank PAR GOLF magazine and International Golf Research of Japan and Bob Wilson of the National Amputee Golf Association for photos, as well as Jeff McBride and Steve Szurlej.

Thanks to the book's photographer, Allan Carlisle, for many of the instructional photographs in the text and to his main subjects PGA Professionals Buddy Antonopoulos, Scott Stilwell, David Thompson and Linda Edgely.

Thanks also to Chuck Passerelli for his beautiful art on the cover and chapter fronts and to GRR/Weston Ganoff Marini, including Greg Ganoff, Senior Vice President; Patrick Cowden, Art Director/Designer; Lynn Wheelan, Proofing Editor; Joanne Mack, Typesetting Director. And thanks to the PGA's Henry Thrower, Director of Research and Information Services, who has read this manual more times than anyone, except the author. Thanks to Colonel David L. Daub (retired) for editing the manual and Des Tolhurst for his assistance. Thanks to Joe O'Brien, Ralph Lima, Pat McCarthy, Martha Ferguson and Alicia Bollman from the PGA national office for their assistance in producing this manual and to the PGA Officers: Pat Rielly, Dick Smith, Gary Schaal and J.R. Carpenter, as well as to the Board of Directors and PGA Executive Director Jim Awtrey for their enthusiastic support of the project. Special thanks to PGA Past President Mickey Powell and other members of the PGA Board of Directors in his administration who approved the proposal for writing this book.

Each member of the PGA should be most grateful to the Tommy Armour Company and its president Mr. Bob MacNally for the considerable financial resources they provided in making the original version available to them.

Finally, thanks to my own family for the extreme patience and unselfishness they demonstrated while I borrowed time away from them to complete this important document for golf.

—Gary Wiren

Tommy Armour
G O L F

As a player, Tommy Armour was the first man to win all of the major championships of his day. His first professional victory was in the 1927 U.S. open at Oakmont Country Club in Pennsylvania, where he beat Harry Cooper in an 18-hole playoff. Three years later, he bested Gene Sarazen in match play one-up to win the PGA Championship. The following year he won the British Open, edging Argentinean Jose Jurado by one stroke. In all, Armour won a dozen professional tournaments in a playing career which spanned only eight years.

Armour was born in Edinburgh, Scotland, and was educated at the University of Edinburgh for a career in business and finance. When Great Britain entered the Great War in 1914, he joined the military, where he eventually attained the rank of staff major in the Royal Scots Army. Convalescing at a military hospital following severe battle wounds, Armour first took a serious interest in golf. Handsome, personable and a gifted storyteller, he probably could have been successful in almost any vocation, yet he chose golf.

In addition to his success as a player, Armour went on to become the greatest golf teacher of his era and perhaps the greatest teacher ever. He gave lessons to both professionals and amateurs during a distinguished teaching career that included such pupils as Lawson Little, Johnny Goodman, George Dunlap, and Babe Didrikson Zaharias. In fact, Armour was one of the first to support the efforts of women in golf, long before women's interests achieved recognition or fame.

As a club professional, Armour served at Medinah in Chicago, Tam-O-Shanter in Detroit and Congressional in Washington. But his best-known tenure, from 1929 to 1948, was at the Boca Raton Hotel and Resort in Florida. As head professional there, he gave lessons from under a large sun umbrella at what he called the outrageous price of $50 per lesson. This was in the days when a cup of coffee was only a nickel. His teaching skills were so renowned that his lesson book was filled six months in advance.

Armour had a unique teaching philosophy that all golfers would be well advised to heed. "Golf is not a simple game," he said. "But it should be taught in a simple fashion." This philosophy allowed him to diagnose and quickly correct the swing faults of his pupils. He never complicated a lesson by concentrating on more than one technique at a time. Tommy Armour's simple teaching philosophy is carried over in this publication.

In recognition of Tommy Armour, the golf company which bears his name underwrote a major portion of the cost of producing the *PGA Teaching Manual* on which this book is based. The original *PGA Teaching Manual* was written to help golf professionals with instructional techniques. Through the financial assistance of Tommy Armour Golf, PGA professionals across the world have been exposed to a sound, simple teaching philosophy through distribution of the *PGA Teaching Manual*. Tommy Armour Golf's support translates into better instruction and a more enjoyable game of golf for the more than 3.3 million amateur golfers worldwide.

INTRODUCTION

The objective of golf is simple, but the game of golf is complex. Moving a ball from here to there by propelling it with a club is a task easy to comprehend. But when you explore all that surrounds and affects this undertaking you have quite another matter indeed! The scope of golf's dimension can stretch even the most inquisitive mind. Consider just some of the major elements essential to golf: equipment, psychology, the human anatomy, rules, course architecture, training and practice, agronomy and course management . . . not to mention the often debated topic of swing technique. This is why teaching the game of golf is a challenge that requires a lifetime of learning. Done effectively, the result rewards both pupil and teacher. The purpose of this book is to help make the learning environment and experience more productive.

As one would expect, the book deals primarily with technique but that's far from the whole picture. There are materials and ideas which are totally new, such as in golf terminology. While many books offer glossaries of golf terms, this is the first time an attempt has been made to compile a "Terminology for the Learning of Golf," i.e., a standardized language. Some of golf's widely used terms such as "strong grip" and "weak grip" are replaced with more accurate ones; and where in the past several terms have been used to describe the same thing, a preferred selection is now made.

Other new offerings are a pupil screening test to help both teacher and pupil identify physical strengths and weaknesses before instruction gets underway. At the close of the book a serious call is made to all golfers to identify those elements that make golf an enjoyable experience and to promote the preservation of these elements.

Any attempt to compile a "complete book" on every aspect of learning golf would be a project ambitious beyond reason. To compile one that identifies and highlights a large number of the elements that constitute "good learning" is not. This is what the author has attempted to do.

The author has had considerable assistance and contributions to this book from a highly select group including some of the PGA of America's most respected teachers: Kent Cayce, Chuck Cook, Manuel de la Torre, Dick Farley, John Gerring, Hubby Habjan, Jack Lumpkin, Bunny Mason, Eddie Merrins, Ed Oldfield, Pat Rielly, Paul Runyan, Craig Shankland, Bill Strausbaugh, Guy Wimberly, and one of the game's great teaching professionals that we tragically lost, Davis Love. It has been an honor for me to work with all of them.

—Gary Wiren
PGA Master Professional and author

CHAPTER 1

HISTORY & EVOLUTION OF GOLF & GOLF TECHNIQUE

IN THE BEGINNING

Where and how the game of golf originated we really don't know. It probably depends on one's definition of terms. If one is talking simply about hitting a ball to a target with a stick, then there are several forerunners to golf, even from its earliest days. The Scots claim golf as "their game" but there have been challenges to that claim.

The Dutch appear to have the closest ties with golf. As early as the 13th century their literature contained references to "golf-like" games with medieval names such as "spel mitten colve" (play with club), "den bal mitta calven te slaen" (to hit the ball with the club) or "kolven" (club) for short. The Dutch master painters have left over 450 paintings and sketches of participants with club and ball playing a game in Holland most certainly resembling golf. (f1-1) (Illus. 1-1)

Commerce between Scotland and Holland over the North Sea route flourished from the beginning of the Middle Ages. However, unfavorable winds or bad weather would frequently result in sailors and traders being "grounded" and spending a generous amount of time in each other's respective country. What better way to enjoy their leisure than participate in the fa-

Illus 1-1 Engraving by Jan Luyken of Holland (1649–1712) entitled "The Club." (from *Early Golf* by van Hengel)

vorite local sports. In a few instances, some of the players shown in the Dutch pictures wore kilts indicating they were Scottish visitors (Illus 1-2) If one compares the written rather than artistic record, he'd see the first written word of golf in Scotland was James I's edict of 1457 declaring golf illegal. In Holland an earlier written record is 1297. It described a cross-country version of a game with four players to a side, playing four holes with the objective being to strike the doors of selected buildings along the way with the ball, the equivalent of "holing out." A barrel of beer went to the victors, indicating that celebrating at the "19th hole" is a long-standing tradition.

f1-1 *Dutch golf historian Steven J.H. van Hengel spent 30 years researching early golf-like games of the lowlands. His work culminated in the book* Early Golf *published in 1982.*

Illus 1-2 The "golfer" preparing to hit is wearing a kilt, yet is obviously playing in Holland. (From Van de Velde painting of 1668)

Scots and Dutch jointly attended festivals, fairs and large market gatherings, where among the items sold were leather-covered balls stuffed with feathers or cow hair, two early-style golf balls, the other being of wood. It is a matter of record that the Dutch provided the Scots with feathery balls for their golf up until the middle 1600s, at which time a ballmaker was appointed by the Scottish king to better balance the trade deficit because feathery golf balls were expensive. Finally, it is also a fact that golf in Scotland was largely an East Coast game, played in the very port towns that harbored the vessels that traded with the Dutch. (Illus 1-3) The connection is obvious.

One might surmise from this information that a strong case could be made for Holland being the true founder of golf. But looking beyond the Dutch border, history records Belgians played a similar stick and ball game called "chole," the French "jeu-de-mail" or "pall mall," which came from Italy. (Illus 1-4) But these were one-club contests, with some of those singular implements being used to perform more than one type of shot. (Illus 1-5)

The origins of all these games very probably stemmed from another stick and ball game played by occupying soldiers of the Roman legions when that empire covered most of Europe. "Paganica" was the name of the game, meaning "leather sphere containing feathers." Is it mere coincidence that the same type ball

Illus 1-3 Golf in Scotland began as an East Coast game in the harbor towns across from Holland. Golf is believed to have been played in these localities before 1650. (from *Golf in the Making* by Ian Henderson and David Stirk)

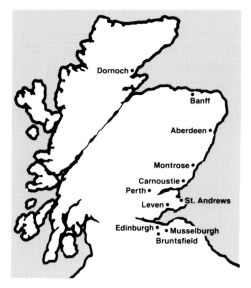

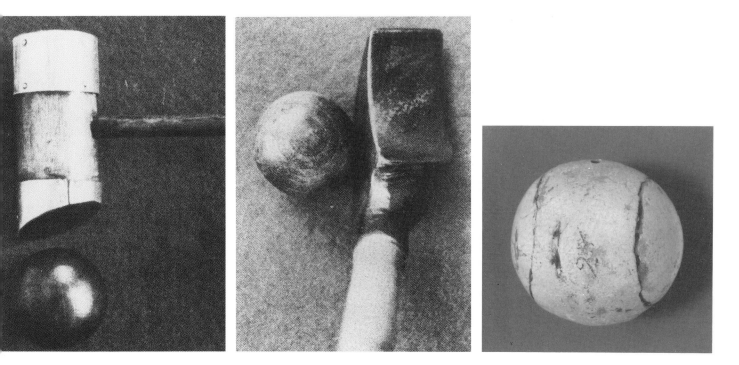

Ilus 1-4 Mallet and ball used for the game of Mail. The flat side was used for driving and putting, the angled side for shots requiring loft. (from *Early Golf* by van Hengel)

Illus 1-5 This club was used in the Belgian game of chole. Like the mallet used in the game of Mail, it had two lofts used for striking the ball. The shape dates from the middle ages. (from *Early Golf* by van Hengel)

Illus 1-6 A "feathery" golf ball from Scotland played until the middle 1800s. Earlier versions were also stuffed with cow hair or made of wood.

was played by the Dutch and later by golfers in Scotland up to the 1850s? (Illus 1-6)

An apocryphal story suggesting that golf was invented by a shepherd who found both challenge and amusement in striking a pebble to a selected destination may not be so fanciful, although the shepherd probably wasn't a Scot. Evidence the fact that in Western Germany, "the hunting law of 1338" stated that the grazing rights for local shepherds could be extended into the forest there as far as they could hit a pebble with one stroke. The length of these drives was marked by permanent stones, the "Hirtensteine" (shepherd's stones). Some of these can still be found today near Frankfort Golf Club. (The long-hitter even had some advantage in the early days.) Finally, a very interesting old print has recently been published in Japan showing a game that certainly looks like golf being played in China during the Ming dynasty, 1368 to 1644. Again, though resembling golf, it, in fact, was not. (Illus 1-7)

Who invented golf? Was it created by the Dutch, French, Belgians, Germans, Romans, Chinese, or some other nation? Certainly all had similar games which may have contributed to the eventual development of the game. (Illus 1-8) But golf as we know it, played with a variety of clubs, not just one, over an extended area, using a small ball and with the object being to stroke it into a hole, is a format not only developed by the Scots but propagated by them around the world. They deserve the credit for the game as it is played today. (Illus 1-9) (For additional information see Appendixes I-A and I-B.)

"Remember, this game was invented by the same people who think good music comes from bagpipes."
—(Sign on Chicago area golf course between an extremely difficult green and the next tee).

Illus **1-7** Ladies playing a "golf-like" game in China during Ming dynasty. (from *Sports in Ancient China*)

Illus **1-8** A sketch of a Chilean Indian boy, taken from Charles Darwin's book of the exploration of South America c. 1835.

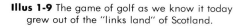

Illus **1-9** The game of golf as we know it today grew out of the "links land" of Scotland.

GOLF'S FIRST BOOM IN SCOTLAND

During the last half of the 18th century golf had a great growth spurt in Scotland, despite the fact that daily life was demanding in this rugged, spartan country. But the Scottish people are tough, industrious and adventuresome. Many Scots left their country to make a living in other lands and took golf, their sport-religion, with them. Those who came to the United States were no exception.

There is considerable evidence that golf was played at several locations in the United States prior to 1888, which is traditionally given as the year golf originated here. The St. Andrew's Golf Club of Yonkers, N.Y., was founded in that year and has been in continuous existence since then. But if 1888 is the year in which golf supposedly originated in the U.S.A., what were they doing in Charleston, S.C., in 1743 when a shipment of ninety-six clubs and four hundred and thirty-two balls came from Leith, Scotland? Why then was there a golf club formed there in 1786 and another in 1795 in Savannah, Georgia? And how does one explain the ad that ran in the Rivington Royal Gazette (Albany, N.Y.) April 21, 1779, which offered golf clubs and balls for sale? The answer, of course, is that someone was playing golf in these locales. Old newspaper clippings, letters and magazine articles exist which describe similar activity prior to 1888 in all of the following states: Massachusetts, Iowa, Nebraska, Kentucky, Pennsylvania, West Virginia, Florida, North Dakota, California, Colorado and Texas. Yes, the Scots liked their golf well enough to introduce it wherever they went.

THE TRANSPLANTED PROFESSIONALS

"Old" Willie Dunn was the first of the Scottish professionals to serve as a golfing "pilgrim missionary." He went south of the River Tweed to Blackheath outside of London in 1851, later to be joined by his twin brother, Jamie. Fittingly, Willie's son, Willie Dunn Jr., was one of the first golf professionals brought to the United States to teach, play, make clubs and build courses. Young Dunn, an early professional at Shinnecock Hills, saw great promise for golf in this new land and stayed to design over 15 courses, among them Jekyll Island, Baltimore Country Club, Scarsdale Country Club, and Philadelphia Country Club. He also designed and made golf clubs, including the now very collectible one-piece driver, and developed the first golf shop in this country at Shinnecock. He personally was responsible for bringing to the U.S. some twenty young Scottish professionals by generously assisting in their passage and early subsistence. Herb Graffis relates in *History of the PGA*, "The Scottish founding fathers of professional golf in the United States disproved the legend that their countrymen are tighter than a warped door. The contrary was generally true—they were inclined to be too generous because they had little experience in handling money." Similar scenarios developed as names like Jim and Dave Foulis, Fred Herd, Harry Turpie, Alex Taylor, William Yeomans, Dave Bell, Jock Hutchison, Bob Simpson and

Laurie Auchterlonie were appointed to golf courses in the Chicago area. In New York, William Gourlay, Robert White, Alex Pirie, Willie Anderson, Gil Nicholls, and Jack Mackie were among the Scots who contributed to the game. Other "apostles of golf" like James and Stewart Maiden, M.J. Brady, William Hoare, George Sargent, J.R. Thompson, Charles Adams and many others were located in New England, the South, the Midwest and California. They were largely a gathering of Scots with a few English joining them. (Illus 1-10)

Some of the new arrivals from famous golfing families in Scotland like The Dunns, Smiths, Forgans and Gourlays were already expert players, teachers and clubmakers. (Illus 1-11) But others were brick masons, carpenters, fishermen, blacksmiths or sailors by trade when they left Scotland. They were golf professionals when they arrived in the United States. Playing the game was their birthright. Add the marvelous accent and it gave them credibility in a country hungry for golf and as yet unini-

Illus 1-10 A group of early professionals and caddies in America, including three-time U.S. Open Champ Willie Anderson, shown with his arm around another Open Champ, Alex Smith. (Photo courtesy USGA)

Illus 1-11 Early Scottish and English professionals advertised their talents as teachers, players and manufacturers.

tiated to its vagaries. As a group these men were honest, hard-working, proud and unquestionably forthright. They had a love for golf that was greatly instrumental in the rapid spread of the game in this country. Evidence of this is that in 1888 American golf was played on a three-hole cow pasture in Yonkers, N.Y. But by 1900 the country could boast of 1,000 courses!

The golfing styles of these immigrant Scot–English professionals were for the most part very individual. What they taught was what worked for them at home, in the British Isles. Several factors influenced choice of style: (1) Course architecture and agronomy, (2) Weather and clothing, (3) Equipment and (4) Styles of the leading players of the day. (f1-2)

f1-2 *One could generally recognize a player's region of the country by his swing. The St. Andrews's swing was long and flowing; Hoylake was an open stance with the ball toward the right foot; North Berwick was with the ball played forward.*

COURSE ARCHITECTURE AND AGRONOMY

God was golf's first architect, man was his assistant. The earliest courses that hugged the coastline of Scotland were known as "links" because they "linked" the arable land to the sea. Nature, using wind and water as its machinery, shaped the dunes, knolls, ridges and hollows. (Illus 1-12)

This terrain was ideal for golf, as it provided open expanses inhabited only by birds, rabbits and foxes. It was adorned by gorse (that unmanageable plant that will tear the club from a player's hands), heather and broom. Add sand, mixtures of wild fescue, marram, bent and meadow grass and you had the "links." Links land was productive for little other than walking the dog, for laying out wash to dry, and for sports, particularly golf. For course construction there was no earth-moving equipment to create elevated greens or to place water hazards and bunkers in the direct line of carry for an approach shot to a green. Bunkers were in abundance, appearing as gaping chasms which often bordered the rough, or demonically placed in the fairways and at greenside. Yet, they did not generally block the entrance to the green. This influenced shot selection, encouraging the use of the run-up shot instead of pitches and the low hook for full shots, rather than a high trajectory style.

Agronomy was not the science it is today. At fabled St. Andrews, "Old Tom" Morris was "keeper of the greens" in addition to his duties as teacher, clubmaker, ballmaker and player. (Illus 1-13) "Keeper of the greens" meant supervising or personally being available for cutting new cups, tending the greens and hoping for nature's cooperation, which provided the only watering system . . . rain. Fairway irrigation was still a century away, so the ground was hard and the low-flying running ball was the shot to hit. Under those conditions and with greens equally hard, today's wedge would be virtually useless. A player had to learn to pitch and run the ball.

Illus 1-12 A true links course, shaped by nature more than by man.

Illus 1-13 Tom Morris, St. Andrews' professional, eulogized as "a man who never had an enemy."

Some of the same factors that molded the techniques of our Scottish pioneer players still exert their influence today. Course design is becoming more penal. There is far more water; housing developments surround most new courses with their accompanying out-of-bounds stakes; more rough and natural grass areas are a trend; greens are elevated, undulating and heavily protected by bunkers; and modern earth-moving equipment can make uneven lies from the flattest swamp or desert. (Illus 1-14) We are returning to some features tht were predominant in the old-style links-type courses.

Unfortunately many of the most talked about modern courses are too difficult for the average amateur player to find enjoyable on a regular basis. If the game is to continue its popularity, golfers must enjoy the experience. Shooting big numbers on courses too hard for all but the most accomplished players is not conducive to "having a good time."

Course conditioning today is vastly improved over the days of knickers and Norfolk jackets. Good lies in the fairway are the rule, not the exception. Putting surfaces are truer

Illus 1-14 Modern earth-moving equipment can provide any type shaping desired. Today golf architects often move millions of cubic yards of earth to create a golf setting. (from *100 Greatest Golf Courses*)

and the Stimpmeter is creating a desire by some to want them even faster—a trend not necessarily advisable. All of these influence playing style. Faster greens promote arm and shoulder putting; rough and out-of-bounds discourage trying for the extra distance that comes from the hooking tee shot; elevated and protected greens call for higher trajectory irons and more frequent use of the sand wedge for pitching.

WEATHER AND CLOTHING

Links courses in coastal towns on the North Sea are accustomed to more than a light breeze. Evidence is the wooden club of the 1800s known as the "driving putter," used for keeping the ball knee-high off the ground on very windy days. The need for such a club is clearly appreciated if one considers the story of Maitland Dougall of St. Andrews, who actually added lead to his ball on a competition day when a near gale was blowing, then came in the winner. In conditions such as these the golfer most certainly was at an advantage by keeping his shots low.

The weather in Scotland is not only windy, but a chill can blow in off the sea during July which makes one think it's December. Thus, heavy clothing was part of the proper golfing costume, but certainly a disadvantage for the swing. Getting a wide extension of the arms to create "high hands" in the backswing was next to impossible with three layers of wool and tweed. ((Illus 1-15) It was far easier for the player to bend the left arm and turn the whole body away from the ball. One popular style was for the club to point across the target line at the top of the backswing and come to rest close to the neck before starting down, then to use a "sweeping style" swing coming forward. (Illus 1-16)

Modern professional golf is a fair-weather game. The players follow the sun. Of course they experience heavy wind and occasional rain, but these conditions are the exception. One of the last events on the present PGA Tour is played on the Island of Maui in Hawaii. Were the Tour to play there every week for two years, the players' swings would certainly change to

Illus 1-15 Golf clothing of the late 1800s was more for fashion than for function.

Illus 1-16 Because the early clubs had so much shaft torque, the most effective swing technique employed a long, gradually accelerating sweeping motion. (from *The Complete Golfer*)

Illus 1-17 A set of clubs from the middle 1800s Only two irons, one for scraping the ball from tight or sand lies and one for extracting the ball from ruts.

combat the wind. The point is, conditions make a difference in the development of a player's technique or style. Playing consistently in favorable weather unencumbered with heavy clothing and free from buffeting winds promotes a freer swing, a wider arc and an aggressive style.

The business suit of the day for the modern professional is a comfortable, non-binding, short-sleeved golf shirt and slacks that can expand and contract to accommodate body movement. When a player can fully wind and extend his arms there is less need to rely on the hands for power, so the hands need only "transmit" the power rather than create it.

EQUIPMENT

The construction of the tools used to accomplish a task influences how they are handled. Golf balls and clubs are no different. In feather ball days before 1850 a set of clubs was composed primarily of woods—a play club (driver), a variety of wooden spoons (i.e., long spoon, mid spoon, short spoon and baffing spoon) plus a wooden putter—and two irons (a small-headed track iron for getting the ball out of wagon ruts or animal tracks, and another large-faced, less-lofted iron for scraping the ball from tight lies). (Illus 1-17) The shafts of the early clubs were first made of hazel and later of ash; both tended to be very whippy. The whippiness greatly influenced how rapidly the player could accelerate the club and still control the direction of the face. With a long-nosed whippy shaft wood, the torque was difficult to manage, particularly if one tried to change direction rapidly. To minimize torque, the ball was swept from the tee with a body and arm motion more than it was hit with the hands. This is one of the reasons why backswings became so long—a very gradual forward acceleration required it to be that way. The long backswing was aided by placing the left foot closer to the target line than the right foot in what today we'd call an extremely "closed" stance.

FEATHERY TO "GUTTIE"

The feather ball gave way to the gutta-percha in the 1850s, economics being one of the overriding factors. A ballmaker laboring ten hours per day could only produce 4 to 5 feather balls, causing them to be very expensive. Thus, golf basically became a game for the wealthy. The "guttie" ball, which could be mass manufactured in molds, changed that. (Illus 1-18) The less expensive "guttie" was a great boon to the spread of the game, but the player found that a mishit shot with this much harder ball produced an uncomfortable shock to the hands. This ball also distressed the face of the woods, creating the need for insert materials because the faces couldn't last under the beating from the harder ball. But the shock remained. Clubmakers sought to alleviate this discomfort by padding the grips with wool underlisting, thus making the grips larger. Larger grips required larger hands or a grip style that grasped the club more in the palms than the fingers. Because the grips were too large for most people to grip in the fingers, the palm grip became widely taught. ((Illus 1-19)

In the 1850s, concurrent with the decline of the feather ball, hickory shafts from Tennessee U.S.A. were introduced in St. Andrews by the clubmaking firm of Forgan & Sons. This was a shaft that was "steelier," had less whip, and allowed the player to hit rather than sweep the

Illus 1-18 The gutta-percha ball revolutionized the game by helping make it more affordable for the masses.

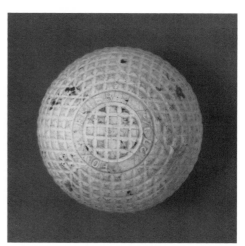

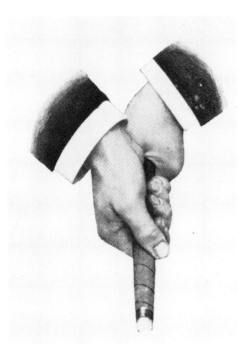

Illus 1-19 Grasping the club in the palms was a necessity from 1850–1900 since the grips were "built up" to cushion the shock from the gutta-percha ball.

ball from the tee. The long-nosed, splice-headed clubs eventually became obsolete (shortly after 1885) because their toe-to-heel length caused too much torque when force from the hands was applied. Thus, a more compact clubhead evolved.

During the 1890s Mr. Henry Lamb proved to golf skeptics that a convex, rather than a concave or even straight face, results in longer, more accurate shots with a wood club. His driver, made by professional Bob Simpson, was called "the bulger."

The "guttie" ball, though then in general use, presented a problem. It was difficult to get sufficient height on the shots. Players found that if they moved closer to the ball and made a more upright swing, the ball would fly higher. The more upright swing was aided by making shorter clubs. When comparing a play club (driver) from the early 1800s with a Vardon driver of the late 1890s, the Vardon wood is three inches shorter. In addition to moving closer to the ball, players changed their stance. Many players, like the great triumvirate Harry Vardon, James Braid and J.H. Taylor, (Illus 1-20) played from an open stance on all shots,

Illus 1-20 J.H. Taylor, British Open Champion, shown playing from an extremely open stance, which suited the "guttie" ball (from *Golf Faults Illustrated*)

Illus 1-21 Harry Vardon, one of the game's great players, demonstrating his effortless swing (top of the backswing) (from *The Complete Golfer*)

Illus 1-22 Harry Vardon (finish of the swing) (from *The Complete Golfer*)

which also assisted in getting the ball "up." This trio amassed 16 of 20 British Open titles between 1894 and 1914, with Vardon garnering six. His effortless style was unquestionably superior to his predecessors and was the model for the next generation of players. (Illus 1-21, 1-22) Backswings became shorter with some players not even reaching parallel with a driver, a position that would have been most unorthodox fifty years earlier. The shorter swing also contributed to the tendency to use the hands and forearms for power, a style that would have been most improbable had the firmer hickory not replaced the whippy ash and hazel shafts. Tight, bulky jackets still made it difficult to fully extend the arms, so a bent left arm at the top of the swing continued to be common among most of the leading players.

THE HASKELL'S EFFECT

Another evolution in equipment that further influenced playing styles was Coburn Haskell's ball patented in 1899. (Illus 1-23) It was a three-piece ball with a center core around which was

Illus 1-23 The three-piece rubber core Haskell ball, because of its greater distance, made many great courses obsolete or necessitated that they be lengthened. (from *Encyclopedia of Golf Collectibles*)

wound rubber thread, then covered with a molded gutta-percha material. It took a few years of experimenting to develop the appropriate core, the best method of winding the rubber thread and the most effective cover material. The cores started small in size, the covers thick. Eventually the cores became larger and the covers thinner as that combination provided a truer flight. Everything imaginable was tried in the ball's center: mercury, human hair, soap, blood, loose steel balls, compressed air, wood, treacle, glycerine, castor oil, honey, pulverized metal, earth, rubber, cork, celluloid and what turned out best, water. Eventually water or glycerine was injected into a rubber circular sac, then frozen so the winding process would not distort the core's shape. The original idea was tested on baby bottle nipples. Once the major imperfections were eliminated, the new Haskell ball proved considerably more forgiving than the "guttie"; it flew higher, it shocked less when mishit, but most important was the fact that it went 25–30 yards farther. The "guttie" was obsolete by 1904.

With the Haskell, it was soon discovered that balata for a cover material created a softer feel off the clubface, which permitted the padding under grips to be reduced, allowing a corresponding reduction in the size of the grip. During this transition period the modern method of gripping the club evolved, more in the fingers than palms. The Vardon overlapping grip, which is universally accepted today, was not really originated by Vardon. Initially, it was used by Mr. F.A. Fairlie of North Berwick, then copied by the first British PGA president, J.H. Taylor, who was Harry Vardon's fiercest competitor. Vardon took notice, tried it and liked it. Being the most famous golfer of his day, he was accorded the honor of the grip's invention.

With the grip more in the fingers, the hands were rotated inward toward the thumbs, which favored a stronger left-hand position, showing three knuckles. (Illus 1-24) This caused most of the leading players to cup the left wrist more at address and at the top of the swing than professionals do today. Because the grip now ran diagonally across the left hand, the player

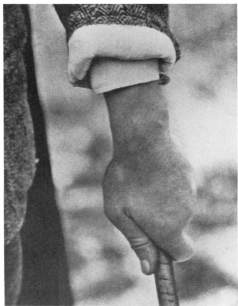

Illus 1-24 The strongly rotated "closed-face position" of the left-hand grip which was popular during the first half of the 20th century.

Illus 1-25 The contrast in face depth between a feather-ball-era play club and a modern "bomber face" driver is extreme.

Illus 1-26 Bobby Jones had a great influence on the teaching and playing style of American golf. (from *The Bobby Jones Story*)

tended to be less firm at the top, even to the point of slightly opening up the last three fingers of the left hand. Some noted professionals, including Vardon, taught that the gripping emphasis should be between the thumb and finger of each hand, claiming that these were the control centers. Keep in mind that what is being described here represents trends. There were a few players in the early 1900s who had elements of a much more modern swing, but they were a decided minority.

One more interesting sidelight to the Haskell ball was that it compressed more than its predecessors when struck and therefore stayed on the clubface longer. This created more backspin and consequently more height. At the turn of the century the average depth of a wood clubface was about 1³⁄₁₆ inches. This new response from the ball, coupled with the shallow-faced clubs then in use, produced skied shots. Accordingly, wood clubs and irons soon began to feature deeper faces. Today's "bomber" face driver can be a staggering 2¼ inches deep compared to Allan Robertson's ¹⁵⁄₁₆ of an inch in his "play club" of the 1840s. (Illus 1-25)

A SHIFT BACK

With a higher-flying ball, the pendulum swung back to a closed stance for long shots, but not as exaggerated as that used by the early feathery player. The new, slightly closed setup allowed players to again have a longer backswing so that the club frequently passed parallel at the top on a driver shot. This was true primarily of players in this country from the 1920s through the 1950s. Not all of the top players adopted the closed stance and long backswing but those who did, like the great Bobby Jones (Illus 1-26), had an influence on millions of others.

THE INTRODUCTION OF STEEL

It was during the end of Jones' competitive career that the next great equipment advance occurred, and what a change it made! Steel shafts were legalized by the USGA for competition in 1925 and by the Royal & Ancient in 1931. The performance of steel may have been no better at the time, but the need for change was critical because the hickory forests were being depleted. Functional steel shafts had been around for longer than most people realize. A patent had been taken out for a solid steel shaft in 1894 and a usable set made then still exists. The Lard patent steel shaft with holes punched in it to lighten its weight and give it some degree of flex was patented in 1914. The drawn tubular version in use today was to come later. Steel reduced torque—less torque meant one could swing harder at the ball and still maintain clubface control. The USGA's fear that the steel shaft would make the ball go farther, thus forcing courses to be lengthened, was not unfounded. That's exactly what happened!

There have been many innovations in golf equipment over the past half century: different materials for shafts, metal woods and graphite heads for iron and woods, frequency matching of shafts, redistribution of weight in irons and putters to provide perimeter weighting, improvements in aerodynamics and materials for balls, and production of continuous sets of iron woods or wood irons. All have contributed to making the game easier, but none has had the significant influence on the swing styles of leading players as did the change in shafts from hickory to steel.

Illus 1-27 One of the game's greatest athletes, Sam Snead, may have made more beautiful in-balance swings over a lifetime than anyone in golf's history.

LEARNING A NEW SWING

The new shaft caused players of the era, the Hogans, Sneads, Nelsons and others, to modify the hickory swing that they grew up with as caddies. Snead's more accurately was not a "hickory swing" but a "swamp maple swing." The legendary story of Sam carving out his own first wood club from a swamp maple is fact, not fiction. Snead's swing, which has some resemblance to that of Jones' with its impeccable rhythm and slightly inside-to-out loop, could work with a rubber hose or a sledge hammer. (Illus 1-27) Hogan and Nelson both fought a hook with the steel shaft. After a recommendation from Henry Picard to learn to "slice the ball," Hogan adjusted his left wrist to a cupped position at the top of the swing (Illus 1-28), thereby opening the clubface and closing the door to inconsistency in his game. The low hot

Illus 1-28 Hogan's cupped left wrist at the top of the backswing allowed him to better control the ball and not fight the hook. (from *Golf With Your Hands*)

hook that he'd grown up with was gone and the controlled Hogan fades became legend. Although naturally right-handed, Hogan began his golf as a "left-hander," because the original club given to him was left-handed. According to Jimmy Demaret, Ted Longworth, the pro at Glen Garden Country Club in Fort Worth where Hogan caddied as a youngster, convinced Ben to switch over to the right side. An equally reliable source says that the real story is that a tough caddie, older and bigger than Ben, didn't like the fact Hogan was swinging left-handed and told him if he ever caught him doing it again he'd "kick the hell out of him." It was

Nelson, also a product of the same caddy yard at Glen Garden as Hogan, worked the hook out in a different way. Early in his career he was employed as an assistant in Galveston, Texas, where it is traditionally very windy. During practice sessions he tried keeping the ball low to control it, while at the same time not hooking. By sitting deeper in his knees during the weight shift toward the target, and making the back of his left hand face the target longer, he solved both problems. His style was

completely unorthodox at the time, upright, flat wrist throughout the swing and overly bent knees at impact. (Illus 1-29) But his style helped lead the transition of the golf swing from the classical era into the modern era.

THE STAR PLAYERS

Historically, golf has presented its brightest stars in clusters of three. The first triumvirate of greats, Vardon, Braid and Taylor, dominated the game on both sides of 1900; from the 1920s it was Hagen, Sarazen and Jones. Beginning in the 1940s, Nelson, Snead and Hogan; finally, the most recent, from the 1960s, Palmer, Nicklaus and Player. There were certainly other names with impressive playing records, in particular foreign players like Henry Cotton, Peter Thompson, Bobby Locke, Roberto DeVicenzo, and Americans Cary Middlecoff, Lloyd Mangrum, Jimmy Demaret, Tom Watson and Billy Casper. Nevertheless, the groups of three seem to stand out. In each era there has been a lull or regrouping between the formation of such trios. If history repeats itself, the next triumvirate would be forming in the early 1990s to dominate until the beginning of the 21st century. If current trends continue it would be a very international group.

THE LADIES' ROLE

One can probably assume that women participated in the games that were forerunners to golf as well as early golf itself. The first written record of a woman playing the game of golf as we know it is, interestingly, a royal example. It is documented that in 1567 Mary Queen of Scots was seen playing golf too soon after the death of her husband, Lord Darnley. This cast a shadow on her character and helped lead to her demise. No further record of ladies at such play appeared for almost two hundred years, although most certainly there was activity. During the 1700s the "fisher lassies" of Mussleburgh, who could do the work of men, played

Illus 1-29 The great Byron Nelson using what at the time was considered an unorthodox "sitting motion" at the start of his forward swing. It was a model for later players. (from *Byron Nelson's Winning Golf*)

Illus 1-30 The first female "immortal" golfer, Lady Margaret Scott, in the typical clothing of the late 1800s. (from *A Pictorial History Of Golf*)

"men's games" as well, including golf. The first ladies' club appeared in 1867, and by 1886 had attracted 500 members. Appropriately, it was named the St. Andrews Ladies' Golf Club.

It was popular at this time for the ladies to have their own courses, which were considerably scaled down in length. Contributing to the need for this practice was the fact that the female golf costume was not conducive to the body positions necessary for long hitting. This was soon to change. With the formation of the L.G.U. (Ladies' Golf Union) in Britain in 1893, women's golf attire and playing standards made a giant step forward. The practice of separate courses for women diminished as they became part of the regular club, to include joining the men in mixed play.

Lady Margaret Scott won the first three British L.G.U. crowns by outclassing the field with scores in the 80s. (Illus 1-30) England later produced one of the greatest women players of all time, Joyce Wethered. Her brother, Roger, was the Amateur Champion and a Walker Cupper. Yet, according to the family, Roger was but 2 to 7 strokes better than sister Joyce *from the same tees*, depending on the type course.

In the United States the first women's championship was conducted in 1895 by the USGA at Meadowbrook on Long Island. It was won by Mrs. Charles Brown with a not-so-impressive 132 for eighteen holes. But that standard, too, was soon to change as women players like Beatrix Hoyt, the Curtis sisters—Margaret and Harriet, Dorothy Campbell Hurd, Glenna Collett Vare, Virginia Van Wie and Helen Hicks won national titles and competed favorably overseas. The women competitors played largely as amateurs until 1948 when the LPGA was formed, led by two incomparable dynamos, Patty Berg and Mildred "Babe" Didrikson Zaharias. (f1-3) (Illus 1-31, 1-32) It didn't take long for the women's circuit to attract many outstanding women players: Betsy Rawls, Louise Suggs and the lady who may have had the best golf swing of all-time, Mickey Wright. Since then, Kathy Whitworth has become the most prolific winner in LPGA history, while she, Joanne Carner and Nancy Lopez Knight have become more recent female additions to the World Golf Hall of Fame. (Illus 1-33)

Golf equipment changes have helped women to find greater enjoyment in the game. The Haskell ball was easier to hit and traveled a greater distance; clothing became more appropriate for the action necessary to produce an effective

f1-3 *Patty Berg turned professional in 1940, prior to the LPGA's formation.*

Illus 1-31 The irrepressible Patty Berg, the first of the women professionals and golf's great ambassador. (See Appendix 1-C)

Illus 1-32 "Babe" Zaharias attracted crowds wherever she performed because she knew not only how to play golf but also how to give the people a great show.

Illus 1-33 Nancy Lopez's presence provided the LPGA Tour with a shining star, a great role model and gallery draw, liked and admired by everyone.

f1-4 *Harry Vardon in his prime played wooden-shafted men's irons but ladies' woods.*

swing; steel shafts became available and being lighter than wood shafts, were easier for women to handle. (f1-4)

Women golfers struggled for equality and sometimes even opportunity at courses which were "Eveless Edens." This, despite their contributions to the game. The ladies gave support to early American clubs like Shinnecock Hills when their great interest in the game helped stimulate male participation. The first workable handicap system was developed by the British L.G.U. and later copied by the men. Women enjoyed golf despite early limitations at some clubs. Rules such as, "Women are allowed to use but one club, the putter," or, "Women can play every other Saturday from May to October," are now passé! Pioneer women competitors were described as "being equipped with 4 or 5 clubs, an India rubber tee, three good balls in respectable condition and ready for all serious competitions for that season."

A MORE RECENT TRIUMVIRATE

Swing changes in the last generation have leaned more toward subtle refinement rather than drastic revolution. Analysis of technique has improved with the availability of high-speed video and photography for both teachers and players to study.

Observing the style of the most recent triumvirate, Palmer, Nicklaus, and Player, would certainly not lead you to a single definitive conclusion as to the one and only acceptable swing model. The principle you *would* affirm is the reality of individual difference.

ARNOLD PALMER

In his prime, Arnold Palmer's swing might not have looked as graceful as the fluid classical motion of Sam Snead, but his technique was

Illus 1-34 Arnold Palmer possessed the strength to fashion an unorthodox but highly effective style.

JACK NICKLAUS

Jack Nicklaus, ''Player of the Century'' and holder of more major titles than any one golfer in history, blended many of the popular modern elements into one swing. He had a neutral hand position for the grip, square on-line setup, one-piece square-faced takeaway, a wide arc, a big shoulder turn with his high hands tending to be upright, flat left wrist position at the top of the backswing, strong leg action with both knees flexed at impact, a feeling of left-side dominance, back of the left hand facing the hole at impact and a big finish with the clubhead pointing toward the ground behind the back, but still with the last three fingers of his left hand holding on in control.

There were some idiosyncrasies of the Nicklaus action. The flying right elbow in his early career was the result of continually trying to get the widest possible arc, but this contributed to his incredible distance. Lifting his left heel so high on the driver swing was caused by a big upper body turn over a lower body that wasn't as flexible as players with a more slender build.

Illus 1-35 Jack Nicklaus used a big turn and ''high hands'' to help generate his great power.

unquestionably effective. He proved one could attack the ball with an aggressive tempo while still successfully timing the clubface back to a square position. Palmer's reputation for accurate driving backs up this observation. One of the important elements of his style was the left-hand grip position. The club was moved slightly out of the fingers and deeper into the palm, where only one knuckle was visible at address. To keep the clubface from opening, the left wrist was arched at the top of his backswing. This kept the hands firm and the swing taut. Power came more from the body and arms with a hitter's motion. Palmer wound the upper half of his body over the lower for greater torque, a style which was to be copied by many. Palmer demonstrated quite dramatically that the left wrist position at impact, ''bowed to the target'' and ''slightly arched downward,'' could be maintained throughout the swing. Granted, it required strong hands and arms, but he had them. (Illus 1-34)

Keeping his head perfectly still gave him a slight reverse weight shift on the long clubs, a position that he altered later in his career. (Illus 1-35)

GARY PLAYER

It is more difficult to critique Gary Player's swing during his most productive years because analysis would depend upon which swing he was using. No player in history has been so successful while changing his technique from one season to the next, sometimes from one week to the next. Player was frightfully inquisitive and would politely listen to anything or anybody about the golf swing—and more often than not, try what was told him. Fortunately, he was very discriminating and could quickly sift and sort the good advice from the bad. More important, he had confidence in whatever he was doing at the time and made it work.

The comment on Player's tendency to try different approaches is not intended to criticize Player's golfing techniques, which for the most part were quite sound, it's just that at times it was difficult to tie them down. He believed that the grip should be in the fingers and the setup

Illus 1-36 Gary Player has always been aggressive in his shot-making style.

of the hands at address nearly the same as at impact. Square alignment in the stance and an extended, almost rigid left arm at address with the right elbow tucked more than most, further characterized his style. This was modified somewhat in later Senior Tour competition. Throughout Player's career he maintained a straight left arm in the backswing and liked to have the right elbow not wander far from his side. A strongly inward-braced right knee at address, a big body turn with the club past parallel with the driver and very active use of the legs to accentuate a "delayed hit" were all swing characteristics identified with the "man in black." (Illus 1-36)

Player's contributions on how to more effectively play the game came more from his attitude than his technique. He was a dogged competitor under all circumstances and would never give up. His dedication to physical fitness has served as a role model to help the next generation of players realize the value of "training for golf."

CONCLUSION

Palmer, Nicklaus and Player were certainly different from one another in many ways, while very much the same in one—they were champions. And so it has been with the top golfers of every era, *a variety in swing style has been the rule rather than the exception.* There have been changing trends in technique that the best players followed. Today, for example, when observing a broad spectrum of the current generation of top players, *there is a decided de-emphasis of active hand action with less forearm rotation. This has been supplanted by increased upper body release with a slightly flatter swing and more lateral motion of the upper body in the long game.* Yet, each is an individual. Many players, past and present exhibit nonconforming fundamentals in play which are actually breakthroughs that became trends in the next generation. It's called *evolution.* It has definitely happened to the golf swing.

CHAPTER 2

SCIENCE APPLIED
TO GOLF:
Cause & Effect

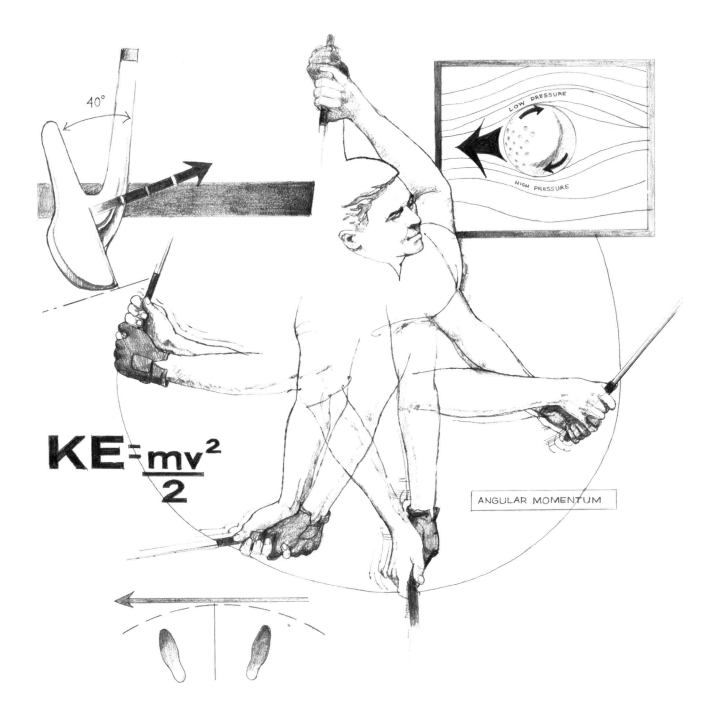

Any in-depth study into the mechanics of golf performance could lead one into several branches of science. *Kinesiology* (also called bio-mechanics) is the study of human motion. (Illus 2-1) The foundation discipline necessary for studying kinesiology is *Human Anatomy*, or how the body is constructed. *Physics*, or a division of physics known as mechanics, has application to kinesiology by investigating, among other things, the mechanical transfer of energy, such as when the clubhead meets the ball. (Illus 2-2) *Geometry*, a science defining, comparing and measuring lines, angles, surfaces, etc., can be related to the study of the golf swing as well. One chapter to cover these disciplines woefully limits their treatment, but

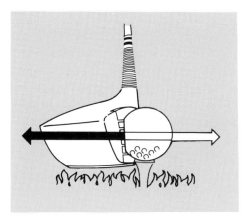

Illus 2-2 There are many opportunities to apply laws of physics when studying the golf swing.

Illus 2-1 The science which investigates and analyzes human movement is kinesiology. *Kinesis* is a Greek word meaning motion and *logy* (from the Greek *logos*) means "science of."

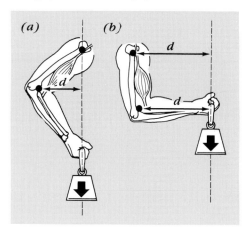

hopefully the reader's interest may be piqued sufficiently to pursue the matter in more depth, by studying of the bibliographical references or sources on these subjects.

Understanding the human body, how it works and how it transfers energy to produce the flight of a ball will not *in itself* make a person a great golfer. In fact, it would be difficult to find among players anything but a handful of individuals conversant in-depth on these subjects. But in this new age of scientific applications to sport, with the use of computerized biomechanical digitizing and three-dimensional simulations complete with analyses, it is a great advantage to have some basic understanding of science, particularly of anatomy and kinesiology.

ANATOMICAL FACTS

The human body consists of some 210 *bones* of a variety of sizes and shapes. Short bones, as in the ankle and wrist; long bones, as found in the leg and arm; and flat bones of the skull and breast. These bones are connected to each other by ligaments. Some bones are arranged in link fashion, allowing versatility in human movement. This linking structure has the capability of producing surprising velocity when applied in sequential fashion such as occurs in a good golf swing.

The body is equipped with over 600 skeletal or striated *muscles* which are attached to the bones and serve to produce the power for movement of the skeletal structure. These act like a cable pulling up a drawbridge or pulling a door closed. Muscles represent approximately 43% of one's body weight and have the capacity only to pull not to push. (f2-1) The term *muscle* comes from the Latin word for mouse. Like a mouse, a muscle has a "body," which is the muscle itself, and a "tail," which is the *tendon*. The tendon acts as an extension of the muscle and attaches the muscle to a bone. (Illus 2-3) To limit the range of motion that a muscle can move a bone, and also to tie the bones together, a series of *ligaments* are attached to the bones at many joints in the body. (Illus 2-4)

Bones and muscles need a blood supply to maintain and repair themselves. The physically

f2-1 *Obviously, the human body can be used to push objects but the muscular force applied to the lever doing the pushing must be a pulling action.*

well-trained person will heal more rapidly than the untrained because of the greater number of capillaries developed through increased blood flow from exercise. This is one of the advantages of walking the golf course. The muscles of the legs massage the blood vessels, aiding in circulation that also helps strengthen bone structure. In addition, such exercise promotes a strong and supple musculature for protection against joint injuries.

Besides helping blood circulation, leg muscles help maintain body balance during the swing. Muscles are also important in creating a good swing posture. But, more frequently we think of muscles as the *motors* that move every part of the body. You can't talk, breathe, eat or blink without using your muscles. All muscles produce movement in the same manner. By contracting they shorten, *pulling* on tendons or attachments which in turn move bones. For example, when the biceps (which is on the front of your upper arm) contracts, the forearm is brought toward the shoulder, decreasing the elbow joint angle. (Illus 2-5)

Muscles also have a variety of shapes. These

Illus 2-3 In golf one hears about tendons when they become inflamed, as in tendonitis. "Golfer's elbow" is a common example.

Illus 2-4 Ligaments, like muscles, are less susceptible to injury when they are warmed up before strenuous activity.

Illus 2-5 Muscles move bones when electrical impulses cause the muscle to contract.

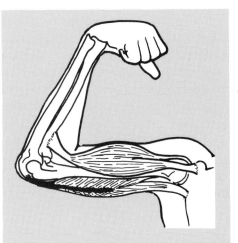

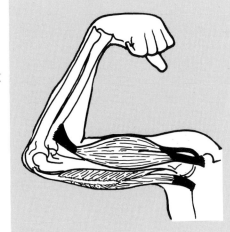

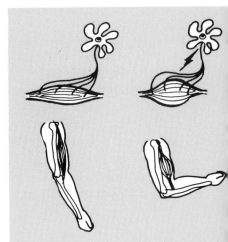

shapes influence their potential force. A muscle's force depends on its physiological cross-section or size and where it is attached to the bone in relation to the joint. The golfer has no control over the attachment location or the length of the bone but, through training, *can* influence the cross-section. Biomechanical scientists are aware of the origin and insertions of the various muscles and can prescribe exercises to strengthen those muscles. They also can analyze the movements to see if they are technically efficient for the activity being performed.

THE STRETCH REFLEX

To gain the best response from a muscle or muscle group, the muscle should be put on stretch. For example, throwing a ball at a high velocity requires the pitcher to reach back with the throwing arm while stepping forward with his leading leg to put the trunk, chest and arm muscles into full stretch. The elasticity of the muscle when positioned near full stretch helps initiate movement. This is known as the *"stretch reflex."* In a golf swing the stretch reflex is utilized when, in the backswing, the turning of the shoulders goes beyond the rotation of the trunk and the swinging of the arms carries past the turn of the shoulders. (Illus 2-6) In this way "extra stretch" is created to aid in initiating motion in the other direction. A person losing flexibility due to age or poor conditioning is unable to create a full range stretch or complete backswing, thus losing a great deal of potential clubhead velocity.

It is also important that muscles can work either *dynamically* or *statically*. Dynamic work results when the origin and insertion of the muscle move in relation to one another as a result of muscular contraction. Flexing your arm with the biceps muscle would be a dynamic movement called "concentric" or *toward*. If the origin and insertion are moving away from each other and the muscle is trying to stop them, you have other dynamic but "eccentric" *away* movement. When a muscle contracts without movement, working statically

Illus 2-6 The top of Payne Stewart's golf swing demonstrates the stretch reflex. (This swing is much longer than his normal swing, as he's competing in the National Long Drive contest.) A chain of resistance (legs, hips, trunk, shoulders, arms) is created to put the various muscle groups into a strong position to return. The correct sequencing is the most critical factor.

rather than dynamically, it is called *isometric*. The pectoral muscles of the chest, for example, may be flexing in the forward swing, but they would be isometric in their contraction, acting as stabilizers, rather than dynamically as movers.

Muscles can develop more force in a concentric motion (foward) if first worked eccentrically (away). For example, a person is given two trials to make a maximum jump vertically. In the first trial, the person squats 90 degrees at the knee joint and leaps into the air. On trial two, the same person stands vertically, then drops to the same 90 degree knee position, then rebounds vertically to jump even higher. The eccentric stretch caused by trying to halt the downward movement makes the upward movement even stronger. This is another example of the stretch reflex. It explains why trying to start the golf swing from a static position at the top of the swing will never generate as much force as swinging to that same position from the ground; the latter has the benefit from an eccentric boost.

Skeletal muscles are organized in pairs, the *prime movers* (agonists) and their *antagonists* or opposites. As in an earlier example, if the desired action is to flex the elbow and raise the forearm, the contraction appears in the biceps muscle on the front portion of the upper arm as the prime mover. Its antagonist, the triceps, is in the back of the arm. If the desired motion is to extend the lower arm, the triceps becomes the prime mover and the biceps the antagonist. To produce graceful, coordinated movement, one must learn to appropriately relax the antagonists when the prime muscles are contracting. When one hears the admonition to "relax" in relation to the golf swing, it really means "relax the antagonists" while the "prime movers" are firing. When muscular tension creeps into a golfer's swing, one problem can be that he is tightening his antagonists, inhibiting a free, flowing motion.

Illus 2-7 A very useful warm-up sequence called a "no ball warm-up," starts by swinging two wedges, beginning with small swings and building to full swings with good tempo.

PHYSIOLOGICAL IMPORTANCE OF WARM-UP

Warm-up is important for getting blood into the musculoskeletal system to enhance movement and to prevent straining or tearing of muscles, tendons or ligaments. The analogy may be made comparing unwarmed or warmed muscles to the pliability of a dry vs. wet sponge. Also, our protective reflex signals contained in muscle spindle and tendon organs travel more slowly when not warmed up and, therefore, can more easily allow injury. Use a basic warm-up routine before playing or hitting balls with a full swing. The following series, called a "no ball warm-up," is recommended. (Illus 2-7, 2-8, 2-9, 2-10)

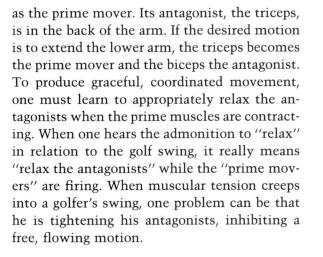

Illus 2-8 The second step is to put the driver across the low back and through the crook of the elbows and make body turns as in the swing, utilizing normal footwork. Next hold the club across the shoulders, behind the neck and repeat. Then drop the club behind the back and, with arms extended, elevate the club and arms and continue to swing. This last exercise loosens the upper-back and shoulder region.

Illus 2-9 Make practice swings letting go with the right hand near impact. This will remind your body to utilize the left side and not let go with the last three fingers of the left hand.

Illus 2-10 Finally, make practice swings with both hands on the grip, focusing on tempo and finishing on the left side with the right heel in the air.

Illus 2-11 Chi Chi Rodriguez with an admiring fan. Who could tell just by looking at Rodriguez that he can generate so much clubhead speed?

MUSCULOSKELETAL WEAKNESSES

Man, in evolving from a quadruped to an erect biped, has had to deal with developmental weaknesses that relate to his golf.

1. To permit more twisting and bending, the vertebrae, over a period of hundreds of thousands of years, have become more wedge-like and they pivot on the vertebral edges which act as hinges. This can cause problems when a person engages in *incorrect lifting*, such as removing a golf bag from the trunk of a car. Also, *the stress on the spine*, due to poor mechanics such as an exaggerated lumbar twist in the swing, can cause severe lower-back pain.

2. The longitudinal shortening of the pelvis has widened the space between the last rib and pelvis, causing a weakened abdominal wall which affects the posture at address. A golfer whose stomach is soft and flabby has a more difficult time keeping his spine aligned correctly during the setup and puts undue stress on his lower back.

Nonetheless, man has a versatile body which, when properly cared for, can accomplish a

f2-2 *Neuromuscular refers to the relationship of nerves to muscles, specifically the transfer of electrical impulses from the nervous system to the muscular system.*

broad range of motor tasks. But there are tremendous individual differences in the inherited physical characteristics of humans. Differences like size are obvious, such as a huge Andy Bean standing next to a slight Corey Pavin or a hefty Craig Stadler compared to a lean Mike Reid. Other physical characteristics are far more subtle. Just looking at an inert Ben Hogan in his prime would not give an appreciation for the tremendous physical strength in his hands and arms. Until one sees Chi Chi Rodriguez in action, it is difficult to appreciate his ability to produce a lightning-fast swing, made possible partly by a great neuromuscular system. (f2-2) (Illus 2-11) The musculoskeletal systems of Seve Ballesteros (extremely supple) and Dan Pohl (more rigid) certainly affect their style. To assess your own capabilities, see the "Preliminary Physical Test" at the end of this chapter.

A KINESIOLOGICAL DESCRIPTION OF THE FULL SWING

The golf swing is similar to the throwing motion of a sidearm/underhand baseball pitcher. This motion, involving a strong rotary action of the body, produces force that is transmitted through the arms, hands and clubshaft outwardly to the clubhead and finally to the ball. While the longer lever of the club introduces considerable speed, it also complicates control. When one considers the small striking surface of the clubface and the timing required to present the clubface both squarely and on line, it becomes easy to see why consistency in shotmaking is both an athletic and mechanical challenge.

The golfer's objective in making a swing should be to hit through the center of the ball on a line toward the target: This has been labeled "the line of compression," the "secret to golf," by Homer Kelley, author of *The Golfing Machine*. This swing is made on an inclined plane with clubs that have variable lofts and lengths for controlling height and distance. Returning the clubhead to the ball on the correct plane (being on-plane) is one of the principles of a good golf swing.

A simple model for the swing is a double pendulum with the hinges at the wrist and shoulder. If the elbow is allowed to be another hinge and is markedly bent in the backswing, the timing becomes more difficult as does consistent clubface/ball contact. While the left arm should not be extended to the point where it causes muscular tension, it will naturally extend in the forward swing due to the pull of centrifugal force. This extension creates a longer lever, and therefore, greater mechanical advantage. Undue muscular tightness or prematurely pressuring the shaft can disrupt this movement.

Coiling or winding the trunk in the backswing creates potential energy for the forward swing. The wind-up or pivot occurs around a center of rotation, the spine. Accompanying the pivot is a transfer of weight from its starting position to an emphasis more on the rear foot. The amount of weight transfer will depend on the player's style and the club being used, less

for short shots than long. The coiling of the trunk and loading of weight over the rear leg increases the potential force that can be transmitted to the ball. The larger muscles of the legs, hips and back are incorporated to add to the power package and to the swing arc, making it longer. Transferring weight to the rear foot creates the opportunity for additional force when the weight is shifted to the forward foot, toward the target. This is a motion common to any striking or throwing action. The transfer of weight which flattens the arc turns it from a circle, into an ellipse. This flattening is important, as it allows the clubhead to travel longer on the target line, thus reducing the potential for error. Byron Nelson, one of the game's straightest drivers, when tested with other tour players of his day, produced a swing that had the clubhead travelling toward the target longer than anyone.

A false pivot, known in golf parlance as a "reverse weight shift," is commonly seen among poorly skilled players. In this action the weight stays over the forward leg during the backswing, and the trunk does not get adequately involved. (Illus 2-12) This causes the player to transfer his/her weight in a direction opposite that of the swing, thus reducing the

Illus 2-12 The player who "reverse pivots" cannot properly rotate the pelvis on the backswing.

Illus 2-13 Nor can they make a strong unwinding move toward the target on the forward swing. Instead, it becomes, "hit with the upper body and fall back."

applied force and creating an incorrect swing arc. (Illus 2-13)

The base of support for a golfer's action is the feet. The transfer of force is affected by the resistance (reaction) from the ground. Slipping diminishes the force, making cleated shoes (spikes) a valuable asset to the player. Width of stance also can influence the effectiveness of the swing. If the stance is too narrow, the foundation of support is not adequate for a powerful swing, causing the player to lose balance. Conversely, if the feet are spread too wide, pelvic rotation is restricted and a full turn cannot be made. In addition, a stance much wider than the recommended "shoulder width" makes it difficult to transfer weight from the rear foot to the forward foot. Weight transfer not only adds to power, but is an important contributor toward setting the club on the correct plane and directing it toward the target. This is accomplished when the center of the swing arc (a point near the left shoulder) moves slightly forward and upward in the forward swing, thus flattening the swing arc. This body movement adds kinetic energy to the rotational force of the club/golfer system, which is imparted to the ball. In golf parlence this is known as a "late hit."

The hands are the only connection between the club and the power source, the performer. Through the hands energy is transferred, and with the hands the clubface is controlled. The choice of grip technique will be influenced mostly by hand size, hand strength and the selected style of swing. If a player seeks more leverage, as in a "hitting swing," then the hands might be spread more, as in a ten-fingered grip (baseball), for the right hand to effectively apply additional pressure against the shaft. Should a player desire to rely more on centrifugal force for a "swinging hit," then the hands should be closer together (as in an overlapping grip), working as a unit, with less pressure felt from the right hand.

CAUSE AND EFFECT— THE RESULTS OF PERFORMANCE TECHNIQUE

Before any serious discussion on technique begins, we should first understand why the ball goes where it does. There is a cause for every result in golf, reason or reasons for every well-executed shot and every miscue. No mystery, no secrets, only cause and effect. Understanding the results of performance technique, or cause and effect, is essential to the progress of any serious golfer.

Golf, like its early contemporaries from Europe (jeu de mail, chole, and colf) is a stick and ball game. The objective is to strike a ball so that it will travel from point A to point B. There are really only two logistical problems which must be overcome to make that happen: (1) to negotiate a stipulated DISTANCE; and (2) to arrive at a selected target in a given DIRECTION. If a player could accomplish these two objectives completely, he/she would play 18 holes in 18 strokes—the perfect round . . . the round which never will be played. All additional strokes above 18 taken enroute to the final score involve a player's attempts to overcome those two elements, DISTANCE and DIRECTION. Whether a two-foot putt or a 235-yard fairway shot, the elements remain the same.

To solve these two challenges, one should understand what is needed to overcome them. DISTANCE has three primary factors and DIRECTION, two that can be controlled by human performance. These can be influenced by technique and are all measured at the moment of impact. (f 2-3)

f2-3 *The "moment of impact" as defined in this book does not refer to the clubface initially touching the ball, but rather the moment at which the full energy is transferred, just prior to separation.*

DISTANCE =   (1) Clubhead speed
                 (2) Centeredness of contact
                 (3) Angle of approach

DIRECTION =   (1) Path of swing
                  (2) Clubface position

Factors like weather (wind and rain), design and construction of equipment and terrain can obviously influence both the DISTANCE and DIRECTION of a shot. But these are factors not directly under the player's control.

DISTANCE—SPEED FACTORS

Of the three primary DISTANCE factors over which the player has control, the first, clubhead speed, is influenced by *five* human variables:

(1) physical strength
(2) body flexibility
(3) swing technique
(4) leverage (body lever lengths, such as the length of the left arm)
(5) neuromuscular coordination

Strength is the most important human factor that influences distance. It's the primary reason why we have different colored tee markers for men and for women. However, we have all seen examples of a physically strong male golfer who couldn't hit his tee shot as far as the weaker local female junior champion. Therefore, there are other factors affecting how far a ball can be hit besides strength.

In a case such as that just described (the strong male and female junior champion), the male may possess sufficient *strength* (variable #1 from the previous list), but have limited body *flexibility* (variable #2), coupled with a poor swing *technique* (variable # 3). The poor technique may not be of his choosing, but stems from his restricted range of motion. He may be a victim of his body condition.

Variable #4 relates to *leverage*. Those with equal horsepower and longer levers (i.e. long arms) have the potential for greater clubhead speed. (Illus 2-14) That is why players are encouraged to have an extended left arm at the moment of impact, though extended does not mean locked straight, for locked would cause tension which inhibits speed. The length of one's arms is an inherited attribute and can't change. All a player can be expected to do is to get the most from what he/she has. One can buy a longer club, but not a longer arm.

Variable #5 is *neuromuscular coordination*, which has to do with the ability of the body to use muscles at the right time and with the correct force. This trait is strongly influenced by heredity. Golfers must concentrate on those factors over which they have the most influence.

It should be evident from these comments that the two factors of strength and flexibility play an important role in helping the player achieve success in his/her technique. Both can be enhanced through training. Combined with technique (the link action which is the most important of the variables), the three, when improved, can produce more clubhead speed and greater distance.

CENTEREDNESS

Speed without contact leaves the ball still on the tee, so speed needs a partner: the center-faced or square hit. A clubhead speed of 100

Illus 2-14 George Bayer, the longest hitter in golfing history, had a great lever length advantage to go along with his strength, flexibility and good coordination.

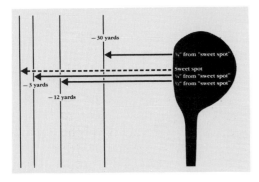

Illus 2-15 The high-handicap golfer seldom finds the "sweet spot," thus decreasing his/her distance.

m.p.h. with a square hit produces a drive of approximately 240 yards. Given the same speed with an off-center or non-square hit, the shot will travel a reduced distance. Off-center shots produce a glancing blow that transfers less energy to the ball. The accompanying chart shows this effect. (Illus 2-15)

ANGLE OF APPROACH

The angle of approach of the clubhead to the ball also affects the distance a ball travels. A steeper approach creates more backspin, more lift and less distance. Also, the more the angle of approach deviates from the arc that produces the launch trajectory for maximum distance the less energy is transmitted to the ball for sending it forward.

Experienced golfers have produced drives which seem to jump off the clubface, yet were made with a swing of less than full effort. There is that special surprise as they walk to the ball and find it well beyond their normal distance. What happened? Very simply, three things. With an unforced, well-timed swing a golfer can: (1) catch the ball with increased consistency in the *center* of the clubface; (2) present an angle of approach to the ball *which enhances the maximum transfer of energy* and produces proper levels of backspin; and (3) *release full power* without experiencing the usual inhibiting tension. This combination of factors is the formula for a player's best length. Speed + squareness + angle of approach = the *cause* that produces the *effect*.

DIRECTION

To explain the two factors which primarily influence DIRECTION (swing path and clubface position), it is useful to have a visual aid. (Illus 2-16) The pointer arm represents clubface path, the other arm depicts clubface position. All ball flight direction is a result of the relationship of these two elements at the moment of impact with the ball. With these two arms at right angles, one *always* gets a straight shot; when they are *not* at right angles, the ball always curves. Notice the statement "always." That's because these are absolutes. *This is cause and effect.* The ball has no choice but to respond in one of the ways it is depicted in the following nine basic shot patterns. (Illus 2-17)

It's no mystery why the ball goes to the right, to the left, curves or goes straight. It's plain geometry and physics. One needn't have received an A in either subject at school to understand how it applies to golf. Under ball flight, the pull, straight and push shots are straight shots—straight left, straight forward and straight right—because the clubface is square to the swing path in each case. All the rest of the shots are curves, because the clubface is either open or closed to the swing path. If it's open a small amount, it's a fade; open a large amount, a slice; closed a small amount, a draw; closed a large amount, a hook.

Face position has a greater potential to influence the flight of the ball than does swing path because it has more possibility for variation. *The direction in which the ball starts will always be the result of a combination of swing-*

Illus 2-16 This teaching aid makes the demonstration of ball flight quite simple. No mystery, just cause and effect.

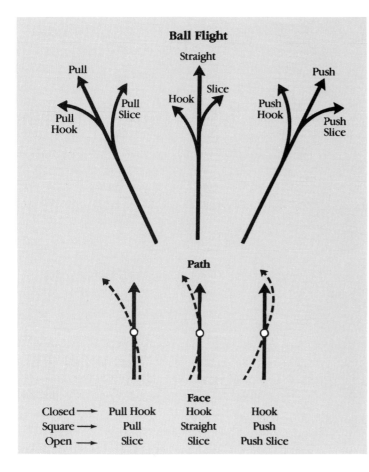

Ball Flight

Closed →	Pull Hook	Hook	Hook
Square →	Pull	Straight	Push
Open →	Slice	Slice	Push Slice

Illus 2-17 Players should learn the nine shot patterns and their basic causes, i.e. inside path + closed face = hook or draw.

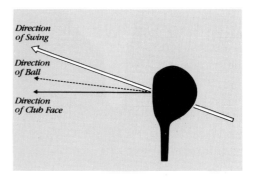

Illus 2-18 Although the path of the swing does influence the ball's starting direction, it is of lesser influence than the face.

path direction and clubface position. Where the ball starts will also be influenced by the velocity of the clubhead. The slower the clubhead is travelling, say in a putt or chip, the more precisely the ball will come off in the direction the clubface is presented. With greater clubhead speed, the ball's starting path will move somewhat closer to the swing-path line than before, but will always fall in between the face and path direction favoring the face angle. (Illus 2-18) It is sometimes incorrectly stated that the ball starts on the swing-path line. This is true only when the face is at right angles to that line. So remember, the face has a greater influence than path, but the higher the clubhead velocity, the greater is that particular vector force moving the ball's starting direction closer

to the swing-path line. This information is particularly helpful when attempting to create the mental image of intentionally hooking or slicing a ball around an obstacle.

LEARN TO "READ SHOTS"

You will be helped in your concept of cause and effect if you learn to "read your shots." After you have played a full shot with a long club, report the result in the following manner: "The shot was a push slice; that means I made an inside-to-out path with a slightly open face." Or, "The shot was a pull; it was caused by an outside-to-in path with the face square to the path." By applying cause and effect, thinking and being able to analyze the basics of ball flight, you will have taken the first step toward understanding some of the elementary influences of science on golf and eliminating the mystery of faulty shots.

WHAT RESEARCH HAS TO SAY

Research exclusively devoted to golf instruction methods, technique and psychological aspects of performance has been rather limited. The majority of what has been done has eluded the popular golf literature. Golf's most ambitiously researched book, *The Search for the Per-*

fect Swing, by Alastair Cochrane and John Stobbs, gives highly readable findings which will be discussed more in Chapter 3. Some of those conclusions are cited in an adapted form here. Unpublished research in the form of doctoral dissertation has not been readily available. If the reader is looking for more information from articles, he/she may contact the Sports Information Resource Center (SIRC) at the address listed here. (f 2-4) Another source of research information not specifically targeted on golf but from which considerable insight can be gained is that which has been conducted in the related areas of motor learning, biomechanics and sports psychology. Many of these research conclusions apply to golf teaching, training, and playing. There is golf research being presently conducted at a number of sites around the country. Reports from Compusport, the biomechanical analysis component of The Golf School at Grand Cypress in Orlando, Florida, (Illus 2-19) and creation of Dr. Ralph Mann, have seen publication and are included in Appendix 2-A. Studying the stick-figure representations of the swing will be particularly useful for an analysis of detail.

Because a subject or problem has been scientifically researched and conclusions drawn doesn't mean conclusions always prove accu-

Illus 2-19 PGA member Fred Griffin, Director of the Golf School at Grand Cypress, teaching with the use of a digitized stick figure comparison swing. (Photo courtesy of Golf School at Grand Cypress)

f2-4 *Sports Information Resource Center*
1600 James Naismith Drive
Gloucester, Ontario Canada K1B5N4
(613) 748-5658

rate. Even a cursory look at the history of science demonstrates that what was "fact" at one time proved later to be incorrect or questionable. The following is a sampling of research findings in golf mechanics and learning, much of which will be covered in more detail in later chapters of this manual.

1. The golf swing requires extensive participation by the larger muscles of the body in order to generate the more than four horsepower required to hit a ball the distance of a top-class player.
2. Learning a motor skill proceeds in stages from a strong beginning emphasis on the detail and mastery of basic techniques (grip, aim, setup, takeaway, top-of-swing, finish), to eventual blending of these parts into the complete motion, and finally, to the highest level, where detail and technique become automatic, and only feel and target are important.
3. By the time the brain senses impact and could respond in some way to bring about a bodily adjustment to an error, the golf ball has already travelled some 15 yards from its original position. (Illus 2-20)
4. To be "on plane" the clubshaft must: be parallel to the baseline (target line) of the inclined swing plane when it is parallel to the ground, or during the other stages of the swing, the end of the club nearest the ball must point to the baseline or an extension of it.
5. Errors in swing path produce only one-half the flight misdirection as do errors in clubface position. In other words, a 4-degree error in the clubface is equivalent to an 8-degree error in the swing path.
6. Skill in motor activities is highly specific rather than general. A golfer may

have excellent perception ability, a good sense of rhythm and a high degree of natural flexibility, but possess poor balance, a low level of strength and slow reaction time. This helps explain why there need to be different swing styles, and why some players are naturally long drivers while others are particularly adept with touch shots around the green. A very few are blessed with talent for all parts of the game.

7. The potential transfer of learning from previous sports experience to golf definitely exists, but the transfer may not always be positive.

8. The margin of acceptable impact error in golf is so small (two degrees of incorrect face alignment at 200 yards places the ball in the rough) that in learning the swing, the utmost in *simplicity* of style is preferred for consistent results.

9. The amount of practice by a golfer influences the amount of learning, although it is not always proportional, due to the ability of the golfer, the quality of the practice time, and the validity of the practice task.

10. Once the forward swing has begun, it will tend to stay in the plane on which it was started. Therefore, the transition move from the backswing to the forward swing is quite important. (Illus 2-21)

11. The most powerful swing results when there is little or no slack in the body coil and when the forward swing sequence has occurred from the bottom upward: feet, legs, hips, trunk, upper chest, shoulders, arms, wrists, hands and, finally, the club. (f2-5)

12. Visualization and mental practice can be beneficial to the learner in acquiring the skill and to the player in producing it in competition. Both skills, however, take practice to acquire.

13. To create maximum force at impact, the

Illus 2-20 Arnold Palmer's brain is just receiving the feedback from impact, well after the ball has left the clubface.

Illus 2-21 U.S. Open, PGA and British Open Champion Lee Trevino demonstrates one of the reasons for his success, a beautiful transition move from the top of the backswing to the left side.

Illus 2-22 Masters and British Open Champion Seve Ballesteros demonstrating a full, in-balance finish, the result of a good swing.

f2-5 *Firm abdominal muscles act as stabilizers for the hips and play a role in producing distance.*

clubhead should never pass an extended line drawn from the left arm, until after the ball's separation from the clubface.

14. A good follow-through in the golf swing serves to gradually absorb the force and help prevent injury. It also contributes toward the attainment of maximum force *at impact* rather than prior to it. (Illus 2-22)

(For additional technical information which may help see Appendix 2-B.)

PRELIMINARY PHYSICAL TESTING— A FORM OF FIELD RESEARCH

It's to your advantage to recognize any physical limitations which might make learning more difficult. Many golfers are physically unable to make the kind of swing that will produce the golf shots they might desire. *They need to know this.* While you should not impose limitations on the potential progress that can be made, you shouldn't be naive. You should not have the false expectation that instruction and practice will eventually make you swing like Greg Norman if you don't have Greg Norman's physical attributes. (Illus 2-23)

One way to objectively confront that reality is to take some tests to discover for yourself that, while you appear to have certain talents, you may also have some inadequacies that could keep you from being a tour professional. You should know the talents to tap and the limitations to deal with—you need to be optimistic, but realistic.

If you want to be a single handicap player and yet can't perform some relatively simple physical tasks, you should know that the road to your goal might be a long one.

This battery of tests will help you recognize what skills you bring to the learning process.

Illus 2-23 Trying to successfully emulate a certain star player like Greg Norman requires a reasonable amount of the physical attributes of that player.

Illus 2-24 Balance is important to sports requiring motion.

Illus 2-25 A flexibility test may help to motivate a senior player with a short backswing to begin exercising. (Note flexibility protractor between feet.)

TEST FOR BALANCE

Balance is a skill which ranks high on the list of essentials for success in many sports. In this manual it is referred to most often as "dynamic balance," meaning the ability to maintain equilibrium while in motion. That motion includes transferring the weight to the right side and back to the left during the course of the swing. Since a good portion of the time that it takes to accomplish that task, however, is consumed with the weight predominantly either over the right leg or the left leg, the test is a one-leg balance test. (Illus 2-24)

Purpose of the test: To measure static balance and leg strength.

Instructions: Stand vertically, feet close together and both arms hanging at your sides. If you are right-handed, lift the right foot so you can balance on the opposite leg. Do so while raising the arms to assist in balancing. Maintain this position for 30 consecutive seconds.

Criterion: Three trials are allowed to reach the 30-second goal.

TEST FOR TRUNK FLEXIBILITY

The ability to rotate the upper trunk by turning in the backswing is widely recognized as being essential to creating maximum clubhead speed. Persons who do not have this ability or who have had it at one time and lost it, will invariably experience a lack or loss of distance on their shots.

Purpose of the test: To measure trunk flexibility.

Instructions: Stand erect with feet at shoulder width. Take a driver and grip it at the hosel with the left hand (for right-handers) and at the end of the grip with the right hand. Now put the club over your head and behind the neck so that it rests on your shoulders. (f2-6) Place a thermofax copy of the enclosed flexibility protractor (Appendix 2-C) between your legs so the baseline runs parallel to your toes and the spokes of the protractor chart radiate toward you (fastening it to cardboard will make it more

f2-6 *Some golfers may even be unable to put the club behind their neck, which indicates they have very poor shoulder flexibility. Instead, hold it in front of the shoulders, just below the Adam's apple.*

stable). Slowly rotate the upper trunk as you would in a backswing and see how far you can turn while keeping both feet flat on the ground. Read the degrees by lining up the position of the butt end of the club with the protractor reading. (Illus 2-25)

Criterion: To see how far you can rotate the upper trunk.

TEST FOR HAND AND FOREARM STRENGTH

Grip is important in golf, as it serves to control the club. This is particularly true in the left hand. As far as producing distance is concerned, strong hands and forearms would be useful to the golfer who is a leverage-type "hitter," but not as critical to the centrifugal force swinger-type. Grip strength, however, is one of the better single measures of total body strength. Hand and forearm strength can be measured best by a grip dynamometer.

Purpose of the test: To identify any marked weakness in the hands and to compare the relative strength of the left and right hands.

Instructions: If grip-measuring equipment is not available, use this more subjective test. Simply request to shake hands with a teaching golf professional. Apply maximum effort, first with the right hand, then the left. Ask the professional for feedback to allow you a general assessment of the relative strength of each of your hands.

Criterion: Kilograms or pounds of pull as measured by the dynamometer or a subjective measure of pressure: weak, normal or strong.

TEST FOR NEUROMUSCULAR COORDINATION

While the tests to this point are generally meant to measure the physical abilities related to a full swing, the following test may be more useful to assess skills in the short game where hand-eye coordination, judgment and touch are particularly important.

Purpose of the test: To identify the ability to judge distance and to assess the style and effectiveness of tossing a ball underhanded to a target.

Instructions: This test for neuromuscular coordination requires six golf balls. Stick a tee in the ground eight yards away and spray-paint a line one yard short of the tee and one beyond it. Place a second tee at fifteen yards, and likewise spray a line short and beyond it but this time two yards away from the tee. Toss a ball underhanded to have it stop as near as possible to each tee: first to eight yards, then to fifteen, three balls being tossed to each.

Criterion: To get the tosses as close to the object tee and as many as possible between the lines.

SUMMARY

There are no norms for these tests. The purpose is to provide a simple, common-sense battery of tests with readily available equipment to help you identify any particular problems which may influence your game.

If you can't achieve 30 seconds in the balance test, you may need leg exercises to develop more strength, or you may adopt a playing style without a great demand for lateral motion.

A golfer whose trunk rotation reading is less than 90 degrees most definitely needs prescribed exercises to increase that particular range of motion. He may need either to raise the left heel more than usual in order to get sufficient arc length in the backswing, or to develop stronger hands and arms for better leverage if he is to be restricted to a short backswing.

A very weak grip strength may suggest the ten-fingered style grip placement rather than an overlap. Or, if the right-hand grip strength is far superior to the left, extra drills and exercises to build up the left side might be appropriate.

Failing to toss the balls anywhere near the objective may tell you that considerable short game practice will be needed to develop superior technical skill should you lack natural "touch."

Poor skill levels can be improved, but first they need to be acknowledged.

CHAPTER 3

LAWS, PRINCIPLES & PREFERENCES:
A Model & Developing a Method to Fit the Model

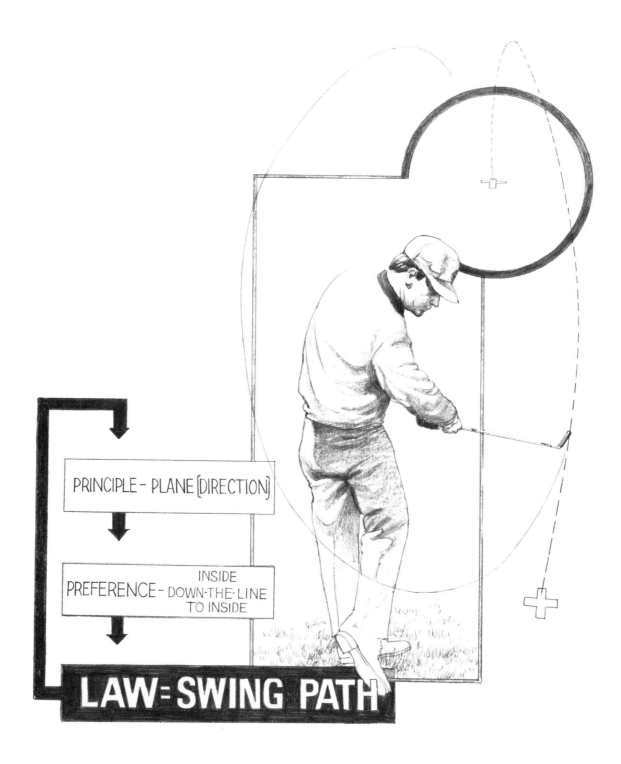

PRINCIPLE - PLANE (DIRECTION)

PREFERENCE - DOWN-THE-LINE INSIDE TO INSIDE

LAW = SWING PATH

It is time to eliminate some of the unnecessary confusion among golfers, time to find a common ground of agreement and do away with the differences which breed such confusion. It's time to organize the teaching and playing of golf into a logical model that leaves room for the individual idiosyncrasies of players. With that in mind, a teaching model is presented here in an effort to move in that direction.

Man always has been fascinated by the challenge of the unknown, the resolution of apparently insoluble problems, some worthy, others capricious. One persistent enigma that has tantalized the minds and tested the skills of sportsmen since the 17th century has been "the search for the perfect golf swing." Legions have committed their time and talents toward this end, but none dedicated his enthusiasm and resources in such a grand manner as did Britisher Sir Ainsley Bridgland.

Like others before him, Sir Ainsley experienced a haunting feeling that there must be a hidden secret that was eluding him, some simple key that would unlock the treasure house of the "perfect swing." Certainly, the secret could be revealed. That is precisely what he set out to do.

Working through the Golf Society of Great Britain, Bridgland helped form a first-rate research team of specialists representing a variety of disciplines: bio-mechanics, engineering, anatomy, physiology, ballistics, medicine, physical education and ergonomics. The team experimented, discussed and analyzed various

elements of the game of golf for more than five years. These sessions culminated in golf's most fascinating technical book, *The Search for the Perfect Swing* (Lippincott 1968), by physicist–author Alastair Cochran and golf writer John Stobbs. (Illus 3-1)

If Bridgland was looking for "the secret" he probably was disappointed (although we certainly may profit from his investment). For

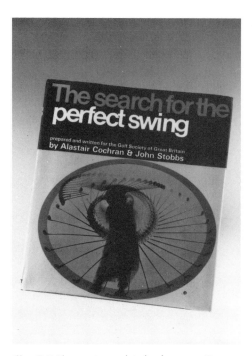

Illus 3-1 The most complete book ever written on golf that was based upon scientific research.

Illus 3-2 Players find a variety of ways to swing a club to answer the problem of Distance and Direction, such as that of Raymond Floyd.

Illus 3-3 Calvin Peete, another style.

Illus 3-4 Bernhard Langer, yet another approach.

what developed from reams of experimental test data, mathematical models, hypotheses and computer printouts probably was not the answer Bridgland sought. The conclusion: *Although a model can be constructed which exemplifies sound principles, there is no perfect swing. Rather, there are a variety of possibilities that are functional and can be considered correct as long as they do not violate physical law.*

From this conclusion there follows a rationale. If there is no one perfect swing to make, then there can be no one perfect swing to teach. That is, no one swing for all players.

There are many people teaching or playing golf in a variety of ways. In itself that is not wrong. Confusing, maybe, but not necessarily wrong. It has been like this for most of the game's history. We have had proponents of one style or another, either as teachers or players, who have drawn battle lines against all approaches that differ from their own. That is wrong! Even a casual study of the game's greatest performers should firmly convince the most stubborn advocate of a single swing style that

individual differences do exist. The only absolute statement you can make about the swings of great golfers is that they are all different. Some look similar, yes. Several around which you could build a system of generalizations, definitely. All sharing common ground in principle, absolutely. But none actually the same. (Illus 3-2, 3-3, 3-4)

These practitioners of a certain method usually offer a stable of stars as final evidence that their way is the best way, or maybe even the *only way*. To support their contentions and reinforce their beliefs, they argue that their method has worked for them and their pupils, particularly those who were successful and came back. (Failures have a convenient way of disappearing.) This type of logic leads to the conviction that anyone who arrives at a different conclusion through another approach has to be wrong . . . or, at least, must have an inferior method.

This position isn't hard to understand. It's a human failing. We can only subscribe to what we know, and we can only know what we have experienced. No one can live long enough to

Illus 3-5 The greatest challenge in teaching is the recognition of individual difference and adapting the message to fit the student. Can the student swing like the teacher? In principle yes, in preference, probably no. (Photo courtesy of International Golf Research)

have experienced everything, nor can he place himself in another's body and mind so as to appreciate fully what the other fellow is experiencing. Consequently, there will always be divergent views on what constitutes "rightness" in an activity such as the golf swing where "right" is measured only by result, not by style.

The following teaching model offers an overview of the cause-and-effect problem facing all golfers and then encourages the development of methods which can minimize or eliminate those problems. Three levels of priority in understanding the golf swing are presented:

- LAWS
- PRINCIPLES
- PREFERENCES

Each is defined for use here in the following manner:

■ LAW is a statement of an order or relation of

phenomena that so far as is known is invariable under given conditions.

■ PRINCIPLE is a first cause, or force. It is a fundamental of high order which must be dealt with and which in this model has direct relation to and influence on LAW.

■ PREFERENCE is the choice one makes based upon liking some particular approach, method, device, etc., better than all others. To be valid in this model, it must relate to PRINCIPLE.

LAWS

When we speak of Law in the model, don't infer that Law deals directly with the golf swing. It doesn't. Law here refers to the physical forces which are absolutes in influencing the flight of the ball. *There are no absolutes in the golf swing, only Principles. Absolutes are reserved for ball flight, that's why they are called Laws.* In the previous chapter we dealt with cause and effect, the factors influencing Distance and Direction. The following five factors are the Laws in this model. The Ball Flight Laws (assessed at the moment of impact) are:

1. **SPEED** The velocity with which the clubhead is traveling. Speed influences the distance the ball will be propelled, as well as the trajectory and shape of the resulting shot. (Illus 3-6)

Illus 3-6 Clubhead speed is a law in this model and the most critical factor in producing distance. . . .

2. **CENTEREDNESS** The exactness with which the ball makes contact on the face of the club relative to the percussion point or "sweet spot." Contact could be either on the center, fore (toe), aft (heel), above or below that "sweet spot." (Illus 3-7)

3. **PATH** The direction of the arc described by the clubhead in its travel away from and then back toward the target. Its line of travel at impact is one of the primary factors influencing direction for a full shot. (Illus 3-8)

4. **FACE** The degree at which the leading edge of the clubface is at right angles to the swing path. It will determine the accuracy of the ball's flight along that line, or produce a left or right curve away from that line.

5. **ANGLE OF APPROACH** The angle formed by the descending or ascending arc of the clubhead on the forward swing in relation to the slope of the gound. Due to its influence on the ball's spin rate, the trajectory and the distance the ball travels will be affected by this angle. (Illus 3-9)

Obviously, there are equipment factors such as clubface loft, construction of the ball, material of the hitting surface, etc., which will influence the distance and direction of the ball's flight. Environmental conditions such as temperature, humidity, wind, terrain and altitude also have an effect. There are also psychological elements which can influence all five laws. But in this model, consideration is given only to the human physical factors and, specifically, those over which we have some control.

Ball Flight Laws rank as the first priority because they are absolute rather than arbitrary. They work every time without fail. The ball is

Illus 3-7 . . . being able to objectively measure clubhead speed gives the golfer evidence of the most effective swing style to produce distance. (Gauge is a Swing-O-Meter™)

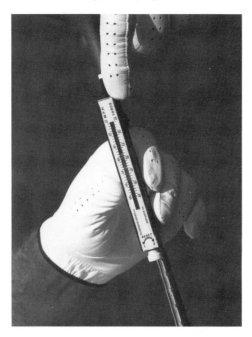

Illus 3-8 The centeredness of ball impact is one of the Ball Flight Laws which influences distance.

Illus 3-9 The *clubface* angle and the *path* of the swing combine to produce the ball's direction. Here, the professional, with the aid of a Shot Maker, shows the student how the two factors, when combined, produce ball flight shape.

not concerned with swing style. It responds to being struck without any prejudice toward the striker. It doesn't ask what particular swing method is being used, nor does it care about one's handicap, club affiliation, sex or age. The ball follows the basic Ball Flight Laws, whether the player uses an open or square stance, has a fast or slow backswing, an overlapping or ten-fingered grip, a firm or cupped wrist, or emphasizes leverage or centrifugal force as the primary source of power. Yet, all these *could have* an important influence on the flight of the ball.

PRINCIPLES

There are fundamental considerations in the swing which have a direct bearing on a player's application of the Laws. In this model they are labeled "Principles" . . . Principles of the Swing. Whereas the Laws are irrefutable and absolute (at least as absolute as we can be in this relative universe), Principles reflect some subjective judgment on the mechanics of the swing.

Listing these elements does not mean the list is all-inclusive. The reader may feel there are additional items needed to improve the model. In fact, this present list of Principles contains an additional two (Connection and Impact) from the original model constructed in 1973. The Principles are divided into two categories: Pre-Swing and In-Swing. The Principle is listed, followed by a description of the Principle, its primary influence on either Distance or Direction and its effect on one or more of the Laws. The Pre-Swing Principles are:

1. **GRIP** (Placement, positioning, pressure and precision related to applying the hands to the club.)
   Primary Influence—Direction
   Effect— Grip has the greatest influence upon *clubface position*.
      1. *Placement* (how far up or down the shaft the hands are placed) can alter the club's effective length.
      2. *Positioning* (the clockwise or counter-

clockwise rotation of the hands on the grip) by altering the hands a half inch counterclockwise from normal on the grip can cause the face to open enough for a 30-yard slice.
      3. Grip *pressure* (the amount of squeezing) influences timing, speed and control.
      4. *Precision* (taking the same grip each time) is critical for consistency.

2. **AIM** (The alignment of the clubface and body in relation to the target.)
   Primary Influence—Direction
   Effect— Aim is one of the most influential yet violated principles. Aim or alignment has a strong influence on producing the correct *path*, though it does not guarantee it. (Illus 3-10)

3. **SETUP** (A player's posture, ball position, stance, weight distribution, and muscular readiness.)
   Primary Influence—Distance & Direction
   Effect— Setup can influence *all five laws*. Ball position, for example, will affect the angle of approach and trajectory of the shot. A ball played forward in the stance

Illus 3-10 The Angle of Approach, or steepness of descent, is one of the five Ball Flight Laws . . . being flattened here with the help of a learning aid.

reduces the angle of approach, adds loft to the face and results in a higher shot. A ball played farther back results in the opposite. Similar examples can be given for each part of the setup.

4. SWING PLANE (The tilt and direction of travel of the inclined plane made by the clubshaft.)

Primary Influence—Direction

Effect— The swing plane is determined by the angle of the clubshaft relative to the ball and to the ground. The swing is in plane when, during the forward swing, an extension from the butt end of the club would intersect a line drawn through the ball to the target. Plane determines *path*. If the butt of the club points outside the intended flight line, the clubhead will travel from inside to outside. If it points inside, the swing will be from outside to inside. Plane also influences trajectory. It can be on a flat, medium or upright approach angle and still be "in plane." The right forearm position strongly influences the plane. (Illus 3-11)

5. WIDTH OF ARC (The degree of extension of the arms and hands away from the center of rotation during the swing.)

Primary Influence—Distance

Effect— If the left arm is noticeably bent at impact, clubhead *speed* is reduced due to a shortened lever. This is similar to the way the middle portion of a spoke on a wheel travels slower than the far end of the spoke although the force from the center is equal.

6. LENGTH OF ARC (The distance the clubhead travels in the backswing and forward swing.)

Primary Influence—Distance

Effect— A short putt needs only a short backswing. On a 20-yard pitch shot a longer swing than on the putt is required but not a full swing. Length of backswing is a contributing factor to swing pace or *speed* and, therefore, distance. If the arc length is shortened in the follow-through that's a good indication of deceleration at impact. (Illus 3-12)

7. POSITION (For a right-handed player, the relationship of the back of the left arm and left wrist to the face of the club and swing plane when the player reaches the top of the backswing.)

Primary Influence—Direction

Illus 3-11 Aim is a principle not given enough attention by the novice.

Illus 3-12 The club is "on plane" when an extension of the butt end of the shaft will pass through the ball on the baseline as the swing is continued forward.

Effect— By either cupping or bowing the left wrist, one can dramatically influence *clubface position*. The simplest style mechanically is to allow the wrist to cock but to keep the left hand and wrist flat throughout the swing. This, however, is not physically possible for every golfer, nor is it desired by all.

8. **LEVER SYSTEM** (The combination of levers formed by the left arm and club during the backswing.

Primary Influence—Distance

Effect— If one swings the club away from the ball without cocking the left wrist at all, it is a one-lever swing. By adding a second lever through wrist cocking the potential *speed* is substantially increased. (Illus 3-13) (f3-1)

9. **TIMING** (The proper sequence of body and club movement which produces the most efficient result.)

Primary Influence—Distance & Direction

Effect— Whether or not the backswing develops in this order, 1) hands, 2) arms, 3) shoulders-trunk, 4) hips, 5) feet-legs, or not, the forward swing should return, 5, 4, 3, 2, 1 in sequence. When it does, this se-

f3-1 *Actually, there are several systems of levers operating in the golf swing, but the primary system incorporates the left arm and the club.*

quential link action summates and maximizes the forces for the greatest possible *speed* and power. The timing of the swing sequence also influences the *path* the clubhead takes to the ball. (Illus 3-14)

10. **RELEASE** (Allowing the arms, hands, body and club to return to and through the correct impact position while freeing the power created in the backswing.)

Primary Influence—Direction

Effect— The momentum exerted by the club will cause the arms and hands and body to make a natural release unless there is interference from undue muscular tension or a premature application of the wrong body part. Attempts to strike excessively hard cause hand and forearm tension, left wrist breakdown or loss of body/arm relationship. Muscle tightness inhibits a natural release and forces the clubface to stay open or blocked, whereas left wrist breakdown results in loss of *face position* control, producing both hooks and slices.

Illus 3-13 The principles of Arc Length and Arc Width, as well as Swing Plane and Position, are vividly demonstrated here. (Bobby Cole)

Illus 3-14 Another principle, the Lever System, clearly showing the preference of two primary levers, the left arm and the club. (Bobby Cole)

Illus 3-15 Showing several principles: Arc, Width, Timing, Dynamic Balance, Plane, etc. The preference for Timing is the delayed hit. (Bobby Cole)

f3-2 *The center of the swing arc of the club is approximately the left armpit.*

11. **DYNAMIC BALANCE** (The appropriate transfer of weight during the swing while maintaining body control.)
Primary Influence—Distance & Direction
Effect— Good players utilize the motion common to all striking and throwing actions: moving from the rear foot (right foot) to the forward foot (left foot) in delivering the blow. Staying on the rear foot reduces power delivered to the ball and alters the path and arc of the swing.

12. **SWING CENTER (ROTATIONAL)** (A point located near the top of the spine around which the upper body rotation and swing of the arms takes place.)
Primary Influence—Distance & Direction
Effect— Technically, the golf swing is an ellipse, but it may be easier to understand by referring to it as a circle. All circles have centers. When the center of rotation moves, the arc of the circle made by the clubhead also moves, and striking the ball

consistently in the *center* of the clubface becomes more difficult. The shorter the shot, the more constant the swing center should stay. Additional lateral freedom can be allowed as greater power is sought, but movements that are up and down, away from or toward the ball are discouraged. (Illus 3-15) (f3-2)

13. **CONNECTION** (Establishing and maintaining the various body parts in their appropriate relation to one another in the setup and during the swing. The opposite of separation.)
Primary Influence—Distance & Direction
Effect— To produce an effective, properly timed link action, the body parts must maintain their correct positions relative to the adjoining part. They must fire in sequence to stay connected. They should also start that way. For example, if in the address the player reaches out extensively for the ball, he partially separates the major power source, his body, from his arms. He is not properly connected. Thus, the sequencing of motion and consistency of that motion would be negatively influenced, causing a loss of *speed* and *centeredness*.

14. **IMPACT** (The position of the body and club at the moment the clubhead delivers its full energy to the ball.)
Primary Influence—Distance & Direction
Effect— There is only one moment of truth in the swing . . . Impact! The *clubface* must be squared at this moment while the *path* is to the target if the ball is to travel there. It is the moment when the maximum speed should be reached and the center of the clubface is contacting the ball from the desired angle. (f3-3)

PREFERENCES

The third and final level of priorities after Laws and Principles is Preference, the choice of swing

f3-3 *The 13th and 14th Principles, Connection and Impact, have been added to the original model.*

fundamentals that constitute style. Listed below are two examples of how the three levels of Laws, Principles and Preferences work.

Example A

LAW: Speed
PRINCIPLE: *Lever System*: When one transfers a one-lever swing (which would occur if one tried to swing the golf club with no wrist cock) to a two-lever swing (which is created by the left arm and club when the wrists are allowed to cock). The potential speed is then multiplied by approximately 1.8 times.
PREFERENCE: If more than one lever in the left arm and club relationship is needed, the question of preference is: where should the player create this second lever, or cocking of the wrists? Early? In midswing? At the top of the swing? On the downswing? Or even before the start of the backswing? (Illus 3-16, 3-17, 3-18) That's a Preference.

The ball doesn't care where the second lever

is created but the golfer might. He must evaluate his assets and liabilities and select the *Preference* that works best which relates to the *Principle* that influences the *Law*.

Example B

LAW: Face (squareness of the clubface)
PRINCIPLE: *Grip*: Grip is the single most important principle influencing the club's face position.
PREFERENCE: Should a golfer use a three-knuckle grip? Two-knuckle? One-knuckle? Overlapping? Interlocking? Ten-fingered? Cross-handed? Strong pressure? Light Pressure? Again, the answer will depend on the golfer. Some experimentation might be necessary to find the right combination of grip elements which produce the desired ball flight.

> "The point is that it doesn't matter if you look like a beast before or after the hit, as long as you look like a beauty at the moment of impact."
> —Seve Balleteros

Illus 3-16 The circled area identifies the location of the swing center for the arms and center of rotation for the upper body.

Illus 3-17 The hinging or "cocking" of the wrists can occur early in the takeaway (an early set).

Illus 3-18 A midswing set.

The decision on grip selection should consider the golfer's strength, flexibility, natural arm hang, hand size, the speed he can generate and desired ball flight. The popularity of a stronger (closed-face) grip position for some PGA Tour players should indicate that there is more than one choice which can produce excellent results. Again, select the *Preference* that works best which relates to the *Principle* that influences the *Law*.

LIMITLESS PREFERENCES

When one gets into the Preference category, which determines one's style, the possibilities are limitless. Consider for a moment which of the following is correct, to have: shoulders aimed left, toward or to the right of the target? Stance open, square or closed? Weight back on the heels or forward at address? Favoring the left or right side? Ball position, variable or standard? Address, relaxed or taut? Flat, medium or upright swing plane? (Illus 3-19, 3-20) Bent left arm or straight at the top of the backswing?

Illus 3-20 A player may swing upright and return on plane . . .

Illus 3-19 The wrists can be further set on the forward swing.

Short or long backswing? Left wrist cupped flat or bowed? Face open, square or closed to the tangent of the arc? Forward swing initiated with feet, knees, legs, hips, arms, hands? Is the hip movement lateral, circular or both? Do the forearms rotate to provide release or is it the wrists, both or neither? Where is the weight distributed during the swing? Does the left knee straighten on the downswing or stay flexed? Does the head move laterally? Does it move up or down? These are Preference choices.

Whereas the Laws are fixed in number (five) and the Principles reasonably limited (fourteen), the Preferences could reach a staggering total. The point is, there are a great many techniques and combinations of techniques which

> "We don't have to force it (the swing) to fit the model. The 'art of golf' lies in allowing your swing to follow the model."
> —Alastair Cochran and John Stobbs, authors of "The Search for the Perfect Swing."

Illus 3-21 . . . or, he may swing flat and return on plane. Note that the clubface looks more closed in the flatter swing yet may be equally square to the upright style.

can work. Ben Hogan could employ a particular grip, stance and swing quite different from Lee Trevino's, yet produce a ball flight that looks almost identical.

PREFERENCE VARIETY AND COMPATIBILITY

This is the key—compatibility. Mixing preference styles when applied to certain principles doesn't work. A player can't use Paul Azinger's grip coupled with Tom Watson's release. This is one reason why we sometimes note a strong difference of opinion among experts on the golf swing over what appear to be clear-cut fundamentals. Because once the player adopts a particular grip style or position at the top, it will dictate several of the moves on the way down and through the shot. The conclusion is, when comparing widely varying styles, each may be right. The test is, *what works for you*?

Above all, recognize that the swing may be simple in theory but the machine which performs it, the human being, is very complicated.

THE COMPLETE MODEL

The complete listing of the three levels follows:

BALL FLIGHT LAWS
  1) Clubhead speed
  2) Centeredness of contact
  3) Clubhead path
  4) Position of clubface
  5) Angle of approach

PRINCIPLES
  1) Grip
  2) Aim
  3) Setup
  4) Swing plane
  5) Width of arc
  6) Length of arc
  7) Left wrist position
  8) Lever system
  9) Timing
 10) Release
 11) Dynamic balance
 12) Swing center (Rotational)

Illus 3-22 An example of working on a good position. The correct position at the top of the backswing includes making a good upper body turn.

13) Connection
14) Impact

PREFERENCES (EXAMPLES)
Early wrist cock
Two-knuckle grip
Outside take away
Flat backswing
Cupped left wrist
Left toe out

Fixed center
High hands
Slow back
Open stance
Lateral slide
Light pressure
Bent left knee
Extended arms
Chin behind
Weight forward
Shoulders closed
Etc., etc., etc.,

CHAPTER 4

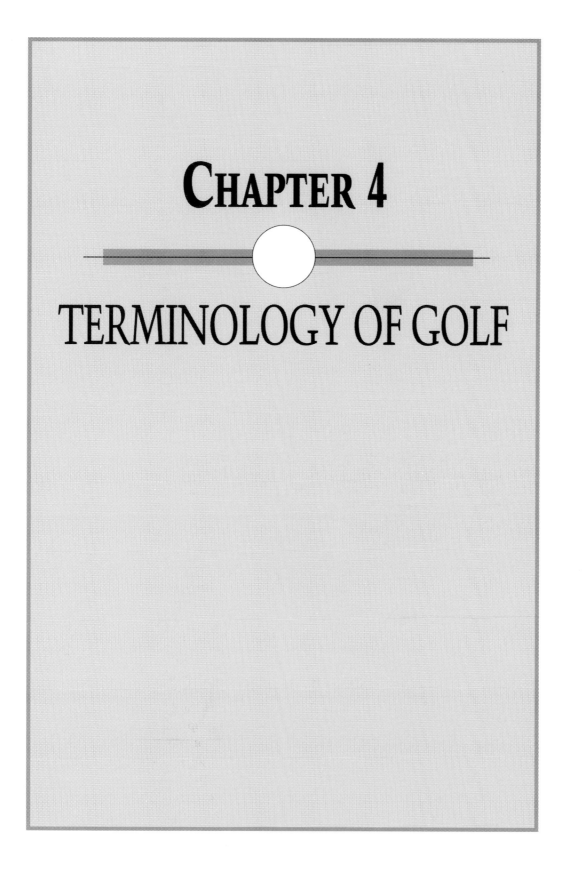

TERMINOLOGY OF GOLF

half-wedge

closed-face grip

lob shot

chip and run

connected

dynamic balance

If golfers are to communicate effectively to one another, they need to be speaking a common language. Presently, much of golf's terminology is inaccurate, misleading and confusing. Take, for example, the common expressions "strong grip" and "weak grip" (which imply pressure but do not mean pressure); "coming over the top" (the top of what?); "coming off the ball" (is one standing on it?); "laying it off" (where is it to be laid, off of what?); (Illus 4-1) "hitting a shot fat" (fat?); "baseball grip" (which is not a baseball grip at all); (Illus 4-2) The list goes on. How well do these terms or expressions communicate? It's time to shore-up our sloppy language, to get more precise; if not perfect, at least consistent.

For that reason, it is proposed that the following terms and their definitions be adopted so communication will be more effective. There are several recommendations for the addition or elimination of certain words or phrases. It is also suggested that multiple usages for a single meaning be reduced to one common preferred term.

Additionally, there are some accepted terms which cause confusion, such as "grip." When one hears the word "grip," is it in reference to the handle of the club or the placement of the hands? It is not clear. Yet, use of the term "grip" as both *hands* and *handle* has such widespread acceptance that attempting change seems insurmountable . . . maybe it's not, but that one is left to future lexicographers.

One serious consideration in proposing a lexicon of terms was to eliminate all references to laterality, i.e., left and right hand, foot or side. Instead of "after placing your left hand on the grip," it might read "after placing your target hand on the grip." In this way all text materials could be read by both right- and left-handed players without the usual instructions for left-handers to reverse all references to sidedness. It was a noble idea but in actual application became extremely awkward and confusing. The idea was dropped. So a reminder to all left-handers must again be apologetically offered. IN THIS TEXT ALL REFERENCES TO RIGHT-HANDED PLAYERS MUST BE REVERSED FOR LEFT-HANDERS.

Illus 4-1 The golfer has allowed the clubhead to "lie down" or be "layed off" so that it is no longer on plane.

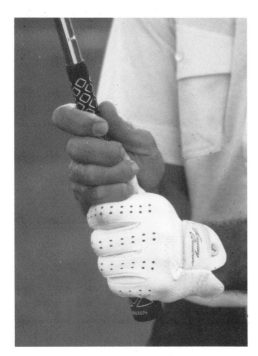

Illus 4-2 Using the term "baseball grip" is a misnomer, since a baseball bat is gripped more in the palms and without the left thumb on the handle. This style is better labeled a ten-finger grip.

GOLF TERMINOLOGY

Acceleration   A positive increasing change in the velocity of an object; in golf usually referring to the hands, arms or clubhead. A major objective of all swings from the beginning of the forward swing to impact.

Address   The process the player goes through in positioning his body and the club for the stroke. From a rules standpoint it is when the player has taken his stance and grounded the club, or if in a hazard, when he has taken his stance.

Aim Line   (See *Target Line*).

Alignment   The arrangement of the parts of

"One of the biggest reasons we can't always translate the *words* of our instructors into effective swings is we really don't understand what our instructor is saying."
—Joseph C. Dey

---

the body and clubface in relation to the target. A part of aiming.

Angle of Approach   The steepness of descent or ascent of the clubhead's forward swing which influences the trajectory and distance a ball will travel.

Approach Shot   A stroke made to or onto the putting green, or one made from the fairway in proximity to the green.

Axis   A straight line around which a body rotates. (There are several axes in the golf swing. The one most frequently referred to is the spine, around which the upper body rotates.)

Backswing   The motion of the club, hands, arms and body away from the ball creating the potential energy to be delivered downward, outward and forward through the ball.

Backspin   The backward rotation of the ball on its horizontal axis influenced by the loft of the clubface, the angle of approach and the clubhead velocity. (A ball struck below its center with any club that has loft, even a putter, will have backspin in the airborne portion of its flight. The greater the backspin, the steeper the ball will fly and more quickly it will stop.) (*bite*)

Balance   Equilibrium in a static position, i.e., at address (see *Dynamic Balance*).

Baseball Grip   (See *Grip: Ten-Finger*)

Bladed Shot   One that has a low "line drive" trajectory as a result of having been struck on the lower portion of the clubface on or above the ball's equator. (*skulled shot*)

Block   To prevent or delay the rotation of the arms, body, wrists or club in the forward swing. (Illus 4-3)

Bobbing   Lowering then raising, or raising then lowering the swing center during the course of the swing.

Borrow   The amount of compensation in aim taken on the putting green when the player has to deal with a side slope, gravity, grain or the wind's effect on the ball.

Break   The curved line a ball travels on the ground because of slope, grain or wind. Also, "break" may refer to the bending at a joint, like a wrist or elbow.

Illus 4-3 Blocking is usually caused either by undue tension in the arms and hands, or a misconception that the face is supposed to remain square to the target line after impact.

Bump and Run A shot around the green deliberately played into a bank or hill to deaden the speed while still allowing the ball to bound forward. (*bank shot*)

Bunker A sandy or grassy hollow forming an obstacle on the course. (*Sand trap* is a term not in the rule book; *bunker* is.)

Carry The distance the ball travels in the air.

Casting A premature release of cocked wrists on the forward swing which causes the clubhead to arrive at the ball out of sequence, ahead of the hands and arms. Also known as "hitting from the top." (*early release*)

Center of Gravity (*body*) The point in the body (somewhere in the pelvic region) where the upper mass, lower mass, right and left sides all balance.

Centrifugal Force The action in a rotating body tending to move mass away from the center. The force one feels in the downswing that pulls the clubhead outward and downward, extending the arms and encouraging the clubhead to take a circular path.

Center of Rotation The axis around which the body winds and unwinds, i.e., the spine. (Illus 4-4)

Centripetal Force The force that tends to move things toward the center, around which they are turning. Gravitation is an example.

Chicken Wing Folding or collapsing the left arm at the elbow in the forward swing so that it is bent, pointing away from the side of the body. (Generally considered a swing

Illus 4-4 Hall of Fame player Nancy Lopez makes a big wind and unwind around her spine with enough force to create this extended follow-through. (Photo by Stephen Szurlej)

fault; however, it can be used effectively to stop clubface rotation such as in a bunker shot, pitch shot or putt.) (*block and fold*)

Chip and Run A low trajectory shot played to the apron, or green, or around the green, in which the roll is considerably longer than the carry.

Chip Shot A short, low-trajectory shot played to the green or from trouble back into play.

Choke A psychological condition producing acute nervousness that keeps the player from performing up to his normal ability.

Choke Down To grip lower on the club for greater control. (should replace term *choke up*)

Chunking A shot in which the clubhead strikes the ground before striking the ball, causing a partial hit, decreasing the distance the ball travels. (*stubbing, scuffing, dunching, sclaffing, heavy and fat*)

Clearing the Left Side Turning the hips to the

Illus 4-5 When during the swing the clubface remains in a right angle position to a straight line which touches the swing arc (tangent), then the face is square. This one is closed to that tangent.

left of the target so the arms may follow in sequence.

Cleek The name given to a wooden club (more frequently now a metal wood) with the approximate loft of a #4 wood. In golf's earlier days it was a light narrow-faced iron with little loft; also, a putter with extra loft.

Closed Clubface (at address and impact) One in which the toe of the club is leading the heel, causing the clubface to point to the left of the target line.

Closed Clubface (swing) Whenever the angle formed by the leading edge of the clubface is less than 90 degrees to the tangent of the swing arc. (Illus 4-5)

Closed-Face Grip An exaggerated clockwise rotational positioning of the hands when placed on the grip; i.e., left hand more on top of the shaft, right hand more under. (To replace the term *strong grip*.) (f4-1)

Closed Stance A positioning of the feet that has the right foot withdrawn from an ima-

ginary line across the toes which is parallel to the target line.

Closed-to-Open A description of the dynamics of the clubhead when the player hoods and closes the clubface in the backswing (pointing more to the ground) then reverses it to open coming through (pointing more to the sky). (*shut to open*)

Cocked Wrists A position in which the left wrist has laterally *flexed* (toward the left thumb side) and the right wrist is dorsally *hinged* (back of the right wrist toward the top of the forearm).

Cocked Wrists, Bowed A position at the top of the swing in which the wrists have cocked as previously described, but the back of the left hand has moved farther away from the top of the left arm (*palmar-flexion*), palm toward the underside of the forearm.

Cocked Wrists, Cupped A position at the top of the swing in which the wrists have cocked as previously described, and the back of the left hand has moved closer to the topside of the forearm. (*dorsi-flexion*)

Cocked Wrists, In Plane A position in which the wrists have cocked as previously described, and the back of the left wrist is flat in line with the forearm, and the right wrist is parallel to the left wrist. (*radial-flexion*)

Coefficient of Restitution The relationship of the clubhead speed at impact to the velocity of the ball after it has been struck. A measure affected by the clubface and ball material.

Coil The circular windup or pivot of the body during the backswing which results in the upper trunk turning farther than the lower, creating a feeling of stretch.

Come Over the Top A move during the forward part of the swing which steepens the plane or arc and throws the clubhead path outside the target line prior to impact. Suggest replacing this term with *Outside-to-In* swing.

Connection Maintaining the various body

---

f4-1 *A closed-face grip does not insure that result but it does encourage it.*

parts in the appropriate proximity to one another before or during the swing so as to produce harmonious movement. The opposite
of separation. (See *Timing*)

Conservation of Angular Momentum (COAM)
A law of physics which allows the player to
produce large amounts of kinetic energy. As
the body shifts its weight and turns toward
the target in the forward swing, the mass
(arms and club) is pulled away from the center into an extended position by centrifugal
force. By temporarily resisting that pull as
well as the temptation to assist the hit by
releasing too early, one maintains the angle
formed between the club shaft and the left
arm and conserves the energy until a more
advantageous moment. It has been referred
to as "the delayed hit," "the late hit," "connection," "lag loading," "the keystone," or
COAM, but when performed correctly may
simply be called "good timing." (Illus 4-6)

Croquet Style A putting stance in which the
player stands facing the hole using the putter
in a fashion similar to playing croquet. Orig-

Illus 4-7 PGA member Angie Alberico using a facing-the-hole croquet style of putting with an extended length putter.

Illus 4-6 Lee Trevino demonstrates the
conservation of angular momentum by
retaining the tight angle formed by the left
forearm and clubshaft until the correct
moment in the forward swing.

inally he stood astride the line but now, by
rule, must stand beside it. (*side saddle*) (Illus
4-7)

Cross-Handed A grip style usually employed
in putting, where the left hand is placed
below the right on the club's grip.

Cuppy Lie When the ball is resting in a cup-
like depression; usually a bare lie in between
patches of grass.

Cut Shot A shot in which the ball is struck
with a slightly open clubface while the clubhead path is traveling to the left of the target.
This produces clockwise spin, as in a fade,
and additional backspin for stopping action
on the green.

Dead Wrists A term used mostly for shots on
and around the green where the wrists do
not cock back or release through; rather,
they stay fixed.

Deceleration A negative change in the velocity of a moving object. In golf it refers usually
to decreasing clubhead speed. It is a major
error when occurring prior to impact. (*negative acceleration; quitting*)

Delayed Hit A golf term used to describe the Conservation of Angular Momentum (COAM).

Divot A piece of turf displaced by a golf club. It reflects a correctly descending swing when taken in front of the ball and is the effect of most good iron shots though not a requirement. Also, the hole left in the turf after the grass has been displaced.

Downswing (See *Forward Swing*)

Drag An aerodynamic force that resists the forward motion of an object. It influences clubhead speed and ball flight. Also a golf shot played that has additional backspin.

Draw A golf shot which curves slightly in flight from right to left. A small hook. The opposite of a fade.

Driving Range (See *Golf Range*)

Duck Hook An exaggerated hook that curves sharply and rapidly to the left. (*snap hook*)

Dynamic Balance Transferring the focus of weight appropriately during the golf swing while maintaining body control. (Illus 4-8)

Early Hit When a player prematurely releases angular momentum in the forward swing, causing a reduction of speed at impact. (*hitting from the top, throwaway*)

Effective Loft The actual loft of the clubface when it strikes the ball. Because of sole configuration, head design, hosel boring and the player's technique, the *built-in* loft can be varied, thus becoming *effective loft*.

Explosion shot A shot made from a lie that is buried in a bunker in which the club digs and displaces a large amount of sand.

Extension Achieving the desired length of the left arm at impact and the right arm at post impact in the swing. (This position can be produced naturally by centrifugal force or willfully by applied leverage.) May also apply to positions at the top of the backswing. (*expansion, extended radius*) (Illus 4-9)

Fade A shot which curves slightly in flight from left to right. A small slice. The opposite of a draw.

Fanning the Face An exaggerated rolling of the clubface into an open position early in the takeaway.

Fat Shot A shot in which the clubhead strikes the ground before the ball. (NOTE: Other shots denoting error are slicing, hooking, topping, skying, shanking, pushing, pulling, etc. "Fat" is not consistent in form nor is it particularly descriptive. Therefore it is suggested that it be replaced by the word *chunked shot* or *chunking*.)

Flange The projected portion on the sole of a club such as on the back part of a sand wedge or putter.

Flat Swing A swing which employs a less vertical, more horizontal plane than considered normal.

Flier A ball that has reduced backspin and therefore more distance, usually struck from long grass. The probable cause is organic plant matter from the leaves of the grass which reduce friction on the ball and, therefore, spin. A similar result can be obtained when water or another friction-reducing substance is introduced to the clubface.

Flip Wedge A short, less-than-full wedge shot (similar to a half wedge) usually played to the green.

Floater A ball struck from deep grass which

Illus 4-8 Adele Moore demonstrates a perfectly balanced finish, having transferred her weight from right side to left side during the swing.

comes out slowly and travels shorter than normal due to heavy cushioning of the blow from excess grass between the ball and clubface. Opposite of a flier. ("Floater" is also a golf ball that will float in water.)

Flop Shot A loose-wristed pitch in which the club is taken abruptly up on the backswing then dropped lazily and steeply down, sliding the clubhead underneath the ball.

Fluffy Lie A ball coming to rest on top of the long grass presenting the potential for the clubface to slide markedly under the ball, giving it little impact and reducing distance.

Fly To hit a shot that completely carries over the intended target. Also, the distance one can carry the ball in the air.

Follow-Through The remainder of the swing once the ball has been struck. (In theory there can be no effect on the shot after the ball has left the clubface. In practice, focusing on a sound follow-through may positively influence what goes on before. (Illus 4-10)

Footwork The action of the lower half of the body (i.e. feet, ankles, knees, legs, hips) when making a golf shot.

Forward Press A movement usually with the hands and arms or some other part of the body which assists the player in starting the club away from the ball.

Forward Swing Once the backswing has been completed, the motion of the body, arms, hands and club in the opposite direction through the ball. This term, "forward swing," should replace "downswing" in golf terminology, as it is semantically parallel ("backswing"/"forward swing") and directs the player in a more positive action toward the target, not the ground. (*downswing*)

Fried Egg A lie in a sand bunker where the landing of the ball has splashed the immediate sand away, leaving the ball resting in the middle of a crater.

Golf Range A facility where a golfer may hit balls to improve his swing. If it also includes a short-game practice area it could better be called a practice center. Golf range to replace the term "*Driving Range.*"

Illus 4-10 The quality of a player's follow-through is a general reflection on the quality of what has gone on before. This Tom Watson finish reflects having made a good swing. (Photo by Jeff McBride)

Illus 4-9 Just as the left arm extends in the backswing, the right arm extends in the forward swing. (Photo by Jeff McBride)

Grain The direction in which the blades of grass grow and lie on the putting green. (Grain follows water runoff, sun, mowing cuts and prevailing wind direction.)

Grip (equipment) That portion of the shaft of the club on which the player places his hands; the material which may be of leather, rubber or a synthetic.

Grip (technique/principle) The placement, positioning, pressure and precision a player employs in applying his hands to the club.

Grip: Interlocking A method of placing the hands on the club which is distinguished by the lacing of the little finger of the right hand with the index finger of the left.

Grip: Overlapping A method of placing the hands on the club which is distinguished by laying the little finger of the right hand either over the left index finger or around the knuckle of the left index finger.

Grip: Reverse Overlapping A popular style of grip used for putting in which all of the right hand remains on the club and the left index finger of the left hand is overlapped across the fingers of the right hand. (Illus 4-11)

Illus **4-11** The reverse overlapping grip puts the entire right hand on the club to encourage a better sense of touch from the dominant hand.

Grip: Ten-Finger A method of placing the hands on the club which is distinguished by the placement of all of the fingers and both thumbs on the club, with the hands abutting but not overlapping or interlocking. (*baseball grip, all finger*)

Groove To develop through practice a sequence of movements, a pattern or path that produces consistent results in the swing. (Also, a linear scoring line on the clubface.)

Ground When referring to the club it is the process of setting the sole on the turf while addressing the ball.

Group Lesson An instructional session which includes five or more pupils with one or more instructors.

Half Shot A shot played with less than the normal length backswing and effort, designed to achieve around 50% of the regular distance for the club. (Illus 4-12)

Heeled Shot One in which the ball is struck on that portion of the clubface which is between the hosel and the center of the face.

Illus **4-12** To produce reduced distances with a club a player may choose to play a "half shot," or one that employs a shorter backswing and follow-through, as Lee Trevino does so well.

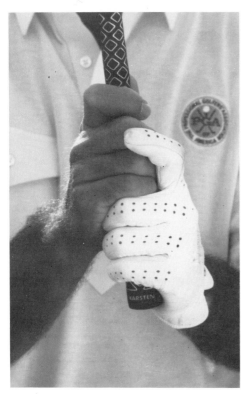

High Side Refers to the portion of the cup which is the highest on a sidehill breaking putt. Sometimes referred to as the "pro side." (The ball has a better chance to drop in from the high side due to gravity and is more frequented by the professional.)

Hitter A player using a style of striking the ball which employs considerable thrust or leverage to power the club.

Hooding Delofting the club by advancing the grip forward toward the target or reducing loft during the swing but keeping the face square to the target line. (It does not mean closing the face, as is so often misconstrued, although when closing the face, the club may be hooded as well.)

Hook A golf shot which markedly curves in flight from right to left.

Horizontal Axis (Ball) An imaginary line running through the center of the ball in a horizontal plane. (Striking the ball with the clubface below this point causes it to be airborne. Striking above it will cause the ball to be topped.)

Hosel That part of the club which joins the clubhead to the shaft. (*neck*)

Impact The moment the clubhead, while in contact with the ball, transfers its energy to the ball.

Inside-to-In The swing pattern which produces straight, on-target shots—providing the clubface is square and the ball is center-face hit.

Inside-to-Out A swing path in which the clubhead approaches the ball from inside the target line and after contact continues forward, crossing that line to the outside before coming around to the finish.

Intended Linge of Flight See *Target line.*

Kinesiology The scientific study of man's movement and the movements of implements or equipment which he might use in exercise, sport or other physical activity.

Kinetic Energy The form of energy associated with the speed of an object. Its equation is: KE = ½ mv²; or kinetic energy = ½ mass × velocity squared. (It is obvious from the formula that increasing clubhead velocity has more potential for producing distance than increasing the clubhead weight.)

Lag Playing a shot intentionally short of the target. (*lay-up*) (Also: see *Conservation of Angular Momentum*)

Late Hit A misnomer which attempts to describe the Conservation of Angular Momentum or the "delayed hit." If it were truly "late" the ball would go to the right, as the clubface would not be squared.

Lateral Shift One of the movements of the body in the forward swing with the purpose of transferring the weight from over the right foot to over the left foot. It accompanies and can be the result of body rotation. (f 4-2)

Lay Off Flattening the plane at the top of the backswing, causing the club to point left of the target and the face to be closed. Literally "laying the clubhead down" so it is no longer square or on plane.

Learning Center A complete golf practice and learning facility. Could include practice areas for full swing, short game, special shots such as uneven lies, putting, physical training, psychological training, equipment testing, video analysis, classroom, learning aids and club fitting.

Lever System The skeletal system is composed of numerous bones which, in mechanical terms, act as levers. The two primary levers in the golf swing are: 1) the left arm, comprised of the radius and ulna of the lower arm and the humerus in the upper arm, and 2) the club when the left wrist becomes cocked.

Lie (of the Ball) The position of the ball after it has come to rest.

Lie (of the Club) The angle the shaft makes with the clubhead as measured from the center of the shaft to a line extending tangentially from the lowest point on the sole.

f4-2 *There is no question there is lateral movement when the weight shifts from the right side to the left side. Some teachers would say, however, that the lateral movement is simply a response from winding and unwinding the body.*

Line The path the player intends the ball to follow on the way to the target. (Illus 4-13)

Line of Flight The direction the ball actually travels.

Lob Shot A short, high trajectory shot that lands softly with little forward roll.

Loft The degree of pitch angle built into the clubface. Also, to lift a ball into the air with a club.

Long Irons Those included in the long iron group are #1, #2, #3 and #4.

Looking Up (See *Raised Swing Center*)

Loop The shape of the arc the clubhead makes when the backswing and forward swing planes don't match. If the forward swing plane is under (flatter than) the backswing plane it is an *inside loop*. If the forward swing plane is over (steeper than) the backswing plane it is an *outside loop*. (Also, caddie slang for a round of golf.)

Loosened Grip Any time during the swing when a player opens his fingers on the grip to cause some loss of control. The most common example would be opening the last three fingers of the left hand at the top of the backswing. (Formerly referred to as a "Piccolo Grip.") (Illus 4-14)

Mechanics The technique elements a player selects and employs in making a golf shot.

Middle Irons Those included in the middle iron group are #5, #6 and #7.

Off-Green Putting A style of chipping which uses a low-to-medium trajectory club in a distinctly putting-like style.

One-Piece Takeaway An early portion of the backswing in which the arms, hands and wrists move away from the ball in nearly the same relation to each other as they were at address. The wrists may cock very slightly but neither fan nor hood the face. (Illus 4-15)

Open Clubface (at address and impact) One in which the heel of the club is leading the toe, causing the clubface to point to the right of the target line.

Open Clubface (swing) Whenever the angle formed by the leading edge of the clubface is greater than 90 degrees to the tangent of the swing arc.

Open-Face Grip An exaggerated counterclockwise rotational positioning of the hands when placed on the club. (Formerly *weak grip*.)

Open Stance A positioning of the feet at address that has the left foot withdrawn from

Illus 4-13 Getting the line by sighting from behind the ball seems to be the most effective method whether it be putting or a full shot.

Illus 4-14 Letting go at the top of the swing with the last three fingers of the left hand is a frequent cause of inconsistency in shot making.

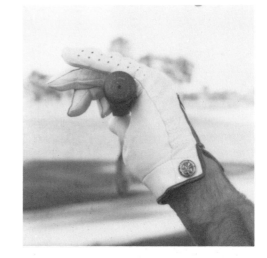

Illus 4-15 One style of takeaway that has been popular for at least half a century is the "one-piece takeaway."

an imaginary line running parallel to the intended flight line.

Open-to-Closed A description of the dynamics of the clubhead when the player rolls the face open during the backswing and rolls it closed during the forward swing. (*open to shut*)

Outside-to-In When the swing path of the clubhead approaches the ball outside the target line, and then, after contact, crosses that line directly to the inside and around to the finish. The forward swing plane with this pattern is invariably steeper than the backswing plane.

Pace The rate of movement in the swing. (Also, the speed of the greens.)

Paddle Grip The grip on a putter that has a flat surface along the top on which the player may rest his thumbs.

Path The directional arc in which the club is swung when viewed from above. Usually identified in the swing zone just prior to and after impact.

Pendulum Stroke A free swing from a fixed pivot point. In putting, a pure pendulum stroke could be with the hands and club swinging from the wrist joint while the arms are stabilized. A more common form is to use the arms and shoulders with the pivot point in the center of the chest.

Piccolo Grip (See *Loosened Grip*)

Pinch Shot A short shot around the green struck with a crisp, descending blow. (Most full iron shots when struck a descending blow are pinched to some degree.)

Pistol Grip The grip portion on the handle of a putter which has extra buildup at the top so that it fits the hand similarly to a small pistol handle.

Pitch-and-Run A short lofted shot having more than a customary amount of roll after it lands.

Pitch Shot A high trajectory shot of short length, played with one of the more lofted iron clubs.

Pivot The movement of the body or a body part around a fixed axis. Most commonly used to describe the body turn around the spine in the full backswing. (*shoulder turn, windup, coil*)

Plane (See *Swing Plane*)

Plumb Bob A pseudo-scientific method of determining the directions a ball will break on the green. It relies on judgment gained from sighting the slope while using a vertical reference line (the putter) as an aid. It does not take into account the green's speed. (Illus 4-16)

Plugged Lie A ball imbedded in its pitch mark.

Press To attempt to hit the ball harder than usual or try harder than normal.

Pre-Shot Routine A procedure which the player completes after selecting a club but prior to initiating the swing.

Private Lesson An instructional session which includes one pupil with one or more teachers.

Illus 4-16 The clubhead represents the plumb bob or weight which will hang vertically when held lightly between the fingers.

Pronation   An inward rotation of the hands toward the body's centerline when standing in a palms-facing-forward position. (The term pronation was inaccurately used for many years to describe the rotation of both hands through the impact area. In fact, one hand, the right, was pronating while the left was supinating. Obviously, it is impossible to pronate both hands through the shot.)

Pulled Hook   A hook which starts to the left of the target and curves even farther to the left.

Pulled Shot   A shot that travels on a relatively straight path but to the left of the target.

Pulled Slice   A slice which starts to the left of the target and curves back to the right.

Punch Shot   A low trajectory shot created by striking the ball while the grip end of the club is advanced well ahead of the clubhead so the club's loft is reduced.

Pushed Hook   A hook which starts to the right of the target and curves back to the left.

Pushed Shot   A shot which travels on a relatively straight path but to the right of the target.

Pushed Slice   A slice which starts to the right of the target and curves farther to the right.

Radius   A term borrowed from geometry used to describe the distance between the center of the swing arc (the middle of the left shoulder) and the hands on the grip.

Raised Swing Center   Elevating the central area in the body (somewhere between the top of the spine and center of the neck) around which rotation takes place. What the novice frequently refers to as "looking up" and which results in a swing that is too high. (*changing the spine angle*)

Rap   To putt the ball with a firm stroke.

Reading the Green   The process of judging the correct path and pace to hole a putt. (This decision must consider all factors which might influence the ball on the way to the target, i.e., length of grass, type of grass, grain, firmness of the ground, slope, dryness or wetness, wind, the ball, the club, the technique.)

Recover   To play from an undesirable ball location to one which is more advantageous.

Release   Allowing or causing the body and club in the forward swing to return the clubface to square and to free the potential power created in the backswing. (Illus 4-17)

Reverse Weight Shift   During the backswing, moving either the upper or lower part of the

Illus 4-17 The release can be checked by noting the position of the toe when the clubhead reaches hip height in the forward swing. When the face is up, it's blocked; toe up, it's square; face down, it's closed.

body in a direction opposite from that which is mechanically sound, i.e., forward (to the left) of the body's centerline rather than behind it (to the right).

Rhythm   A harmonious movement in the swing with a regular and repeating pattern.

Scramble   The attempt to recover from erratic play and produce effective results. (Also a form of competitive team golf play.)

Semi-Private Lesson   An instructional session which includes two to four pupils with one or more instructors.

Separation   When the body, arms and legs get out of sync or position and lose the desired relationship to their contiguous parts. (Also, may be the ball leaving the clubface.) (Illus 4-18)

Setup   The mechanical procedure other than grip and aim prior to initiating a stroke. It includes positioning the body and clubface, alignment in relation to the ball and establishing the body's overall attitude or posture.

Shanking   To strike the ball on the hosel of the club. Usually this causes the shot to travel sharply to the right, but it could go

Illus 4-18 The left arm is out of position, having separated from its correct location nearer the left side.

straight or to the left as well. (*socketing, hoseling*)

Shape of Shot   The ball's actual line of travel, i.e., left to right, right to left or straight.

Short Game   That part of golf played near the green to include all types of shots that may be used to get the ball holed in as few strokes as possible, i.e., bunker shots, putting, chipping, pitching and all special variations of these.

Short Irons   Clubs included in the short iron group are the #8, #9 and pitching wedge. Consider the sand wedge as a specialty club.

Shut   (See *Closed Clubface*, etc.)

Sky   To hit under the ball on the upper part of the clubface, sending the ball high and a short distance.

Slice   A ball which curves markedly from left to right.

Smothered Hook   A hook that drives quickly to the ground, usually directly to the left, but may possibly start to the right. Caused by an exaggerated closed clubface.

Sole   The bottom of the clubhead. (Also, the process of setting that portion of the club on the ground.)

Splash Shot   A shot played from a good lie in a sand bunker in which the club bounces or splashes through the sand, cutting it from beneath the ball.

Spoon   The earlier name for a lofted fairway wood, presently the #3 wood.

Spot   To mark the position of a ball on the green before lifting it by placing a coin or small object at the back side of the ball.

Spot-Putting   Using an intermediate target on the line to the cup, such as a discoloration of grass or ball mark, as an aiming point for the putt.

Square   A term with several uses in golf. May refer to the clubface when it is positioned at right angles to the target line; to the stance when a line drawn across the heels is parallel to the target line; to the shoulders, hips and knees in aiming when they are also parallel to the target line; to center-faced contact with the ball when it is struck. Also, when the club is at 90 degrees to the tangent of the arc, anywhere on that arc.

Stance The position of the feet when the player addresses the ball.

Steer An exaggerated attempt to control the shot which results in losing the desired distance and/or direction.

Straight-Faced An iron club with little or no loft on the face, or a wood without normal bulge and roll.

Strong Grip The currently used expression to describe the exaggerated rotation of the hands in a clockwise (toward the right shoulder) position when placed on the club. (Suggest this be changed to *Closed-Face Grip*: This is more descriptive, does not imply tight pressure and is parallel in its application to other golf terms such as "closed stance.")

Supination An outward rotation of the hands (thumbs turning out) away from the body's centerline when standing in a palms-facing-the-body position. In the golf swing it is the right-hand rotation motion on the backswing and the left's on the forward swing.

Suspension Radius The distance when measured from a point at the base of the neck to the ball that is used as a reference to determine the spine angle inclination and whether or not the swing center has moved. (Illus 4-19)

Swaying A general description of exaggerated lateral body movement in the backing or forward swing.

Sweet Spot That point on the clubface where the club does not torque when struck with a sharp object. (To check, hold the club loosely at the top of the grip between two fingers. Let gravity hang it vertically. Then poke the face at various points with the leading edge of a coin until you find the spot which gives no feeling of torque in your fingers. That is the "sweet spot.") (*percussion point*)

Swing Arc The entire path the clubhead follows in its complete motion away from and toward the target. It has the dimensions of both length and width.

Swing Center A point around which the roughly circular motion of the swinging of the arms and upper trunk are made. It is located between the base of the neck and top of the spine. (Not necessarily fixed, it remains generally constant in the small swings, with some movement allowed as the swing gets longer. Nevertheless, if the movement of the swing center is too great, the overall timing of the swing becomes more difficult.) (*hub*) (f4-3)

Swinger A player using a style of striking the ball which primarily employs body rotation, light grip pressure and good rhythm to maximize centrifugal force.

Swing Plane An imaginary flat, thin surface which is used to describe the path and angle on which the club is swung. Plane has inclination or tilt, i.e., flat, medium, upright, as well as direction—inside, down the line, or outside.

Takeaway The early portion of the backswing.

Target Line An imaginary straight line drawn from behind and through the ball toward the intended target. (*Intended line of flight* or *Aim-line.*)

Tempo The rate of the swing—fast, slow, etc.

Illus 4-19 If the suspension radius length is altered markedly from address to impact, then some other compensating move would have to be made in order to achieve consistent centerface hits.

f4-3 *Not to be confused with the center of the clubhead's arc, which is located nearer the left armpit.*

(Most swings take around two seconds from takeaway to finish.)

Texas Wedge A putter used from an unusually long distance off the green. The term developed on Texas courses where the ground was so hard one couldn't effectively pitch the ball with a wedge.

Three-Quarter Shot A shot played with less than the normal length backswing or effort, designed to achieve around 75% of the regular distance for that club.

Timing The sequencing of the body parts and club to achieve the most effective motion. (*proper sequential motion, connection*) (Illus 4-20)

Toed Shot Any shot that is struck away from the club's center nearer the toe end of the club.

Topped Shot A rolling or low-bounding shot caused by striking the ball above its equator or horizontal axis.

Touch A delicate sense of feel, usually alluded to when referring to skill around the greens.

Trajectory The path a ball takes in the air. In golf it refers primarily to the height of a shot.

Transition The change of direction in the swing from back to forward, from away to toward.

Uncock To allow or cause the wrists to release or straighten in the forward swing.

Upright A swing plane which is steeper than normal; an address position which is more erect than normal; or the lie of the club in which the shaft is inserted more vertically than in a club with a normal lie.

Vector A quantity or measure related to force that has both magnitude and direction. An important factor in determining the distance and direction a ball travels.

Visualization Forming a mental picture of the correct swing or desired result prior to swinging the club. (*mental imagery, visual imagery*) (Illus 4-21)

Waggle A movement or series of movements made prior to the swing with the purpose of staying relaxed, establishing comfort or setting pace. In its most common form it con-

Illus 4-20 Timing is one of the *Principles* Betsy King, LPGA superstar, exhibits weekly on the Tour. (Photo by Don Furore)

Illus 4-21 Imaginative positive visualization is one of the strengths of golf's most traveled champion Gary Player.

sists of moving the clubhead over or in back of the ball in small wrist-cocking motions of the hands with accompanying movements of the arms or other parts of the body.

Weak Grip The currently used expression to describe an exaggerated counterclockwise (toward the left shoulder) rotational positioning of the hands when placed on the club. (Change to *Open-Face Grip*. This is more descriptive, does not imply an over-relaxed

hold, and, in its application, is parallel to other golf terms such as "open stance.")

Whiff A complete miss when attempting to strike the ball. (*air shot*)

Yips A psychological condition affecting the nerves which causes the player to lose control of his hands and the club. Usually associated with putting, it can also intrude upon other parts of the short game such as chipping, pitching or bunker play. (*twitches*)

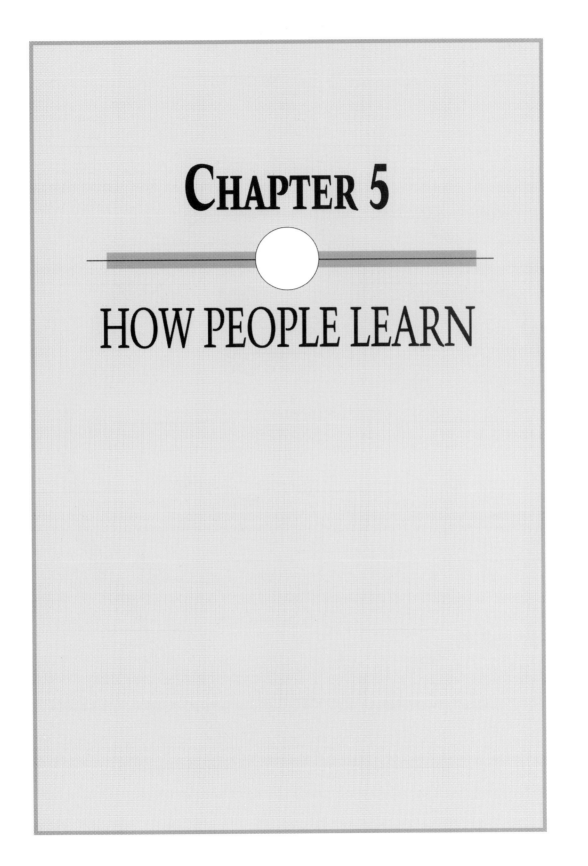

CHAPTER 5

HOW PEOPLE LEARN

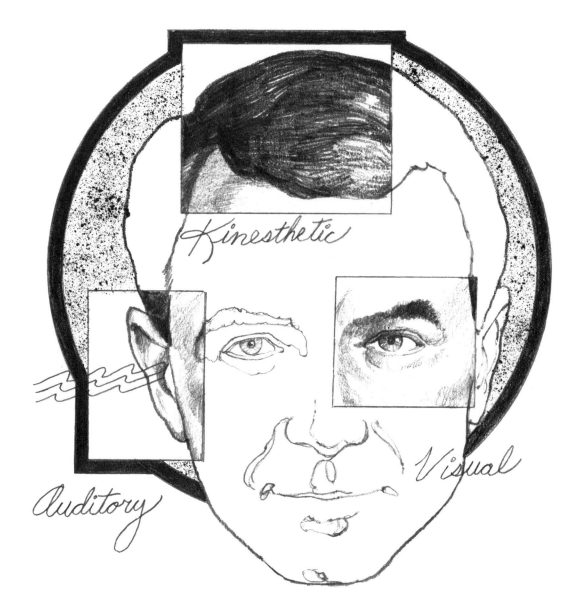

Kinesthetic

Auditory

Visual

The novice golfer reaches one of the game's early mileposts when he makes the observation, "There certainly is a lot of psychology associated with learning and playing this game." Making that discovery and successfully coping with it are two different matters. Golf is psychology personified. In any sport the more time you have to think about your performance the more susceptible you are to becoming "psyched." Playing golf provides that opportunity from 60 to 160 times a round. In fact, you really can't separate the physical and psychological when considering one's performance. Together they are present in the execution of every shot. Nonetheless, we can identify and discuss facets of learning which relate more to the mind than the body.

How *do we* learn a motor skill, any kind of skill like typing, ping-pong, or playing the piano? The honest answer is we're not absolutely certain, at least not as far as the details of what happens precisely from the brain to the nerves and muscles to produce a given movement. Motor learning *theories* do exist which attempt to explain the general pattern of the learning process, be it basketball free-throw shooting or swinging a golf club.

HOW WE LEARN

How do we learn? Learning is a process that has stages, and the process of learning starts by perception . . . perceiving through our senses . . . using the ears, eyes, and body's internal sensory receptors. The stimuli that the teacher gives to the student are called CUES—they are classified as either verbal, visual, or kinesthetic, to correspond with our senses of hearing, sight, and feel. (Illus 5-1, 5-2)

COMPARING THE THREE FORMS OF LEARNING

Think of learning how to ride a bike. Someone telling you how would not be very useful. Seeing someone else ride would help. But actually doing it and developing the feeling

Illus 5-1 The weakest way to learn a motor skill is by listening.

Illus 5-2 Golfers learn visually, with demonstration being the most commonly used visual form.

Visual

If a picture is worth "a thousand words" then visual cues must be more effective than verbal cues, and they are. Be it videotape, movies, still pictures, a mirror, demonstration or visual imagery, the golfer will definitely profit if visual aids accompany verbalized instruction. The visual aid may be as sophisticated as the latest multidimensional computerized graphic reproduction of the golfer's swing overlayed or placed side-by-side on the screen and compared to a current PGA Champion. Or, it may be as simple as a cut out from a recent golf magazine picturing a champion in a certain swing position compared to what the golfer sees in the mirror in his own production of a similar swing. In either instance visual learning is a powerful tool.

Kinesthetic

Kinesthetic cues are considered a strong means of communicating information to assist the learning of a motor skill because they help transmit "feel." They can take the form of drills, manipulation or teaching devices, but their primary purpose is to create within the player the illusive quality of feel, the one which all golfers must have to play well, no matter how mechanically proficient they are. Add kinesthetics to the visual and verbal and it constitutes a powerful potential learning combination. Through all three senses the golfer can best obtain information.

through one's kinesthetic senses (f 5-3) is the answer. So, while words are an easy way for the teacher to present information, they are not as effective, particularly for the beginner or less experienced player, as *visual learning* from still pictures, video movies, mirrors and demonstration or *kinesthetic learning* from drills, manipulation and learning aids. The advanced player can, on occasion, communicate with his teacher over the telephone or just sit and talk together and be helped, but this would hardly be effective with the novice.

Verbal

One very good reason why listening is a poor way to try to learn golf is that the game *does not have a precise language.* This has been identified and dealt with in the previous chapter. Its terms range from inconsistent to inaccurate, and from ambiguous to confusing. Verbalizing the golf swing as the primary means of instruction has many shortcomings.

A LEARNING MODEL

In the learning theory model shown here the professional's cues or information received by the golfer are defined as INPUT. (Illus 5-3)

INTEGRATION is the mental and physical processing of the cues (like data in a computer) that the golfer must undertake. If the information is simple and clear the golfer will have a better chance to understand or gain insight.

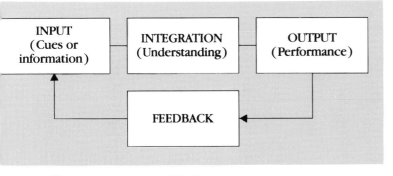

Illus 5-3 A schematic model of the learning process.

The golfer's ability to integrate the information will determine the quality of his *OUTPUT* or performance. When the performance (the swing or the shot) is completed, there is a result ("good" or "bad") which gives the golfer *FEED-BACK* on the degree of success. This process is repeated in some form or other on every trial that is made.

THE LEARNING CURVE

The acquisition of a skill improves as the golfer acquires accurate information, practices and assimilates. The learning is not a linear activity. Improvement is not constant. There are plateaus and regressions which must be experienced and these become the most critical times for the golfer. A golfer's simulated learning curve is illustrated below.

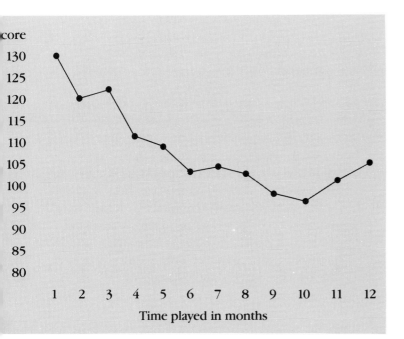

During extended periods of plateauing (6–9 mos.) and particularly at times of regression (10–12 mos.), you may need encouragement. The rate of improvement slows, and the "law of diminishing returns" takes over, particularly in the mechanical realm. But improvement can continue as long as the elements of motivation, practice and proper technique are in place.

> "There are no mistakes in communication, only outcomes."
> —Richard Bandler & John Grinder

The primary causes of plateauing or regressing can be found in one or more of the following reasons:

1. Loss of interest or motivation
2. Focus on incorrect cues
3. Fatigue
4. Emotional interference
5. Change in technique
6. Lack of understanding
7. Physical deficiency
8. Low level of ambition
9. Period of assimilation and transition

If your progress has come to a halt or has regressed, study this list, determine the cause and apply a remedy.

VISUAL AIDS
TO ASSIST VISUAL LEARNING CUES

There are other visual cues which can be provided by using free or low-cost visual aids. A scrapbook of pictures that are cut out from used golf magazines showing the various positions and moves of great players may help to construct a correct visual swing model. Those of Tour stars contained at the end of this book are an example. Tees, balls or clubs placed on the ground or spray-painted lines to help visualize path, strings, two-by-fours and mirrors also

Illus 5-4 Visual aids can take many forms such as painting lines on the ground or on a mat.

come under the "not so expensive" yet worthwhile aids that can improve visual cues. (Illus 5-4)

One of the very best visual aids which can be obtained quite reasonably is a mirror. A large full-length mirror placed where you can swing and view your positions is a wonderful visual aid. Putting taped vertical, horizontal and angled swing plane lines on the mirror provide excellent reference tools to monitor alignment, spine angle, a reverse weight shift, position, path, etc.

There are, of course, more expensive and in some cases more effective aids available to communicate visually. Thirty-five mm reflex cameras equipped with a motor drive will provide 5 pictures per swing and freeze the action. Of course, one has to wait for the film to be processed but it provides a reliable record.

Videotape is the most widely used of the sophisticated aids to provide visual feedback. It invariably proves to be an attention-getting and motivating tool and is extremely effective *when used correctly.* In a complex action like

the golf swing it is particularly useful to be able to watch the act repeatedly and focus on individual segments. The major limitation had been video's inability to freeze detail, particularly in the hitting area. But non-blur pictures using freeze action in the hitting area are now available in moderately priced video equipment.

PRERECORDED VIDEOTAPES

Watching videotapes of a good player's swing would be helpful for most golfers, particularly if the golfer is a predominantly visual learner. Sybervision™ is a sophisticated example of visual learning which shows star performers making a variety of repeated successful shots. The visual presentation is enhanced by using different speeds, auditory sounds, graphic representations and changing perspectives to imprint your brain with what you see. It is the modern-day scientific equivalent of caddies watching good players and copying what they saw.

IMPROVING KINESTHETIC CUES

Are there ways to learn the feeling of a golf swing without actually making the swing and striking a ball? The inventors and manufacturers of teaching aids must believe in this, judging by the number of teaching devices advertised in the golf literature. Long before the 1940s when Ernest Jones tied a pocketknife onto a handkerchief and swung it to demonstrate centrifugal force and timing there were commercial training devices to help teach "feel." We are just starting to see swing "teaching machines" which literally program the golf swing motion into the pupil by mechanically manipulating him and/or the club through what the inventor considers the proper positions. These machines won't teach a person to play, but they *may* teach him to make a certain swing. In the meantime, anything you can add to your program which helps teach "feel" as well as program the muscles to perform correct repetitive action would seem useful.

THE VALUE OF TEACHING AIDS

In the minds of some, teaching devices fall into the category of gimmickry, running from questionable to worthless. True, there are bad ones which tend to drag the good ones down, but this attitude seems to be changing. It is easy to understand that a player generally does not seek change if he's satisfied with what he's doing, but the use of valid learning aids can make it easier to learn.

LEARNING STYLES

Variation in learning theory and method should not be considered a negative. In fact, just the opposite is probably true. There is variety in the players who come to the practice tee. Should there not be variety in how a particular player should learn? The fundamentals may be standardized but the approach to learning can be varied according to the golfer's needs. Teaching styles vary among professionals, and learning styles vary among students. The engineer might be taught more effectively using mechanical examples than a musician or salesman. For example, one PGA professional, Chuck Cook, was explaining two approaches he has used with TOUR players to get more extension through the impact area. With Tom Kite, the analytical type, he described the exact position of the hands, their relationship to the body and the angle of club inclination. To Ben Crenshaw, the more sensory type, he simply said, "Just picture driving the ball underneath a bench placed out in front of you." Both methods were effective, but they needed to match the student.

Are you a primarily visual, cognitive (verbal-auditory) or kinesthetic learner? Acknowledging your occupation may be of help. People in the sciences tend to be more cognitive. They need detail to fully understand the "why" of what they are being asked to do during a lesson. Reading about golf and studying teaching and playing methods is enjoyable for them. A book like Homer Kelley's *The Golfing Machine* might be of more use to the cognitive learner than Toski's and Love's, *How To Feel A Real Swing*, which would be ideal for the "kinesthetic learner." Video instruction like Sybervision would seem totally appropriate for the visual learner, while at the same time it can easily be understood why the other learning types might find it of less value. (Illus 5-5)

INDIVIDUAL DIFFERENCE

Not only do we learn with different styles but at different rates under different conditions and at different rates at different ages. What takes one golfer two lessons to achieve may take six lessons for another. What a player could accomplish in a given period of time when he was twenty years old may take him three times as long at age sixty.

THE MOST IMPORTANT FACTOR IN LEARNING

Having the most accurate information, the perfect facility and all the available learning tools would be of little value if you had no desire to

Illus 5-5 A visual learner would appreciate this concept of a bunker shot.

Illus 5-6 One can overcome formidable odds when motivated, as did Calvin Peete.

cultural ghetto community, his future portended little hope other than that of a migrant farm worker, unless he could find "a way out." Peete read in the newspaper that Jack Nicklaus had made $1,000,000 playing golf, so Peete decided that he would try to make a living in the same manner. Using a high school athletic field on which to practice he laid a paperback golf instructional book on the ground, studied the pictures, copied them to the best of his ability and hit balls. Though he had a deformed left arm from a childhood accident, no advantage of a golf facility on which to practice or play, very limited financial resources and no teacher, he succeeded. What does that say about learning? That the most important factor is *desire to succeed*. Theoretically, learning can continue to infinity, stopping only when the person loses his motivation to continue. When that happens, learning stops and deterioration in performance sets in.

learn. On the other hand those people who are intensely motivated will, in the most primitive circumstances, without easy access to any tutorial assistance, find some way to learn. One of the game's all-time straightest hitters, Calvin Peete, became a PGA Tour winner strictly out of the determination to do so. (Illus 5-6) He was motivated by circumstance. Being one of thirteen children and living in a Florida agri-

THE OVERALL OBJECTIVE

What's the value to the world in lowering your handicap or winning a tournament? There is none, unless in doing so you further develop as an individual . . . more self confidence, perseverance, appreciation for the effort it takes to obtain reward, more tolerance of others, etc. Golf can be not only a builder of golf technique but of people.

CHAPTER 6

PRE-SHOT
FUNDAMENTALS:
Grip, Aim, Setup

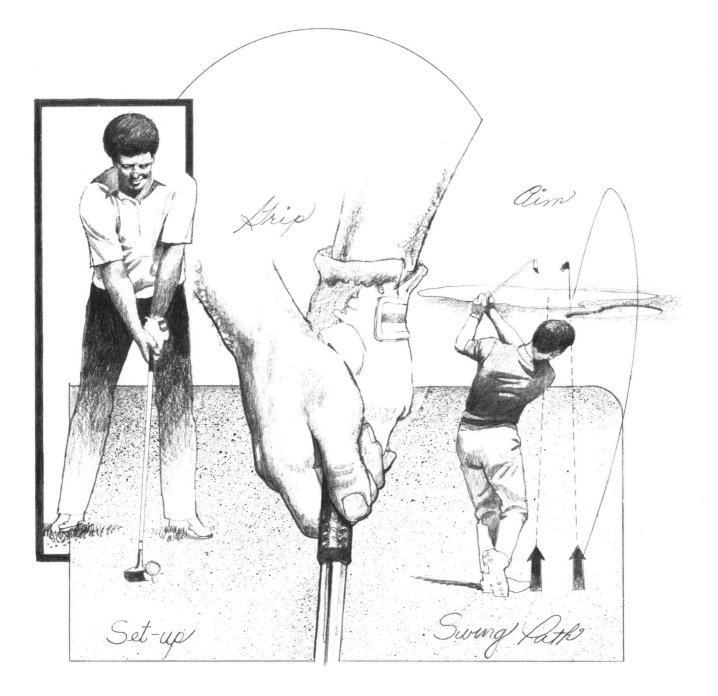

Set-up

Grip

Aim

Swing Path

Full shots constitute less than 45% of the scoring in golf for almost all levels of players. Yet whenever golfers gather, the full swing monopolizes the practice time, the effort and the conversation. "The swing," as it is more commonly called (as though there were just one), can be made in a variety of angles, shapes and sizes while still being effective. (Illus 6-1, 6-2, 6-3) Because there is no one solution for finding a swing style that fits all, there is no universal agreement on which style is best. So people keep searching and expounding upon their results, which explains titles of books like *The Search for the Perfect Swing*. The swing mystique continues because there is no simple solution. (Illus 6-4)

Therefore, when we discuss "The Swing" in the ensuing chapters we are referring not to any particular swing style, but rather to many of the preference choices that the player makes in placing his hands on the club, positioning the clubface and his body to the ball and target, and setting the club in motion in an attempt to propel the ball to the target. From those preference choices we hope to demonstrate some patterns and draw conclusions which may help the reader in his search for an effective technique.

WHAT IS A SWING?

Understanding the word *swing* itself as it applies to golf would be useful in attempting to perform this action. Dictionary definitions of swing use descriptive phrases like "back and forth with a regular motion," "to hang or sus-

pend," "to cause to turn in alternate directions," "cause to move in a curve," "to move freely," all quite applicable to a golf swing. Whether the player attempts to get results with a hitting swing (a more right-sided, leverage-dominated action) or a "swinging hit" (more left-sided with a centrifugal force emphasis) is of no concern to the ball. The important point to grasp is that in order to get the best results, some type of swinging action must take place. The ball only responds to the clubface, path, centeredness, speed and angle of approach, not to how they were produced. The ball doesn't care. The word swing, however, appears in every instructional book ever written, so whatever style the player prefers, the idea of "making a swing" should be a part of any instructional plan. (Illus 6-5)

TWO PHASES TO THE SWING . . .

The swing has two distinct phases: (1) *preswing*, before the major motion begins, and (2) the *actual swing* itself. One of the hardest lessons to learn is the importance of the three preshot or pre-swing principles: grip, aim and setup.

THE GRIP—ITS IMPORTANCE

How can anything so bland, so inert, so preliminary as *The Grip* in golf be so important to performance? Take a poll among the millions of golfers who have received instruction and you'll find that the grip wins "Golf's Dullest

Illus 6-1 Professional golfers exhibiting three different finish positions. Note the variation in elbow separation among the three. Arnold Palmer. (Photo by Jeff McBride)

Illus 6-2 Larry Nelson (Photo by Jeff McBride)

Illus 6-3 Mike Reid (Photo by Jeff McBride)

Principle Award" hands down (no pun intended).

Yet, PGA teachers and tournament players line up in dutiful respect to extol the importance of grip as a Gibraltar-size rock-solid PRIN-

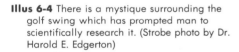

Illus 6-4 There is a mystique surrounding the golf swing which has prompted man to scientifically research it. (Strobe photo by Dr. Harold E. Edgerton)

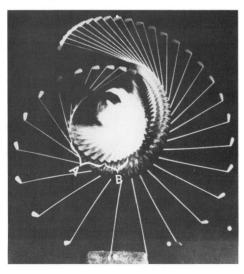

CIPLE around which to build a golf swing. Don't take our word for it, read the captions surrounding this chapter.

One of the game's great teacher/player professionals, Tommy Armour, after a career of watching thousands of swings, said, "If I could stand the strain I would devote at least a couple of weeks to the grip in golf instruction." He may have been exaggerating, but it showed how serious he was in expressing his feelings on the absolute high priority that grip plays in good golf.

If one were endowed with hands like Armour's—strong and supple—he'd enjoy a distinct advantage in his potential to control the club. These attributes are an advantage, but anyone, even with untalented and unathletic hands, can learn to position them in a workable manner. Despite this fact, if an inspection were called for on the way most of the world's golfers place their hands on a golf club, it would reveal that faulty grips prevail. Ask the top 60 PGA Tour money winners participating at the

Illus 6-5 A sample of a swinging motion in which there is rhythm, acceleration and consistency.

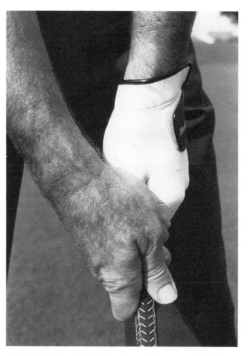

Illus 6-6 "Good golf begins with a good grip." (Ben Hogan)

weekly pro-ams in the U.S. and they'll attest to the scarcity of sound grips among their amateur partners. It explains how an old chestnut like "you never see a good player with a bad grip or a bad player with a good grip" achieves credence. Grip does make a difference! If one is seeking a higher authority on the issue, someone in the golfing immortal class, then let's wrap up this case for the grip's importance with the quote of a man who, when discussing golf, didn't waste words on trivia. He said simply, "Good golf begins with a good grip." Ben Hogan has spoken. (Illus 6-6)

A GOOD GRIP

What is a good grip? Which style should be selected? Being bombarded by tips, hints, secrets from books, newspapers, magazines and TV must raise some basic questions for the player seeking golfing truth about grip. What should the player do? Interlock or overlap? Grip

tightly or lightly? Use a long thumb or a short thumb? Show three knuckles or two knuckles? Lay the grip in the roots of the fingers or diagonally across the hand? Try to keep the hands quiet or active? Apply constant or changing pressure? And how about all of the variations within and choices beyond these examples? There must be countless combinations.

Back to the question: What is a good grip? *It is the one which lets the player hit the most good shots!* More specifically, it maximizes the number of shots that meet the criteria for distance and direction. Since solving the problem of distance and direction is golf's ultimate and absolute challenge, then whatever combination of PREFERENCES a player utilizes to accomplish that objective becomes a "good grip."

> "I have to rate a faulty grip as the most common cause of bad golf."
> —Tommy Bolt

ACCEPTED GRIP STATEMENTS

Actually there are more areas of agreement than disagreement on grip among teachers and players. These areas of consensus are listed below:

Areas of General Agreement on the Grip

1. Even though there is a natural position in which the hands should hang, the correct golf grip does not seem to come naturally to the novice player. When the club is first placed in the hands of a beginner, he invariably holds it in a position which will either fail to return the face to square consistently, or will not provide for the greatest clubhead speed. Therefore, the grip must be *learned*.
2. If a golfer learns the grip incorrectly from the beginning, he can always change his grip, but it will take longer than he realized for it to feel natural. In addition, he can expect that during stressful situations, he will instinctively want to return to the former grip. Whatever discomfort or repetitive practice one must experience in achieving a proper grip, it is worth the effort.
3. The palms of the hands for most players should basically face each other or be turned slightly inward because that is the way most arms hang, but there are exceptions. In some cases, particularly with heavy barrel-chested people, the hands can work effectively if each is rotated slightly outward, i.e., weak left, strong right, provided the rotation is equal, i.e., the same number of degrees. (f6-1) There is variation of opinion on where the V's should point and how many knuckles one should see. These are only guidelines anyway, since it is easier to see more knuckles from a low hand address position than a high one. But

f6-1 *Extremes in rotation must be avoided, as such a position would hinder natural forearm rotation.*

"The basic factor in all good golf is the grip. Get it right, and all other progress follows."
—Tommy Armour

even among those who disagree on how "rotated the hands should be," the majority feel that when the palms are not aligned close to, or in, a parallel fashion, "they work against each other." For those teachers who allow one of the hands to be further adjusted, it is usually the left that is turned clockwise to a more closed-face position while the right palm still faces the target.

4. Grip pressure should be light enough to encourage clubhead speed without losing directional control; it should be firm enough to keep the club from turning in the hands on contact, yet not so firm that it destroys feel or speed.
5. The placement of the hands should facilitate their working together as one unit, with no slippage or repositioning.
6. Ultimately, the player should become comfortable with his grip and confident about the position of the clubface during the swing.
7. The grip in the left-hand should be one where the last three fingers of the left hand capture the club handle against the butt portion of the palm, while the grip in the right-hand cradles the club handle more in the fingers.

These are guidelines that one could use to develop a philosophy on grip. But there is so much more. This part of the chapter also deals with the recognition of PREFERENCES—those little variations within the PRINCIPLES that can make a big difference.

GRIP OPTIONS—OVERLAP, INTERLOCK OR TEN FINGERS

There are four basic points within the PRINCIPLES of grip where one can make choices and

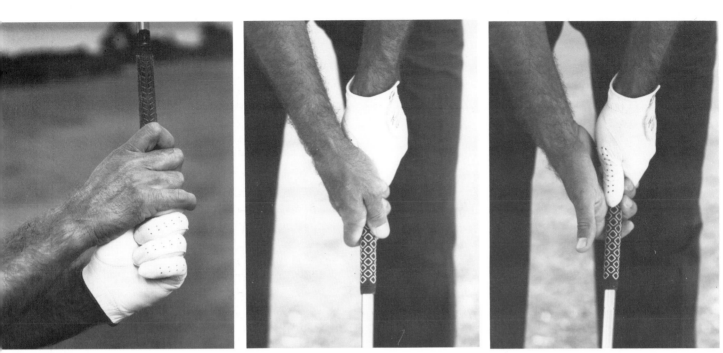

Illus 6-7 One of the elements of grip is the placement of the hands relative to one another high or low on the shaft. This placement is too high, over the end of the grip.

Illus 6-8 Another element of grip is positioning, or the amount of rotation of the hands, clockwise or counterclockwise. Here is a natural arm hanging position grip with 2½ knuckles of the left hand showing and the "V" of the right hand pointing to the right ear.

Illus 6-9 Pressure is a third element of grip. It is more probable that the correct pressure will occur in the right hand when the grip is carried in the fingers rather than the palm.

demonstrate PREFERENCES. They are: (1) Placement, (2) Positioning, (3) Pressure, and (4) Precision. (Illus 6-7, 6-8, 6-9, 6-10)

Illus 6-10 Another element, and maybe the most important one in grip, is precision—doing it the same way each time.

Point 1

"Placement" is the location of the hands on the grip in a vertical axis. How far up or down the shaft is each placed? Should a player choke down on the grip or go up slightly over the butt end? Are the hands spread apart? Are they flush with each other, overlapped, double overlapped, one on top of the other (a putting grip for some) or cross-handed? These are examples of placement choices.

The choice of grip *placement* will be affected by the size of the player's hands, their strength and suppleness. For example, the Vardon overlapping grip has been passed down from one of the game's early great players, Harry Vardon, a man with large fingers and strong hands. Its use by a majority of golfers with these attributes can hardly be questioned.

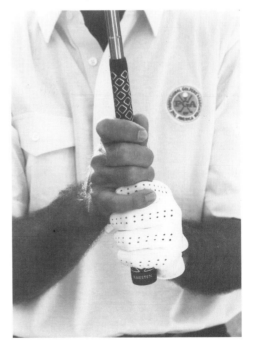

But what about the people who don't have athletic hands—the short-fingered, those weak in grip strength, the junior player, a large percentage of ladies and others who find the overlap position less suitable for their hand structure? That's when the other options need to be considered. Two U.S. Open Champions from the 1980s, Andy North and Jack Nicklaus, use the interlocking grip. Both feel the hands more secure and unified with this grip. Unquestionably, it is useful for some players. However, be certain that the locking of the right little finger and left index finger do not get so deep as to force the right-hand grip on the club into the palm rather than the fingers. This would tend to limit wrist joint mobility.

The *ten-finger* grip, sometimes called a "baseball grip," is natural for most new players. (Illus 6-11) They seek to cover more of the grip surface in an effort to use the right hand and exert pressure against the shaft so as to square the face and provide power. Obviously one gets more right-hand leverage in a *ten-finger* grip (no overlap or interlock), since more of the grip surface on the lower portion of the shaft is covered. That's why this grip is often recommended to young golfers and to ladies whose smaller hands

Illus 6-11 When the player lacks strength, or wishes to apply more right-hand leverage, a ten-finger grip should be considered.

occupy less area on the grip. These are the players who cannot generate sufficient speed through centrifugal force using their large muscles. Additional emphasis on the right hand by putting more of it on the grip can be a disadvantage, however, if the player still hasn't trained his left side to be an equal partner in the swing. The tendency to put early leverage pressure on the shaft by the right hand when using a ten-finger grip is why it is generally recommended only for those groups previously mentioned. That is why it is important to understand the relative advantages and disadvantages of the three grips: overlapping, interlocking and *ten-finger*.

How to Choose

How do your hands compare with each other in strength? A golfer may have a left-hand grip strength of 127 lbs. measured on a hand dynamometer (grip-strength gauge) and a right-hand reading of 166. One can see which hand will dominate. Should he emphasize left-sidedness in the swing, in which case he would subjugate the right in the grip, setup and swing to equalize the two; or, should the emphasis be on the stronger right hand, developing a right-sided dominant action?

The choice of right-side or left-side emphasis could hinge on several factors. Right-side emphasis with a ten-finger grip might be the choice, a) if the player has a limited backswing length and is unable to recruit the large muscles of the trunk and back, b) if the player has adequate flexibility to turn but low levels of strength in the trunk and back and needs right-side leverage both for power and to square the face.

A left-side emphasis with an interlocking or overlapping grip might better fit the individual with a) reasonable strength levels who also possesses the flexibility to make a full turn and

> "It is impossible to play good golf without a proper grip."
> —Sam Snead

recruit the large muscles of the back and trunk; or b) one who is very dominant in the right side and causes the left side to break down continually.

Strive for Balance

Golf is neither a right-sided nor left-sided game. Golf is a two-sided (bi-lateral) game. What we are striving for is the correct balance of each side, left and right, to produce a swing that is timed properly and produces maximum power. The difficulty of the task is that players have different levels of strength, flexibility and dominance patterns. What works for one is not necessarily the best for the next. The challenge is to find one's strength and limitations, maximize the first and minimize the second to find the best balance of a right- or left-side emphasis by encouraging the right or left side or by focusing on the two sides together. But we do know that the left side is the leader; it *must arrive first*.

Point 2

"Positioning" in the grip is the amount of rotation of the hands clockwise or counterclockwise, generally referred to as "strong" or "weak." Positioning is dependent upon the size and strength of the player's hands plus the shape of the shot he/she is trying to hit. The terms "strong" and "weak," when used in a golf grip context, are both imprecise and misleading. Traditionally, a strong grip is one in which the hands are rotated clockwise on the shaft so the left hand shows more knuckles (three or four) and the right hand will have the V pointing to the right shoulder, or even farther to the right. In this text this grip positioning will be called a "closed-face grip," a grip position that encourages a hook. One redeeming value of a hook is that it does produce less backspin on the ball and therefore frequently results in more distance. (f6-2) Most of golf's great players hooked the ball when they were young. That fact simply demonstrates that these players

f6-2 *A hook does not produce topspin, only less backspin. Only a topped shot or rolling ball produces topspin.*

were physically talented enough to generate a lot of clubhead speed with rotation of the shaft and clubface. To curb the tendency to hook excessively, the physically gifted player may move his grip counterclockwise into a "weaker" position. He shows fewer knuckles of the left hand, so the back of the left hand faces the target more squarely. If a golfer sees fewer than two knuckles we'll refer to that positon as an "open-face grip." (Illus 6-12) With a "neutral grip" the player's arms and hands hang naturally, with the hands rotated so the thumbs point slightly inward toward the body's centerline. Gripping the club from this position would find each thumb resting slightly on the opposite side of the grip's centerline. Generally two knuckles would be visible on the back of the left hand, one knuckle on the back of the right.

What about you? Are you a strong player . . . do you fight the hook? Ask a teaching profes-

Illus 6-12 The left-hand positioning where only one knuckle was visible to the player with the right hand matching would encourage an open clubface.

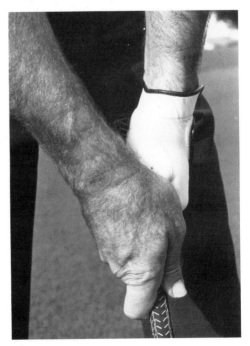

> "The grip is the crucial junction point from which all the body's strength and rhythm are transmitted to the club."
> —Arnold Palmer

sional that question and probably 75% of the answers would be: "No, more of my pupils slice the ball rather than hook it." You have some choices. One is to stay with what you have. "If it works, don't fix it." But if the slice causes a distance loss which is critical, then a change *may be* necessary. Tom Watson's one-knuckle grip position is generally for a physically talented, strong, highly supple striker of the ball. If you can match Watson's physical ability, then you can copy his grip. Lacking this ability, chances are you'll need to employ a grip with more clockwise rotation—show two knuckles, three, or in extreme cases, even more in the left hand. Whatever the choice, the right palm must be positioned behind the shaft because the player will always exert pressure on the shaft in the direction the palm is facing. Try to avoid extremes because any extreme rotation of the hands to either a closed-face or open-face position will limit the degree of wrist cock available.

Point 3

"Pressure" is not difficult to describe; it's simply how hard one is squeezing the club. It is extremely difficult, however, to explain the proper amount of grip pressure and to communicate that feel. We hear words such as "light" and "firm" which, of course, are only relative. Light pressure for a strong person may be "squeezing the club to death" for someone with weak hands; besides, the correct pressure is relative. A club which is traveling at a higher rate of speed (the driver) will exert more pulling force away from the player and require a stronger grip pressure to hold than one moving more slowly (the putter). The player, however, does not need to consciously grip tighter as

speed increases; it happens instinctively. This can be demonstrated by gripping the club in the left hand and raising it to waist height in front of you. Have a friend take hold of the head and pull the club from your hand; you should resist. When the friend tugs, you automatically increase the grip pressure commensurate with the amount of pull. The same thing happens in the swing. It's a wonderful example of the adaptability of the human mind and body.

Because of the importance of achieving the correct feel, it's good practice when working on a grip change to do so in the presence of a professional instructor who can see and hear the swing to determine whether the correct pressure is being applied. Analogies seem to work well when trying to communicate feel. For example, if seeking light pressure for a more centrifugal force-type swing, "You are exerting the right amount of pressure if the weight of the clubhead can actually be sensed as though it were a rock on the end of a rope that is about to be swung." Or, "Imagine the grip portion of the club is a tube of toothpaste. Don't squeeze so hard as to squirt the paste all over the bathroom, but do apply enough pressure to let it come out gradually and evenly." Basically we should grip the club tightly enough to hold onto it. As the club changes positions, the pressure should be increased or decreased depending upon the resistance of gravity, inertia and centrifugal force.

Where in the grip should the pressure be exerted? Those players who employ a conscious striking action with the right hand usually describe more firmness in the grip and often a sensation of pressure by the fingers against the shaft. In their hand placement they may trigger the right index finger slightly down the grip for greater leverage and will have a pronounced callous on the right index finger where it rests

> "A correct grip is a fundamental necessity in the golf swing."
> —Bobby Jones

> "Without a proper grip no player can expect to hit accurate shots with even a fair degree of consistency."
> —Gary Player

against the grip. Obviously, with either an "open-face" (weak) or "closed-face" (strong) grip style, there will be some leverage exerted against the shaft with that part of the finger at impact. What we are talking about is the degree of leverage which is consciously applied.

Some leading players of a half-century ago felt that the primary pressure should be between the pincers of the thumb and forefinger of each hand. Today's imperative, "Hold on with the last three fingers of the left hand," was not as critical a factor in their day because of the swing style which employed a great deal of hand action. That former style is seldom seen or talked about today, yet it may have some rare application to the "rigid-hands player" who needs more freedom in his swing.

Point 4

The last of the four points under discussion is simple, yet critically important. It deals with *"precision"*; it's an either/or situation. That is, either one grips the club in a precise fashion (the same way each time) or is careless about the grip so that it is seldom the same.

Altering the rotational positioning of the hands a half-inch in either direction from one swing to the next can result in a tee shot that travels 30–40 yards off line. Subtle changes in a grip can be the difference between driving the ball in the fairway or into the water, hitting the green or the bunker, making the putt or lipping it out. Golf is a game of consistency. The foundation for consistency is a *repeating* swing that must start with *a repeating* grip. Hogan, in further commenting on the subject said, "In golf there are certain things you must do quite precisely, where being half right accomplishes nothing. This certainly applies to grip."

GRIP ROUTINE

Consistency is a by-product of having a routine. You should develop your own routine for taking the grip, one that you perform the same way before every swing. One possibility is to come in from the side; grip the club in the fingers of the right hand alone and sole it behind the ball, checking carefully to see that it is at right angles to the target line. Then swing the left hand from a natural hanging position onto the grip. (Illus 6-13) See that the club is securely braced against the heel pad and palm of the hand by the last three fingers. In this position the player can exert the greatest control. Use markings on the grip portion of the club to check correct hand positioning. From there, you can waggle the club while adjusting the feet, body and the hands. The club is now ready to be swung.

Two other grip routines are also pictured. (Illus 6-14, 6-15) Your grip or grip routine may not be exactly the one prescribed by Watson or Nicklaus, but one that is compatible with your needs. (Illus 6-16)

Illus 6-13 Developing a grip routine is important for consistency. Here is an example of a right-hand-first style.

Illus 6-14 Another grip routine, starting with the left hand at the side.

Illus 6-15 And another, starting with both hands on the club, held in front to check the face.

Illus 6-16 The style is not so important, just as long as the end result is correct.

Some of these decisions are reached by trial and error. After making adjustments, you should settle on a grip that becomes so comfortable that the hands fall naturally into place each time. Once the best position has been chosen, make sure you stay with it. *No thought in golf is more fallacious than believing the grip is something to alter every time you wish to correct a faulty shot pattern.*

MORE OBSERVATIONS ON THE GRIP

1. The reason one needs strength in golf is so he can produce speed without great effort. The reason one needs strength in the hands is so that he can grip without tension.

2. Here are some simple drills to tell whether you are changing your grip during the swing. To check for regripping, place a dime in the fleshy pad between the thumb and knuckle of the index finger of your right hand. If the dime falls out, you have

regripped on the backswing. To see if you are letting go with the last three fingers of the left hand, place a tee (point first) between the club and the pad of the left hand. If it falls out during the backswing, you have opened your left-hand grip.

3. Players who have spells of erratic shot-making sometimes eliminate this malady by shortening grip placement (choking down) and improving timing and squareness of contact.

4. If you quickly wear holes in your glove on the heel pad area of the left hand, you are loosening your grip in that hand, causing friction and wear as the grip handle rubs against the glove.

5. Using an interlocking grip and placing the thumb of the left hand outside (off the

> "Unless a player gets his or her grip correct, trouble begins immediately."
> —Bobby Locke

grip) provides more flexibility in the wrist for those who may be arthritic, exceptionally rigid, or have had a left thumb injury. For a person with a normal range of motion, however, it tends to encourage more freedom than is normally desired, promoting spells of wildness in shot-making.

6. There are three acceptable variations of the Vardon overlapping grip; laying the little finger of the right hand on top of the index finger of the left, as Vardon himself did; placing the little finger in the space between the index and middle fingers, a variation which is probably more common than the original; hooking the little finger of the right hand around the knuckle of the index finger of the left.

7. The strong, supple player can learn to draw the ball without a grip change. That's the preferred style of many good players. They would rather draw it with a modification of the swing or setup, not by modifying the grip. The former could include different body alignment, repositioning the ball in the stance, more hand and arm rotation in the swing or bowing the wrist at impact. They all are possibilities. For the less-gifted player, a grip change may be necessary to produce a draw.

8. The degree of extension of the left thumb (long or short) is an indication of how the club has been placed in the left hand. A "long thumb" is the result of a placement where the club shaft runs perpendicular to the fingers, almost straight across their base. A long thumb placement encourages a longer swing while restricting wrist action and forearm rotation near impact. A "short thumb" will find the club shaft running more diagonally across the hand. This placement restricts backswing length and encourages more hand action and forearm rotation near impact. Both extremes should be avoided if a natural swing is desired.

9. Two very useful suggestions for determining the grip are: a) Develop a natural grip in which the arms hang at the sides, re-

> "The grip is the most important single consideration in learning to play winning golf."
> —Byron Nelson

laxed, with no tension. Then bring them together directly in front of you, allowing the right to hang slightly below the left; b) Make sure the grip matches the swing action.

AIM AND SETUP

Golf is a target game. Granted, distance must be overcome—often long stretches of it—but it is distance to a precise location. Considering the size of the target (4¼ inches in diameter) and its relation to the size of the playing field (generally over 100 acres), it is obvious that direction must always play a critical role. A good golf swing produces the ball/club contact which overcomes the problems of distance and direction. Although scoring in the game is determined by a high percentage of skills other than the full swing, golfers nonetheless tend to get caught up in the intricacies of the elusive swing motion. However, many who follow this quest fail to recognize that no matter how efficient and precise the swinging mechanism becomes, it is of little consequence unless aimed correctly.

Is aim important? Consider this. A perfect swing made in the wrong direction will produce a most imperfect shot. Timing, rhythm, speed and square contact are of little value unless they produce a shot that travels toward the target. What a waste to make a good swing and come up with a bad shot because of faulty aim!

What does one need to aim in golf? First the clubface, then himself. The "himself" includes the eyes, shoulders, hips, knees and feet. Don't think that correctly lining up one part of the body automatically aligns the others. Most assuredly it does not.

If the player's objective is to hit a straight

shot to the target, it will have to be accomplished in the following way: the clubhead must be traveling on a path toward the target at contact and the face must be square or at right angles to that path. *Whatever combination of body and clubface positions which consistently accomplishes these objectives is the correct aim for the golfer.* Read the above last sentence again! It doesn't say you *must* assume your setup with your stance or clubface square, open or closed. It says, "Whatever combination of body and clubface positions which consistently accomplishes these objectives" . . . these objectives are "path to the target and face square" at impact.

HOW WE AIM

You may be better able to appreciate the problems associated with developing a consistent aim in golf if you compare it to aiming in other sports.

Think of how a rifle is aimed. The barrel of the delivery system at short range is pointed right at the target. Look down the barrel (or sighting device) with the sighting eye. When the barrel is lined up with the target, fire! In golf, if the eyes, feet, hips or shoulders were the delivery system (equivalent to the gun barrel,) one would aim them at the target. But they are not. The delivery system (the clubhead) can be positioned on a line as far as two-and-a-half feet in front of the sighting device (the eyes).

The eyes have a different perpsective than the clubhead or even the left shoulder, which is a primary controller of the clubhead's path. The eyes view the shot from a place in-between the clubhead and shoulder. The fact that the right eye is farther from the shoulder line than the left eye when your head turns to look at the target may be part of the reason that right-handers frequently aim their shoulders too far to the right. They are trying to put their shoulders on line with what their sighting eye sees as it looks from its perspective.

Now, add that to the fact that the positioning of the feet, knees and hips has an influence on the alignment of the shoulders at impact, and it is easy to understand why even the greatest players in the world have one question they ask teachers more than any other, "Where am I lined up?" If they have trouble with aim, then certainly the average golfer will. Aim is one of golf's most important fundamentals. Strangely enough, it takes the least amount of natural talent but requires the greatest amount of attention.

The aiming of the left shoulder is, indeed, important to anyone trying to make a pure golf swinging motion. When employing this swing style, the direction the clubhead travels will be influenced by where the shoulder is aligned prior to impact because the shoulder will tend to return there. That alignment in a pure swinging motion influences the direction in which the left arm is moving. The swing path tends to follow the shoulder alignment. *Those who make a free-swinging motion with no manipulation should definitely align their shoulders at address parallel to where they want the clubhead to travel.*

AIMING THE CLUBFACE

There is general agreement that what we must try to align on the clubface of an iron is the leading edge. (Illus 6-17) On a few iron club brands, the top line corresponds with the leading edge and can be used in aiming the face, but that's not true of most. Almost all irons have scored horizontal lines, but not all have vertical bracketing lines. Some brands have special lines to help you aim, which can be useful, particularly to the new player.

On wood clubs, the top line on the face is the aiming line. Decals that run at right angles to that line can be helpful if they are put on correctly (which is not always the case).

A few companies place a T-line or arrow on top of their woods to help in aiming; others use a contrast-colored insert which can serve as an alignment aid.

Whether playing an iron or a wood, the aiming process should start at some point away

Illus 6-17 Aiming the clubface (in particular the leading edge) to the target is one of the first steps in a good pre-shot routine.

Illus 6-18 Aiming or aligning the body consistently and correctly is one of golf's more subtle and difficult problems.

Illus 6-19 It is the dream of golfers to produce the kind of consistent shots that come from an "Iron Byron," which is the result of being able to repeat basic fundamentals or principles. (Photo courtesy of True Temper.)

from the ball (preferably behind it). Visualizing the shot you are about to play is the first step in aiming. If you plan to fade or draw the ball, that decision will have an influence on where to aim. If there is trouble to play *away from* or an advantageous place to play *toward* rather than on a line to the pin, visualizing the desired shot will help produce the correct aim.

AIMING THE BODY

When we speak of "aiming the body" we are referring to the *alignment* of the various body parts in relation to the target. (Illus 6-18) Aiming the body is more difficult than aiming the clubface. There are several components to aim, and they aren't necessarily aimed at the same place.

The aiming of our body is strongly influenced by what we see. The eye is a marvelous and complex mechanism, and sight is a won-

derful gift, but we are not all equally gifted. Two people looking at the same object may not perceive it in the same manner. There are great individual differences in visual acuity, breadth of field, depth perception and the ability to aim at a target.

AN EXAMPLE OF PARALLEL AIM

Look at the ball-hitting machine in the illustration. (Illus 6-19) The swinging arm (the equivalent of a player's left arm) repeats, with the same path precision, time after time. It is directed on its path by the alignment of the upper structure of the machine (the equivalent of a player's shoulders.) The lower part, the base support structure (equivalent to the legs and hips), happens to be parallel to the upper part but does not have to be. It could be anchored with the base supports pointed to the right or left of the target without severely affecting the machine's performance. The human body can do likewise (Lee Trevino is an example), but only to a small degree compared to the machine. Any large deviation from parallel in the lower part of the body will influence the upper body's alignment during the swing.

VARIATIONS

What about the not-so-natural golf swings—the ones that are manipulated? The arms are capable of independent movement from that of the body. Though influenced by both shoulder alignment and shoulder inclination, the arms can operate on quite a different plane and path if directed to do so. Manipulators of the club can have a shoulder alignment that deviates from the conventional parallel left, and still get the job done. In other words, they could aim somewhere other than where a more natural swinger of the golf club aims and still make the clubhead travel in the correct direction.

The shoulder line could be square (parallel left) with the hips and feet progressively more open, as in the case of Hogan, or the shoulders, hips and feet could be closed (aiming right), as with Sam Snead. But a swing accommodation can still produce an on-line repeating action. The question then arises, "What is wrong if the ball flight is consistent and correct?" The answer is, nothing. It's not wrong, only different.

SPOT AIMING

If one is to copy an aiming procedure, one might use that practiced by the best, Jack Nicklaus. Start from behind the ball, visualizing the shot. Then draw a line from the direction the ball is to start, back to the ball. Pick a spot on that line somewhere three to six feet in front of the ball and sole the club so that the leading edge is square to the spot out in front of the ball. (f6-3) It may be a divot mark, some discolored grass, a broken tee, a clubshaft stuck in the ground and used as a ball starting line, whatever. Complete the setup by using that inter-

f6-3 *Some players use a 1- to 2-ft. target; others 20 to 30 ft. in visualizing the ball-path starting direction.*

mediate target spot as a reference point, then visually checking the line all the way to the target, and finally making a swing to send the ball over the spot. Visualizing the swing path approaching the ball as a slightly curved, painted stripe on the grass could help. Actually painting the stripe there will help promote this practice.

Experimenting with aim and alignment should be limited to determining how your body most naturally produces an inside to on-line to inside swing. Then stick with it. If the ball still does not go where desired, make the changes in grip or setup rather than developing a new swing path to compensate for some other error. You will literally then be on the "path to better golf."

THE NORM

The alignment pattern of feet, knees, hips and shoulders parallel left of the target is probably the most sensible standard from which to start. It may not be where you end up. Adjustments to this standard may need to be made because ligaments, bones and muscles function or are structured differently from one golfer to the next or they may have been damaged by injury or suffer from disuse. Therefore, the correct alignment pattern will need to be arrived at by some experimentation.

The target at which you are aiming is not the ball. The target is where the ball is to be sent. Focusing too much on the ball tends to cause a hit impulse and create tension in the impact area. Swing the club *through*, toward the target, not *to* the ball.

VISION

Several visual factors can influence one's ability to aim. The effect of eye dominance on aim, for example, has been discussed for quite some time by those exploring the intricacies of golf performance.

If you don't know which is your master eye (more correctly, sighting eye), hold a pencil at arm's length, aligning it with both eyes on some object across the room, then alternately close one eye, then the other. The image that remains the same when viewed with one eye or both eyes identifies the master or dominant eye. Is this useful? Noted opthalmologist Dr. Curtis D. Benton Jr., also a golfer and contributor to *Sr. Golfer Magazine*, makes this observation: "The concept of a dominant or master eye has received more emphasis than it deserves. The test described identifies the sighting eye, but not necessarily the dominant eye. A golfer who usually sights with his right eye may sight equally well with his left eye if something is blocking the line of sight of his right eye, for example his nose, eyeglass frame, or a tree. With both eyes regarding a distant target, the flag on a green for example, the line of sight from each eye is so nearly parallel that the difference is negligible. The primary function of the two eyes together is to more accurately judge depth and to detect subtle variations in contour. A player with two good eyes looks at the ball with both eyes nearly from start to finish of his golf swing. While putting, a golfer may tip his head to right or left, seeming to emphasize one eye more than the other, but that probably makes little real difference. (f6-4) Many golfers have one eye that has defective vision (from refractive error, injury or disease), but it makes no difference which eye is good or bad in the execution of his shots. We know golfers with one blind eye who aim quite accurately."

As age progresses, sight deteriorates. Vision problems and glasses become a reality in the senior golfer's world. (Illus 6-20) To get a better understanding, see Appendix 9-A.

f6-4 *Though tilting the head may not make a difference in aiming, it does in the stroke or swing. Cocking the head to the* right *encourages an inside swing path, to the* left, *the opposite.*

SETUP

Part three of the pre-swing trilogy after grip and aim is "setup." Though not a new golf term, *setup* is still less well-known in the game's lexicon than *stance* and *address*. While address and setup may be quite similar in the minds of some, in this book "Setup" is used in a more comprehensive way. It includes foot placement, ball positioning, the body's total posture, muscular readiness and weight distribution. A player has a successful setup when he has adjusted his body to the correct attitude in relation to the ball, the lie and the desired shot.

BALL POSITION—IMPORTANCE

Take the "perfect ball-hitting machine" like the USGA's "Iron Byron" (made by True Temper®) and move the ball three inches forward from its normal tee location, and the machine will produce "grounders." Move the ball two inches away from the programmed swing arc toward the toe and the result will be sideways squibs to the right. There is no magic to a per-

Illus 6-20 When golfers have to wear glasses to aim correctly it presents added problems, particularly in rainy weather. Yet PGA Tour players like Hale Irwin (pictured) and Tom Kite have overcome those problems.

fect swing if the ball is not in the desired position for the clubface to collide squarely with it. The ball must be positioned to get in the way at the right part of the swing.

BALL POSITION—LOCATION—FORWARD AND BACK

There is no one universal ball location for everybody, but there are some guidelines. Assuming the ball is in a normal flat lie on the ground and a standard trajectory with an iron shot is desired, where should a player locate the ball? The answer is, "just prior to the clubhead reaching the bottom-most portion of the forward swing arc." That will generally be somewhere to the left of the center of the stance. How far will depend partly upon the degree of lateral weight transfer the player makes from the right to the left side on the forward swing. If the player's lateral motion is limited, the ball should be closer to the center. Likewise, if the player has poor flexibility or balance problems due to heredity, age or physique which allow for little weight shift, then the ball location would also be more centered, but this is a compensation. Those preferring a more rotary swing with an emphasis on swinging the arms and hands also generally play the ball farther back; whereas those with more body weight shift, using more arm and body swing, play it more forward. (f6-5) A *constant* ball position method as opposed to a *variable* ball position is where the ball is played in relatively the same location to the left foot for all shots. Nonetheless, constant ball positioning does have a variable, the right foot. (Illus 6-21) For the longer shots like the #2, #3 and #4 irons, where bigger swings require a wider base for better balance, the right foot is spread far-

f6-5 *Even the constant ball position players will occasionally move the ball location for the shorter iron shots back to alter the ball's trajectory. When a specialty shot such as low into the wind is called for, then all normal ball placement is dismissed.*

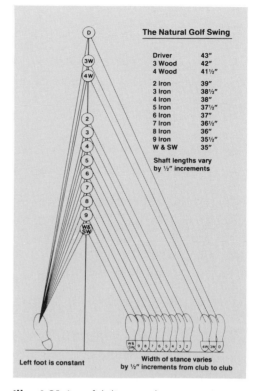

Illus 6-21 A useful diagram showing a constant ball position and a variable foot placement. (From The National CPGA Teaching Manual, authored by George Knudson.)

ther from the left. This moves the swing center and center of body rotation (the spine) farther to the right and makes the angle of approach to the ball shallower, thus taking a shallower divot. Conversely, with the same ball position but the right foot drawn closer to the left for a #8, #9 iron or wedge, the swing center and center of rotation move forward, steepening the angle of approach thus taking a deeper divot.

With a ball placed on a tee peg the angle of approach should be decreased as the height of the tee is increased. When hitting a driver, a steeply descending approach arc to the ball provides less effective force, more backspin and a shorter driven ball, making the shot undesirable. To decrease the approach angle to make it closer to zero degrees, the ball can be moved farther forward, nearer to the inside of the left heel, or the swing center can be set farther back by spreading the right foot farther to the right.

The left foot is the most common reference

point for ball location. Some players and teachers, however, suggest that the positioning of all shots be related to the lowest point of the swing opposite the middle of the left shoulder. For a wood shot, this puts the ball also directly opposite the left shoulder with the hands covering the line of sight to the left toe. For a short iron the left shoulder still is in line with the swing's low point, which is now an additional 3 to 4 inches farther forward; thus the ball position ends up farther back. The hands now block the line of sight to the left heel.

Most teachers prefer all woods to be played either off the left heel or up to two inches back, toward the center; the irons 2 to 4 inches back from inside the left heel. Some want all irons played from the middle of the stance and all woods from two inches inside the heel. There is yet to be an absolute consensus on this topic.

Whether the choice is a fixed or variable ball position, using the feet, the club or some other part of the body as a reference point, this fact should be made clear: *Ball position is an important factor that must be given precise consideration on each swing if one is to hit consistent shots.* Locate it, measure it and check it frequently, just as one would do with the grip.

BALL POSITION—AWAY FROM OR TOWARD THE BODY—CLOSE OR FAR

The next decision is the distance a player should stand from the ball. This is influenced by the golfer's body structure, posture, length of club and his swing style. It's obvious that a bulky person will need more room to swing his or her arms in order to clear the chest. A tall, angular body-type can clear with the ball quite close. This distance from the ball affects the upper body tilt, causing most tall players to lean

forward more and have upright swings, and short, stockier players to lean forward less and have flat swings.

Body shapes alone don't determine distance from body to ball; technique also has an influence. The hand and arm hitter-type player, particularly the very dominant right-hand strikers, tend to throw the club arc away from the body in the forward swing. Consequently, they compensate and place the ball farther away. This ball position is frequently used to offset the error of hitting behind the shot. While moving the ball farther away does reduce the chance for this error, it increases the possibility of some other type of mishit, in particular a poorly directed swing path. The body players who feel more connected let the legs and center of the body initiate the forward swing and don't "throw the club away" from the body. This allows them to place the ball nearer to them.

To find that "correct distance," starting from the erect position, bring your arms down onto the chest until slight pressure is felt. Next, bend forward at the hips until the club nearly touches the ground. At this point you should "settle-in" with a slight flex in the knees. (Flexing too deeply in the knees moves the center of gravity back on the heels rather than in the middle of the feet.) The back will now be reasonably straight, the arms hanging so they are extended but relaxed, shoulders over the toes, the hands a little inside a vertical line dropped from the eyes. There should be no sensation of reaching or being crowded. The butt of the club should be pointed reasonably close to 90° to the spine angle, as an object swings fastest at 90° to its axis. The most important check is that you are in balance. It is common to find golfers who stand too far from the ball, but rare to find them too close. Simply stated, the correct distance from the ball in the setup position should

Illus 6-22 A good setup position allows the player to move with power yet stay in balance.

allow you to make contact with the ball without having to search for it. (Illus 6-22) No mid-swing manipulations or corrections, just a proper body attitude that puts the clubface on the ball when you turn in one direction and return in the opposite direction.

POSTURE, BALANCE AND MUSCULAR READINESS

One of the most common words used in teaching golf is *relax*! While the golfer in setting up to the ball should not be tense, neither should he be relaxed in the sense of being limp. Golf is a game of differential relaxation, of muscular reciprocal enervation (one group of opposing muscles is relaxing while its opposite is contracting). This is certainly true in the setup. The body should look "proud," head up, not slumped on the chest trying to keep it down, arms extended, but not locked, back straight but not rigid, grip firm but not tight, legs and feet solid but not wooden. It's an athletic, "at-

ready" position common to any sport before movement begins.

Think of a baseball shortstop getting ready to field a grounder, a basketball player in a defensive guarding position, a football quarterback about to receive the ball from center, a skier on a downhill run, a swimmer preparing to dive into the water at the start of a race—all ready for action; they are bent at the knees, balanced, with the weight slightly favoring the balls of the feet in anticipation of movement. There are some differences, but there are enough similarities to show that golf, like other sports, requires that the performer prepare the body for action. The only difference is that golf is motion without locomotion. It's movement without the body traveling "anywhere." Golf requires both precision and power. Both are influenced by how the swinging apparatus is "set up" to perform.

WEIGHT DISTRIBUTION

Balance is critical to athletic performance. In golf, one deals with balance in two directions, left-to-right balance and front-to-back balance.

As in the other sports examples of athletic "at-ready" positions, the forward-to-back balance in the setup will be near the balls of the feet for the full swinging motion. The heels and toes are used as stabilizers like training wheels on a child's bike. Once the swing begins, the weight then shifts toward the right heel on the backswing and toward the left heel on the forward swing.

Only in the short game (chipping, pitching and putting), where the ball is played closer to the body, does the center of balance shift more

"Yes, you're probably right about the left hand, but the fact is that I take the checks with my right hand."
—Bobby Locke (Commenting on criticism of his left-hand grip position).

toward the heels in the setup. There is, in fact, a progression of weight distribution from the balls of the feet to the heels as a player works from a long to a short club. It is a natural adjustment. But, if one is not sure that he is adjusting properly, here is an easy way to check. On short shots, the forward-to-back balance should allow one to wiggle the toes when set. For full swing shots, one should be able to comfortably tap the heels on the ground.

VARIATIONS

There are exceptions. The hand and arm players tend to balance more toward the heels on their shots. However, the body player is more on the balls of his feet for all shots (even chips and pitches). Of course, a player can go too far in either direction.

For women, here's an additional note. To get the weight more toward the balls of one's feet one must counterbalance the upper trunk's forward bend with an equal action in the opposite direction. In other words, allow the derrière to protrude. Since women are conditioned to regard this posture as "unladylike," it may not feel comfortable at first, either physically or mentally. But, pulling one's seat in and shifting the weight too far back on the heels will hurt a player's golf more than pushing the seat out will hurt a player's pride! (Illus 6-23)

LEFT-RIGHT BALANCE

What about left-to-right balance in the setup? Should one favor the left foot, right foot, or a balanced weight distribution in the setup? Hand players will tend to stay more left, from the setup through the swing. Some weight will shift to the right but not as much as with other players, since hand players look for their power from the leverage of arms and hands. Body players will start more balanced or to the right in the setup and shift more to the right in the backswing, before moving through to the left.

Illus 6-23 It may be more graceful to have the seat pulled in, but it encourages an upper body that is too vertical plus more weight on the heels and a deeper knee sit than is correct. This is poor mechanics.

One criterion for left-right balance is the angle at which the player plans to make contact—more left in the setup when needing descent, less left for a shallower angle of approach.

Width of foot placement influences left-right balance. The closer the feet are together, the easier it is to place the weight over the left foot, toward the target. Too narrow a stance, however, increases instability when greater force and more motion in the swing are needed. As the stance widens, one's center of gravity lowers and shifts more to the right in relation to the ball, influencing the swing's angle of approach. Doug Sanders, for example, is a low ball hitter. He has an extremely wide stance, causing his swing angle of approach to flatten, putting less backspin on the ball and reducing its rise. Too wide a stance will restrict the pelvic turn over the right leg. And because of this, the shoulder turn, too, will make it more difficult for the player to transfer weight effectively.

Width of foot placement should be determined not only by the desired weight distribution but also by the amount of balance necessary to support the swing effort. Chip shots and putts can be executed with the feet together because the physical effort and accompanying body motion is minimal. *As the golfer's motion increases, so must the width of his foot placement. The maximum width is exceeded when it diminishes one's ability to readily turn and* *transfer weight from one foot to the other as one must in the full swing.*

f6-6   *An alternative to Grip, Aim and Setup that may be easier to remember is PGA—Posture, Grip and Aim.*

THE IMPORTANCE OF GRIP, AIM AND SETUP

It should now be evident that even "Iron Byron" becomes a hacker by making any one of three pre-swing errors: 1) taking a poor grip, 2) aiming in the wrong direction, or 3) putting the ball in the incorrect position in relation to the swing. The essential pre-swing principles of Grip, Aim and Setup are an integral part of every golf stroke. (f6-6)

CHAPTER 7

IN-SWING
FUNDAMENTALS:
The Remaining Principles

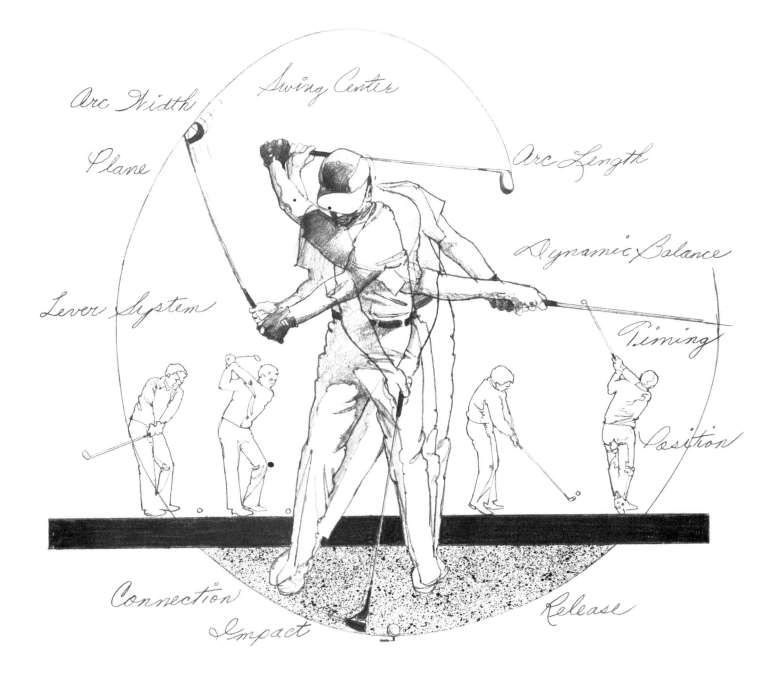

Golfers live on hope and promise: the hope that tomorrow will be better, and the promise that a newly discovered swing tip will contain "the secret"—the key that will unlock the mystery of the repeating, power-filled, yet effortless golf swing. If they are looking for a perfect golf swing, that fits everyone, it should be made clear that it won't be found anywhere, given a lifetime to search. That quest falls into the "Fountain of Youth," "Shangri-La," and "Meaning of Life" classification—seemingly there, vigorously pursued, yet never quite attainable. Good advice is: Don't chase that myth! There is no *one* perfect golf swing for everybody.

If they are looking for help to find their best swing, that's a different story. Everybody has a swing style that is best for them. (Illus 7-1) Finding it is a challenge, maintaining it is a struggle, and adjusting it as they age is a necessity. That is a worthy goal.

Each golfer is unique with his special natural talents, some deficiencies, and more than likely a few idiosyncrasies. The approach in learning should be to discover that "best golf swing." This discovery can be aided by understanding the Ball Flight *Laws*, dealing with the *Principles* which influence those Laws and selecting the appropriate *Preferences* to produce the desired results.

There is a best swing for every golfer, which includes a specific grip, alignment, setup and swing pattern which best suits: (A) one's abilities, (B) one's temperament, and (C) one's body. It is important to recognize these three as keys

Illus 7-1 Miller Barber has had a most successful career with a unique swing style.

in the search because the answers chosen will vary according to the traits.

WHAT IS SIMPLE IS NOT ALWAYS EASY

Swing styles of even the greatest players vary in their mechanical efficiency. Some are composed of a complex series of adjustments, ma-

"His swing reminds me a lot of a machine I once saw at a country fair making saltwater taffy. It goes in four directions and none of them seem right."
—Buck Adams on Miller Barber's swing

nipulations and compensations. Others are simple and straightforward with minimum chance for error. What is mechanically efficient may be extremely demanding physically. "Keeping it simple" may require the strength and flexibility of a conditioned athlete. Using the position at the top of the backswing as an example, we find that a flat left wrist position throughout the swing is mechanically simple, but for many, physically difficult. They may find the cupped (concave) left wrist position much easier to perform even though it may be more complex from a purely mechanical standpoint. (Illus 7-2) Conversely, a bowed (convex)

Illus 7-2 PGA Tour professional Fred Couples prefers a cupped left wrist position which encourages this more "relaxed" finish. (Photo by Stephen Szurlej)

left wrist position used by some Tour players might for the average golfer be physically *impossible*. The plain fact is that some swing styles are more physically demanding than others. If a golfer is attempting to perform a swing style beyond his current physical capabilities, he has the option of: (1) conditioning his body to perform this action, or (2) continually failing when attempting it in his present physical state, or (3) changing the swing style.

FINDING A BEST SWING

There are five important steps you can take to help find your best swing: (1) *Learn cause and effect relationships* in determining the outcome of golf shots, (2) *become familiar with the principles* of making a golf stroke and how variations affect the result, (3) through experimentation, logic and with professional help, *choose a style* or technique compatible with what you are trying to accomplish and what you have with which to accomplish it, (4) learn to *appreciate your physical assets and liabilities*, how to use the advantages and compensate for disadvantages, and (5) once the preferences have been selected, *stay with them and practice*.

DEVELOPING AN UNDERSTANDING

Cause and effect, which has been mentioned in Chapter 2, may be gradually learned through lessons, observation, visuals from articles or books and teaching aids. Learn to become increasingly self-sufficient by hitting shots and describing the root causes, i.e., *Laws*. "The ball started left of target and moved markedly right, so it was a left-of-target swing with a wide-open

"I do not advocate unorthodox golf but I make provisions for it."
—Homer Kelley

"The good player swings through the ball while the
awkward player hits at it."
—Ken Venturi

club face." Learn to "read" and describe your
shots to understand cause and effect.

Next comes an understanding of *The Principles*. One approach is the "ABC Method":

A. The preparations before the swing. (Illus
   7-3)
B. Shift the weight to the right as you swing
   your arms over your right shoulder. (Illus
   7-4)
C. Shift to the left and swing your arms over
   the left shoulder. (Illus 7-5)

That is a nice approach if one wishes to keep
it simple. of course, those three things incorporate the following principles:

A. Preparation: 1) Grip, 2) Aim, and 3) Setup
B. Shift weight to the right and swing arms:
   1) Dynamic Balance, 2) Swing Plane,
   3) Lever System, 4) Position, 5) Swing
   Center, 6) Arc Length
C. Shift to the left and swing arms: 1) Timing, 2) Release, 3) Arc Width, 4) Connection, 5) Impact.

Listed below are the In-Swing *Principles* followed by an explanation of their importance
and some observations on their applications.

"Those commonalities of the good players are the basic
fundamentals of golf technique. They haven't changed
much in an awful long time, and there aren't a whole lot
of them. But they have to be understood and mastered if
you are to play the game consistently at or close to the
maximum of your potential."
—Jack Grout

Illus 7-3 The "ABC Method"—a simple
approach—A is the preparation to swing.

Illus 7-4 B is the top of the swing.

Illus 7-5 C is the finish of the swing.

> "If a great golf swing put you high on the money list, there'd be some of us who would be broke."
> —Ray Floyd

In-Swing Principles

Dynamic Balance	Width of Arc
Swing Plane	Length of Arc
Lever System	Swing Center (Rotational)
Release	Connection
Timing	Impact
Position	

DYNAMIC BALANCE

In reviewing the physical talents necessary to play any sport, it would be difficult to study the subject without mentioning "balance." Adding the word "dynamic" simply lends the idea of motion to what could otherwise be thought of as a static position. For an example of dynamic balance, take a ball in your dominant hand and imagine that you are going to throw it a long distance using a sidearm motion. As you prepare to throw, the body will coil and the weight instinctively shift to your rear foot. Now the body is primed for action, like a boxer ready to punch, a quarterback ready to throw, or a shot-putter ready to release. Completing the imaginary throw, the weight will transfer to the forward foot. *In every striking or throwing motion, maximum power is achieved when the motion is directed toward the target by transferring the weight from the rear foot to the forward foot.* (Illus 7-6, 7-7) That principle is no different in the golf swing. Yet golfers will frequently neglect footwork, trying to strike with arms only, or using a weight transfer that is the reverse of what it should be, going from the forward foot to the rear foot. (Illus 7-8, 7-9)

Being able to transfer weight by using one's feet and legs correctly is so high on the scale of golf priorities that it is senseless to continue until you can accomplish a basic weight shift. Why? What does dynamic balance contribute to a swing? Using the legs properly does three vital things in the golf swing:

(1) It provides the platform for the rotation of the body and swinging of the arms.

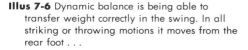

Illus 7-6 Dynamic balance is being able to transfer weight correctly in the swing. In all striking or throwing motions it moves from the rear foot . . .

Illus 7-7 . . . to the forward foot.

Illus 7-8 An upper body reverse weight shift will have the upper body angled toward the target. The major cause is "trying to keep the head down."

Illus 7-9 The upper body should either be straight (usually on the shorter shots) or angled away from the target (more on the longer shots).

(2) It adds impetus to the total movement.
(3) It places the body in a position to strike the ball with a clubface that is traveling in the right direction at the correct angle of approach.

Dynamic balance is one of golf's fundamentals which doesn't allow for much latitude. Either one transfers the weight from the back foot to the front, or one doesn't. But within the movement there are some details worth examining. When the weight has reached the right side in any of the examples we've used—underarm throw, football pass, shot put, punch, or golf swing—the right leg is: 1) always flexed, and 2) never rolled to its outside. When these two positions are not observed, either power or control is lost. The amount of flex may vary individually. The hands player of a couple of decades ago, who had an open-face position at the top of the swing, straightened the left leg more in the forward swing and called it "hitting against a firm left side." By using this straightening action the player braced to halt the forward motion of the body and left arm so the clubhead could be "whipped through" with the face closing. This was done in conjunction with the head kept down and back, further encouraging "whipping through the hands." The

> Follow-through is an important element in skill involving powerful propulsion of an object.
> —Tom Ecker

player produced an emphasized rotation of the clubface so that the toe passed the heel and literally guaranteed a draw or hook, the popular shot shape of the classic era.

The modern Tour player keeps the forward pivot point (the left knee) slightly flexed as he unwinds and moves through the shot. (f7-1)

This strong rotation and moderate lateral movement coupled with a more level upper body allows the arc of the clubhead to approach the target line more closely and stay on it slightly longer. But many golfers who aren't on Tour have hips that barely turn and knees that flex only on demand; for them a more classic style may be the solution. *Club players with average or less-than-average talent may be served better by instruction that does not follow the style the Tour player is employing.*

The Importance of the Legs

There is some confusion about what the legs can and can't do in the golf swing. For example, you may have heard and read of fine players who attribute their length off the tee primarily to their legs. They may feel this, but it's a misconception of the extent to which the legs can actually deliver power to the club and subsequently to the ball. Let's repeat, "The legs in the golf swing are primarily the platform for balancing the trunk and swinging the arms." True, without the stability of the right foot and leg anchoring the swing, the power which comes from the motion of the arms, the turning of the powerful hips and trunk and the ability

f7-1 *The amount of lateral motion is one of the distinctions in preference. Some players have very little (more rotatory), others have a good deal (more lateral).*

of the wrists to hinge and release would be greatly diminished. With a solid base these four elements normally make up 70–80% of your power package. The momentum developed by the legs in the weight shift accounts for the other 20–30% of your distance, significant but not dominant.

This conclusion may be hard for some to accept when they have heard so much about "leg drive for distance." However, its truth is easily demonstrated. Watch a trick shot performer hit balls while sitting on a chair or kneeling on the ground. (Illus 7-10) Any strong player, with practice, can do this and drive the ball 230–240 yards, compared to his normal tee shot of 260–270 yards. In the chair, the player uses the feet and legs only for support. Hitting off the knees (which is more difficult) requires the performer to rely entirely on a well-timed upper body and arm-swinging and trunk motion with a little help from the hips . . . but still no legs, yet 70–80% of his total distance is produced.

So, the majority of golfer's power does not

Illus 7-10 Seve Ballesteros can drive a ball over 240 yards while on his knees. (Photo by Stephen Szurlej)

come from his legs. Establishing the desired position of the lower body from which to deliver that power does, however, require the legs. That's why so many teachers emphasize good footwork.

Which Influences Which?

Another misconception is that a good arm swing automatically produces good footwork. Not true. It helps, but it doesn't do it alone. The arm swing going away from the ball helps the player to transfer his weight to the right, and an arm swing through the ball assists in the finish. But the critical weight shift from over the right leg to over the left is not purely a result of the arm swing. Getting the left heel down and transferring the weight of the lower body from the right leg to the left are necessary actions that produce a good forward-swing weight shift. It's very similar to the weight transfer used in throwing a ball. The arm doesn't throw and the body follow. Instead, the body initiates, helping to propel the arm, which then pulls the body around to a finish. (Illus 7-11) In fact, they are best visualized as moving together, not exclusive of each other. (f7-2)

A proper weight transfer can be learned if it's not natural. It is such a critical move in golf that, if necessary, players should specially practice it until mastered. For practice, take a 7-iron and first rehearse the grip and setup routine. (Gripping and establishing the setup is like playing musical scales; even accomplished performers rehearse and repeat, repeat and rehearse.) Then, visualizing the target line, waggle and swing, trying to feel that right combination of body actions for a good weight transfer both back and through. Most important is the move from the right foot to the left. Once

f7-2   *This move right to left is a critical part of good footwork. It not only puts the golfer into a powerful striking position, but also promotes a swing that travels on line to a centerface hit with the correct angle of approach.*

Illus 7-11 The body initiates, the arms and club follow. But it should feel all together, as one motion, so the levers are timed correctly.

the golfer's coiled body is poised over the right leg he is ready for golf's most critical action, initiating the downswing or, better, "establishing the platform."

It's the same delivery used in the previously mentioned side-arm throw. The left heel is planted as the weight transfers to the left foot. There is rotation of the trunk and a dropping of the arms and hands into position for their important contribution. This reversal of weight from primarily over the right leg to settling over the left is the foundation of golf's footwork. It is initiated under and through the right foot and leg. Unless the lower portion of the right leg is solidly braced, the powerful movement to the left is flawed. Once this body attitude has been reached, the momentum of the swing itself will carry the player forward into a satisfactory finish position. A true swing will always create a full finish with the hands and arms over the left shoulder.

SWING PLANE

The least understood and least appreciated of the golf swing's principles for many years has been swing plane. One aspect of it, the base line, indicates the direction of the swing path.

The other, the tilt or steepness of the club shaft during the swing, determines the angle of approach.

The angle of approach aspect of this plane is easy to recognize. Does the swing tend to be flat like a merry-go-round or more upright like a Ferris wheel? Either can produce accurate shots, albeit with different trajectories: flat for lower, upright for higher. Until recently, golfers hadn't talked much about swing plane. If they did, it was usually relegated to arguing the merits between the two swing positions, upright or flat. The second but more critical aspect of swing plane is the line on which the clubhead is traveling. *Downswing plane controls the clubhead path;* the clubhead path is half of direction; and direction is half the game.

Recognition should be given to Seymour Dunn, whose photos of the swing plane, as published in *Golf Fundamentals* (1922), still serve as a model that other writers of golf books could follow. (Illus 7-12) Recently, PGA professional

Illus 7-12 Seymour Dunn was an innovative teacher from a famous family of golf professionals. Here he demonstrates the plane angle's degree of steepness. (From *Golf Fundamentals*)

Hank Haney has created additional interest in the importance of the swing plane. According to Haney, an advocate of Ben Hogan's *Five Fundamentals,* you swing parallel to an imaginary sheet of glass on the backswing and under it on the forward swing. This visual description stuck with thousands of golfers, who saw illustrations of this plane in Hogan's book. There are many great players, however, whose forward-swing shaft plane is *slightly* over their backswing shaft plane. This is usually because the takeaway was inside (Snead, Palmer, Leitzke, Lyle). *The important point is that literally all fine swings approach the ball from the inside in the impact area whether over or under the backswing plane.*

Dunn, Hogan and now Haney have made it clear that in the forward swing the directional plane dictates the path. It does for this simple reason. In a golf swing, the head of the club will always follow the line on which the club's butt end is pointing and will intersect the baseline halfway into the forward swing. (Illus 7-13)

For examples, let's look down from a position above the golfer. The player pictured in Illus 7-14 is in the most common improper forward swing position. Halfway through the swing, the player has incorrectly used the hands and arms, causing the butt end of the club to point to the left of the target—the eventual direction the swing path will take. In Illus 7-15 the player is overusing "knee drive," thereby dropping the

Illus 7-13 Here Dunn demonstrates how the butt of the club points to the plane's baseline. (from Golf Fundamentals)

Illus 7-14 Example 1: The butt of the club is pointing left of the target in the downswing and the clubhead follows.

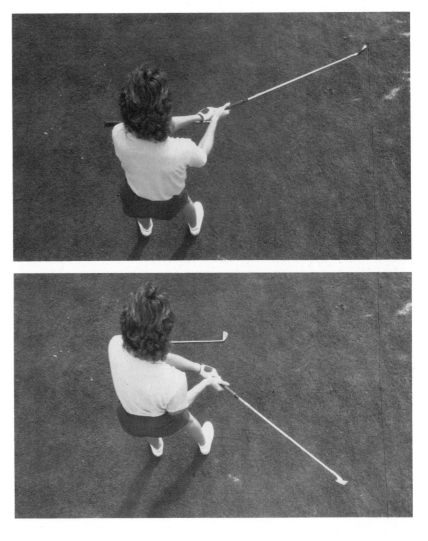

Illus 7-15 Example 2: The butt of the club is pointing to the right of the target in the downswing and the clubhead follows.

club to the inside so that the butt end points well to the right of the target. This is where the clubhead will follow. Remember, THE CLUB-HEAD WILL ALWAYS FOLLOW THE BUTT END. As the club reaches a position horizontal with the ground, an extension from the butt end should point through the ball and extend toward the target. If it stays in plane it will point back along that same line well into the follow-through.

This may help explain the line of travel of the clubhead along the plane, but what about the inclination or tilt? The greatest players of all time have had swing planes that have ranged from very flat—Hogan, Player, Trevino—to rather upright—Nicklaus, Weiskopf, Watson. There are some tradeoffs which may help a player gravitate toward one preference or the other.

The flatter swing may have a better chance of staying "connected" than one in which the arms try to reach high in the backswing. Staying "connected" makes it easier to time the swing. A more upright swing, however, wanders less from the aim line, and if timed correctly allows a good chance to hit the ball straight.

Swing plane influences the angle of approach and therefore, trajectory. A flatter plane results in the ball coming off the clubface on a lower trajectory, with a tendency to draw. This can be an advantage in wind but a liability on courses which favor longer tee shot carries and soft-landing iron shots.

The plane of the swing is influenced by the angle of the right forearm, as is seen in Illus 7-16. Note how the forearm position influences the plane in Illus 7-17, 7-18. Both at the top of the swing and midway through the downswing, the positioning of the right forearm will largely dictate the shaft plane. This angle can vary dramatically from the backswing to the forward swing. In many players' forward swings, the pattern seen is a slight flattening of the club-shaft plane as the motion begins toward the target. This occurs even though the plane line of the hands may be slightly outside and steeper than that of the backswing.

A Bonus—Distance

Only the effects of plane on *Direction* have been mentioned to this point. The bonus is that if the player can get his swing plane geomet-

Illus 7-16 The right elbow is at right angles to the desired swing plane, helping to set the club "on plane."

Illus 7-17 Note how the elevated right elbow has forced the club shaft to point right of the target line, "across the line," encouraging an inside approach path.

Illus 7-18 With the right elbow down, the club points left of the target, "layed off," encouraging an outside approach path.

rically correct, he'll not only be on the correct line for direction, but on a line which produces the best leverage, the power channel which produces the strongest hits.

If there is any one position in golf that could qualify for adjectives like "secret," "magic" or "keystone," it is the one pictured in Illus 7-19. This position produces both accuracy and power. It is common to both hand players and body players, swingers and strikers, flat planes and upright planes—it's an on-plane forward swing with the power being delivered at the proper moment.

That power package has some elements common to other sports. Like a catapult, there is a sling-like action which can unleash great power when the right elbow leads the hand. Think of a football passer, baseball pitcher, or javelin thrower. The power is contained as long as the elbow leads, but when the hand passes the elbow, the power is unleashed. The key in creating this position is to get the club shaft "on-plane."

LEVER SYSTEM

Mechanically, the body can be looked upon as a series of levers which contribute to the swinging of a golf club. These levers, when connected to one another, constitute a linkage system. The leverage from this system is multiplied progressively as the rotational acceleration of the trunk, transfer of weight and swinging of the arms affects each link (body part) until the club is thrown centrifugally outward.

When a golfer addresses the ball with the club and left arm in a straight line from the shoulder to the clubhead, a single lever has been created. A swing made from this position without cocking the wrists might hit the ball straight, but certainly not far. (Illus 7-20) However, by cocking the wrists so the club shaft is positioned at approximately 90 degrees to the left arm, the player has created a second lever and immediately can substantially increase the potential force. This reflects the importance of a *second* lever. (Illus 7-21)

Illus 7-19 The first PGA champion, Jim Barnes (1916), demonstrates the principle of delivering a swing down the "line of compression," both powerfully and accurately.

Some novice players have stiff-looking backswings and they seem afraid to cock or hinge the wrist for fear of losing control of the club. In the forward swing they appear to be shoving the club at the ball. The result is that they hit tee shots with so little force it appears that their drivers have cashmere inserts. This could be eliminated immediately by cocking the wrists and creating a second lever, the club.

A third lever in this arm-hand-club link combination could be added not only by cocking the left wrist (thumb in plane with the forearm) but also in "dorsiflexing" or cupping the left wrist (back of hand toward forearm), or by bending the left arm at the elbow in the backswing. (Illus 7-22) Both moves have some potential for greater distance but tend to cause such additional problems in timing and consistency that the result is usually counterproductive. (f7-3)

f7-3 *They may not be counterproductive if the player who desperately needs more distance is extremely inflexible, with little ability to turn the trunk and shoulders.*

Illus 7-20 With the wrists hardly cocked, this could be classified as a one-lever swing, with much less power available.

Illus 7-21 A two-lever position; simple, yet potentially powerful.

Illus 7-22 A three-lever swing; more difficult to time and to locate the ball.

If a player wants distance, it is not a question of whether or not he prefers to cock the wrists . . . he must. But when, in the swing, should he cock them? That's not quite as clear cut.

When to Cock the Wrists

At the turn of the 20th century, the great players of the world first started their right hip and arms away in the backswing, letting the hands and clubhead follow as though they were being dragged. The clubhead would catch up and pass the hands in a reflexive fashion, cocking the wrists in the process. In the 1930s and 1940s the "one piece takeaway" became the vogue and players started to cock their wrists in the backswing somewhere between their right leg and right hip, until they were fully cocked when they reached the top of the backswing. In the last two decades we've seen players like Jack Nicklaus and Miller Barber who wait almost to hip height before cocking their wrists. It does encourage a wide arc, but can result in an occasional "rebound" of the hands from this late cocking at the top, causing timing of the impact to be more difficult for the average player. More recently, a trend is to have the club nearly pointing vertically by the time the left arm is horizontal, as in the style of Seve Ballesteros. (Players with a low hand position at address, like Ballesteros, essentially have their wrists partially cocked already.)

Some players also complete the wrist cock after the forward swing has already begun. Ben Hogan was perhaps the best example in this category. This move, the further cocking of the wrists on the forward swing, by the way, is characteristic of most long-hitting players. A possible viable option for the future is the preset. In this style the wrists are cocked before the backswing is in motion, a precocking method. The player must select a preference. If based on today's popularity, it would be a combination of "one piece" with a little "early set" action blended in.

THE RELEASE

The term "release" sometimes creates controversy. There are those who don't believe such a word should exist in describing the golf swing. Let's call it a difference in semantics. The release may be described as the returning of the arms and clubhead and body to the position similar to that in which they were at address. Not the same position, but similar. This return allows expenditure of the energy potentially created in the backswing, i.e., "releasing it." The release comes from a rotational/lateral return of the body, unhinging of the wrists and a natural return rotation of the forearms. In the backswing the trunk has been turned, the wrists have been cocked and the left forearm rolled. This is where most of the controversy arises, in the concept of forearm rotation. Some professionals talk about the position of the forearms *relative* to the upper trunk, during the swing. Of course, the forearms turn but so does the trunk. In other words, in the approach the forearms maintain the same basic relationship to the trunk in a good part of the backswing and follow-through as they did in the address. (Illus 7-23, 7-24) Teaching professional Jim Bal-

lard describes this concept by using the analogy of carrying a sack of flour in front of you with your palms facing upward, then turning and returning the body as though to toss it. This type arm movement is a part of his "connection" theory that the arms and upper body maintain the same position relative to what they were at address.

The other way to look at the idea of release is to look at the impact position as a constant, with the forearms and hands close to right angles to the target line at address and the body parallel to that line. The hands and forearms are not at right angles to that line in the backswing or through swing, but have rotated roughly 180 degrees from halfway into the backswing to halfway into the forward swing. The body has turned roughly 45° to 90° away from the target line, depending on what part is being observed and what player is doing the turning. It rotates similarly in conjunction with the arms and hands into the through swing. These actions of body, forearms and hands in the through swing are labeled a "release" in this text.

The terms one uses to describe the proper positions are not so important. It's getting to

Illus 7-23 A release emphasizing hands while the body stays back. This would encourage a hook.

Illus 7-24 A release emphasizing more use of the body so hand and arms remain in a position relative to that at address.

the positions that counts. A simple illustration like, "shake hands to the right," "shake hands to the left," using the right hand might do the job, in describing release. (Illus 7-25, 7-26) Whatever your semantic viewpoint, when you make a proper swing from the "shake hands" position on your downswing and continue to impact position, the left forearm returns 90 degrees to its original position, and the left wrist unhinges. Some teachers consider this a natural move, some teach conscious left forearm rotation, some teach "connection," and others a right-hand hit to make it happen. *Whether the right hand impels it, follows it, or supports it is a matter of preference. In the experience of many professionals it is natural for some golfers but must be taught to others. As long as the geometry is correct, the ball doesn't care.*

Failure to Release

One of the most common errors related to release is lack of it. "Blocking a shot out"—leaving it to the right for a right-handed player because of the failure to square the clubface—is one problem that can be solved by having a

better release. "Blocking" is the basis of the slice for many golfers and results in compensations such as a bad grip and a worse swing path. Two common causes of the "block out" are: 1) tightness in the forearms, which destroys the freedom to let the arms, hands and clubhead "go" or rotate along with the body. Blocking stems from trying to hit hard and squeezing the grip "too tightly." Firmness in the grip is desirable but tightness is destructive since it inhibits release. And, 2) moving the swing center ahead of the ball so that the arms, hands and clubhead cannot square up or release in time is another common cause of "blocking a shot out."

TIMING

Whatever number of levers is used and however the player employs a release, the swing has to be timed correctly. An accurate description is PGA Professional Paul Bertholy's PSM (Proper Sequential Motion), when all of the elements of the swing are assembled in their correct order. PSM is experienced when a golfer hits an extremely solid shot that goes farther than ex-

Illus 7-25 Demonstrating the position of the clubface by using a "shake hands" . . .

Illus 7-26 . . . to "shake hands" position.

pected, yet the execution seems effortless. That's when the linkage system is operating most efficiently—good levers, good release, good timing.

Remember taking a group of dominoes and standing them up so that when one fell, it knocked the rest over, one by one? When setting them up, the sequence of placement was not critical as long as they finally were in place. But in knocking them down they had to fire in sequence. So it is with the golf swing. Firing in sequence causes efficiency in movement.

If we take the force of the swing to its source we'll find that once a player has loaded the gun—that is, when he's reached the top of a fully wound backswing—there is a series of sequential movements like a domino chain that produces a power-efficient swing. The feet and knees lead by transferring weight, followed by the hips and the lower trunk, then the back and shoulders, and finally the arms and hands. Yet the feeling is that "it is all together." By timing the sequence in this fashion, there is a summation of forces with each part contributing some share. When the body parts fire in precisely the right order and right amount, the best swing is produced. Paraphrasing the great Bobby Jones, there will be changes in swing style over the years, but there will never be a change in the sequence of movements in the forward swing.

The backswing can be 1–2–3–4–5 or some other combination but it should be followed by a reverse 5–4–3–2–1 forward swing to be correct. If on the return the sequencing is 5–4–1–2–3, the linkage system is not being used correctly. Timing is lost, a good deal of the force, and possibly the ball.

"Boy, my timing was sure off today," is the comment one frequently hears from golfers. Or, "Just didn't have any rhythm." Or, "I lost my

tempo." Though they are probably referring to timing, these three—rhythm, timing and tempo—are not the same. To set the record straight and avoid confusion of these terms, *rhythm* in the movement arts means *a harmonious flow resulting from the proper relation of parts.* A rhythmical swing "looks good." It may not be as productive, however, as one of lesser beauty. *Timing is the sequence of movements. Tempo is the rate of movement—*fast or slow—but has nothing to do with the sequence. You could have a fast tempo like Lanny Wadkins, but be in perfect sequence. His swing may have perfect timing, but would not generally be considered rhythmical. Good rhythm and tempo are desirable, but *timing is critical. It is the most important!*

Finding a Workable Tempo to Improve Timing

"As ye shall waggle, so shall ye swing," is one of the oldest sayings in golf. It means that people with quick waggles will tend to have quick swings, and vice versa. A person's tempo, whether it be in the waggle or swing, will generally relate to his nature. Some people are more tightly strung and do everything quickly. Others are phlegmatic, and fast moves are foreign to their nature. A player's swing should match his nature—within reason. A fast backswing and quick change of direction can present considerable problems in timing. Otherwise, the hustler's saying, "Just find me a guy with a fat wallet and a fast backswing and I can have a very enjoyable day," would never have gained credence. On the other hand, a swing that is too slow may never get up enough steam to produce effective clubhead speed. Or, if it is a very deliberate backswing, the player may rush the change of direction in an effort to generate speed. This rapid change of tempo can lead to inconsistency. A good image would seem to be somewhere between the tempo of Lanny Wadkins and that of Gene Littler. If you can make it a habit when your timing is off to picture a rhythmical swing like Payne Stewart's

> "There is no one right speed for everyone . . . if I tried to play at his (Tom Watson's) breakneck speed . . . I'd self-destruct before I finished the front nine."
> —Nancy Lopez

> "When, through practice, you have grooved a good position at the top; practically all you'll have left to do to perfect your swing is to get your timing right."
> —Anon

or Larry Mize's, and then apply your own natural tempo, you'll stand a good chance of achieving a swing that is also well timed.

POSITION AND THE SLOT

Another principle influencing direction, is the *position* of the arms, hands and club at the top of the swing. (Illus 7-27) In particular, the term *position* in this model refers to the relationship of the back of the left hand and forearm. At the wrist joint is the *position* flat, cupped or arched? It is possible to play first-rate golf from

any of the three positions. At the 19th hole or in the locker room, one may hear better players talk about how they couldn't get it "in the slot." The "slot" is the position the hands and arms "drop into" just after the body's forward motion begins. It's the "transition" period of the swing. (Illus 7-28) It is most easily found when, at the top of the swing, the player has the club, his hands and left wrist in such a location that he can simply return to the ball without manipulation and produce an on-line, center-faced, square-bladed hit. "In-the-slot" for the Tour performer most often finds the back of the left hand, the forearm and clubface being in a single plane. A flat left wrist position is what the player is seeking at impact. One of the worst golfing faults influencing the face position of the club is a breaking down of the left wrist in the impact position. If the wrist is flat at the *top* it has a better chance of returning that way at *impact*.

Illus 7-27 Good position at the top allows Gene Littler to . . . (Photo by Chuck Brenkus)

Illus 7-28 . . . get the club "in the slot." (Photo by Chuck Brenkus)

The ball-hitting machine mentioned and pictured earlier in Chapter 3 has swing characteristics that fit the Laws, Principles and Preferences model to a "T." The club has to be gripped, even though it's a clamp-like device. The machine must be set up and aimed correctly. It needs arc, length and width to produce distance. It swings in-plane for direction. The plane is a single plane since there is a single fixed axis, whereas the human golfer uses both left and right legs as axes for the lower body movement, causing a change in planes. Balance, footwork and a steady center are not problems because the machine is bolted to concrete. Its linkage system, consisting of a well-timed, two-lever, properly released swing is built into the mechanism to produce correct impact. But one of the greatest advantages it has over the human body is that the machine does not have a wrist. The movement in that part of the machine is limited to an on-plane hinging action and 180-degree rotation like a person's forearms. This is produced by a sleeve-like device which keeps the face square to the tangent of the arc throughout the entire swing. The machine does not have a left wrist that will cup, arch or rotate out of plane. So, while humans have the luxury of a complex wrist joint for accomplishing infinite daily manual tasks, for swinging a golf club it would be simpler if the wrist only flexed laterally.

ARC WIDTH

The path of the clubhead describes an arc during the swing that is basically circular with some flattening at the bottom. Both the length and width of that arc affect the distance a ball can be hit, or if it will be hit at all.

> "The only purpose of the golf swing is to move the club through the ball square to the target at maximum speed. How this is done is of no significance at all, so long as the method enables it to be done repetitively."
> —John Jacobs

Arc width, like the radius of a circle, is measured from the rotational swing center to the end of the clubhead. If one measured clubhead velocity for a given swing and at the same time measured velocity of the club midway up the shaft, he'd see that the head is moving faster than the mid-shaft point because it has a greater distance to cover. Given an equal force, the velocity at the end of a lever will always be greater than any other point along that lever. Therefore, when a player shortens his lever lengths, potential clubhead speed is lost. The left arm may be bent in the backswing if the golfer is unable to maintain extension without tightness, but the arm should return to a more extended position at impact.

Arc width not only influences speed but also is critical in centered clubface/ball contact. Imagine the hitting machine's performance if the lever arm swinging the club shortened by just two inches as it neared the ball. It would hit a bushel full of grounders. A human can compensate for shortening the leading lever arm (the left) by lowering his swing center. But the result is inconsistency, because it adds to the complexity of the swing. Also, the player experiences loss of distance even if the ball happens to be struck squarely, because it's hit with a shorter lever. An extended left arm at impact should be the result of centrifugal force pulling it into extension. This result is the release from a properly timed swing that is free from muscular tension. Trying to keep the arm straight produces unwanted tightness in the arms and shoulders.

Two forces in nature, gravity and centrifugal force, are working to help golfers achieve extension at impact. If you hold a club in the air, then release it, it hits the ground . . . gravity. If you swing the club with tension-free arms and hands, the club will try to pull out of your grip—centrifugal force—causing the arms to extend. With continuous repeating swings and the help of gravity, centrifugal force and a swing center that is not moving up until after the shot, you will be able to locate "mother earth" and brush the grass with the clubhead. It's the natural consequence of extension or arc width.

ARC LENGTH

How far back and through should a player swing the club for a putt, pitch, short iron, driver? This distance is called the "arc length." The arc length will most often be tailored to the length of the shot: short shot = short swing, long shot = longer swing.

Too Long

There is a law of diminishing returns regarding the general formula of "longer swing produces longer shot." The standard most often used is when the club shaft is horizontal at the top of the swing, with a plus or minus five degrees, which includes most of the great players in the world. An overly long swing encourages inconsistent contact rather than longer drives. (Illus 7-29)

Illus 7-29 Although players who are not as strong may need more arc length in the backswing to give them more time to build up speed, there is a point at which control is sacrificed and no distance is added. Here is Marlene Bauer early in her career. It is to her credit she played so well, considering this position, which has long since been corrected.

When seeing a full swing with a long club that markedly has passed parallel, it is usually assumed correctly that in order to get there, either the left arm had to bend excessively, the swing center has moved too much, the left hand has let go (loosened grip), or the arms have lost effective connection with the body. Few players possess the flexibility to drop the club below parallel without resorting to one of these four technique flaws, all of which tend to reduce consistency and control.

Too Short

On the contrary, when the swing with a long club becomes too short, the player cannot effectively incorporate the larger muscles of the back and trunk into the swing. (f7-4) If power is desired it must come from somewhere else. The player will usually try to get the power from the arms, shoulders and hands, which is potentially the cause of several additional problems. Most of these relate to hitting out of sequence with the right side causing the club to be cast outside the target line, pushing the right shoulder upward and forward, resulting in a premature loss of angular momentum (the "early hit"), a lack of weight shift and early breakdown of the left arm and wrist—all because of inadequate arc length. A swing that is too short tends to become a hit.

Ideally, the golfer is strong and flexible with fast neuromuscular response and can take a long club slightly short of parallel and still produce good distance. But most golfers aren't so blessed. Less physically strong and/or flexible players need a longer swing to allow additional time to build up speed. This is the swing that one sees more frequently on the LPGA Tour. In some golfers the backswing may need to drop lower than five degrees past parallel. The aggressive, shorter, faster change-of-direction

f7-4 *Flexibility exercises like those demonstrated in Appendix 10-B can do wonders for this problem after a few months' work.*

swing of Arnold Palmer is not the style this type of player should emulate. *Make arc length fit your needs.*

SWING CENTER

Swing Center in this model relates to the body's "center of rotation." It is the center of the swinging of the arms. The objective of the backswing on a full shot is to wind up (coil) the upper body and place the majority of the weight over the right leg. That windup is made around a swing center or "center of rotation" which, when controlled in its movement, adds to both balance and consistency. (f7-5) The rotational "swing center" should not be considered an absolutely immovable and finite point. It is a reference point between the top of the sternum on the front of the body and the top of the spine on the back of the body. On short shots, such as a full wedge or short iron, the center would show either a small amount or no movement. On a drive it could move more noticeably to the right on the backswing, returning in the forward swing. The degree of centering depends on how much lateral movement the swing style employs. The swing center can move in combinations of six directions: left (toward the target), right (away from the target), down (toward the ball), up (away from the ball), forward (toward the target line), back (away from the target line). If the swing center has moved from a correct initial address position, it must return to the correct position at impact to consistently hit good shots.

If during the backswing the player moves his swing center forward toward the target (a reverse weight shift), then that center must move backward in the downswing to produce an effective result. Likewise, if the center goes up,

f7-5 *The actual center of the swing arc varies between the center of the chest and the left armpit depending upon the ball's location.*

"If everybody could learn to hold his head still there wouldn't be any golfers around still trying to break 100."
—Arnold Palmer
(Editor's note: apparently this was before Curtis Strange appeared on the Tour)

it must come down; forward, it must move back. If it does not return to somewhere near its original location, some mechanical compensation must be made in the swing. For example, if the center moves down, the left arm may need to bend to accommodate the reduced length of the suspension radius. That radius is defined in the address position by the player's forward body tilt and distance from the ball. (Illus 7-30, 7-31, 7-32, 7-33) Maintaining the swing center relates not just to lateral body movement but also to any movement that disrupts the body's correct posture bend, or tilt, measured by the suspension radius. Maintaining the upper body's proper forward tilt for a particular club is one of the critical factors in consistency.

IMPACT—THE MOMENT OF TRUTH

In many of life's endeavors, whether running a company, cooking a meal or playing a musical instrument, there are different styles that work. This is also true in golf. There is a great variety in preferred swing mechanics, as demonstrated by the game's best players. Some golfers prefer to overlap, others interlock, and a few use all fingers on the grip; good players can make a one-piece takeaway, cock their wrists quite early or very late; champions use flat, medium and upright swings. The player's choices represent his swing style and attempt to make all things "right" at impact. The outcome of these choices is the "moment of truth." All that leads up to or follows simply detracts from or contributes to that instant. *The goal is to eliminate as many compensating moves as possible.*

Does the ball care that a player's right foot is still on the ground just prior to impact like

Illus 7-30 The swing center controls the angle of body tilt forward. From the base of the neck, or top of the spine, to the ball may be labeled the "suspension radius." Moving it markedly up or down during the swing causes contact problems.

Illus 7-31 Here it remains.

Illus 7-32 The swing center may lower slightly, but not raise at impact.

Illus 7-33 It releases after impact.

Miller Barber's, or higher in the air like Raymond Floyd's? (Illus 7-34) Not really. It only responds to where the clubface is at *impact*. Certainly the position of the right foot can influence the clubface; but a golfer doesn't hit the ball with his right foot . . . he hits it with the clubface. Please understand the point!

> "Trial and experiment demonstrated to me that the necessary whirling motion of the club was produced only when the force activating the club had its origin in the center of the body."
> —Bobby Jones

Those considerations can be important, and they do affect ball-clubface contact. The point is, know what's most important. The moment of impact is the *most* important. Get that right and the ball won't care how you did it. The end, in this case the ball's flight, justifies the means.

There are common positions exhibited repeatedly by world-class players in every impact picture: 1) left arm more extended than bent, 2) left wrist flat (not cupped), also arched slightly upward, 3) body weight favoring the left side, 4) right elbow pointing toward the right front trouser pocket, 5) left arm and clubshaft in a straight line, never with the clubhead ahead of the arms and hands. (Illus 7-35)

Illus 7-34 Raymond Floyd in excellent impact position although the right heel is fairly high in the air.

Illus 7-35 Classic characteristics of effective impact: 1) left arm extended, 2) flat left wrist, 3) weight on left, 4) right elbow pointing to pocket, 5) left arm and shaft in a straight line. (Photo by Stephen Szurlej)

Impact

How does one learn this critical impact position? The golfer with the correct position at the top of the swing, a well-executed forward motion and a good finish may automatically produce correct impact. But if a player regularly collapses the left wrist and elbow, or blocks the release, consider this: Henry Cotton, five-time British Open champion, had his students hit a tire to strengthen their hands and provide the

"I discovered that by keeping the back of my left hand toward my objective—from the time the clubhead entered the hitting area . . . until it had completed the early stages of the follow-through, I naturally increased my accuracy" . . . "The full swing is the same with all clubs. I don't feel the iron swing is basically any different than the swing you use with a wood . . . you should not consciously try to make any modifications."
—Byron Nelson

needed resistance that gives the proper feeling for the position of the left wrist at impact.

But a tire can produce too much shock and possible injury to the joints. What is needed is something softer. You can use everything from pillows to old seat cushions until you literally knock the stuffing out of them. There is also a tough vinyl bag on the market that serves the purpose even better. It may look like something to sit on, but when you strike it, there is an instant kinesthetic revelation, the feeling of solid, square contact. Practice of this type can be particularly helpful for the golfer who has one of the following problems:

— Allowing the clubhead to pass the hands before impact.(f7-6)
— Deceleration near the ball and producing "powder-puff hits."
— Pulling the arms past the ball and leaving the face open.
— Letting the right elbow fly away from the right side on the forward swing, making

f7-6 *When the clubhead passes the line of your left arm, it is decelerating. That shouldn't happen until the transfer of energy at impact.*

the path of the clubhead approach the ball from outside the flight line.

Whether using a bag or something similar, heed two imporant suggestions: 1) Indicate the aim line by placing a club beneath the object to be struck. Swing from inside the line to develop the feeling of the right forearm and elbow on the correct path to the ball. The right forearm should be in plane with the shaft, and the right elbow pointing toward the right front pocket. "Put your elbow in your pocket" was the phrase often used by one of our earlier great PGA professional teachers, Harry Pressler. This is the result of proper sequential motion between the upper and lower body. And, 2) after feeling the impact position against the bag, step away and focus on swinging to a full finish with a feeling of reaching speed just past the ball. The drill with this bag can help ingrain correct impact position. But no drill should ever distract you from making a full swing *through* the ball.

Whether drills to work on, tips to try, devices to employ or fundamentals to adhere to, the ultimate objective is still the same—to be right at the one moment that counts—IMPACT!

CONNECTION

Connection, as a term describing the body's movements in the swing happening in their correct sequence, has been quietly used since the early 1900s. But the term has been expanded upon and popularized more recently by teaching professional Jimmy Ballard.

In this model the term "connection" does not include the entire "seven common denominators" from the Ballard system. What it does refer to is proper positioning of body parts both before and during the swing. If a player in his setup has over-extended his reach to the ball,

he is partially disconnecting his arms from the more powerful producer of power, the trunk. If during the backswing the arms and club are moved outside the target line in a lifting action, they are partially "disconnecting." If in the forward swing the body stops turning toward the target prematurely and the arms and hands are impelled forward, they are doing so without maintaining their connection.

Some of the uses of the term "connection" in this text could be interchangable with "timing" and "setup." But connection communicates well and works better in many specific situations to describe what is or isn't happening. In learning connection the following comments may be useful:

1. Connection should begin at address.
2. The triangle between the shoulders and arms stays relative to the rotational swing center (upper chest).
3. Sequence and position can be maintained by keeping the elbows in relatively the same relationship they were to one another at address.
4. The body is as much a part of release as the hands and arms if the swing is to stay connected.
5. Connection can apply successfully to the short game as well as the full swing.

Two Additional Useful Words

Two words you may find useful on the practice tee are *transition* and *rotation*. *Transition* describes the change in the direction of the swing from the backswing to the foreward swing. It may well be the most critical move in golf. The reason it's not listed as a principle is because it can be incorporated within the terms timing, connection, plane and dynamic balance.

Rotation is the primary motion to develop power in golf. Like a Mazda's Wankel engine, the golf swing relies on rotary power. There is also power from lateral motion and it is necessary but it does not provide anywhere near the force that comes from making a pivot,

> "It is wrong for a person to think power comes primarily from strong hands and strong arms. It absolutely does not! Power in the golf shot comes from body action . . . The function of the hands is simply to square the face, not provide the power."
> —Anon

winding and unwinding the body. This coiling move incorporates the large muscles of the hips, back and trunk, some of the strongest in the body. Rotary movement is also useful in helping to minimize the vertical lifting of the player's center of gravity. In addition, there is rotation of the forearms and hands, which must square the face but also can provide power. This hand and forearm rotation may be either a natural free-wheeling motion or a more conscious leverage-thrusting action. The term "rotation" is incorporated into dynamic balance, arc length, arc width, connection and release.

So What's Important?

So what's important? Is it better to have a "good-looking swing" or a swing that produces "good-looking results?" Generally, they go together. A golf swing that is correct in *Principle*, one that effectively solves the problems of Dis-

Illus 7-36 LPGA Tour star Ayako Okamoto has a swing that is mechanically efficient and aesthetically appealing. (Photo by Dom Furore)

tance and Direction through the five Ball Flight *Laws*, will employ *Preferences* that are most often pleasing to the eye. (Illus 7-36) But it's important also to remember that "the ball doesn't care how you do it; it only responds to whether or not you did." (See Appendix 3-A for additional valuable material.)

CHAPTER 8

PUTTING

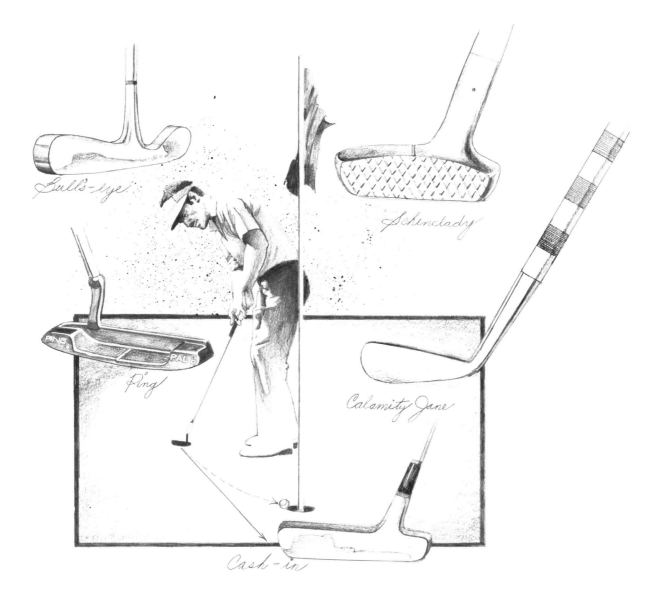

Bull's-eye

Schenectady

Ping

Calamity Jane

Cash-in

Harry Vardon once called putting, "The game within a game," acknowledging the fact that it is a skill unto itself, utilizing specialized techniques and talents, some of which are quite apart from those required for the rest of golf. This miniature part of golf, which brings a conclusion to every hole, has been castigated by some, "Golf would be a great game if it weren't for putting," and praised by others, "Putting is the great equalizer in a game that otherwise would be dominated by the strong and the mechanical." (Illus 8-1)

Percy Boomer, *On Learning Golf (1961)*, has put a different twist on the opening quote, saying, "Putting is *not* a game within a game, it is the game." His view was that the putting stroke is still a swing of the club as in all other shots, but a smaller swing. Certainly the players who claim to have "played great, but putted badly" delude themselves about the nature of the game. Putting *is* a vital part of the score and, therefore, most certainly, part of the game. If you don't putt well you don't play well—period! Yet, of the hundreds of thousands of golf lessons given worldwide in the past year, how many were on putting? There are no statistics, but anyone close to the game knows that the percentage is ridiculously low considering the importance of putting to scoring. Is it because the student shows little interest in putting? Is putting instruction not promoted by the professional? Does putting seem so simple that lessons are considered unnecessary? It may be these factors as well as others but, whatever the reasons, golfers need to spend a greater per-

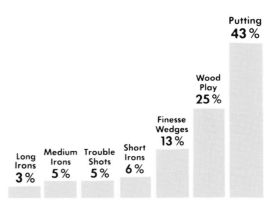

Illus 8-1 Putting consumes some 43% of the strokes for the better player, thereby serving as a "great equalizer" between the power hitter and the finesse player.

centage of practice time on their putting than they do. It is the fastest way to improve one's score.

HISTORICAL

During the early 1800s, successful putting left as much to chance as to skill due to the condition of the greens. This becomes obvious when one reviews the rules then in effect. They stated that a player *must* tee off *no more than* one club length from the cup. After completing

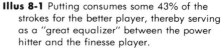

"The best way to putt is the way you putt best."
—Old Adage

play of a hole the caddy or competitor would reach into the bottom of the hole (there were no liners or "tins" at the time), scoop out enough sand on which to place or "tee" the ball, then "play away"—right from the green! (Illus 8-2) The rule was later altered, extending the distance to two club lengths. Finally, around 1875, a separate tee ground was created, leaving the greens exclusively for putting. Imagine the condition of the greens when they served this dual role! As British golf writer Peter Dobereiner so aptly put it, "Putting then must have been more like chipping the ball in a bunker." This appears to be a reasonably accurate description because the greens were maintained not only as nature made them but as nature kept them. Today, we expect verticutting, topdressing, aerifying, watering, plus a lot of other "*ings*," including a 3/16-inch cutting. As we create improved putting surfaces, "good putting" increasingly becomes science, practice and skill rather than luck.

GREAT PUTTERS

The first famous practitioner of putting was Willie Park, Jr., twice British Open Champion and the first professional to write a golf book, *The Game of Golf (1893)*. (Illus 8-3) He was also the creator of the original goose-necked putter, his being called "Old Pawky." It is Park

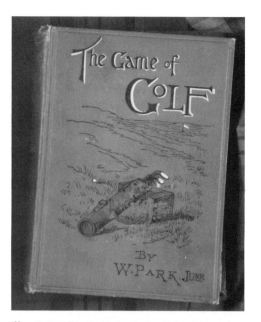

Illus 8-3 Willie Park's book describing his putting and playing style.

who gave us the saying, "The man who can putt is a match for anyone." The stories of Park's putting prowess are legendary. One tale describes Park dropping nine balls on the green at a distance of three yards and not only holing them but also having called whether the ball would enter on the left side, right side or middle of the cup. In his book, *The Art of Putting* (1920), Park says, "I believe I have devoted more time to the study and the practice of putting than any other golfer." And it's been documented that Park would practice putting up to eight hours a day, which may give an indication of one of the secrets of success in putting . . . *an abundance of practice.*

The next great putter to receive considerable notoriety was Walter Travis, the U.S. Amateur Champion in 1900, 1901 and 1903, and the British Amateur Champion in 1904. His story of being the first American ever to win an international title is legend and is certainly worthy of being briefly recounted here.

Travis was born in Australia, came to this country as a boy and didn't take up golf until the age of 34. In only four years he became the American Champion. A more unlikely cham-

Illus 8-2 Prior to the invention of the peg tee, a player had to get the sand from the bottom of the cup and then tee off one club length away, right from the green, leaving it in a rough condition.

pion would be hard to imagine. He was a small man, standing only 5'6" and weighing 138 lbs. Travis wore a beard, smoked a cigar while playing and was a notoriously short but accurate driver.

It was said that he could beat anyone in the world on a course 10 yards wide with a 30 knot wind blowing. It was also said of Travis that he could hole a ball from 60 feet putting on peanut brittle. Thought to be thoroughly outclassed and overmatched in the British Amateur of 1904, this bespectacled, business-like Yank proceeded to mow down one opponent after another of Britain's finest. This success was due largely to the amazing accuracy that he enjoyed on the greens, utilizing a new putter loaned to him at the last minute by a friend from Schenectady, N.Y. This devastating center-shafted implement became known as "The Schenectady Putter." Travis went on to upset long-hitting Ted Blackwell in the final. Later, in 1910, the R & A declared the center-shafted putter illegal in their competitions, and it remained that way for over 40 years.

Another great putter, who had a name similar to that of Travis, was Jerry Travers. He won the 1916 U. S. Open and, coincidentally, played out of the same club as Travis, the Garden City Golf Club on Long Island. If a chronological list of great performers on the green is to be continued it would have to include the man with the gentle touch and golden wand, Bobby Jones. A contemporary, Walter Hagen, was also brilliant on the greens as were later arrivals Paul Runyan and Horton Smith. (Illus 8-4) In the next generation the triumvirate of Hogan, Snead and Nelson, though having periods of solid, if not brilliant, putting, were better known for their shot-making skills. A foreigner, Bobby Locke of South Africa, was the greatest putter of that era with close competition from players like Dr. Cary Middlecoff, Lloyd Mangrum and that master of the short club, Jerry Barber. Another foreign player who brought his putting prowess to everyone's attention was Bob Charles from New Zealand. Those who compete against Billy Casper concede his wizardry on the greens and acknowl-

Illus 8-4 Walter Hagen, one of the game's great putters, demonstrating his style.

edge that he is one of the all-time best. Before his late career doldrums, Arnold Palmer was better than "just good." When he had it going— he was *great*. And finally, few would choose anyone other than Jack Nicklaus to make the putt that counted under pressure; he did it again and again to win major titles. There are others who are, or may have been as good, maybe even better: Deane Beman, Bob Rosburg, Ben Crenshaw, George Archer, and Doug Ford. Characteristics of some of these great putters' styles are included in the following text.

PAUL RUNYAN

Grip—Each hand positioned so that if opened the palm would face upward and inward at 45 degrees. Reverse overlap grip with equal hand pressure.

Setup—Eye line over the ball, forearms in line with an extension of the putter shaft and flexed at 45 degrees, feet parallel to target line, ball opposite the left big toe inside the shoe, weight evenly distributed, feet slightly less far apart than the shoulders.

Stroke—Firm-wristed, eliminating any wrist action using the forearms to swing. Stroke is an arc moving inside the target line as it gets longer. The face stays square to the arc but not to the target line throughout the stroke. (Illus 8-5)

Special Thoughts—Great putters stick with one method and one game plan. "Never up, never in," should be a part of a player's philosophy for all short putts as well as those in reasonable makeable range (providing the green is not too slick). Visualize the entire trip the ball takes right into the cup, but pick a spot about a foot from the ball over which the ball is to start its journey.

HORTON SMITH

Grip—Preferred not to use a glove. The left hand holds and steadies the putter as a guide, the right supplies the feel and hit. Used a re-

Illus 8-5 Paul Runyan, both an expert putter and an expert teacher of putting.

"Compared to the rest of golf, putting looks easy . . . Putting is not that simple. It demands constant attention to practice."
—Paul Runyan

---

verse overlap, with both thumbs pointing squarely down the shaft. Palm and finger grip in the left; fingers in the right.

Setup—Make sure that the clubface, right hand and back of the left hand face the target. A square stance, almost even weight distribution but favoring the left side slightly, eyes over ball, left elbow to cup, right elbow to the side, ball played off the left toe.

Stroke—"Keep it square, keep it low, keep it smooth." Break the right wrist in the backswing but do not let the left wrist break in the forward swing. Seek a right-hand action with no body movement. Visualize hitting the ball with the back of the left hand and palm of the right. Use an intermediate target on the green over which to stroke the ball.

Special Thoughts—The clubface of the putter is the right hand. Limit the body parts involved to be more accurate. "One of the reasons people thought I was a good putter was because I never complained of it." He believed in having two putters, one with a firm shaft, medium flat lie and some loft in the face that is used on slow greens, the other more upright, a bit softer shaft and less loft for fast greens. Finally, adopt a sound method and stick to it.

BOBBY LOCKE

Grip—Left-hand grip normal except thumb down the center of the shaft, right hand also

---

"The teacher experiences no grave difficulty in having a student understand the importance of putting. Getting them to *practice* it is quite another matter."
—John Duncan Dunn

---

with thumb down the shaft but regular overlap style. Grips lightly in the fingers. Never changes grip length up or down shaft for various length putts.

Setup—Feet are placed four inches apart, left foot three inches ahead of the right in a closed stance and the weight is evenly distributed. Ball position directly opposite the left toe. Addresses the ball on the toe of the putter then hits it in the middle of the putter face so as to prevent cutting across the putt from the outside.

Stroke—Inside takeaway, no wrist action, putter face stays square to hole all the way (hooded). Keeps putter blade low, head stays down. Follow-through equal in length to the backstroke, like a pendulum. (Illus 8-6)

Special Thoughts—Pays particular attention to reading the green in the area around the cup within a three-foot radius. On fast greens will aim at an imaginary hole 6 to 12 inches short of the cup. On longer greens or going uphill will try and rap it into the back of the cup. Make

Illus 8-6 Bobby Locke, the man with the unorthodox style, was unrivaled in his putting performance. He putted with an inside stroke as though he were trying to hook the ball. (from *Golf with the Experts*)

> "Billy Casper is currently one of the best putters from four hundred yards into the hole that the Tour has ever seen."
> —Tony Lema

up your mind on the putt's line and pace and don't change it.

BILLY CASPER

Grip—Tries to confine the feel to the right thumb and index finger. Uses a reverse overlapping grip so the two hands feel as one. Grip pressure "easy but firm." More grip in the fingertips than the palms.

Setup—Weight equally distributed over each foot. Varies his stance and setup according to what is comfortable that day.

Stroke—Makes the wrists act as hinges so the head of the putter goes more abruptly up on the backswing than most players' putters do. On the short putts, he keeps it low. Likes to feel the putter head moving freely and then time the face to arrive squarely at the same instant the blade is even with his hands. "Taps" or "pops" the short putts with a bit more stroking action on the long ones. Feels the left hand should be dominant in the stroke.

Special Thoughts—After completing his surveying and reading of the green he sets up to the ball and putts quickly and positively. Casper was endowed with an excellent sense of touch and perception about his surroundings. He practices putting as much as any of the modern-day players. Putts in a calm and confident manner, which is a reflection of his priorities in life—he doesn't feel *he has to make the putt*—it really isn't that important when compared to family and faith. Focuses on speed rather than line, once the line is established.

GARY PLAYER

Grip—Player removes his glove for better feel. He uses a reverse overlap grip with his left

> "The ball doesn't care how positive you are thinking
> when you hit it with a putter moving and aimed in the
> wrong direction."
> —Dave Pelz

index finger pointing toward the ground and the hands quite close together, as one unit. He is not adamant about grip style as long as it's comfortable and effective.

Setup—Eyes over the ball (anything else to him doesn't make sense) and weight strongly over the left heel. Stands fairly close to the ball so likes an upright putter.

Stroke—Prefers a shorter "tapping" stroke on the shorter putts and a more flowing stroke on the longer ones. Keeps the body absolutely steady and the head down well after the ball has been struck. The putter blade stays close to the ground both on the backswing and throughswing and goes slightly inside on the backswing, never outside.

Special Thoughts—Player spent many hours on a friend's practice green in South Africa in friendly but serious competition. He feels practicing in a competitive fashion was most useful in developing his present skill level. Is meticulous in his green-reading preparation, taking the time to get enough information by looking from both sides of the cup. Likes to putt over a spot on the line to the hole. Prefers a heavy-feeling putter. Like the rest of his game he strongly believes in positive attitude, visualizing success.

JACK NICKLAUS

Grip—Reverse overlap, fingers firm, right palm parallel to the face. Back of the left hand slightly to the left of the target and hands at the same height for all lengths of putts. Right forefinger important for touch.

Setup—Stance and posture insignificant to Nicklaus if comfortable and stable. Eye line over the ball or over a line extending back from

the ball. Putter shaft vertical, hands never behind ball. Ball positioned off the left toe.

Stroke—A leisurely paced sweeping action impelled by the right hand working from behind the shaft in a piston-like fashion. Prefers "dieing" the ball in the cup. Has used open-to-closed, closed-to-open and square-to-square stroke styles all in the same season based on the green conditions. Tries to keep blade low on back-and-throughswing.

Special Thoughts—The long time spent crouching over the ball ready to stroke is not to focus on mechanics but to wait for the right feeling that the putt is going in. Uses spot putting for direction. Practice strokes are copies of what the real one is to be. Before a round the time on the putting green is merely to get the pace—maybe 10 minutes or less.

ARNOLD PALMER

Grip—Reverse overlap, light pressure with control. Removing the glove to grip in putting is more habit than important principle. Right hand is the touch or master hand.

Illus 8-7 Arnold Palmer: when at his best he was the best. (from *All About Putting*)

"Putting is like wisdom, partly a natural gift and partly the accumulation of experience."
—Arnold Palmer

Illus 8-8 The putting style of Seve Ballesteros, a simple arm swing pendulum style . . . (Photo courtesy of Golf World

Illus 8-9 . . . without trying to keep the blade low in the finish. (Photo courtesy of Golf World)

Setup—Early in his career, knees inward, pigeon-toed stance to lock body from moving. Weight basically equally distributed, but to the insides of the feet. Eyes directly over the ball.

Stroke—The most important principle is "hold still," a totally motionless body except for arms and hands. A charge putter who is never concerned about the length of the "comebacks" that miss the hole. Stroke is close-faced going back, square at impact, open at the finish. This is made possible by wrist action in the swing. (Illus 8-7)

Special Thoughts—"We learn to read greens in the same way that we learn to read books, by mastering the basic rules and then reading, reading and reading." A closeup look at the hole will psychologically reinforce the ample size of the target. Putting control should be focused in one hand as the master. Under pressure, grip lightly, swing slowly and make sure to complete the backswing.

SEVE BALLESTEROS

Grip—Reverse overlap, index finger of the right hand extends down the shaft farther than normal. Light pressure that is even in both hands.

Setup—Comfort is number one, so Ballesteros changes somewhat from time to time. Putts from a slightly open stance with the feet less wide than the shoulders. Eyes are over the ball, ball in line with the left heel.

Stroke—Watches the heel of the putter to keep the face square. Tries to hook putts that break from right to left and slice ones from left to right. He believes in his touch. Uses a pendulum stroke, making the putter swing at the same speed, the same distance, at the same height. Counts 1–2, 1–2, 1–2 for rhythm. (Illus 8-8, 8-9)

"... it seems to me that we must practice a lot or not at all. The half-hearted, infrequent, casual practice spells just before a tournament usually serve only to confuse a player, by awakening him to the fact that he can hit the ball in a dozen different ways and *still miss* them."
—Henry Cotton

Special Thoughts—Thinks distance putting important. Has practiced in the dark when he couldn't see the cup, just to get the sense of the stroke. Feels that higher handicap players are very poor green readers and aim badly as well. Marks the top of his putter blade in line with his intended ball contact point.

BEN CRENSHAW

Grip—Reverse overlap grip with the thumbs on top for better feel. Palms face each other and work together. The thumbs are the feelers so should be put in a position to get the maximum feel.

Setup—Eye line a bit inside the flight line with the upper back slightly horizontal. Hands underneath the shoulders. Stance almost square, slightly open, feet six inches apart, weight almost even, favoring the left.

Stroke—A definite arm and shoulder stroke with the hands solid throughout. Accepts a little wrist action on the long putts. The putting stroke should fit the personality and resemble the full swing. Keeps the head steady, feeling it's one of the "absolutes." Very even, unhurried pace in pendulum fashion, but inside to one-line to inside. (Illus 8-10)

Special Thoughts—The ability to hole short putts is largely mental, i.e., fear of missing

"If there's one thing certain about putting, it is that it's an individual business. The great putters have used every conceivable type of grip, stance and stroke."
—Ben Crenshaw

Illus 8-10 There seems to never be any left wrist breakdown in Ben Crenshaw's stroke.

causes most of the missing. The most common mechanical reasons for missing short putts are deceleration and raising up to see the result. Develop a clear mental picture of the perfect putt, otherwise uncertainty will ruin the stroke. Take practice strokes to help establish a positive attitude and make them rehearsals of the stroke you plan to make. Think in the present tense of simply making your best stroke, letting the results take care of themselves.

PUTTING—THE PRINCIPLES

Lee Trevino has observed that if a player is putting badly, then one of four things is wrong:

1. A bad stroke.
2. A bad system of planning and reading putts.
3. A bad attitude.
4. A bad putter (club).

All four will be covered here, starting with technique. As is the case with any specialized skill, there is not universal agreement on how putting should best be performed. Players develop their own putting mechanics, which become important to their success, but these mechanics may not be to someone else's liking. For example, Arnold Palmer preferred the knock-kneed, toed-in stance to stabilize the body. Another player may find a more effective but different way to accomplish the same thing. There may be no single element of overall putting *technique* that every great putter agrees upon, but there are a few that a majority support. They are:

1. *Eye line over or slightly inside the ball.*
2. *Set the clubface square to the target.*
3. *Position the ball forward of center.*
4. *Keep the body motion limited.*
5. *Use an accelerating stroke.*
6. *Be comfortable.*
7. *Make solid contact by hitting the ball in the putter's "sweet spot." (Illus 8-11, 8-12, 8-13)*

There are exceptions. Bob Rosburg, a great putter in his own right, said, "One *unswerving fundamental* is that the toe of the putter *must be* on the ground not in the air." Apparently this was before Isao Aoki or even Deane Beman hit the tournament scene. "Keep the body motion limited" is on the principles list and is good counsel. However, Bobby Locke, one of the greatest performers on the greens, percep-

Illus 8-11 Tom Kite exhibits the seven principles that the majority of teachers agree upon for putting. (Photo by Dom Furore)

Illus 8-12 Back with no body motion. (Photo by Dom Furore)

Illus 8-13 Through farther than back, suggesting acceleration. (Photo by Dom Furore)

tibly moved his body as did Bobby Jones. There are further exceptions to the above list of maxims, so golfers should not be totally dogmatic about the seven preferences listed here. Yet, by using them as a guide, you will not vary far from proven convention.

WHAT'S IMPORTANT IN PUTTING

The body's physical requirements for putting are minimal. Golfers with low levels of strength and flexibility can be accomplished putters, though not able to drive a golf ball over 200 yards. In fact, putting and the accompanying short shots around the green are the beautiful equalizers between the power and finesse players in this game of golf. *It is not the mechanical requirements that separate the poor from the great putters.* With practice, anyone can develop a solid, repeating, mechanical stroke. The problem is that few will make the effort, and even if they do, they still may fall short of being superior putters because there are requirements beyond the mechanical stroke which they fail to master. *A successsful putter must also have the ability to judge slope, the sensitivity to feel the proper speed and the courage to act on his decision once it has been made.* So, the requirements for superior putting are more challenging than may first appear to the new player. However, by themselves, the mechanics are relatively straightforward.

THE REQUIREMENTS

Simply stated, what one must do to produce a successful putt is: a) roll the ball on the correct path, and b) do so at the right speed, i.e., the same requirements as for all other golf shots. To start the ball on the proper path, one must first decide what that path is. In other words, one must "read the green." The decision will be determined by slope, green speed, grain, length of putt, the ball and the putter itself. (These factors will be covered further toward the end of this chapter.) Assuming the player

"Don't spend your golfing life in one putting experiment after another. Too often a golfer will continue experimenting simply because he is too lazy to perfect a technique through practice. For lack of practice his putting remains uncertain and he continues to look for some magic putting system."
—Charles B. Cleveland

has read the green correctly, the ball must be struck with the putter blade at right angles or "square" to the correct starting line. How does one do that?

GRIP—AIM—SETUP

In putting, there is a minimal need for power so the stroke is the shortest of all golf swings. With a shorter stroke, less opening and closing of the clubface is produced. To reduce hand rotation, use a different grip from that used in the full swing. You can find a functional grip by first bending slightly at the waist so the arms hang extended. Then, raise the hands by bending the elbows until the hands reach the desired location on the putter grip. The more the elbows are bent the more the hands will rotate to a palm upward or skyward facing if you are to be in your most natural position. Most teachers today recommend a taller posture than in previous generations, meaning a longer arm hang. This produces a natural grip that finds both thumbs pointing more down the shaft. Because the player stands closer to the ball and the lie of the club is more vertical, the grip will run more diagonally across both the left and right hand. This helps to reduce wristiness and clubface rotation.

You have quite a variety of grip styles from which to choose, starting with the overlap, interlock or ten-finger grip, one of which you probably will use for the full swing. But, since the velocity required in hitting a putt is so low, several other variations are possible, such as: reverse overlap, split-handed, cross-handed, left-handed, finger-down-the-shaft, hands-

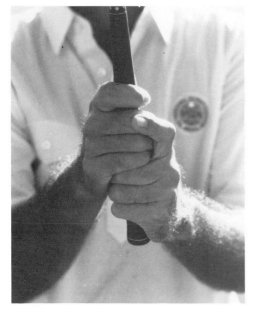

Illus 8-14 The reverse overlap grip, where more of the fingers of the right hand are on the club, is the most popular today.

overlapped plus many other individualized exotic styles, as well as the grips that are used for the side-saddle and the extended-putter-length technique. (Illus 8-14, 8-15, 8-16, 8-17) Most common among all grip choices is the reverse-

overlap, which puts the entire right hand on the grip and brings the two hands quite close together to better work as one unit. Among the others, the advantage of cross-handed and split-handed is that the left wrist is less likely to collapse in the forward stroke. All the grips mentioned are viable options, particularly if the conventional reverse overlap style is not effective or comfortable.

Aiming accurately may be the most difficult and most important element in the mechanics of putting. One of the greatest putters who ever lived was amateur golfer Mark G. Harris, a retired clothing manufacturer from Chicago. He took up golf at the age of 66 and set about practicing for several months with a carpenter's square until *he could tell a right angle from a half mile away.* Harris realized that to consistently hit a 4¼" target one had better be able to aim precisely. He was very correct in his thinking.

One setup similar to Harris' that is quite functional is as follows: (a) ball forward of cen-

Illus 8-15 Split-handed with a long putter is easier on the back and the nerves for Charlie Owens and many others. (Photo by Jeff McBride)

Illus 8-16 The cross-handed grip for putting has its adherents in both professional and amateur ranks. PGA Tour star Bruce Lietzke is one of the most successful adherents. (Photo by Stephen Szurlej)

Illus 8-17 Split-handed, croquet-style putting is not a totally new idea. (Photo by H.W. Neale)

ter (check by putting a shaft in the ground to locate the center), (b) eye line over the ball (check by dropping a ball from between the eyes), (c) weight focused and stabilized on the left foot (check by raising opposite foot momentarily), (d) feet, shoulders and arms square (check by placing a shaft across them), (e) be comfortable.

Grip pressure in any style varies from light to firm depending somewhat upon what fits the player's philosophy. Are you a touch putter, a "jammer," wristy, or an arm-and-shoulder type? Whatever the choice, whether gripping firmly or lightly, the idea of keeping the grip pressure constant throughout the stroke is a valuable asset.

DIRECTION CONTROL

There are two problems with which to deal—Distance and Direction—first we will work on Direction. To get the proper direction one must deliver the club toward the target and present the clubface at right angles to the target. To do

> "Mechanics are about 10 percent of putting—feel is 90 percent. But good mechanics lead to good feel."
> —Tom Watson

this, use a 2 × 4 as a guide for the stroke. Three-foot lengths of 2 × 4 wood have been widely used by such noted putting specialists as PGA Professionals Labron Harris, Sr., and Conrad Rehling. These learning aids can help promote a sound stroke technique from the beginning. Draw or paint a line across the top of the board, in the middle at right angles to the board's length. Use that line to see if the clubface is square. Find a level spot on the green. Place the board so the line in the middle of the board is one foot from the middle of the cup. Rest the heel of the putter against the board so that it can ride back and through against the board's edge. (Illus 8-18, 8-19) The board will guarantee that the path is correct at impact; you must simply return the face to square. If the stroke is a pendulum-type, natural stroke (f8-1), with no manipulation of the hands, the face will open slightly on the backswing, square itself at impact and close slightly on the throughswing.

Illus 8-18 Putting with the heel of the putter riding on a 2 × 4 is an effective practice task for the beginner and professional alike, providing the distance of the putt is limited to 3 to 4 feet.

Illus 8-19 If a 2 × 4 is not available, a club will do.

f8-1 *A pendulum stroke is one of equal length both back and through.*

After a few trials without a ball, place the ball opposite the line on the board so that it will be at the sweet spot, theoretically, the middle of the putter head. Use the same stroke used as when the ball was not there. With the face square at impact and the path on the board, the ball will go into the cup, i.e., success. After a few more successful attempts, move the board back to two feet, then three feet. Do not use the board when putting from a longer distance because the clubhead must naturally start moving to the inside on the backswing as the swing gets longer and back to the inside in the follow-through, assuming it's a nonmanipulated stroke from a natural setup position. (f8-2)

Step away from the board. Then with no ball and *eyes closed* you should be able to feel the pattern of the swing.

Then, *open the eyes* and repeat. Next, set up on a T-square from three feet to establish correct alignment and reproduce the pattern you have been doing. This can be a chalk line, string, or a manufactured teaching aid. Assuming the T-square is aimed correctly toward the target and you match it with the clubface, the rehearsed stroke will again produce success. After several trials, move away from the T-square to putt at the same distance from the cup, but with no guide or alignment aid. Practice from there, occasionally return to the board and complete the already rehearsed cycle.

The basics of *Direction* have now been covered, i.e., a center-face hit, with the blade at right angles striking the ball while on a path

f8-2 *There are putting devices which have you stay on a straight edge all the way back and through, keeping the face square the entire way, even on the longer putts. This requires, however, that the player manipulate the face by closing it going away and opening it going through, or setup so the hands are directly under the shoulders, which is not natural. It's more a manufactured technique, but it does work.*

going toward the target. The next problem is *Distance.*

DISTANCE CONTROL

Already you have experienced that short putts only require short backswings with enough pace to get the ball to the cup. Now it's appropriate to demonstrate that an important controller of distance is backswing length. Place balls at three feet, six feet and 12 feet. Retain the same stroke that was used on the board, but gradually increase the backswing to provide the extra energy to get the ball to the hole from longer distances. If made in a natural fashion, the stroke will gradually increase in speed, creating acceleration to and through the ball. This acceleration is one of the fundamentals in all golf strokes. *Deceleration, in anticipation of making contact with the ball, or from fear of missing the putt, is a stroke killer.* Experience the judgment of distance by taking several long-distance targets of varying length. Place tees in a six-foot-diameter circle around each cup. Focus on rolling the ball into the circle so your next putt will be of three feet or less.

ATTITUDE AND THE "YIPS"

There is no skill in golf where lack of confidence demonstrates itself so dramatically as in putting. Good putting starts with a good attitude, and that attitude is—I CAN PUTT! (Illus 8-20)

Although the reader may not believe in psychokinesis (the ability of the mind to move an object without using physical means), it almost appears possible in putting at times. Any golfer who has experienced the special feeling that a particular putt was going to drop, even before he hit it, and then makes it happen, gets the sensation that one can literally "will the ball into the hole." What's happening, of course, is that a positive attitude is allowing the player to make his best stroke, which markedly increases the chance for success.

Illus 8-20 To be a good putter you must feel you can putt, like PGA Professional Kevin Cashman.

pectation level is experienced as the putt becomes shorter and the "yipper" feels greater levels of self-imposed pressure. It is this pressure to "not fail," which, when it gets out of hand, expresses itself in many of the classic symptoms of acute fear—tremors in the hands, increased heart rate, shortness of breath, perspiration, shaking knees, hollow feeling in the stomach, difficulty swallowing and arms of lead. *The fear of missing putts comes from having missed putts and over-remembering the misses.* (Illus 8-21) Theoretically, every experience a person ever has in life is stored in the brain. Most experiences are, for all intents and purposes, lost because they made no particular impression and no attempt was made by repetition or reinforcement to store them in the active recall memory. But a traumatic missed putt or a series of missed putts in competition which caused a player to lose a title or a check can make a vivid impression that is easy to recall. In fact the player may frequently and

Illus 8-21 The fear of another short putt missed has caused Bernhard Langer to seek creative putting styles to steady the hands. (Photo by Stephen Szurlej)

On the other end of the spectrum is the feeling that "there is no way I'm going to make this putt." Such an attitude can cause dire consequences, especially on short putts.

The spasmatic reflex action that is produced in the hands of some golfers when faced with a short shot on or around the green is called "the yips." Its cause—fear of missing. Since this psychosomatic condition (a body response caused by one's thoughts) is most prevalent in putting, that is the context in which it will be discussed.

Players seldom "yip" long putts because they are not expected to make them. A higher ex-

> "The hole will not come to you: Be up!"
> —Young Tom Morris (to his father Old Tom, notorious for leaving putts short).

> "It takes steadier nerves for that good, long stroke. A nervous individual can't putt that way."
> —Harvey Penick

unwittingly recall and refer to it. The mental recall of the negative experience causes a physiological response: the player "yips." Here are some suggestions to help a player who develops this problem:

1. Employ a selective memory. Forget the bad experiences and shots; focus on the good ones.
2. Get things in perspective. Making or missing a putt has little influence on mankind or the course of history. A miss will not cause the player to lose his life, health, family, home or anything of real value, so what's to fear?
3. Change putting styles, for example: (a) left-handed; (b) cross-handed; (c) place the right hand in a bent wrist locked "piston-like" position, gripping the left wrist or holding the grip against the forearm; (d) overlap three fingers of the right hand over the left to reduce the right hand's involvement; (e) look at the hole rather than the ball or, just as the stroke is being made, look backward away form the cup; (f) close the eyes; (g) or with a widely split-hand position, stroke short putts with one hand; or (h) squeeze the grip tighter with both hands.
4. Change putters. A new putter may give hope which leads to success, building confidence and destroying the yips. Heavier, thicker-grip putters or the long putters that require a split-hand grip are now in vogue.
5. Develop a routine that totally occupies the mind so that the act of putting short ones becomes very mechanical. Using a number counting system can help where the player hits the ball on, say, six—(1) see the line, (2) rehearse the distance, (3) square the blade, (4) set the feet, (5) exhale, and (6) stroke the ball.
6. Look into psychological counseling geared toward restoring your confidence and self-esteem as a putter. Post-hypnotic programming has been demonstrated to be effective with golfers in curing competitive problems like "the yips."

EQUIPMENT

Up to the last half of the 19th century all putters were made of wood. A putter created by the craftsman Philip was considered the top-of-the-line and is today a rare collectible. Other makes were developed later such as McEwan, Morris and Forgan, providing players with choices of style. The first great break from the traditional wooden putter to be broadly accepted and become a commercial success was the Park Patent "Wry-Neck" putter, 1894, the prototype for designs that are still used for many blade putters today. The Braid Mills putter became popular at the turn of the century, selling hundreds of thousands. These aluminum mallet putters were named after five-time British Open champion James Braid, and made by the Mills Company of Sunderland, England. A putter of similar design, the previously mentioned Travis' "Schenectady," took the golf world by storm and was a center-shafted mallet-style putter with an aluminum block head.

Like the Schenectady, the next famous putting instrument was a second-hand gift, but this time it was a goose-neck blade style, an offshoot of Park's original patent, given to Bobby Jones while visiting the Nassau Golf Club on Long Island. He immediately found it to his liking and became so "deadly" putting with it that it

> "The prime requisite for putting? An abounding confidence in one's ability."
> —Walter Travis

> "No amount of eccentric implements will make a bad putter putt better."
> — W. T. Linskill

was christened "Calamity Jane," named after the sharpshooting female Wild West performer.

Just prior to World War II, Spalding and Company brought out a center-shafter blade putter, called the "Cash-In" putter, that dominated the putter market. It reigned supreme shortly before and after World War II, when it gave way first to the Tommy Armour "Iron Master," followed by John Reuter's "Bull's-eye," Wilson's "Arnold Palmer," and finally the champion of today, Karsten Solheim's magic wand, the "Ping." There have been others, of course, from Basakwerds, T-line, Zebra, Response, Potato Masher, Otey Crissman, T.P., Mills, and Freddie Haas—some steady sellers, others bright flash-in-the-pans. Less than a dozen putters in a hundred years have dominated the market. Two things are clear: 1) *Not everyone agrees on what is "the best putter," 2) all great designs have been able to dominate the competition during their heyday, yet were eventually replaced by a "new kid on the block."* (Illus 8-22)

SELECTING A PUTTER

Choosing the right putter can be very important. But how do you know what's right for you? And, if it's right today, will it be right tomorrow or next month? You'd think Arnold Palmer, who has a collection of some 3,000 putters, might possibly be able to answer that question, but he, too, is *still searching* for the perfect tool with which to putt. Other players like Bobby Jones and Bobby Locke found a favorite and kept it for a lifetime.

Selecting a putter is a very subjective exercise. What looks great to one touring professional looks horrible to another; what is functional to one amateur is useless to another. Aesthetics are a part of preference, and beauty is in the eye of the beholder. That's why we have such a wide variety of putters. Look at Illus 8-23 and you'll see just a sampling of man's efforts to design the infallible putting tool. The best putter designs, coupled with the best advertising, capture the highest share of the market, but no one brand gets it all because everyone's taste is not the same.

Here are some of the choices available to the consumer:

Head

Blade (style)
Blade with Flange
Mallet
Heel-Toe Weighted
Sole Design

Illus 8-22 Some of the most popular putters in the game's history, from right to left: McEwan wooden putter; Park Wry-Neck; Braid-Mills; Schenectady; Calamity Jane; Bull's-eye; Cash-In; and Ping.

Illus 8-23 A variety of putters that work for a variety of people.

"All I can do is start it. The Lord handles it from there."
—Jimmy Demaret

Loft
Material (brass, aluminum, wood, etc.)
Shape
Lie Angle

Shaft

Length
Goose Neck or Offset
Center-Shafted
Material (steel, graphite, wood, aluminum,
    etc.)

Grip

Material (rubber, leather, composite, etc.)
Size (standard, over- or undersized)
Shape (round, square, paddle, pistol)

Other

Overall Weight
Total Design
Color
Materials for Insert

Traditional advice on putter selection has been to choose a heavy putter for slow greens and a light one for faster greens. Yet, in practice you see few Tour professionals switching putters from week to week based on green speed. More realistically, they simply adjust their thinking and pace. However, if your home course has consistently slow greens and that's where you play the majority of your golf, choosing a putter with more weight certainly would make sense.

Green speed may also have some influence on putter loft. The heavier and rougher the green, the more loft is advantageous. Smooth, slick greens will call for less loft. Remember your hand position at impact will also influence the effective loft. The setup position with hands forward reduces loft; the position of hands back increases it. (Illus 8-24, 8-25)

Illus 8-24 Advancing the hands de-lofts the putter.

Illus 8-25 With the hands pushed to the right, loft is added to the face.

PUTTER GENERAL STANDARDS

	Loft	Lie	Length	Weight*
Less Than Average	2.0	69	32"	10.0 oz.
Average	4.0	73.5	35.5"	11.5 oz.
More Than Average	6.0	79	37"	13.0 oz.

*Length of shaft would make a considerable difference in swingweight.

> "But as I see it, the thing that hurt my putting most when it was bad—and it was very bad, was *thinking too much about how* I was making the stroke and not enough about getting the ball in the hole."
> —Bobby Jones

GREEN READING

Reading greens is the next subject. Until now, all practice should have been conducted on a flat surface with the aim line always being the center of the cup. Next, add uphill and downhill putts. Note the difference in distance the ball travels downhill, then uphill using the same length backstroke. Experience the effort needed for a six-foot putt on a level surface, then a six-footer downhill and uphill. Shorten the backstroke putting downhill, but lengthen it for uphill. Take note how much less or more stroke length for that distance is needed.

Move to sidehill lies. Roll the ball across a slope just by tossing it underhand from distances of 20 feet, then 10 feet and five feet. Note that on the longer rolls the aiming point is higher above the hole because gravity has a longer period of time to pull the ball down the slope. Practice first rolling then putting the ball. Next, putt over the same distances in reverse, with the opposite break from five feet, 10 feet, 20 feet. This practice demonstrates both the need for a gradually longer backstroke and a progressively higher aiming point and it will acquaint you with left-to-right and right-to-left break. *The concept here is to treat all putts as straight putts.* The ones on sidehills simply have a different aiming point than the cup itself. You should learn to start the ball along a line straight to that aiming point, letting gravity take over to provide the curve to the cup. (f8-4) Proper distance, the right direction and good "reading skills," all can be developed through this kind of practice. (Illus 8-26)

f8-3 *For the most complete explanation of the science of green reading see Vector Putting, by H. A. Templeton.*

Illus 8-26 Nick Price looks for the correct starting line. (Photo by Stephen Szurlej)

GRAIN AS A FACTOR

Bent grass, rye grass, Bermuda grass and poa annua more than likely are the only types of greens you will face. Whereas bent, rye and poa have negligible grain, Bermuda has a broad blade, presents the most grain and will noticeably influence the direction and distance a putt will roll. Newer strains of Bermuda, like Tiffdwarf, are less likely to develop strong grain because the leaf is narrower. Useful information for reading Bermuda with heavy grain could include the following:

1. When the grass looks shiny the grain is going away and the putt will be fast; dull, it's coming toward and will be slower.
2. When one side of the cup looks browned-out, that is the direction the grain is growing.
3. Rough the surface up in the collar grass to check the grain. (You can't do that on the green, as it is against the rules.)

4. Find the setting sun and the grain will generally follow its growth pattern in that direction, although it can also follow water drainage and prevailing winds.

One man who has devoted considerable time to the science of green reading is Mr. H. A. Templeton of Ft. Worth, Texas, author of the book, *Vector Putting*. Here are some of his conclusions:

— Gravity and slope are going to influence the roll of a putt proportionate to the length of time it is rolling across the green. Faster greens require putts be sent off at slower initial speeds, taking longer to reach the hole, thus allowing gravity and slope to influence them more.
— A putt, at the beginning, rises out of its nestling place and skids the first 15% of its travel before starting its rolling phase. During this time it rides along the tops of the blades of grass largely impervious to spike marks and other irregularities. During the last, slower phase of the putt, however, it begins to nestle back down into the grass where green imperfections can deflect it from a true course.
— Off-center hits on the putter face have significant effects on the distance and direction the putt will travel. We may get upset with off-center hits on full shots, but they may be even more important to scoring in putting.
— Attempting to impart additional topspin to a putt is at best inconsistent and if accomplished, adds but approximately ¾ of a foot extra roll on a 25-foot putt.
— Aggressive putters who charge the hole and leave their putts more than 3½ to 4 feet beyond are exceeding the top speed that would allow the putt to drop if it hits the center of the cup.
— Players who attempt to "die the ball in the hole" fall victim to the grain, irregularities, slightly elevated cups, spike marks, ball marks, etc., due to the ball losing its speed and settling.

— A very playable putting thought is to judge the speed, so if the ball were to miss, it would finish one foot past the hole.
— Sixty percent of the break of an average putt is going to occur within three feet of the hole. Except in unusual cases the slope at the beginning of the putt has very little influence. This means study more closely the finish portion. (Illus 8-27)
— X-out golf balls are generally the most poorly balanced and can affect a six-foot putt by as much as three to four inches on either side of the hole. The effect is like having a tire out of balance on your car.
— Although grain on the greens can influence the speed when putting against or with it, there is much less effect on the break until the decay phase or last foot of roll.
— When slope is introduced, the initial velocity tolerance for error is drastically reduced. On steeply sloping greens a 12-foot putt becomes as difficult as a 50-foot putt on a level green.

Illus 8-27 Green speeds are quite different from one course to another, even when slopes may be the same. Therefore, the practice of plumb bobbing to determine the correct direction is far from a true measure. Players, nonetheless, use this system to get general information and to *confirm* their selected line.

—On a putt 2.5 feet from the hole, the permissible error in alignment is a generous plus or minus four degrees, indicating these putts should be automatic—*were it not for indecision.*

And that is where the next writer of a putting book should pick up, dealing with indecision. For even with a laser reading, a chart of the green, a perfect ball, the most scientifically designed putter, and a good stroke, it is to no avail if one doesn't have the confidence to use them. Putting is primarily inspirational, allowing the marvelous computer in the brain to take over and handle the breaks, speed, gravity, vector forces, friction and line. The inspiration, however, will be developed only with practice.

IDEAS AND THOUGHTS ON PUTTING

—Placing the ball either outside or inside the eye line will distort perception of the path to the hole. Outside moves it left, inside to the right.
—Positioning the hands forward or back of the way the putter was made to be soled affects the loft on the putter face. Forward also tends to close it, back to open it.
—Wind can be disturbing to a putting stroke by altering balance. One strategy is to wait until a feeling of steadiness is achieved. Widening the stance and crouching will help.
—Players can become as "ball bound" in putting as in the full swing. Remember the stroke is through the ball, not to it.
—To reduce the chance of deceleration, do the following: On a putting practice stroke make the follow-through twice as long as the backswing, i.e., four-inch backswing, eight-inch follow-through.

> "When putting sense and inspiration desert me, I resort to putting by aid of mechanical theory."
> —Seymour Dunn

> "Natural golfers are bad golfers but natural putters are good putters."
> —Percy Boomer

—Focusing on making the hands pass the left leg in the forward stroke will also help reduce the tendency to decelerate in the stroke.
—Aligning the putter shaft with the left forearm will provide a useful hand/arm position in the stroke.
—Practicing putting with the leading edge of a sand wedge helps develop precision in the stroke.
—Some players pace off their putts to get a better idea of how hard to make the stroke. If the greens are long, wet, or the putt uphill, they add paces to their count; downhill, dry and fast, they subtract.
—The putting stroke, like the full swing, can be successful with either a light grip and free-flowing swing, or a firmer grip using a leverage-type stroke.
—The choice of putter should be influenced by style. A firm, quick stroker will generally favor a shorter, stiff-shafted putter. A light-gripping, touch-type stroker will generally favor a slightly longer putter with a little more shaft flex. Center-shafted putters are usually better for players who tend to hit on the toe, as there is less torque with the center shaft.
—On very fast greens it may help to grip lower on the shaft to reduce the clubhead speed.
—The ball position (forward or back) is critical in putting if the stroke is anything but straight back, straight through. It affects the timing of the clubface.
—Some players are firmer in their grip on short putts as the lighter touch needed for distance discrimination on a lengthier putt is no longer needed.
—A caddy or partner can *help* with the line but only the player himself can *establish*

the line, since only he knows how hard he's going to hit it. (Illus 8-28)
— There are players who suspend the putter slightly in the air at address, which helps them in the following ways: a) focuses on a shoulder and arm stroke rather than hands, b) prevents catching the sole in the grass in the takeaway, and c) causes them not to receive a penalty stroke if the ball moves since they have technically not addressed it.
— Some players hit right-to-left breaking putts off the toe of the putter and left-to-right ones off the heel to reduce the tendency to leave the ball below the cup.
— The shoulder line can influence the path of the putter, both back and through. Closed shoulders will encourage an in-to-out stroke, open shoulders an out-to-in pattern. Square shoulders help in producing an on-target-line stroke.
— Focusing the body weight on one spot, like the back of the left heel, will help keep the body from moving.
— Practicing long putts to develop good

> "Develop a pattern and follow it!"
> —Joe Dante

Illus 8-28 It takes considerable experience to learn to read greens well. (Photo by Stephen Szurlej)

> "What separates the men from the boys on the putting green is *confidence* in knowing what they are doing."
> —Bob Rosburg

rhythm can also be helpful in establishing rhythm in the full swing.
— Players who wear glasses to play golf may find it easier to putt wearing contact lenses. Distortion frequently comes from the spectacle lens, whereas the contact lens follows the eye movement so the wearer views through the optical center.
— Practicing putting to a smaller target like a tee, another ball or a reduced-size cup can sharpen a putter's focusing skills and help psychologically by making the actual cup appear larger.
— Focusing on a spot an inch or two in front of the ball on the correct line helps to start the ball on that line and encourages hitting through the ball.
— Even perfectly stroked putts don't always go in, due to: a) a poor read, b) a poor aim, or c) a poor green.
— Face-angle errors are 70 percent more influential than path-angle errors on affecting the ball's actual line of travel.
— Some players who were great putters have advocated the feeling of hitting up on the ball on the forward stroke, whereas experts of equal stature have recommended hitting the upper half of the ball but doing it on the downstroke portion of the arc.
— When aiming in golf, particularly in putting, keep the head level. Tilting the head to the right or left distorts the perspective.

For more information, including a Putting Matrix by Dave Pelz and a test, "How Well You Should Putt," see Appendixes 4-A and 4-B.

> "Bad putting stems from thinking *how* instead of *where*."
> —Jackie Burke, Jr.

CHAPTER 9

CHIPPING & PITCHING

The greatest golfers in the world, those who play on the PGA and European Tours, average hitting approximately thirteen greens per round in regulation figures. That means that four to five times a round an accurate chip or pitch will be needed to save par. At that level of competition, where the difference between winning $50,000 per season and $500,000 can be but one stroke per round, the result is significant.

The high-handicap player whose golf is for fun may hit only two or three greens per round in regulation. This provides him with many more opportunities to save or lose strokes by the quality of his short game. For example, assume that a player has twelve pitch or chip chances in the round. By getting up and down in two strokes rather than three on only 50% of the occasions, the player saves six strokes per round. That's not even counting the times he'll "mess up" and take *more* than three. So, whether one plays for pay or for pleasure, developing additional skill on the shots near the green will be reflected in significantly lower scores.

HISTORICALLY—FROM RUN-UP TO FLY-ON

Even in golf's early days when most of a player's clubs were made with wooden heads, the chip or longer "run-up" shot was a part of his arsenal. Due to playing conditions up to the middle 1800s the high-lofted pitch was largely unknown. Greens were small, unwatered and

quite firm, causing the high trajectory shot to simply rebound into the air and over the green. In addition to size and firmness, the earliest greens were rarely elevated or bunkered in front. (Illus 9-1) Add windy conditions and one can understand why the "run-up" shot was the preferred style. With changes in green design, the availability of iron clubs that could be forged with greater lofts (f9-1), and the watering

Illus 9-1 Early greens were largely open in front and encouraged a run-up shot with a middle-loft iron. (Picturepoint photo)

f9-1 *The evolution in pitching clubs was "rut iron," niblick, wedge.*

of greens, the pitch shot evolved. As a result, today's golf is played more in the air, with the pitching wedge and sand wedge used frequently around the greens. (Illus 9-2)

Illus 9-2 Today's game requires frequent use of the wedges for pitching over obstacles and to land softly on the green. (Photo © Walt Disney Productions, 1980)

CHIP AND THE PITCH—THE DIFFERENCE

What is the difference between a chip and a pitch? One common expression is that a pitch "has more air time than ground time," i.e., it is a lofted shot which flies a greater distance than it rolls. Conversely, a chip has "less air time than ground time," rolling a greater distance than it flies. *Trajectory* is therefore a factor in the description: a pitch is high, a chip is low. *Style* can also help distinguish the shot. Chips are usually firmer-wristed, one-lever strokes, while pitches may use more cocking of the wrists and hands to create a second lever—an observation generally, though not universally, true. So trajectory and style are two ways to distinguish between a chip and pitch. (Illus 9-3, 9-4, 9-5, 9-6) (f9-2)

WHEN TO CHIP AND WHEN TO PITCH

Consider the following rule of thumb: *Putt when you can, chip when you can't putt, and pitch only when you have to.* The basis behind this statement is that it's easier to roll the ball

Illus 9-3 A classic chip: weight left, hands ahead of the ball . . .

Illus 9-4 . . . one lever, back of left wrist solid, remaining ahead of the ball through the shot.

Illus 9-5 A classic pitch: two levers, weight left . . .

f9-2 *One may play a loose-wristed chip or firm-wristed pitch.*

than to loft it. There is more chance for error whenever one has to lengthen the backswing and add velocity.

The chip is used whenever the player is near the green but feels he can't putt due to heavy or uneven grass between the ball and the putting surface. In this situation the ball should clear any intervening terrain and land on the green. This is to achieve the truest bounce and greatest ball control. The pitch is played when height is needed to reduce the ball's roll once it has landed. For example when: 1) the cup is cut close to the fringe; 2) there is considerable expanse of grass, sand or water to carry; or 3)

> "One secret to scoring is sticking to a simple, consistent setup and swing. For all short shots, I stand open, play the ball in the middle of my feet with my hands ahead, and put most of my weight on the left foot."
> —Seve Ballesteros

the green slopes away and a soft-landing shot is desired. (Illus 9-7, 9-8, 9-9)

Finally, there are times when one cannot safely execute a normal chip or pitch due to the ball's lie, the location of the cup, or the slope

Illus 9-9 This ball, in the rough, should be pitched.

Illus 9-6 . . . swing the arms, keep the hands quiet.

Illus 9-7 This ball, just off the edge of the green, should be putted.

Illus 9-8 This ball, deeper in the fringe, should be chipped.

of the green. When it is not possible to land the ball on the green and stop it short of the hole, the chip-and-run or pitch-and-run is the correct play. This shot is intentionally played to land short of the green to reduce some of its forward momentum. If the player understands these shots, (chip, pitch, chip-and-run, and pitch-and-run), and knows when and how to play them, he'll be able to handle most situations. (Illus 9-10) A look at the fancier shots will come later.

THE CHIP—A TECHNIQUE

Assuming that putting is a part of your repertoire, it is an easy transition to convert the putt into the chip.

Question 1	What is the difference between the putt and the chip in how I place my feet?
Answer	*In the chip the stance is open with feet closer together.*
Question 2	Why is the stance for the chip open?
Answer	*It is easier to sense the target and to swing the club back*

Illus 9-10 There are situations where a special shot is required, like a chip-and-run.

closer to the intended flight line.

Question 3	Where are my hands placed on the grip to play a chip shot?
Answer	*Farther down—shortened.*
Question 4	Why are my hands farther down on the grip?
Answer	*For better control of the club.*
Question 5	In the chip, where is the emphasis in the placement of lower-body weight?
Answer	*Over the left foot.*
Question 6	Where does the upper body's vertical centerline fall in the chip?
Answer	*A line measured through the golfer's sternum (breast bone) should fall about two inches in front (to the left) of the ball. (f9-3)*
Question 7	In the chip, where are the hands in relation to the clubhead at address and at impact?
Answer	*Slightly forward, ahead, leading the clubhead. (Illus 9-11)*
Question 8	Why are the hands placed this way?
Answer	*So the low point of the swing arc will be reached after ball contact rather than before. This helps guarantee a center-face impact. Having the weight left and the centerline ahead of the ball also promotes descent.*
Question 9	Is the stroke made with wrists hinging and hands active or wrists firm and hands quiet?
Answer	*The basic chip is a one-lever stroke with the wrists and hands quiet and the arms swinging from the shoulders.*

f9-3 *This is influenced by the lie. The more the ball is sitting up the less the centerline needs to be to the left.*

Illus 9-11 A vertical line from the center of the body will fall approximately two inches ahead of the ball on a normal chip and on the ball for a pitch from a good lie. Note: Hands ahead of the ball, on the inner left thigh.

Illus 9-12 Setup for the chip: ball centered, weight left, hands ahead of the ball, feet slightly open (could be more), grip shortened down.

Place an extra club on the ground with the grip end pointing just to the right of the cup. Set a ball in the grass as a reference ball position. (Illus 9-12) Take your grip, aim and setup with a #6 or #8 iron. Then check to see if your hand placement on the grip has been shortened, weight is setting left, hands ahead of the ball, and stance open. From that position, you should be able to step back and swing with a pendulum, single-lever motion, making consistent brushing strokes through the grass just ahead of the ball, with a slightly descending stroke. After brushing the grass several times, move forward so the ball is now in the way of the stroke. The club's path will travel slightly inside on the back stroke, returning to the flight line, then continuing to slightly inside on the forward swing. It may appear that the back-and-throughswings are straight along the shaft of the club lying on the ground, but this is due to the perspective of sighting from above at an angle. Repeat the procedure by making three types of practice swings: one over the club on the ground following the direction line; one stepping back from the club and brushing the grass ahead of the ball with hands and wrists firm, though not rigid; and one to feel the pace for correct distance. Then allow the ball to get in the way of the "feel swing" just rehearsed. It is this rehearsal swing that you need to utilize on the course to get the feel of distance for the shot.

> "To save shots around the green . . . 1) visualize your trajectory, 2) in all cases, align the hands directly beneath your swing center, and 3) make an unhurried motion."
> —Jack Lumpkin

THE BASIC PITCH

The transition from chip to pitch can be made in a simple way. Continue the same one-lever chipping stroke with a pitching wedge. Since the purpose now is to achieve a higher trajectory, the centerline of the body can now be moved directly over the ball (assuming the lie of the ball is good). This will move the club's handle slightly back to the right, adding a small amount of loft to the club's face.

Here is where you face a psychological challenge. You are aware the shot is to have a higher trajectory. The club in your hand has a deeply lofted face. So the instinctive thing to do is to try and lift the ball up. This causes the right hand to prematurely uncock, the left wrist to break down and the clubhead to pass the hands so that it bottoms out too soon, either striking the ground behind the ball or striking the ball with the leading edge of the club rather than with the face.

To help overcome this tendency, here are three suggestions:

1. Use an extender inserted from the butt end of the club and maintain the extender the same distance from the left side of the body at the completion of the swing that it was at address. (Illus 9-13)
2. Have a friend kneel in front and to the side of you and hold a club by the clubhead, with the shaft and grip horizontal to the ground, a couple of feet in the air, like a hurdle. Attempt to pitch the ball just under the club. This "attempt" produces a descending stroke allowing the clubface to contact the ball, actually lofting the shot over, rather than under, the club. (Illus 9-14)
3. "Block the face" or pull in the left arm by bending the left elbow at impact and into the follow-through. This encourages the left arm to stay ahead. (Illus 9-15) All three are possible ways to keep the right hand from passing the left.

ADDING THE WRISTS

Once you are able to negotiate the one-lever pitch, repeat the same stroke but add a small wrist break in the backswing. Make certain you

Illus 9-13 An extender from the club's butt end will tell the player whether he/she has let the left wrist break down and the clubhead pass the hands.

Illus 9-14 Select a wedge. Have a friend create a hurdle about a foot off the ground and attempt to strike the ball on the face so it goes under the hurdle. This will encourage you to make a descending stroke, getting the clubface on the ball and actually causing the ball to go over the hurdle.

finish the shot just as you did when no wrist break was present, i.e., with the left wrist still flat. With this additional wrist-cocking added, the backswing of the club will lengthen and the shots carry farther.

Think of the chip stroke as "arms back—arms through" and the pitch stroke as "hands and arms back—arms through." The hands will return the face squarely without conscious effort as long as too much grip pressure is not applied. There is also a style for both the chip and pitch which might be called a "body chip/ pitch." The arms and hands are kept relatively (though not totally) quiet while the trunk is turned to the right in the backswing, finishing well up over the left foot in the follow-through. It's a style which attempts to take the small muscles (the hands) out of the stroke by fixing the impact position, then turning away and returning through that position. The player employing this method will feel more firmness in the abdominal and lower back region. (Illus 9-16)

The wristy chip style, which gives a sharp "rap" or "tap" to the ball, has been quite effective for professionals like Gary Player and Isao Aoki. Mastering this style takes a sensitive touch developed by countless hours of practice and is not strongly recommended for most golfers.

CONTROLLING DISTANCE FOR THE CHIP AND PITCH

Distance control on short shots will be determined largely by clubhead speed, which in turn is influenced mostly by the length of the backswing. The longer the swing, the greater the potential speed of the clubhead and the longer the resultant shot. Vary the backswing length to see the difference it makes in the distance the ball travels. Strive for a consistent, accelerating, but unhurried, pace.

When your practice routine produces solid contact and good results, add the requirement to complete a routine before each stroke. The routine could include five steps:

1. *Survey*—check the lie, the terrain, the conditions.
2. *Visualize*—see the shot and result.

Illus 9-15 Blocking the face by letting the left elbow bend and pulling slightly inward is one method to resist left wrist breakdown.

Illus 9-16 A body-style chip or pitch where the arms and hands stay passive and the shot is made with more emphasis on the body turning to face the target.

3. *Rehearse*—make practice swings or re-hearse mentally, or do both, until the correct feel is established.
4. *Execute*—produce the swing that was rehearsed. (Illus 9-17)
5. *Evaluate*—if the shot was good, put it in your memory bank; if bad, make a correct practice swing.

THE ESSENTIALS

There are a variety of styles that one could use to accomplish a successful pitch or chip. But there are only a few essentials which command universally strong support. Let's examine them:

1. *Shorten down on the grip for greater control.*
   The clubs used for chipping and pitching are not really designed specifically for these two purposes. They are made for the full swing. We only "adapt" them for the shorter shots. The adaptation process is a

Illus 9-17 Once the mind is made up and the feel is there, trust the feel and execute as PGA Champion Bob Tway is doing. (Photo by Jeff McBride)

shortened grip position also called "choking down." The player should move the hands down the shaft to about the hand height that would be taken on a standard putter. Most players go about halfway down the grip on chips; some go even lower. Only a few Tour players chip or pitch from a full-grip-length position.

2. *Grip pressure may be firm or light but it is never tight.*
   Tightness destroys touch and touch is necessary to play well around the greens. Use a firm grip with no wrist break for the straightforward chip of short and medium length. This style is mechanically simple and minimizes error. The firm one-lever-type shot can also be used for short pitches when a soft, dead-ball landing is desired. A firmer grip slows clubhead speed, a lighter grip encourages more clubhead speed.
   Where a greater swing length is needed, for an 80-ft. chip or a long or high pitch, the hands need to lighten their pressure enough to allow for wrist cock. This does add another movement which requires timing. With practice, however, this hand motion provides the player with a better feel for distance. The player should first develop a good, firm, one-lever technique before attempting to add the second lever.

3. *The feet and hips are open to the target.* (f9-4)
   The best position from which to toss a ball underhanded to a cup on the green would be to stand facing it. It's best because the underarm swing is on the target line through the whole motion and aiming is simpler when one faces more to the target. Opening the hips and feet for use in a chip and pitch a) makes it easier to see and swing to the target, b) causes the backswing to be more on the target line

f9-4 *The shoulders remain more parallel to the target line than the feet and hips, which are open, unless the player is trying to cut the shot to make it stop quickly.*

rather than inside, and c) restricts the backswing length, which provides for better control.

4. *The stance is narrower than in a full shot.* By narrowing the stance (bringing the feet closer together) the player can establish a predominance of weight on the left foot. This left-side focus helps the player avoid overshifting to the right side. A wider stance is used when more body movement for a more forceful or a more level swing is desired.

5. *The ball is played in the center of the stance for normal chips and pitches.* (f9-5) For the standard pitch and chip this is solid, simple advice. Obviously, a varia-

f9-5 *Players can play the ball more forward of center but should compensate by leaning more to the left to get their body centerline in correct relation to the ball's position.*

tion in the lie or the type of shot desired could require an adjustment. For example, if the player finds the ball on a bare spot with little or no grass underneath (Illus 9-18), the ball is moved back in the stance. This adjustment advances the grip farther in front of the head of the club, causing a steeper angle of descent and giving the clubface a better chance to hit the ball before striking the ground. With a cushion of grass beneath the ball this adjustment is not necessary. In fact, if the ball is sitting high up in the grass the player should adjust by moving the swing center more to the right to level the angle of approach and reduce the descent.

When a higher-than-normal trajectory pitch shot is desired, the ball is positioned more forward in the stance. This moves the hands back in relation to the clubhead and adds loft to the face. (Illus 9-19) For a lower shot, the procedure is reversed. (Illus 9-20)

Illus 9-18 From a tight or bare lie (simulated on the practice green) the ball is played farther back in the stance.

Illus 9-19 A basic principle: Moving the grip back adds loft.

Illus 9-20 Moving the grip forward reduces it.

6. *A vertical line drawn down the center of the body, splitting it in half, would fall a couple of inches to the left of the ball on a standard chip and fall directly on the ball with a standard pitch.*

Leaning the body encourages the hands and arms to angle in the same direction. By leaning the body left for a chip shot so the centerline is approximately two inches ahead of the ball, a natural pendulum arm swing from the shoulders with no hand action will produce a slight and desirable descending arc. In the pitch, where more height is desirable, the centerline of the body can fall right on the ball or can even be slightly behind, assuming a good lie. This moves the hands slightly back, adding loft to the clubface. Again, make adjustments when the lie is not normal or a particular trajectory is desired.

7. *The arms hang comfortably from the shoulders.*

The arm hang is straightforward and simple, no reaching, no crowding. The hands will hang about one fist width from the left thigh. If the arms already hang extended in the address, they won't extend farther during the swing, a fault which could cause hitting the ground behind the ball. It is acceptable, however, to chip and pitch with bent arms at address, providing they are kept that way and not allowed to extend during the swing.

8. *The small shots around the green require positive acceleration to and through the ball.*

Premature deceleration of the left arm is a shot killer in the short game. One major cause of deceleration is the ball itself. It acts as a psychological barrier for the player, something to swing the club *to* rather than swing the club *through*. When the left arm slows or decelerates, the clubhead strikes the ground before reaching the ball. Arm acceleration must continue through the ball.

ADDITIONAL OBSERVATIONS ON CHIPPING & PITCHING

1. If positive acceleration is important in chipping and pitching then a backswing that is a "bit too short" is better than one a "bit too long."

2. Players may go through three stages developing their technique for chipping and pitching.

   a. Beginner level—firm grip pressure—no perceptible wrist break.

   b. Intermediate level—firm grip pressure, but allowing a little wrist break to add touch.

   c. Advanced level—light, soft hands for touch shots when needed.

"You should never release your wrists as you go through impact. Hold them firm right into the finish."
—Ken Venturi

3. The more touch and judgment a short shot calls for, the more visualization and physical rehearsal is necessary.

4. Novices will need work on reading the greens for chipping and pitching to visualize what happens to the ball once it's on the ground.

5. After visualizing the shot and rehearsing, execute! Don't stand over the ball "too long." "Feel" has a very short retention time. Tom Watson hit his famous "in the cup" pitch on #17 at Pebble Beach three seconds after he felt it.

6. Is it more advantageous to use one club and vary the swing or use one swing and vary the club? Generally, it is easier to use one swing and vary the club. But, if a person gets very adept with a single club, he should use it whenever it will produce the desired result. Familiarity with and confidence in the club means a lot.

7. An alternative to the single club versus varied club selection debate is to compro-

"I recommend that you weaken your left hand (open-face grip) on the club so that your palms are in a facing position. This keeps the back of your hand and the clubface always facing the target."
—Byron Nelson

mise. The one-clubber could use a sand wedge to pitch and a #8 iron to chip. The varied-club player can simplify his choices by using every other club, i.e., #6 iron, #8 iron, pitching wedge and sand wedge for his chipping and pitching arsenal. Of course, using odd-numbered clubs instead of even is just as feasible. (Illus 9-21)

8. The more upright the address and swing, the higher the shot's loft. A flatter address and swing produces a lower trajectory.

9. Putting the left-hand grip in an open-faced position (weakening) helps prevent rotation of the blade in the chip and pitch, softens the shot and helps keep the left wrist and back of the left hand from breaking down before impact.

10. When pitching or chipping to the green, select a spot at least three feet beyond the fringe to land the ball, thus allowing for some margin of error.

11. A ball sitting well in the grass will generally come out softer than a ball sitting tightly, which may come out "hot." This is partially a result of setup. We tend to deloft the clubface by moving the hands ahead with the tighter lie situation, whereas we add loft as the hands move back closer to the center with the better lie.

12. The difference a ball will roll when chipping on a *medium speed green* with a #7 iron going slightly uphill vs. slightly downhill is 10–12 feet. It is much farther on a fast green, so recognize this possibility before playing the shot.

13. The length of the backswing should be

Illus 9-21 One system that simplifies club selection is to use only the even-numbered clubs and select the appropriate one according to the amount of carry needed and run allowed. Note: Estimates of carry and roll will vary by a player's style.

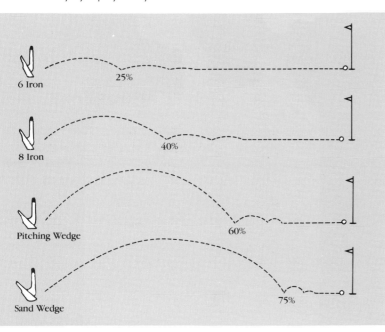

6 Iron — 25%

8 Iron — 40%

Pitching Wedge — 60%

Sand Wedge — 75%

matched by the length of the follow-through on a normal chip or pitch.

14. Soft, high pitch shots will usually be made with a slower tempo. Knockdown pitches, which employ a great deal of backspin, have a faster tempo and more hand action.

15. The center of gravity in the body on chips and pitches stays almost constant. Shifting laterally to the right foot in the backswing is extremely dangerous and results in inconsistency.

16. The statement, "The left hand never stops moving to the target," although technically not totally accurate (it does obviously stop at some point in the follow-through), is a useful thought for chipping and pitching. (Illus 9-22)

SPECIALTY SHOTS

If a player likes the simplicity of using a stroke similar to the putting stroke for chipping, he may wish to try another closely related technique.

Off-Green Putt Style—Off-green putting with a chipping club is a useful technique for

Illus 9-22 As long as the left hand stays ahead of the right, the left wrist will remain flat.

> "I would say that 90 percent of golfers have already uncocked their wrists before they reach the ball. This early hit accounts for most of the fat (chunked), topped and misdirected short shots that you see."
> —Jerry Barber

some players. It is quite simply a putt from a chipping setup. The club is held almost vertically so the grip is more across the palms than normal. (Illus 9-23) This closer-to-vertical setup discourages clubface rotation and helps keep the club on-line. Because the club is now held more vertically, it may rest with its heel off the ground when soled. The hands and grip are still inclined toward the target, ahead of the clubhead. The arms may be somewhat bent at the elbows as in a putting stroke. A firm-wristed pendulum stroke—again, much like a putting stroke—is used to make the shot.

Cut shot—For the higher-handicap player,

Illus 9-23 With an off-green putting-style chip shot, the shaft runs more vertically so the club is soled on the toe.

whose wedge shots have the trajectory of a #7 iron, learning a high shot that lands softly on the green is like getting a cherished toy for Christmas. The high-handicap, low-trajectory player usually has a strong (closed face) grip at address and a delofted clubface from an exaggerated hands-forward position. *Without* a grip change a player can get at least normal trajectory by opening his stance and opening the blade. To produce a cut shot, aim left *first*, then open the face of the club *before* taking the grip. The swing is made with "hands and arms" on the backswing and the feeling of "arms and body only" on the forward swing. The release (to square the face) is automatic when the correct grip pressure is employed. It doesn't need more help from the hands. The swing path should parallel the body's alignment while the clubface sends the ball toward the right in the direction of the target. The most difficult part of the cut shot for the player new to it is finding the correct ball position and trusting the feeling of the "new" longer swing for that distance.

Lob Shot—The lob shot is a high, soft shot played primarily with a long, slow-paced arm swing and very little hand action. It is made from a forward-ball position so the hands are hanging toward the middle of the body rather than ahead toward the left thigh. Make sure you keep a firm grip when playing the shot.

Cut-lob—Combines the cut and lob shot; ball forward, open clubface and stance, arm swing, dead-handed motion.

Chip-and-Run or Pitch-and-Run—Faced with a steep bank in front of the player and the flag just beyond, the chip/pitch-and-run is the shot. Select what part of the bank you'll use as the target. If the grass is quite heavy the shot will need to land high on the hill because more than one bounce will kill it in the grass. If the grass on the bank is sparse or trampled down, a low-trajectory shot followed by a couple of bounces will be required, using a less-lofted club to get the job done. Besides selecting the correct club, you must judge how much momentum the bank will take off the shot so you can determine how hard to swing. If the shot doesn't require much speed, a firm-wristed stroke could suffice. If the shot needs more force, a cocking of the wrists would be in order.

Flop Shot—A wristy pitch is used when a very soft landing is needed. The wrists are cocked abruptly in the backswing, encouraging a steep descent. The club drops to the ball and the left wrist breaks downward to add loft to the club as it slides underneath the ball. It can be a risky shot, requiring a decent lie and considerable touch but it is very useful once mastered.

A USEFUL CONCLUSION

If one could characterize the essential difference in the practice habits between a touring professional and an average club player, it would be in the allocation of time devoted to the long game versus the short game. The golfer who plays for a living, the professional, devotes a considerably higher percentage of practice time to the short game than the club player. And that is one of the fundamental reasons that professionals score better. Chipping and pitching is never taken lightly by the serious player.

CHAPTER 10

BUNKER PLAY

One golf shot which strikes fear into the hearts of some otherwise brave people is the bunker shot. (f 10-1) Nevertheless, it has been said by no less a champion than five-time PGA winner Walter Hagen that, "The bunker shot is the easiest shot in golf—you don't even have to hit the ball." But if the player lacks the knowledge and skill for execution of this shot, apprehension prevails. Combine poor technique with a lack of confidence and failure is imminent. However, those who understand the principles of bunker play (including the design of the sand

f10-1 *Bunker shot, not trap shot. The word "trap" is not in the rule book.*

Illus 10-1 An example of the treacherous bunkers that are mighty enough to earn a fearsome name. (from *Ind Coope Book of Golf*)

wedge) can, with a modest amount of practice, become quite comfortable in playing the shot.

There are a great variety of bunker styles, yet most employ several of the same principles.

HISTORICAL

The early "links land" of the Scots was ideally suited for golf. It *linked* the mainland to the sea, having a sandy base and providing no shortage of natural bunkers. The ever-present wind, with time, would hollow out what may have started as resting places for rabbits or sheep but were transformed into gaping holes which became hazards on the course. Stories which describe bunkers growing from a large divot not replaced are a bit unbelievable even with the erosion potential on the windy links, but nonetheless do suggest how "natural bunkers" were created. Some of those bunkers were so forbidding, they were given their own descriptive names, like "Hell Bunker" at St. Andrews, "The Crater" at Portrush, "The Graves" at Musselburgh and "Sandhills" at Troon. (Illus 10-1) More recently, the awesome bunker at the 16th of PGA West has been called "Pete's Fault," referring both to the diabolical design of architect Pete Dye and the nearness of that man-made hazard to the geological San Andreas fault. (Illus 10-2) Most modern bunker designs, for practical maintenance purposes, are confined to a design that will accommodate a bunker raking machine. A raking machine can't be driven into a steep pot bunker, which

Illus 10-2 The awesome bunker at the 16th of PGA West's Stadium Course. It has a 19-ft. elevation to clear. (Photo courtesy of PGA West)

means one either has to hand maintain it or not maintain it. Lack of maintenance is frowned on in this country, while hand labor is very expensive. Therefore, maintenance budgets partially dictate our golf course design features, including bunkers. For this reason, the average player today encounters mostly flat or saucer-type bunkers.

EQUIPMENT

Prior to 1931, a golfer facing a greenside bunker shot with the ball sitting on top of the sand had a formidable challenge. It took great nerve and skill to cut the sand out from beneath the ball and land it on the green with only a sharp-bladed niblick to accomplish the task. But what happened in the winter of 1931 at New Port Richey, Florida, would change that. Gene Sarazen came up with a clever idea. Aware of his upcoming summer trip to the British Open and the prospect of facing a multitude of bunkers, Sarazen was concerned about his bunker play. One day while taking a flying lesson, he noticed that in order to make the tail portion of the plane rise, the elevator on the horizontal part of the tail needed to be turned downward. This meant that the trailing edge of the elevator was lower than the leading edge. The air resistance against this surface forced the tail up. Could the same principle work on a golf club so the club wouldn't dig? After the lesson, Sarazen went to a machine shop and had solder put on the sole of several niblicks. After hundreds of trial shots accompanied by numerous adjustments to weighting and loft, Sarazen was satisfied that he had a workable solution to the sand shot. He quietly practiced with it at the 1932 British Open, hiding the head of the club by placing it upside down in his bag and then taking the club to his hotel room each evening. Sarazen won the British and the U.S. Opens that year with excellent bunker play contributing to the wins. The secret was out. A new club had been born, the bounce sole sand wedge.

UNDERSTANDING THE CONCEPT

Sarazen's observations were accurate. The principle that works in the air with airplanes also works in water with boats and in sand with golf clubs. A hydrofoil on a boat such as the hovercraft that plies the English Channel causes the boat to rise in the air when the foil's trailing edge is turned downward to resist the water. Whether you are cutting air, water or sand, the principle is the same. On a golf club, the fixed design component featuring this reversal of the clubhead's sole, which provides the bounce, is called "inversion." On all other irons in the bag, the leading edge of the flange is lower than the trailing edge. These iron clubs are built to penetrate or dig first before leveling. Not so in a properly designed sand club. A sand iron is designed to glide, skid or bounce rather than dig. The sole or flange has three important characteristics which make it work: 1) sole inversion, 2) camber, and 3) breadth. (Illus 10-3) The wide flange, inverted sole, and increased camber are all resistive to digging. Additionally, the sand wedge has more loft. Normally the loft angle is from 56 to 60 degrees compared to the pitching wedge at 50 to 54 degrees. The sand iron is heavier than any of the other irons by four to eight swingweight points. Also the toe-to-heel camber of most sand irons gives an oval-shaped look to the face and helps prevent the

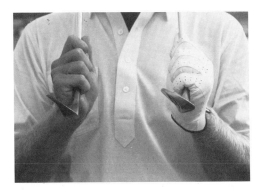

Illus 10-3 Two sand irons displaying the elemental characteristic of sole inversion, but each having slight differences in loft, camber, sole breadth and weight.

toe or heel from catching, thus diverting the intended face direction. What makes one sand wedge effective under certain conditions also can cause it to be awkward in others. Since using the sand wedge to pitch from grass is also desirable, it's important for a player to find the right combination of club characteristics of inversion, width, sole camber, loft, weight, face progression and face design to suit these different uses. The correct choice will be affected by the design of the bunkers the player regularly faces, the nature of the sand, the type of grass he plays on, the firmness of the ground and the player's technique.

THE GREENSIDE BUNKER SHOT

It doesn't take an extensive review of literature or observations of various good players' styles to discover that some very effective results are coming from a wide variety of bunker-shot styles. One sees, hears or reads about the following preferences: "play down the flight line"—"play across the line"—"use an earlier wrist cock"—"use your regular pitch swing wrist cock"—"set your weight to the left"—"set your weight to the right"—"hit one inch behind the ball"—"hit six inches behind the ball"—"play the ball off your left heel"—"play the ball in the middle"—"use a steeper 'V'-shaped swing"—"use a normal 'U'-shaped swing"—"use the same length backswing for all sand shots"—"vary the length of backswing to the length of the shot"—"start with the face square and block the finish"—"start with the face open and use a normal release." The list could continue. What is the best style? The technique recommended here is probably the easiest, safest, most dependable for the greatest number of players. Granted, there have been and will continue to be genius performers in the bunker who use highly individualized styles which they have mastered. But these styles would probably be difficult for the average player to emulate. The techniques which appear to be accepted by a majority of golf's most successful teachers and players are these (for a greenside bunker with the ball sitting up):

1. *Establish a firm footing that will support the swing without slipping, yet will not dig the feet too deeply. Longer shots require a better base.*
2. *Take an open stance to restrict backswing length and to steepen the swing.*
3. *Open the clubface to match the address position. (Illus 10-4)*

Illus 10-4 Take a slightly open stance to match the slightly open clubface. Play the ball forward, toward the left hand.

4. *Start with the weight favoring the left side at address for the normal shot.*

5. *Swing the club like a full "cut pitch shot," matching the length of the backswing and the follow-through to the force needed for that shot.*

6. *Strike the sand from two to four inches behind the ball, although slightly more or less distance can still be useful. (Illus 10-5)*

7. *Do not let the face close (toe pass the heel) until after impact if at all. (Illus 10-6)*

8. *Continue to accelerate through the ball to a natural finish. (Illus 10-7)*

For buried shots—

1. *Play the ball farther back in the stance than a normal sand shot to get more penetration with the clubface.*

2. *If the ball is buried deeply, turn the toe in to make a knife-like leading edge for easier entry, or use a pitching wedge for better penetration. (Illus 10-8)*

3. *Accelerate well into impact, providing concussion adequate for the ball to exit the bunker. A follow-through is not necessary, but can be helpful in sustaining force.*

4. *Consider using a pitching wedge or #9 iron for buried shots where a longer distance is required.*

UNDERSTAND THE DESIGNS

First understand the purpose and design of the sand club and other irons. Take your #9 iron and sand wedge to demonstrate the principle of bounce and dig.

Hit behind the ball with the #9 iron and the clubhead will dig deeply and abruptly stop, imparting little force to the ball, leaving it in the bunker. Then, with the bounce sole of the sand iron, hit the sand behind the ball and the club will skip through the sand, throwing the ball easily onto the green. This is the difference between bounce and dig.

The modern sand wedge will produce this bouncing or skipping rather than digging ac-

Illus 10-5 Strike the sand approximately 2-4 inches behind the ball.

Illus 10-6 Do not let the toe pass the heel of the club until after impact.

Illus 10-7 Accelerate through the ball to a natural finish on the left side. If you frequently leave the ball in the bunker, try t make the hands reach shoulder height in the follow-through.

> "The height of a bunker shot will be regulated by one's ability to displace the sand upward . . . the direction, by one's ability to displace sand toward the target."
> —Pat Riley

tion, as long as the student doesn't improperly use the club. "Improper use" for a ball sitting up would be eliminating the sand wedge's built-in bounce advantage by closing or hooding the face either at address, or during the swing prior to impact. Two sure tip-offs for a "digger" are a closed-face grip (strong grip) and hands placed well in advance of the clubhead at address.

Visualize the basic shot. Watch the whole activity performed by a professional first so you can: 1) visualize the fullness of the motion, 2) see the carryover in form from the swing with other clubs, and 3) watch the reaction of the ball in the air and after it hits the green. If time permits and the occasion calls for it, try several wedges that produce different trajectories and action to emphasize that all sand wedges are not the same. You should now have a good concept of the club's design and purpose, plus a picture of the overall shot, and be ready to learn the fundamentals of how it should be performed. Know your tech-

nique goals. They should be few in number and simple.

An example might be:

BASIC BUNKER TECHNIQUE

Here are some basics on which to focus to develop a sound bunker technique:

a. Set the face slightly open at address.
b. Aim the body line open to offset the face position to produce a steeper swing.
c. Splash sand from 2–4 inches behind the ball out of the bunker onto the green with a swing path traveling parallel to the body's aim but across the target line.
d. Let the length of the follow-through be at least equal to the length of the backswing.
e. Finish with the weight on the left foot as in other golf shots.

CHOOSING A STYLE

Preferences in bunker style among good players can vary drastically. So trying to choose a simple method of bunker play has its limits. One

Illus 10-8 For a deeply buried shot penetration is needed, so toe the club in.

Illus 10-9 The professional explaining how a sharp-bladed club digs and a round-soled club bounces.

very simple approach to this shot is to make a normal pitch shot from grass, but move the ball forward in the stance so the alignment is pointed left of the flag, the backswing becomes steeper and the club enters behind rather than on the ball. Former PGA Champion and short-game expert Paul Runyan once described the approach to bunker play as simply "nothing more than a controlled fat shot." Yet, Runyan and most players and teachers agree that bunker shot consistency improves when adjustments are made to the normal pitch swing. Let's look at some of those adjustments.

GRIP

For a normal "splash type" bunker shot, the *placement* of the hands should be at the same length on the shaft as that used for a full sand wedge shot. *Positioning the hands is not as straightforward.*

To encourage a soft bunker shot and to protect from letting the toe of the club pass the heel and dig into the sand, some players alter the normal grip by rotating the left hand counterclockwise (toward left shoulder) to an "open-face" *position* before placing it on the grip. This one-knuckle grip with the left thumb straight down the shaft and the right-hand palm in a matching position will literally guarantee that the face will not be closed at impact. (Illus 10-10) A similar effect is achieved if the face is set markedly open prior to placing the hands on the club in their normal grip position. With either adjustment, the objective is to keep the toe from passing the heel prematurely. If the toe is allowed to pass the heel before contacting the sand, the bounce is lost, replaced by a dig.

Grip *pressure* will reflect and largely control whether the player is basically an arms-and-body player or arms-and-hands player. A firm grip encourages less hand activity; a light grip, more. The advocates of a firm grip claim this style produces more consistent results and greater precision. The light-grip players opt for their method for better touch or feel. The

choice is definitely one of preference, but more of the great players today emphasize the arm swing rather than hand action.

When the clubface is opened to compensate for the aim to the left, more inversion is created, giving increased bounce to the sole. This reduces the chance of the player digging the club into the sand too deeply and stopping the clubhead so that too little energy is transferred to the ball to get it out of the bunker.

AIM

There are two definite schools of thought on the principle of AIM. One would have the player align almost square to the target line with the face of the sand wedge square and playing down the line to the target on all shots. This style has the shape and direction of the swing which matches a regular pitch shot. (Illus 10-11) The second would make more adjustments, aiming left of the target line with every-

Illus 10-10 A closed-face grip will make it difficult to execute a "splash" sand shot because the toe will tend to lead and dig.

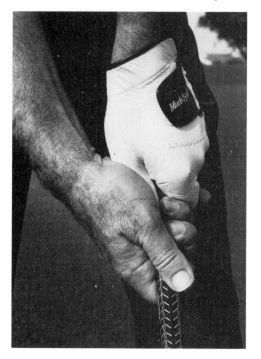

thing but the clubface, then making the swing parallel to the body line, left of the target. (Illus 10-12) The open clubface, however, would send the ball toward the target with a bit of slice spin.

Both methods are effective. If a player tends to close the face at impact and dig excessively, then the "aim left, open-face, steep, swing-across-the-target-line method" would seem to be effective. This is the more widely taught technique, since it helps alleviate the devastating error of penetrating the sand too deeply and leaving the ball in the bunker. Too much descent, however, can also be a problem if the angle of approach is so severe that the club simply buries, giving inadequate force to the ball and leaving it in the bunker. A sharply descending approach can also be dangerous in coarse, packed or firm-based sand, in that it can bounce the club too abruptly off the sand's surface, rather than sliding it under the ball, which may cause the ball to be bladed over the green.

There is a difference of opinion as to what causes the ball's direction leaving the sand. Is it the swing path or the clubface which determines the ball's direction? Swing-path advocates claim that since the clubface does not touch the ball, the former does not affect the direction the ball travels. Clubface-direction advocates feel that wherever the face is aiming at impact will be the direction the ball travels. The correct answer is the one that applies for every golf shot. *Direction is the outcome of the combination of path and face.* However, since this is not a high-velocity shot (the sand slows the clubhead, cushioning the force), the ball direction will be more influenced by face position than path. If you close the clubface and hit the sand, the particles will fly left (the law of rebound); square the face and they'll go forward; open the face and they'll go right. The influence of face position holds true for the ball. Watch the direction in which the sand is displaced to know where the ball will go.

By opening the stance and aiming left the player steepens the angle of approach, which

Illus 10-11 A setup position which is the same as the player uses for a normal pitch, where the player swings down the line to the target.

Illus 10-12 An open-face, open-stance setup where the player swings across the line to the left of the target.

helps to insure he'll hit the sand with enough descent to get the blade under the ball. Players who swing from sharply inside the flight line approach the ball on a shallower plane, increasing the possibility of the club's leading edge glancing into the middle of the ball rather than cutting the sand from beneath it.

When the clubface is opened to compensate for the aim to the left, more inversion is created, giving increased bounce to the sole. This reduces the chance of the player digging the club into the sand too deeply and stopping the clubhead so that too little energy is transferred to the ball to get it out of the bunker.

SETUP

Firm footing is particularly helpful if the player is using considerable force in the swing. If the swing base falters and the feet move, the shot will most likely be misplayed. Therefore, a first step in the setup is to work the feet into the sand. This puts the golfer's feet slightly lower than the ball, at about the level where the clubhead easily passes beneath the ball.

Most players agree that the ball placement should be forward, in line with the instep of the left foot. But what really matters is where the ball should be placed in relation to the vertical centerline of the body. Players who set their weight on the right side at address tend to center the ball between their feet. (Illus 10-13) Those who favor their weight to the left side will have the ball more forward—approximately four to six inches left of the vertical centerline. But again, ball placement can also depend on how much lateral weight shift accompanies the swing. Those who favor setting left, besides having the ball forward, will tend to have a steeper angle of approach, will hit closer to the ball and prefer broad-soled, bounce-type sand wedges. A balanced setup position or one more to the right will encourage the player to take a longer, thinner cut of sand, with a shallower swing. The player using this style will generally select a narrower-flanged sand iron.

SWING

From the discussion thus far we know that grip, aim and the setup will influence the swing style and that swing styles differ among players. But swing shape will also differ. Some players prefer an early, pronounced wrist cock to get steepness in what has come to be described as a "V"-shaped swing. Those who prefer to swing the club as they would in a normal pitch shot could refer to their swing pattern as a more "U"-shaped swing. The steeper "V" shape pops the ball up higher, softer and shorter. Its "U" shape counterpart produces a lower trajectory and equal distance with less effort. Picture making the "U" swing as standing in a larger saucer of sand, the "V" swing in a large teacup. These swing shapes are also one type of distance control which will be discussed in a moment.

As in the full pitch shot swing, there are players who play a bunker shot using a lot of body with firm hands and wrists as their style. Others employ a looser grip pressure with more

Illus 10-13 If the player's setup is a bit more to the right or his release early, the ball must be farther back than the left heel.

"Do not flip the wrists, the ball should come out slowly."
—Gene Sarazen

wrist action and an aggressive arm swing. Strength has something to do with style choice. It takes strength to be consistently firm. So one usually associates firmness of grip pressure and the use of more body action with physical strength and a looser arm swing style with a less muscular player. But keep in mind there are many exceptions to this general observation.

CONTROLLING DISTANCE

There are five ways to control distance in the bunker shot:

1. *Angle of Approach*—Use a steep angle for short distances; use a shallow angle for longer distances.
2. *Blade Position*—Add loft by opening or laying back the face for short distances; reduce loft by closing or hooding for longer distances. (Note: As in shots from grass, ball position also influences loft; back for less, forward for more.)

3. *Backswing Length and Pace*—A long backswing has the potential for creating more force than a short swing and, therefore, will generally send the ball farther. The pace, however, also affects that result. A player could use a slow pace with a long backswing or a fast pace with a short backswing and hit the ball as far or farther with the short swing than the long one. So, pace and length of backswing need to be blended.
4. *Amount of Sand*—Shorter shots result from taking more sand by hitting farther behind the ball (four to six inches) and longer shots result from hitting closer to the ball (one to three inches), taking less sand. Keep in mind, however, that hitting close to the ball, though sending the ball farther, will spin it more and make it stop quicker on the landing area.
5. *Length of Follow-through*—A short follow-through is generally the result of reduced speed at impact, whereas a long follow-through usually means more speed and greater distance. Keep the backswing about the same length for both types of follow-through. (Illus 10-14)

Frequently, a player will use a combination of two or more of these control styles to play a specialty shot from a difficult position.

Illus 10-14 PGA champion Lanny Wadkins lets the follow-through length match his backswing length. (Photo by Stephen Szurlej)

FAIRWAY BUNKER SHOTS

When the ball is in a fairway bunker and the objective is to get greater distance, a fundamental principle changes. Whereas in the normal "greenside bunker" shot, a player should always contact the sand first, *in a fairway bunker he should always contact the ball first.* Most of the adjustments are related to this objective.

Once a player has selected a club with adequate loft to safely clear the lip of the fairway bunker, he should then make the following adjustments:

1. First, check the lie. A good lie will allow a normal swing with few adjustments. A medium lie may require more descent, a poor lie may require a "pitch out" to the fairway. (Illus 10-15)
2. Establish solid footing, especially with the right foot.
3. Choke down on the club the same number of inches the feet have been worked into the sand.

Illus 10-15 In the fairway bunker, the player needs a perfect lie to attempt a wood. Then the ball should be played slightly back and the grip shortened down on the club.

4. Position the ball more toward the center of the stance.
5. Place the hands slightly ahead of the ball as with a normal shot, not sitting too much in the knees, even playing slightly "stiff-legged."
6. Sweep the ball from the sand as though it were resting on a sheet of glass. It may help to visualize making contact with the ball "below its equator, but above the sand" as Bel Aire professional Eddie Merrins suggests. If the lie isn't good and more descent is needed, open the clubface slightly, aim left and use one more club. This will help the heel to lead, encouraging bounce, rather than the toe to lead, and causing dig.
7. Look not at a spot behind the ball as some do in a greenside bunker, but look rather at the front edge of the ball, or just slightly ahead of it, to help assure ball contact is made before sand contact.

PSYCHOLOGY IN THE BUNKER

Probably the hardest thing to overcome is one's fear of the bunker shot. This fear is a result of past failures, a lack of confidence and a feeling of uncertainty. The best way to avoid that frame of mind is to understand the principles behind executing the shot and to practice until you have enough confidence in a method that you know will get the ball out. Visualizing a successful result is one of the important steps in playing the shot. Fear of making a mistake produces muscular tension. Tension produces shortening of muscle fibre or tightening up. When you tighten up, you inhibit the swing and reduce the chance of making a successful shot. Thinking negatively and seeing poor mental pictures can destroy one's ability to make a good swing in the bunker. You must stay loose and relaxed, and that comes only when you know you can successfully execute the shot.

One of the touring professionals with exceptional confidence in the bunker has been Gary Player. Several years ago, he was warming up before a tournament. While walking by the practice bunker he was seen by Australian Bruce Devlin. Gary Player had the reputation for tireless practice in the bunker and for being one of the world's best at the shot. Devlin saw the opportunity to pick up a tip. He said, "Gary, come here a minute. Give me a rundown on what you do in the bunker."

Gary said, "Let me have your club." He took Bruce's club and proceeded. "Well, here's what I do. I dig my feet in first, take a bit of an open stance; I choke the club down; lean into it with the weight on my left side; open the face up just a little, and then I swing and cut it out."

Bruce said, "OK, let's see it." Gary went through the routine, swung the club—and poof—two skips, boom, right in the hole.

He said, "That's how I do it," and handed the club back.

In the meantime, Devlin was saying to himself, "This lucky stiff—there's no guy that good." So, he countered, "Just go through that once more for me."

"All right," said Player. "Choke the club down a little, get yourself settled in the sand, lean into it to the left, open the face just a little, and do like this." And he hit another shot which floated up, took two skips, hit the right edge of the cup and just lipped out. Then Gary looked at Bruce and said, "But you don't want to open the face too much, mate."

Much of a player's success in the bunker depends on confidence. Visualizing good results is one of the tools to create confidence.

ADDITIONAL THOUGHTS ON BUNKER PLAY

1. The term "splash" rather than "explosion" is a word which may better describe the preferred swing action when the ball is sitting up on top of the sand. "Dig" is a descriptive word for the swing when the ball is buried.
2. Good results from a bunker, like good results on the putting green, depend greatly upon the ability of the player to "read the sand," like "reading the green." The only means within the rules that the player has for reading the sand are his eyes and feet. The feet are the "feelers." Walking to the ball and taking a stance will provide information on sand depth. Sand depth and condition can also be partially determined visually. If the sand is coarse or wet that means it is firmer and will cause more bounce; fluffy and dry sand will cause the club to dig more. Therefore, for firm lies use less bounce from the sole; for soft lies use more bounce.
3. Vary the depth of cut by setting the club's grip-end forward for a deep cut or back for a shallow cut.
4. Chipping from sand is difficult and is not widely taught. Players who do execute this shot play the ball back in the stance and try to keep the swing level and wrists firm.
5. In the follow-through for a bunker swing the player can either hold the arm rotation or release it, depending on his setup. The more open the face in the backswing, the greater the arm and hand release. If the face is square the tendency will be to hold or just "body release." (Illus 10-16)
6. Some of the factors determining the type of shot to be played are lie, distance to the flag, sand composition and condition, slope and speed of the green, height of the bunker lip and type of bunker club that is being used.
7. A visual image to help the player from closing the face prematurely is to picture balancing a glass of water on the clubface, without spilling it, until well into the follow-through.

> "If I am one of the greats, it's for one simple reason; no bunker shot has ever scared me and none ever will . . . Approach every bunker shot with the feeling you are going to hole it."
> —Gary Player

Illus 10-16 The follow-through shows some upper body release and less hand and forearm release. U.S. Open winner Scott Simpson demonstrates an effective style. (Photo by Stephen Szurlej)

8. Uneven lies in the bunker are played like those from grass using similar adjustments. For example, align the shoulders parallel to the slope of the ground for uphill or downhill lies. An exception to this is when the slope is severe, i.e., having the ball plugged in the face of an uphill bunker where a parallel-to-the-slope shoulder position would cause the player to fall over. In this case lean into the hill and hit closer to the ball than in a normal sand shot. The vertical bank will still allow plenty of sand between the clubface and ball.

9. A player should learn how far he can hit a sand wedge from a bunker under different sand conditions so that he'll know when the target is out of range and a different club is needed.

10. Fear produces tension, which in turn destroys swing motion. The bunker shot is a natural for causing this psychological reaction, particularly in players who have experienced only occasional success in escaping from a bunker. What is the effect on technique when players execute this shot in a fearful state? They release prematurely, trying to scoop the ball up and catch the sand too far behind the ball with a shallow approach. The clubhead is then allowed to pass their hands too early in the forward swing, resulting in a bladed shot. Or they tighten and decelerate, causing the club to lose its impact force, leaving the ball in the bunker. Eliminating fear will improve results. Confidence will destroy fear. Confidence comes from knowing what one is doing.

CHAPTER 11

THE IMPORTANCE OF PRACTICE DRILLS

THE STRENGTH OF HABITS

A habit is a difficult thing to change. Imagine a person who is accustomed to turning a doorknob clockwise with the right hand because he's been doing it all his life. Then someone says, "If you'll learn to turn the knob counterclockwise, it will take less effort and you'll do it faster." So the person tries. Each time, his first instinct is to put the "old clockwise move" on the knob, but he stops and thinks, "counterclockwise." After a while, "counterclockwise" begins to replace "clockwise" as his habitual way of opening a door. *That is, until someone yells "FIRE!"* Our person runs to the door and "clockwises the knob," a complete reversion under pressure. Golf is a lot like this. We can adopt a technique change (*on the practice tee*), sometimes quickly, but will it "hold up" when we are on the course? What appears to work on the range often fails when tested under the pressure of the game. How can golfers overcome this? The most powerful answer is practice—*overlearn*, if there is such a thing. Practice makes permanent. (Illus 11-1) To get a better understanding of this essential part of golf improvement, let's use a Who, What, Where, When, Why and How approach.

Illus 11-1 The practice range may be crowded with serious competitors but the majority of golfers seldom practice. Do they need to be convinced that motor learning comes about only by practice?

WHO

Who should practice? Anybody and everybody who wishes to improve. In fact, anybody who wishes to simply retain his present skill level needs to practice. (Illus 11-2) Golfer, musician, artist, public speaker, surgeon, trial lawyer, mechanic, pilot—all must practice to perform well. If a player is going to compete, he will have to practice even more than for mere skill retention. (Illus 11-3) The improvement one gets will be in direct proportion to the time spent in practice, if:

1. What one practices is mechanically correct.
2. One's practice time is used properly—is it quality time or just time?
3. The time is divided into frequent periods rather than devoted to one long session.

WHAT

A famous Tour professional has commented that there aren't enough hours in the day to practice what one needs in order to stay on top

"Goal-less practice is worse than no practice at all because it builds a cavalier approach to the game."
—Thomas Simek and Richard O'Brien
(authors of *Total Golf*)

of all parts of the game. Since there are considerably fewer hours a week available for most amateur golfers to practice than for professionals (to practice), the choice of what they practice becomes that much more important. If improved scoring is the objective, then players should spend at least 50% of their practice time on the short game—*at least 50%*.

A PRACTICE PLAN FOR THE SERIOUS PLAYER

Practice sessions should have a purpose. The serious player should have a written schedule of *what* he is going to practice. In planning practice time (Schedule A) the player should concentrate on what he and his professional have agreed needs the most work. The player has a definite *what* to practice. The schedule may include both the short and long game, specific shots, remedial work, physical and psycholog-

Illus 11-2 Practice is essential both for improvement and maintenance of present skill.

Illus 11-3 Strike a balance in practice between the time spent on full shots and the short game. Here, Tom Watson works on some short-iron shots under the experienced eye of Byron Nelson. (Photo by Stephen Szurlej)

SCHEDULE A
ONE WEEK PRACTICE & PREPARATION SCHEDULE (PROFESSIONAL LEVEL)

	Mon.	Tues.	Wed.	Thurs.	Fri.	Sat.	Sun.
Short Game (Chip & Pitch)	1 hr.	2 hrs.	30 min.	2 hrs.	1 hr.	1 hr.	15 min.
Putting	30 min.	1 hr.	15 min.	1 hr.	X	2hrs. (Pre-shot routine)	15 min.
Irons	30 mins. (Short & Mid.)	1 hr. (Pre-shot routine)	15 min. (Short only)	1 hr.	30 min.	1 hr.	10 min.
Woods	15 min.	45 min. (Pre-shot routine)	15 min.	1 hr. Fairway	15 min.	30 min. (Pre-shot routine)	10 min.
Bunker Play	30 min.	15 min.	X	30 min.	15 min.	30 min.	X
Play & Course Mgmt.	9 holes	X	18 holes	9 holes	18 holes	9 holes	18 holes
Mental	Read golf & watch videos 1 hr.	Relaxation, meditate, & visualize 15 min.	Relaxation, meditate, & visualize 15 min.	Read golf & watch videos 1 hr.	X	Relaxation, meditate & visualize 15 min.	Read Rules 30 min.
Physical	Aerobics & stretching 1 hr.	Strength 30 min.	Aerobics & stretching 1 hr.	Strength 30 min.	Aerobics & stretching 1 hr.	Strength 30 min.	REST
Miscellaneous	Trouble shots, (select) trajectory, curving the ball, uneven lies, left-handed, rough, recordkeeping 15 min.	Trouble shots & left-handed	X	Uneven lies 20 min.	Take equip. for lie angle check	Curving the ball	Recordkeeping & schedule
Notes	Run errands	Shopping	X	Haircut	X	Errands	

ical training, playing and information gathering. This is the type of schedule that someone contemplating a career in golf or who is training for national-level competition might follow. For other serious golfers with more modest objectives, or more serious time restrictions, this sample schedule can be used as a guide.

PRACTICE FOR THE WEEKEND AMATEUR

The majority of golfers practice only occasionally. (f 11-1) but even the avid amateurs will find that time constraints limit their opportun-ities. The *what* to practice for them has to be more limited in scope than for the aspiring tournament player. Here are some suggestions:

1. Make practice swings whenever possible. Place old clubs around the house in various locations so that it will be convenient to pick one up and swing it.
2. Without a club, make imaginary swings with the arms and hands in front of a mir-

f11-1 *Statistics indicate that 47% of high-handicappers* **never** *practice.*

SCHEDULE B
ONE WEEK PRACTICE & PREPARATION SCHEDULE (AMATEUR—MODERATE LEVEL)

	Mon.	Tues.	Wed.	Thurs.	Fri.	Sat.	Sun.
	Health Club Workout 12:30–1:30, include golf drills	Evening Swing club at home in front of mirror or window.	Health Club Workout 12:30–1:30, include golf drills	Evening Swing club or chip.	Health Club Workout 12:30–1:30, include golf drills	Practice 1 hr. and play 18 holes	Watch Golf Tournament T.V.
	Putt on rug 15 min.		Read golf magazine, watch a video 9:00–10:30 P.M.		Practice range 5:00–6:30 P.M.		Practice 30 min. Play 9 holes Sun. evening
Notes	Work on keeping left wrist from breaking down in putting stroke		Watch for preshot routine in video		Practice keeping the driver in play		

ror or window. Picture and feel the correct positions.

3. Grip a club while watching television. Swing during commercials.

4. Create a practice area in the house or office which makes practice more convenient. Include short-game practice.

Schedule B is for the weekend player who wants to improve but has full-time work, family or other obligations. (For a list of personal golf objectives for competition see Appendix 6-A.)

WHERE

The obvious place to practice is at the "golf range," referred to for many years as the "driving range." Of course, all practice needn't be confined to that area. Consider the following possibilities:

> "A golfer should put in the same amount of time on the practice tee as he does playing."
> —Lee Trevino

1. *At home* (outside)—If a survey were taken, one might be surprised at how many players who do practice do some of their practice at home. A golfer can chip, pitch or make a full swing in the yard. Home nets and pitching targets are made for that very activity. (Illus 11-4) Former Tour star Ed Sneed grooved his swing as a youngster by watching himself in front of a large window in the family home. Bob Toski built a miniature course in his yard as did Hall of Famer Chick Evans. Jack Nicklaus has his own green and bunker in the backyard for family practice on the short game.

2. *At home* (inside)—Basements with high ceilings, or garages can become practice ranges. Who can say how many golfers in the past have used the front room carpet as simulated turf from which to pitch onto a sofa or chair "greens" and then sunk the putt in a glass "cup" placed on the floor? Video offers a new and exciting opportunity for a vicarious type of practice at home. Watching with club in hand can become an effective way to learn and practice.

3. *At work*—If practice is possible on the job,

Illus 11-4 Ernest Jones, one of golf's great teachers, felt that learning a swing indoors could be more effective than outdoors because the student focused on the movement rather than the ball flight. (Photo courtesy of Golf World, U.S.)

a golf club placed in the corner which can easily be picked up and swung during a free moment may be a viable means of stress reduction or a stimulating break from a tedious task.

4. *In the car*—Audiotapes on golf can provide another medium for learning. There are several commercial tapes on the market that provide golf tips and coaching. One amateur in California who was a busy physician had his professional give him a two-hour lesson with the most important points put on audiotape. The "doc" listened regularly for several weeks to that personal audio lesson until the points were so clear that his performance improved even though he'd had no ball-hitting practice.

5. *At the health club*—If you regularly "work out" at a health club or gymnasium, leave a golf club or a specially weighted training club stored there for

> "I never hit a shot, not even in practice without having a very sharp, in-focus picture of it in my head."
> —Jack Nicklaus

practice swinging during a workout session.

These examples highlight the point that practice can take place in many different locations. You can modify your daily routine to find more practice time using one of these suggested alternatives. If you use your imagination, you'll find a place to practice. (Illus 11-5) Mental practice, in particular, is always possible, since it can be done anywhere, almost anytime.

MENTAL PRACTICE

Expansion of the mental practice concept will be the next giant stride in learning golf. Consider the stories that came from prisoners of war in Vietnam. Men who were incarcerated

Illus 11-5 By using one's imagination, practice can be accomplished almost anywhere. (Photo courtesy of Golf World, U.S.)

> "The purpose of practice is to tell the brain as accurately as possible, how to organize the movements of the body."
> —John Syer & Christopher Connally

for several years learned to play a guitar by practicing chording on a homemade "stick and box with strings." There were no sounds, but they learned to play. Musical pieces were also performed on a "wooden board piano" with keys drawn on the board. There was no key movement and no sound, but the pupils mentally "heard" the songs and they learned to play. Closer to our subject of golf is the story of a U.S. military officer who was in a prisoner-of-war camp for six years and carried a four handicap before his capture. Although he did not hit a golf shot while he was imprisoned, he did practice mentally every day. Three weeks after his release, he shot a 75 in a pro-am. *He hadn't hit a ball in six years, but he had practiced— in his mind!* Where can people practice? Anywhere!

WHEN SHOULD YOU PRACTICE?

You should practice whenever you can. Frequent short practice sessions are proven by research to be more productive than an equal amount of time spent in only one session. A productive time for practice can be right after a lesson while the ideas are fresh and you are trying to acquire a new feel. What about before and after a round? Before a round, it is usually better to focus on warm-up rather than on practice, although you can use this pre-play time to rehearse and practice your routine for various shots which may have caused you a problem on the course.

Playing and practicing before going to work is not very common, but may be possible when the course is close and the workplace easily reached. Thirty minutes to an hour of regular practice is amazingly effective. Lunchtime practice is a possibility, even in the cities, if indoor golf centers or a nearby range is available. After work is the favorite among the golfers who work normal hours.

HOW TO PRACTICE

The most important advice that can be given about practice other than to do it is: *make it as similar as possible to the real thing*, actual play. How can this be accomplished?

1. Make it competitive. Set goals; for example, six out of ten balls from the bunker onto the green, successive putts from one to ten feet, or eight out of ten drives between two target trees. Practice with someone else of similar or higher skill and have contests—closest to the cup, best in line with the flag, fewest strokes up and down. On occasion, practice with only one ball around the green. No shag bag or bucket, just one ball played from various locations, until you get it in the hole as you must on the course. The number of ups and downs in two strokes from ten different starting positions becomes a contest and, therefore, provides competitive pressure similar to that experienced in a round of golf.
2. Create realistic situations. Don't always take preferred lies. Play balls where they land, particularly around the green. Hit shots from uneven lies and out of the rough. Practice the full swing by playing a shot with one club, then another club and then another, as is done in a round of golf.
3. Practice as you would play. Sloppy practice habits will produce sloppy play on the course. This takes a lot of discipline, but treat each practice shot as though you

> "Practice is the only golf advice that is good for everybody."
> —Arnold Palmer

were on the course. That means picture or visualize the shot first, make the images vivid, complete the routine, swing and then assess the result.

4. Practice to a target. *Hitting balls is exercise; playing to a target is practice.* Aim is so crucial to the result, you must have something at which you aim during practice. (Illus 11-6)

5. When working on changing a position or movement in the swing, it may be more effective to not make the whole swing, but rather work on the part that's defective. Isolate it and repeat it correctly until it can blend naturally into the whole.

WHY SHOULD YOU PRACTICE?

Practicing to establish a correct and lasting "groove" is like running a trickle of water down a dirt bank. With enough volume and repetition, the water makes a channel. The longer the water runs down that bank, the deeper the channel gets. If it stops running, the channel

Illus 11-6 Golf is a target game, so practice should always include targets.

> "I figure practice puts your brains in your muscles."
> —Sam Snead

begins to fill in. Sometimes the channel is not the most direct one and the water takes a circuitous route. Eventually, the water gets to the bottom, even though it takes longer and the route is inefficient. That circuitous channel, like a technically flawed swing, can be altered to become more direct and efficient, but a lot of water must be run down the new route before its course becomes set. For a while it may go in both directions. It works much the same for changing the course of a golf swing.

The analogy demonstrates that if you want to groove a swing, *many* swings must be put in that groove. The swings can be on the course, at the range, in the basement or in the mind, but they have to be made and they have to be made correctly. Some swings are mechanically complex, others more efficient, but all swings can be changed. It's just not easy. It takes repetition and practice. In the words of Jack Nicklaus, player of the century, "Nobody—but nobody—has ever become really proficient at golf without practice." (Illus 11-7)

NATURAL ABILITY ISN'T ENOUGH

Golf may be the greatest game for practicers. Some good golfers may be "naturals," born with exceptional physical talents, but proficient players can also be developed from people with very modest talent. The natural athlete may find golf more frustrating than expected when he or she doesn't experience immediate success. This lack of quick success frequently leads to quitting and seeking another activity. The athlete's less-talented counterpart who is patient and does not expect overnight success can make gradual improvement with persistence and practice, until one day he could be the club champion.

Former PGA Champion and Ryder Cup

Illus 11-7 There wouldn't be any seekers of Jack Nicklaus's autograph had he not practiced countless hours to develop his skills. (Photo by Stephen Szurlej)

player Jerry Barber was certainly in this latter category. He epitomized the person with average talent and great determination who devoted himself to practicing hour after hour. It is easy to see why, after someone called him "lucky," Barber made the statement, "Yes, and the more I practice, the luckier I get." (Illus 11-8)

Peter G. Cranford in his book *The Winning Touch in Golf* gives further insight into the value of practice with the story told by a member from his club. "Although Betsy Rawls, the great woman golfer (now a PGA World Golf Hall of Fame member), was endowed with considerable natural talent, much of her success

> "The player who expects a lesson to 'take' without subsequent practice just isn't being honest with himself or fair to his professional."
> —Gary Player

was due to her early attitude toward practice. While the rest of us would be playing at the old Austin Country Club, she would take her habitual stand under a tree on the 13th hole and hit balls by the hour. It was only on rare occasions that she would play with us, even though she was already the equal of most male golfers. Before we realized it, she was the U.S. Women's Open Champion."

GOLFERS ON PRACTICE

Why do people involved in other motor disciplines such as playing a musical instrument expect to improve only if they apply the axiom of *effort and reward*, while golfers look for miracles? The golfer must be aware of the reality that there are no swing secrets or instant methods to achieve competency.

Ben Hogan once said to a young player attempting to garner a thought from him on how

Illus 11-8 One of the game's most diligent practicers was Jerry Barber. His physical talents were limited but his determination was not. He demonstrated that determination by untiring practice, particularly in the short game.

to become a champion golfer, "Son, do you have a practice bag?"

"Yes sir," was the young player's reply.

"Use it!" was Hogan's advice.

GENERAL OBSERVATIONS ON PRACTICE

1. Selecting wind conditions in which to practice is important. The most desirable wind conditions are: wind into the player, right-to-left, or no wind at all. Less desirable is a following wind, and the least desirable is left-to-right. A left-to-right wind blows the ball off-line to the right. To this the body instinctively reacts by releasing the "hit" prematurely and swinging outside-in to the left of target. In downwind practice the drawback is that the player's errors are not always evident. On the plus side, a right-to-left wind encourages an inside path to the ball and into the wind clearly would magnify error.

2. One purpose of practice is to develop confidence. If the time available for full-shot practice is quite limited, you should just practice making your best swing and work on establishing a routine until both routine and swing are indelible.

3. Practicing golf can be a very pleasant, relaxing experience as well as a mild physical workout. One could call it *work*; but if so, it's most enjoyable work.

4. An interesting practice experience on the course to test a player's consistency and patience is a "worst-ball scramble." Find a quiet time on the course when you can play two balls with management approval. After the tee shots, select the poorer one and play two shots from there. Again select the poorer. This will direct your attention to work on consistency. You should practice the worst-ball format only rarely, because it can be as hard on your confidence as not breaking 80 is for a scratch player. It's better to experience "best-ball" practice if you need to build positive feelings.

5. When full-swing practice time is *limited*, the psychology of hitting the easier clubs to build confidence makes sense. When *longer* practice periods are available, you should focus on your weaknesses. The only way to overcome a weakness is to practice the correction, probably with the clubs which have given you the least success.

6. Practice in the following manner: deposit the bucket or bag of practice balls at least one step away so there is no thoughtless, rapid-fire swinging. Having to take a step to rake the ball in is more conducive to completing a pre-shot routine.

7. Times *not* to practice are:

   a. When one is tired. Fatigue makes people sloppy. It also promotes more chance for error, poorly hit shots, and a loss of confidence.
   b. When one loses interest. This is when bad habits creep in.
   c. In bad weather conditions, which can cause one to alter the swing.
   d. If things are going poorly and it seems progress isn't being made. Tomorrow is another day. That may be all that is needed.

8. There are also other times when practice can make one worse. An example of this is in putting. It you have learned a solid technique, but then begin experimenting with other methods, you can lose what you have. This kind of experimentation can cause confusion, tentativeness and a loss of confidence.

9. Do not spend valuable practice time on shots that rarely confront you. Try these

> "The golf swing is muscle memory."
> —Patty Berg
> (Editor's Note: Muscles do not have the ability to remember. But the neuromuscular system's pathways, which carry messages from the brain, can be developed to be more efficient through practice.)

occasionally, but to spend 30 minutes around the practice green hitting super cut shots that rise almost vertically and descend the same way is wasting good pitching and chipping practice time.

10. Avoid long practice sessions before play. Playing when tired leads to poor performance and a loss of confidence.

11. Finish a practice session on a good note—several consecutive, successful shots.

12. Practice a varied club selection by teeing off with a club other than the driver, such as a #3, #5 or #7 iron. It makes a familiar course offer entirely new challenges.

13. Keeping a log or record book of practice provides a means for expressing, understanding and remembering what was learned at the session. (Illus 11-9) A log is a great reference for recalling what you were working on, including your feelings, during a particular practice time. This bit of practice "history" may help to recap-

Illus 11-9 A practice log can capture useful ideas, feelings, insights and adjustments that may otherwise get lost or forgotten.

ture one of those inspirational moments that we occasionally experience, then later find hard to recall.

DRILLS

Think of a sport other than golf. Now picture a practice session for that sport. One of the images that comes to mind is the performer either putting himself, or being put through, a series of drills. If your image was a baseball practice, the coach may have been observing the infield practicing their moves in different game situations. They might "walk through" how and when the pitcher covers first base, where each player goes on a "run-down" between third base and home plate or who calls the play on a pop-up around the mound. Why does a coach do this? So that player reactions under game conditions will be appropriate. The correct reaction becomes habit through repeated drills.

Drills, done correctly, have value in learning golf skills. They can:

1. Cure specific problems or weaknesses by replacing bad habits with good ones. (Illus 11-10)
2. Teach position, motion and feel.
3. Isolate a portion of the swing or a body segment on which to train.
4. Reinforce existing good habits.
5. Provide exercise while practicing technique.

"Done correctly" is an important phrase. A novice not fully understanding a drill may practice incorrectly. This will result in having to undo the damage again before moving on, thus wasting precious time. Drills to the golfer, like scales to the musician, are forever. That is why one sees top tour players rehearsing positions and using drills that are given to beginners in those first weeks of instruction. As long as one is trying to improve or maintain his skills, he must do his exercises. Performance deteriorates when practice stops.

Illus 11-10 When a student has the problem of getting the weight to the right side in the backswing, a drill having them lift the left foot can give them a better feeling for it.

There are hundreds of drills with different objectives and multiple variations of each. A limited list of drills based on laws and principles, as well as drills for specific shots, plus games and contests are listed in Appendix 6-B. Crediting the originator of every drill would be an impossible task. There are drills used today which are modifications of those depicted in books written in the 1800s. Let us give thanks to all the teachers of golf who have contributed drills to the game. Those who see drills listed which they feel are their original creation, we thank you in particular.

Illus 11-11 Products that are more highly engineered will obviously be more expensive than those that are simpler.

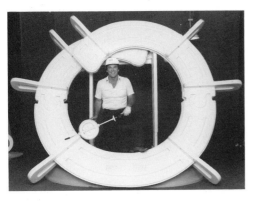

LEARNING AIDS

Any object or device which can assist the player in learning could be called a learning aid. Some are useful, others frivolous. To be able to distinguish between the beneficial and useless is not always easy without first being able to test it.

To evaluate a learning aid, apply the following criteria:

1. Is it valid?—Is the premise upon which the learning aid is based actually helpful to the golfer? For example: A device which keeps the left arm ramrod straight in the backswing may actually produce additional tension in the arm and shoulder and produce weaker golf shots than before its use.
2. Does it do what it says it can do?—If the product claims to keep one's left wrist flat, does it really do this or just look like it does?
3. How reliable is it?—Do you get consistent results from the product? If it measures clubhead speed and other swing components, for example, and a player produces two identical swings, will the same readings appear?
4. How well is it made?—Does the product meet all the previously mentioned criteria, but fall apart after two weeks of use?
5. What about the cost?—Based on how useful it is in the learning process, is it worth the price? (Illus 11-11)
6. Is it easy to set up and use?—If it is a marvelous piece of equipment, but requires considerable time to assemble or activate, and in addition, is complicated or highly sensitive, the hassle may not be worth it. (Illus 11-12)

f11-2 *A collection of over 200 golf learning aids and 116 drills are demonstrated on a series of six instructional videos called Gator Golf Instructional Video Library by PGA member Wally Armstrong. Contact Gator Golf, P.O. Box 1911, Maitland, FL 32751.*

Illus 11-12 These stacked shafts can be set up and taken down in a matter of seconds.

In brief, learning aids should be simple, effective and reasonably priced. The player can find many learning products advertised in golf trade and consumer magazines. (f 11-2) Three companies that deal in a variety of learning devices are:

The Golf Works
Ralph Maltby Enterprises, Inc.
4820 Jacksontown Road
Newark, OH 43055
(614) 323-4193
(800) 848-8358

Practice House of Golf, Inc.
3801 W. Linden Avenue
P.O. Box 1496
South Bend, IN 46624
(219) 288-4991
(800) 348-5162

Golf Around the World
564 Greenway Drive
North Palm Beach, FL 33408
(407) 626-4176

CHAPTER 12

SPECIAL SHOTS & UNUSUAL CONDITIONS

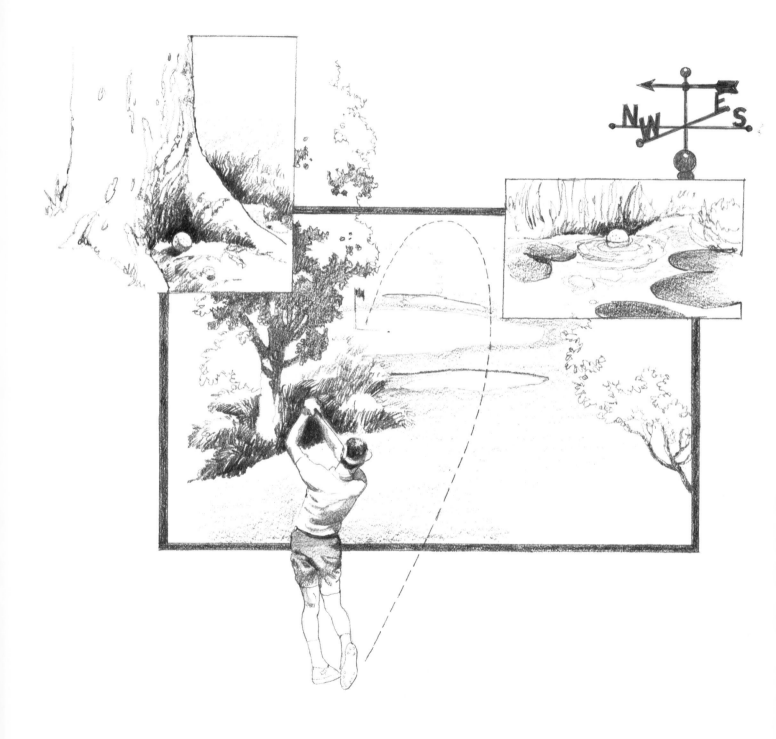

One of the fascinating elements of golf is that conditions are constantly changing, from one course to the next, one day to the next and one hour to the next. The terrain, the grasses, sand texture, course layout, wind, temperature fluctuations, rain, ground firmness, growing trees and foliage all contribute toward making the playing of golf a continually changing and challenging experience. Learning to handle a variety of conditions is a requisite for being a competent player.

UNEVEN LIES

Most golf is practiced on "flat as a pancake" terrain, but hardly any of it is played there. The four most frequently encountered uneven lies are uphill, downhill and the two sidehill (ball above the feet and below the feet). Here are the basic considerations and adjustments for these four:

Sidehill—Ball Above the Feet

All uneven lies create a tendency for the player to err, resulting in incorrect distance, faulty direction or both. When the ball is *above the player's feet*, on the side of a hill, the three most frequent errors are *chunking, pulling* and *hooking*. The chunk is easy to understand. The ball is elevated and closer to the player. This requires the player to either assume a different body tilt than that to which he is accustomed

Illus 12-1 Note the body tilt is more upright and the player (Jerry Pate) has choked down on the grip when the ball is higher than his feet. (Photo courtesy of *Golf Digest*)

and/or to shorten his hand position on the grip. (Illus 12-1) If neither is done, the club will hit the ground first rather than the ball.

The other two errors that are frequently made when the ball is above the feet are pulling and hooking. A simple but graphic illustration is to take a putter and sole it so there is literally zero degrees of loft in the face and so that it is "looking" or facing at right angles to the target.

Where will the ball go if it is struck with the face in this position? "To the target" is the answer. Now elevate the putter 1½ to 2 feet in the air, keeping zero degrees of loft in the face. Where will the ball go if struck now? The answer again is, "to the target." Next take a lofted iron, like a #9, and repeat the previous routine. With the #9 soled normally, the answer to where the ball will go is "to the target." But when it is elevated, you can readily see that the loft in the face when tilted upward is now directed to the left. The ball will *not go to* the target, but to a spot quite a bit to the left of it. With the ball higher than the feet, a more horizontal swing plane is created, promoting more hand and forearm rotation. With an inside swing path added to a clubface "looking" left, it is easy to see why a pull or pull hook from this lie is a common tendency. Another factor which encourages a pull to accompany the hook is gravity. Whenever a player is on uneven terrain, gravity will try to pull him toward the lower point of the slope. In this case, the low point is behind him so the pull is backward. Because of the backward pull of gravity, the swing path can travel several degrees to the left, resulting in a pulled shot. Here are some solutions to offset these three negative tendencies when the ball is positioned above the feet:

1. Stand as perpendicular to the lie as possible so the body position in relation to the ground approximates a normal lie, yet the weight favors the balls of the feet.
2. Choke down on the club so the club can clear the ground.
3. Position the ball near the middle of the stance, since weight transfer won't be as strong.
4. Keep the suspension point (the distance from the ground to the base of the neck) constant to maintain balance.
5. Take a couple of practice swings to get the feeling of clearing the ground at the right height.
6. Allow for the pull or hook by aiming to the right. The steeper the ball lies, the more you must compensate.

7. You should swing within yourself. Trying to hit hard from an awkward lie is difficult. Always swing with less than full effort. This may require using a stronger club to provide the added distance needed.

Uneven Lies—Ball Below the Feet

Playing a shot where the ball is lying *lower than the feet* is one of the harder shots in golf and it's easy to understand why (Illus 12-2). Beginning golfers find it easier to contact the ball if it's raised in the air on a tee, more difficult when it's on the ground. Now, in the ball-below-the-feet lie, it's actually *lower* than ground level. The tendency is for the ball to be topped, pushed or push-sliced. The procedure is the same as the one with the ball above the feet, but the result reversed. To make the proper compensations for a ball positioned below the feet the player should:

Illus 12-2 When the ball is lower than the feet, it takes an adjusted address position (sitting deeper), a full-length grip and a concerted effort to stay seated through the shot. (Photo courtesy of *Golf Digest*)

1. Go to the full length on the grip.
2. Stand close enough to the ball to reach it easily with the clubhead.
3. Angle the body close to perpendicular with the ground, but sit deeper in the knees at address and let the weight feel more on the heels.
4. Keep the suspension radius constant. Don't pull up or fall forward.
5. Aim to the left an amount relative to the tilt of the clubface and allow the ball to go to the right.

How much should a player aim right or left on these shots? The answer will come from practice, but here is a way that may help. After you have selected a club, mimic with the palm of your hand in the air the club's loft and the soling of it on uneven terrain. Carefully note the amount of deflection the face presents from the target line. Compensate that amount plus a bit more for the curve, then swing naturally.

Uphill Lies

The most common tendencies from the *uphill lie* are pulling, chunking and underclubbing (Illus 12-3). This is due primarily to the force of gravity attracting the player toward the low ground or the player's right. It is difficult from the uphill lie for the golfer to transfer his weight to the front foot as he normally would. When the weight stays back, the swing path travels left, causing a pulled shot. In addition, the natural slope of the terrain tilts the golfer's stance upward, adding loft to the face of the club. This causes the ball to go a higher and shorter distance. Increasing this tendency even further is the reluctance of the weight to transfer left, allowing the head end of the club to pass the grip end too soon. To neutralize these tendencies when faced with an uphill lie the player should:

1. Set up basically perpendicular to the ground level but with a bit more focus of weight to the left. Resist gravity's pull by

Illus 12-3 Gravity will resist the player's attempts to transfer weight to the left foot from the uphill lie.

seeing the weight transfer up the slope with the swing.
2. Play the ball near the middle of the stance to make it easier to contact.
3. Take a stronger club to reach the target.
4. Choke down on the club for better control.
5. Aim to the right an amount sufficient to compensate for the slope.
6. Take a couple of practice swings to adjust to the different condition, then make a comfortable, controlled swing.

Downhill Lies

The *downhill lie* shot is difficult because the ball is below the normal stance level (Illus 12-4). This shot requires more concentration than any of the others. The tendencies are a push or push-fade and the topped shot. A push or push-fade is largely the result of not squaring the clubface. It is difficult to produce clubface rotation and not top the shot while trying to fol-

Illus 12-4 The downhill lie is made easier if the player moves the ball back in his stance.

Illus 12-5 Keep the shoulder tilt matching the terrain with a flexed right knee.

low the slope of the terrain. Further adding to this tendency to push or slice is gravity pulling the player's swing center ahead of the ball. Some solutions (used in combination) are:

1. Play the ball slightly back of the middle of the stance.
2. Set up perpendicular to the ground, but resist being pulled down the hill past the ball.
3. Tilt the shoulders as much as possible to match the slope of the ground to make it easier to stay with the shot. (It helps to sit more in the right knee.) (Illus 12-5)
4. Allow for the club being somewhat delofted, which will cause the ball to go lower, hotter and roll farther. A ¾ controlled swing from a downhill lie may send the ball the same distance as a full swing with the same club for a normal lie.
5. Aim to the left an amount commensurate with the slope.
6. Take some practice swings until there is a

comfortable feel, then make a controlled swing, following the level of the ground. (Illus 12-6)

Uneven Lies—Short Shots

The same ball flight tendencies will also apply to the short pitch, chip and bunker shots. In fact, it is quite important to learn how to adjust to severe slopes around the green where a lofted club is frequently used. (Illus 12-7) In these situations the face angle will be even more misdirected in relation to the leading edge than on longer shots. Some general guidelines for pitches, chips and bunker shots from uneven lies appear on the facing page.

In the adjustments to the short shots, notice that an option was given to open the face instead of aiming right or to close the face instead of aiming left. This is possible, of course, in the full swing as well. On a full shot, you could also block the release when the ball is above

Illus 12-6 Follow the level of the ground as does Jerry Pate.

Illus 12-7 Players are often surprised when playing a shot from an uneven lie around the green, that it travels in a different direction from where they have aimed. An experienced professional like World Series of Golf champion David Frost can handle it. (Photo by Stephen Szurlej)

your feet to counter a hook, or roll your hands to counter a slice when the ball is below your feet, though the latter solution is quite difficult and not generally recommended.

SHORT SHOTS AROUND THE GREEN

Tendencies	Adjustment
BALL ABOVE FEET	
—Ball will go left	Aim right, or open the face.
—Chunk	Shorten grip, make practice swings, weight toward balls of feet.
BALL BELOW FEET	
—Ball will go right	Aim left, or close the face.
—Top or blade the shot	Sit deeper, weight on heels, make practice swings, stay down.
UPHILL	
—Shot travels high and short	Aim right, take straighter-faced club.
—Shot pulls left and hit behind	Lean into hill, take practice swings, follow terrain.
DOWNHILL	
—Push shot to right	Aim left, or close the face.
—Hit behind, skull or top	Position ball back, sit more in knees and follow slope.

WEATHER—WIND

Wind adds a special challenge to golf and has even helped make some particular courses and holes famous. The par 3, 12th hole at Augusta over Rae's Creek, though only 155 yards long, is considered one of golf's toughest, partly because its wind patterns are unusually difficult to read. Revered St. Andrews on first look appears to be a modest challenge as players blithely trek outward on the front nine. It is a different story when they turn the corner to fight the wind coming inward. (f 12-1)

Like uneven lies, the wind has four general directions:

1. against
2. following
3. across from left to right
4. across from right to left

Quartering winds and varying velocities further test the player's judgment on windy days. The basic four wind patterns and the needed adjustments are as follows.

Wind Against

"When it's breezy, swing easy" is one of those golf sayings that has a simple but emphatic message: play within yourself in windy weather.

But this is not *easy* to do, particularly when the wind is against you. Every human instinct pleads for you to swing harder, but this response only courts disaster. Harder swings produce more chance for error, and errors made into wind are severely compounded. Attempting to hit harder usually results in: 1) an early hit with the right hand at a steep approach angle causing

more than normal backspin and a high (rather than low) shot, 2) too much tension in the right side of the body inhibiting release and producing a push-slice (disaster when played into a strong wind). So, rule number one is: Instead of trying *to hit harder and farther into the wind, learn to swing with normal effort, or even shorten the grip and swing more conservatively.*

There are those who recommend that the ball be teed lower on a driver shot into the wind. This advice has some inherent danger. 1) When the ball is teed lower, it encourages a more descending blow, which adds backspin. (Illus 12-8) 2) A ball teed low makes it more difficult to square the clubface. The tendency is to leave the face open, resulting in a push slice. It is better to tee the ball at a height which encourages a shallow or level angle of approach to the ball. Descent causes additional backspin, while ascent adds more loft. You want neither. Therefore, the most effective tee height is that which allows you to square the face with a more level approach angle.

Another option when playing from the tee into a stiff wind is to play the ball three to four inches farther back in the stance. This position closes the left shoulder, presents less loft on the face and encourages a slight in-to-out path,

Illus 12-8 If teeing the ball low causes the player to steepen the angle of approach and create more backspin, then the purpose of teeing low has been defeated.

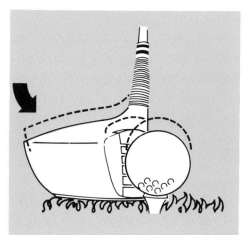

f12-1 *St. Andrews' "old course" is responsible for the origin of the terms OUT and IN, which still are found on 18-hole scorecards. The first nine holes go "out" away from the clubhouse and the last nine "in" toward it.*

for a lower running draw. When you tee the ball too far forward, the opposite, a high slice, is often the result.

One of the most frequent errors made by all golfers, professionals included, is leaving the approach shot to the green short when playing into the wind. Wind is universally an underestimated force. Keeping the ball flight low is fundamental to playing effectively in windy conditions. A simple way to create a lower trajectory for an iron shot is:

1. If the shot is normally a #7 iron distance but now is against the wind, choose a stronger club like a #5 iron and choke down the grip from one to two inches. Each inch down produces about one club shorter in distance.
2. Move the ball two ball widths farther back in the stance. The grip end is now more advanced toward the target past the clubhead. This decreases clubface loft.
3. Take a ¾ length backswing with normal rhythm. This will also produce a ¾ finish with the upper body finishing a bit more vertical.
4. In the forward swing return to the ball with the hands and clubhead address relationship (hands well advanced of the clubhead) still intact. Make a normally paced swing, but one that is shorter. This is not necessarily a downward punch. You should be trying to minimize the backspin so the ball doesn't "upshoot." The shot should be an abbreviated version of the normal swing with an adjusted setup. The reason this is not described here as a "punch shot" is the word "punch" connotes a sharp, steep blow that causes additional backspin.

On wood shots and long irons, special effort should be made not to "rush" to get the shot "over with." Use a normal pace into the wind. Also on wood shots a widened stance will lower the center of gravity to help maintain balance and will level the angle of approach.

> "I love rotten weather. The founders of the game accepted nature for what it gave, or what it took away. Wind and rain are great challenges. They separate real golfers."
> —Tom Watson

Downwind Shots

When the wind is following, it will not only help propel the ball forward in the air but also reduce the backspin. So, when the ball lands, it will roll farther. This may be an advantage on the drive. However, it may pose a problem on the shot to the green. Unless the downwind approach shot has a very high trajectory and/or an unusual amount of backspin, the ball should be played short, bounced onto the green and rolled to the flag, if the terrain allows. If the ball has to carry a hazard, you may play the ball a bit more forward, open the face slightly and take a longer, slower swing to produce a high fade that falls softly.

On the downwind tee shot, there is some difference of opinion on strategy. The following is a sampling of these opinions:

1. Tee the ball higher. Stay behind it in the swing to get greater height in the shot and take advantage of the wind for length. Be careful not to exaggerate the changes.
2. Hit a normal shot rather than risk trying to do something different that can cause trouble off the tee. The wind will make the ball go farther.
3. Use a #3 wood to get a higher trajectory for distance while also having good directional control.

All three approaches have certain advantages. The choice will be influenced by hole length, tightness of the fairway and potential problems of an errant shot. Stay with the normal shot downwind and accept the added distance as a bonus. If the driver is inconsistent, go with the #3 wood.

Side Winds

On the tee with either a left-to-right or right-to-left wind, stand closer to the side from where the wind is coming and aim down that portion of the fairway. Let the ball ride the wind, not fight it, to maximize distance. Some players try to fade the ball with a left-to-right wind or draw it with a right-to-left wind in order to get more distance on a tee shot. Assess the risk before attempting this. The fade can turn into a slice; the draw, a hook; and with the wind's help, the ball can go totally out of control. That is the key word in wind conditions: *control*. Basically, keep the ball at normal or lower trajec-

Illus 12-9 Most golfers do not compensate adequately for the effect of wind on their shots.

WINDSPEED CHARTS

Carry and Total Length of Shot*

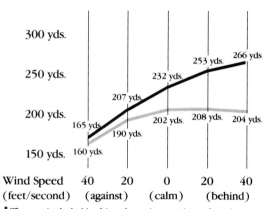

```
300 yds.
                                              266 yds
                                253 yds.
250 yds.                232 yds.
                207 yds.
200 yds.
        165 yds.        202 yds.  208 yds.  204 yds.
                190 yds.
150 yds.  160 yds.

Wind Speed   40    20    0    20    40
(feet/second) (against) (calm) (behind)
```

*The run included in this column is an estimate based on the forward speed of the ball when it first hits the ground. It will in any event depend on ground conditions.

Time of Flight

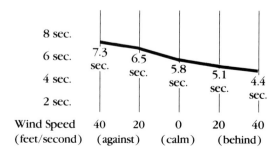

```
8 sec.
6 sec.  7.3    6.5
        sec.   sec.  5.8
4 sec.                sec.  5.1
                            sec.  4.4
2 sec.                             sec.

Wind Speed   40    20    0    20    40
(feet/second) (against) (calm) (behind)
```

tory, swing within yourself, take extra club when necessary and remember that the wind will probably affect the shot more than you expect. (Illus 12-9)

Finally, one of the most subtly astute comments ever made about playing in wind came from PGA Hall of Fame professional "Chick" Harbert. He said, "When playing *into the wind*—just try and make your very best swing and solid contact. When playing *downwind*—just try and make your very best swing and solid contact." Need we say more?

COLD AND WET WEATHER

Be prepared is the best advice for playing in inclement weather. You should absolutely have the following items available during play: (Illus 12-10)

1. One or more dry towels, depending on the severity of the rain. Hook the towels under the umbrella so they'll stay dry. Losing control of the club is potentially the most serious bad-weather problem related to performance. You can't swing a golf club when you can't hold onto it. Keep the hands and grips dry. (Illus 12-11)

2. A golf umbrella with a 58" spread, and a golf-bag cover to help keep the rain from entering the bag so that the grips will stay dry.

3. Though not essential, a hand-warmer certainly is useful when the temperature is in the 40s or 30s. The new instant chemical disposable variety is the most convenient. But remember, it is illegal to heat golf balls with a warming device during play.

4. Dress for the occasion. Staying warm and dry are the objectives, providing you do not lose the mobility to swing effectively. (Illus 12-12) The solution is to have a good rain suit that permits freedom of movement, is waterproof and warm while still "breathing." The best suits are expensive; the inexpensive products keep a person neither warm nor dry.

Illus 12-10 The player who plans to compete needs to be prepared for inclement weather. (Photo by Jeff McBride)

Illus 12-11 Keeping the hands dry in wet weather is absolutely necessary.

5. In cold weather consider wearing underneath the suit the following: thermal underwear, a turtleneck, loose-fitting sweater or sweater vest. For the lower torso, include heavy trousers (not made from wool) and two layers of socks. A player's hands, head and feet are the most critical to keep warm and dry. A wool stocking cap that can be pulled over your ears or a water repellant hat with a brim or bill is a must, as well as spiked shoes that are waterproof or at least water-resistant. Several golf gloves, some of the wet-weather variety, should be in your bag. Sheepskin gloves or one of the newer thermal-type gloves can be worn in between shots for hand warmth.

Playing in wet, cold weather also calls for some adjustment in technique and strategy. Cold weather dictates that you warm up and stretch more than usual before the round. Particularly, stretch the back muscles so a full turn can be made. When wearing extra layers of clothing, the swing will tend to shorten. This, coupled with playing a cold golf ball, requires that you take more club to reach the desired distance.

If the greens are very wet and you are in chip or pitch range, choose the lofted shot which lands close to the hole. Judging roll on wet greens is chancy. (Illus 12-13) Also, when playing iron shots from soaked turf, it is a good practice to play the ball a bit farther back than

Illus 12-12 Being prepared for play on a cold day can make a great difference in the player's comfort, enjoyment and performance.

Illus 12-13 On wet greens, pitch to land the ball close to the hole on the fly, since trying to judge speed is difficult. (Photo by Jeff McBride)

normal in the stance so as not to catch the ground first. The sole of the iron club will not bounce on a drenched fairway; instead, it will dig. Fairway woods like a #4 or #5 wood are easier to use from wet turf than long, straight-bladed irons like a #2 or #3.

HOT, HUMID WEATHER

An important tip that applies to both hot days and rainy days is: *keep the hands and grips dry.* Have a towel handy for hot days as well as rainy ones. Like playing in cold weather, you should also keep your head covered, preferably with a cool, reflective material. (Illus 12-14) You should avoid overexposure to the sun if you have not previously played in hot weather, and particularly if you are on a winter vacation and going south to play. (Illus 12-15)

Be aware of the sun's damage to your skin and sight when you are frequently exposed. A sunscreen of at least a 25-rated protection may

Illus 12-14 The man under the towel is PGA champion Larry Nelson, who is drying his perspiration on a hot day using one of two towels his caddy is carrying.

Illus 12-15 U.S. Open champion Curtis Strange knows it's important to keep cool on very hot days and does so here by pouring cold water on his neck. (Photo by Stephen Szurlej)

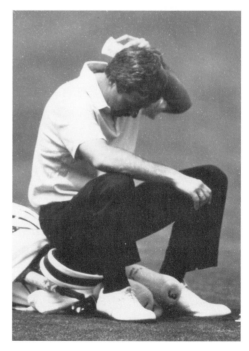

prevent skin cancer and avoid wrinkling from over-tanned skin as you grow older. As a preventive measure, wear a visor, cap, hat or dark glasses when the sun is particularly strong. Regular exposure of the eyes to the sun can do serious and irreversible retina damage. This is serious business for anyone who gets frequent, long exposure to the sun's rays. The sun may appear to be one's harmless friend, but long-term effects of overexposure are no laughing matter.

LIGHTNING

From 1959 through 1989, over 120 golfers were killed on golf courses by lightning, and 308 injured. In storm conditions where lightning is present, golf can become dangerous. Too many players disregard this danger. Demonstrate a healthy respect for lightning by finding shelter or leaving the course when the threat appears. See Appendix 7 for further information.

GENERAL OBSERVATIONS ON WEATHER

1. If your home course is quite windy, you should consider choosing clubs and balls that favor a lower trajectory.
2. A strong wind can have a definite effect on short pitch shots, chips and even on putts. Chip more than pitch in strong winds and be aware of a powerful wind's influence, even on putting.
3. Players seldom realize that, when pitching into a strong wind, they can stop the ball almost immediately with a lofted club. They need to land the ball closer to the hole than usual in this circumstance. The opposite is true downwind.
4. It is easier to curve the ball intentionally hitting into a headwind, and more difficult to curve it going downwind.
5. On a cold day, walking briskly will help you stay warm and loose.
6. Wind affects not only the ball but also the body. Maintaining balance on both long

and short shots, particularly putting, can be aided by slightly widening the stance. This lowers the body's center of gravity and gives you a more solid base.

UNUSUAL SHOTS

The need to "scramble" may not be a desirable situation, but being able to scramble proves beneficial when the score is posted. Scrambling can simply mean good, straightforward "up and down" short-game play, or it can include more creative shots that save strokes. Here are some of those special shots:

Intentionally Curving the Ball

Golfers frequently play a shot that curves around an obstacle to the target. Knowing the principles behind such a shot and having the ability to perform it provide the player with a very useful skill.

The *laws* are basic: swing path and clubface position. If you wish to hook the ball, you need a face position that is closed to the swing path at impact. That combination can be accomplished using several different techniques.

1. Sole the face squarely but assume a closed-face grip position; line both the feet and shoulders to the right of the target.
2. Align the body to the right of where the ball should *start* and close the face so that it is at right angles to where the ball is to *finish*. (Illus 12-16)
3. Take a normal grip and setup, but during the forward swing make the path travel on an inside-to-out line while allowing the normal rotation of hands and forearms to close the face.

Options one and two are achieving the result by prepositioning, in other words "setting up the result" before the swing begins. The trick, then, is to trust the geometry and make a normal swing that matches the alignment. Option

Illus 12-16 The teaching aid is set up to let the player produce a draw, i.e., inside path with the face slightly closed to the path.

three, which is used only by the more talented players, is made with motion rather than position. It is done by experience, feel and imagination. The ball doesn't care which style or combination of styles is used.

When a small curve is desired, only small alterations are necessary. Large curves require large departures from conventional technique. Visualization of the shot prior to execution is an important part of achieving the desired result.

When hitting the intentional hook, the ball will go farther than normal for that club; conversely, shorter for a slice. Also, when playing the sharp hook, you must leave enough loft in the clubface to get the shot airborne; when slicing, not so much loft that the ball goes "nowhere." The hardest thing to do in order to curve the ball successfully is to alter one's normal swing path. An inside-to-out swinger has difficulty in hitting a cut around a tree-lined "dogleg right." The problem is that although he sets the face open and aims left, he then swings from inside-to-out to the right with a

resulting push into the trees. Path and face must combine correctly to get the desired result.

RECOVERY FROM ROUGH

When the ball lies deep in the rough, the element which makes the shot difficult is the grass which gets between the clubface and the ball. (Illus 12-17) You should learn how to minimize the amount of grass and make allowance for its effect.

A steeper *angle of approach* will reduce the tendency to catch the grass too early in the forward swing. A large amount of grass cushions the blow. It also reduces the clubhead speed, resulting in a totally fluffed shot, or generally a weak result.

Aiming the body left, opening the clubface and playing the ball a bit forward will help create the loft and steep approach angle needed to escape the grass. (Illus 12-18) The open face also helps to offset the effect that long grass can

Illus 12-17 Allowing too much grass between the clubface and ball will kill the energy applied to the ball.

Illus 12-18 Steepening the approach angle in deep rough helps to reduce the grass between the face and also gets the ball up quickly, as PGA star Tom Kite demonstrates.

produce by grabbing the hosel and closing the face. Expect sharply reduced distance out of the shot. Therefore, if there is a great deal of rough or other trouble to carry before reaching the target, it may be wiser to play out, into the fairway, which is more easily reached.

When faced with greenside rough, the principle of steepening the angle of approach is one method, but another is made possible because a long distance does not have to be covered. In greenside rough, a simulated bunker shot may be played. Here, you can take a bigger than normal swing for the distance required and intentionally hit behind and through the grass as you would on a bunker shot. If the grass is thick, the shot should be played aggressively, similar to a lie in fine sugar sand. If the grass is less thick, the effort should correspond to a bunker shot played from firm sand. The direction in which the grass is growing also has an effect on how the shot should be played. If the nap is into the player, it will tend to catch the club, slow it down and leave the ball short of the target. When the nap of the grass is inclined toward the target, it makes the greenside shot easier, but it may offer another challenge to the player attempting a full shot. The challenge is the "flier."

FLIERS

If you play from longer than normal fairway-length grass or wet turf and are continually surprised when the shot goes over the green, you should become educated about the flier shot. Anytime one reduces backspin on a ball it will tend to lower that shot's trajectory and cause it to roll farther than normal after it hits the ground. When a player gives up backspin on the iron shot to the green, he gives up control. The first step is to recognize flier situations. When the ball is in grass or clover that is high enough to get between the ball and clubface, but not so high as to reach to the top of the hosel, you should expect a reduction in backspin and a "hotter ball," a flier. This holds true, as well, if water (dew, rain or liquid from plant material) reduces the friction which is necessary to promote backspin. Like a "spitter" in baseball, the ball will do "funny things."

Once the conditions are recognized, you can either allow for added distance on the shot or make some mechanical adjustments. Allowing for greater distance would mean either taking less club or swinging at less than full effort. If adjustments are preferred, you can steepen the swing arc or open the face and play a high fade.

HARDPAN

Bare spots on the golf course that are largely devoid of turf and quite firm underfoot (such

> "The difference between a sand bunker and water is the difference between a car crash and an airplane crash. You have a chance of recovering from a car crash."
> —Bobby Jones

as those caused by golf-car traffic) have come to be called "hardpan" in the golfer's lexicon. A golfer who finds his ball on such a lie can be helped by knowing some of the tricks in playing this shot. If the distance to the green is within chipping or pitching range, it is wise to take a less-lofted club than normal and play a chip-and-run or pitch-and-run shot. This is the safest choice for two reasons. First, the flange of the club will be narrower and tend not to "bounce" into the ball; second, but more important, the clubhead speed for the less-lofted iron will be slower than for the deep-faced, wider-flanged pitching club, so that if the ball is mishit the error will be far less severe. Chipping, or even putting, from hardpan off the green is generally good advice.

If the ground is "rock hard," and you must use a sand wedge, be sure the minimum bounce from the sole is presented. This is accomplished by squaring the face up at address. Play the ball back in the stance so the contact point for the clubface will be at the very base of the ball where it meets the ground. Make no attempt to lift the ball. Instead, maintain the shaft angle that was established at address. It takes considerable trust to execute this shot because the margin of error is close to zero.

Golf, by being a game played out-of-doors, in the natural elements and on individually unique facilities, presents the participant with ever fresh circumstances which challenge his ingenuity and skill. That's what helps make golf a great game.

CHAPTER 13

INDIVIDUAL DIFFERENCES/
SPECIAL POPULATIONS:
Women, Srs., Jrs., Left-handed,
Physically Challenged

In art and architecture we are accustomed to hearing the phrase "form follows function." In describing the relationship of a person's body to his style in golf, we might say "function follows form." A person's body build and composition have a significant influence on how he swings the club. Knowing that and making the proper allowances can be most useful for the golfer.

VARIETIES OF HUMAN PHYSIQUE

In his 1940 Book *Varieties of Human Physique*, Dr. W.H. Sheldon presented a system of classifying the various shapes of human bodies. It was called "Somatotyping." Though far from a pure science, it did provide insight into performance traits and personality characteristics which might be associated with different kinds of body builds. The three major classifications were:

Endomorph—A body that is round and soft, soft-boned, low in muscle tone and generous in fat deposits around the hips, abdomen, buttocks, thighs and arms. This body type is usually poor in athletic events requiring speed, agility, endurance or jumping.

Ectomorph—A body that is thin-muscled and thin-boned, frail and delicate. The trunk is short and the neck, arms and legs are long. Very little fat is on the body. This body is usually good at endurance activities and tends to shun body contact sports.

Mesomorph—Muscular and big-boned, moderate height, broad shoulders, large-chested with a relatively slender waist and hips best describes this body type. An individual with this build tends to be strong and excels in sports requiring strength.

Whereas certain sports will favor a special body type (gymnastics, swimming, basketball, distance running, etc.) golf attracts all three, even at the championship level. Ectomorphic tendencies prevail in players like Paul Azinger, T.C. Chen and Bill Rogers; endomorphic tendencies in Craig Stadler, Ed Fiori and Bob Murphy; mesomorphic in Arnold Palmer, Greg Norman and Dan Pohl. None falls purely in any one category, but each has a swing style influenced by his body form. (Illus 13-1, 13-2)

BODY TYPES

If "function follows form," it would generally be a mistake for a Davis Love III to try and swing like a Lee Trevino, or for an Andy Bean to emulate a Chi Chi Rodriguez. People adopt a style usually for good reason. It fits them! For example, short people tend to have flatter swings because the plane of the shaft starts flatter at address with the grip end lower to the ground. In addition, the forward tilt of the upper body is less. Taller people have the opposite, a higher hand position and more bend. There is no one set swing plane for everyone for these and other reasons. The swing plane for each golfer should be as natural as possible and comfortably fit the player's build.

Poor balance as well as good balance can be found in all body types. But *shorter people* find it easier to balance in golf. They are closer to their work and that is an advantage. Because their center of gravity is lower, they are less affected by wind or unusual lies and can enjoy more freedom of movement in their swing center while still returning to the ball with consistency. They are more likely than a taller person to use a "ten-finger grip" as they seek leverage and rotation for clubhead speed. A flatter swing plane and shallower angle of approach is natural, since the upper body is shorter and there is less bend from the waist than with a tall player. For this reason, they will tend to draw the ball. This should be encouraged if length is the objective.

Taller people have the advantage of a wider swing arc for greater distance, but have to be more concerned about balance, timing and control. The higher the center of gravity, the more difficult it is to maintain good balance—one of golf's important fundamentals. (Illus 13-3) A tall player would need to control the swing center more and would find it easier to simply turn back and through in an Al Geiberger-like fashion. (f 13-1) A natural, more upright swing favors a high trajectory ball flight that encourages a fade. There is a tendency, however, for the tall player to pick up the club abruptly in the takeaway and "break down" the left arm.

Wind and uneven lies are harder for the tall player, again because of balance. The swing tempo will tend to be slower and more rhythmical than that of a short player, who generally can move more quickly.

The heavyset golfer frequently has a different natural arm hang position. For this thicker, stocky type, the arms and hands may hang in a more outwardly rotated position. If this is the case, the grip should reflect this natural arm-hang position when the hands are brought to-

f13-1 *Al Geiberger's Sybervision swing is a beautifully simple model for the tall player.*

Illus 13-1 Golf attracts a variety of body types, all of whom can be excellent performers, such as a lean T.C. Chen . . .

Illus 13-2 . . . or a muscular Greg Norman.

Illus 13-3 At 6'4", U.S. Open champ Andy North must work harder on rhythm to keep good balance.

gether in front. If the player fights a slice from this natural position, it may be necessary to turn the left hand clockwise to show an additional knuckle. But for many, the natural hang position, which rotates a bit more outward, though slightly unorthodox, is correct. If the heavyset player has short fingers, the interlocking grip could be more functional.

The heavyset player will usually be more successful with a ball position played closer to the middle of the stance. Lateral movement for this type player can be more difficult than rotary movement; therefore, a more centered ball location would be favored. Be aware that an extended left arm at the top of the swing is almost impossible for this body type to accomplish. Bulk in the arms and chest will not permit the degree of extension available to the less massive player.

In the setup it can be helpful for the stout player to let the rear foot turn outward slightly to the right. This position will encourage the player to turn the hips more fully on the backswing, one of the hardest moves for this body type to make. Making a good body turn rather than simply lifting the arms is critical for the stout player.

WOMEN—STRENGTH AND ENDURANCE

The principles that apply to the development of a sound golf swing and game are the same for both men and women. The way they are implemented may need to be different.

While some women have more strength and endurance than men, this is not common. Because women have less muscle mass (roughly ⅔ that of comparable males) and because their limb levers are shorter, it is difficult to generate equal clubhead speed and, therefore, produce equal distance.

If a golfer lacks strength, this has several implications. One is equipment. The player's set of clubs might start with a #3 wood rather than #1, since she would be unable to get a driver shot high enough in the air to take advantage of its potential distance. Similarly a #5 and #7

> "If a teacher ever tells you there is only one way to play, he's not the best."
> —Gary Player

wood should replace some long irons. A lightweight shaft with a low kickpoint, perimeter weighting and low center of gravity in the head may also help. The lack of clubhead speed means the trajectory on all shots will be lower, since the ball has little backspin speed and therefore less lift. Strategy on the course becomes much different for the weaker player. Approach shots to greens where a bunker has to be carried may require playing away from the bunker. Shots played from long grass or soft sand in bunkers could call for a style different from one employed by a strong player. For example, a weak woman player may not be able to hit an open-face cut shot from a bunker because the force she generates is not great enough to even get the ball out of the bunker from that kind of setup.

So one can see that lack of strength is a disadvantage not only in the long game but, surprisingly, also in the short game. It is generally felt that women professionals do not perform as well around the green as men professionals do. Why this is the case is difficult to ascertain, but could it be that strength influences control as well as distance?

WOMEN'S ADVANTAGES

Women golfers do have advantages over males. A lower center of gravity helps them to balance easier. Also, having potentially greater flexibility than their male counterparts means it is less difficult for them to make a full turn in the backswing and follow-through. Greater flexibility, however, can present a problem if not accompanied by muscular support. An example of this occurs with women who are doubled-jointed at the elbow, which allows the elbow to hyperextend or, more graphically, "to bend in both directions." This results in a loss of stability and control. In a similarly built flexible-type woman, the left wrist may also be able to assume an extreme palmar-flexed (palm toward underside of forearm) position at the top of the backswing, causing the clubface to be set in a wildly closed position.

A low handicap woman's swing is frequently more appealing and technically more accurate than a man's of equal handicap. Mickey Wright, LPGA Hall of Famer, who finished her competitive playing career in the early 1970s, may have had the best golf swing of any player in history. (Illus 13-4) Mechanically, the principles are the same for either sex. However, for many female golfers who don't have the physical talents of a Mickey Wright, these modifications should be considered:

Grip—Make sure you have the proper grip size on your club. If the grip diameter is too large, you'll fight an open-face position. If measurement indicates a smaller size is necessary, taking a .600 grip and stretching it on a .580 diameter shaft would provide a smaller grip size. Consider a clockwise rotation of the hands (closed-face grip) so the V's point farther to the right and three knuckles of the left hand show.

Illus 13-4 Mickey Wright may have had the best golf swing of any player in history, male or female.

This common adjustment from standard helps to rotate the face so that it squares correctly at impact.

Aim—Align the clubface to the target, but with the shoulder alignment slightly closed to encourage a draw for greater distance.

Setup—Be careful not to address the ball with the seat tucked in and weight back on the heels. This is a more "lady-like" posture but no good for golf. A woman with large breasts could close and elevate the left shoulder so her left arm can extend more over her breast at address. She might position her right arm (which is more folded at the elbow) slightly under and at the side of her. This will preset what will be close to the desired impact position and a path from the inside rather than steep from the top. (f 13-2) Or, she may choose to use a more connected style with the upper arms held in and rely more on body rotation to square the clubface rather than forearm rotation.

Swing—The principles stay the same for both sexes but some adjustments should be considered. Those lacking in strength will need the more clockwise, closed-face grip position. This means that the left wrist will not be as flat at the top of the backswing. Most women cannot change direction as quickly as men, so their backswings *may need* to be a bit longer in order to build up forward speed. (Illus 13-5) In addition, women's wrists will have to begin uncocking sooner in the forward swing because they do not have the strength to square the face if the wrist cock is held until very late in the forward swing.

Many of the accommodations suggested here are for women who fall in the norm area of a bell-shaped curve. (Illus 13-6) Those falling on the low end of the scale need even further accommodations and will find golf a difficult game.

For the athletic woman on the opposite side

f13-2 *Don't take the backswing too far inside or it will encourage a steep forward swing path. Take it in a more natural arc without separation and return inside on the forward swing.*

Illus 13-5 A longer backswing may help the female golfer build up the forward speed her swing needs.

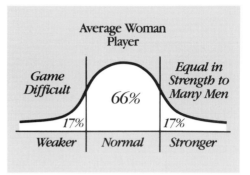

Illus 13-6 Normal distribution curve applied to the matter of strength.

of the norm, few, if any, technique accommodations from the standard are necessary. They can handle whatever would be given to a stronger, male player. (Illus 13-7, 13-8, 13-9)

SENIORS

The senior golfer, along with the woman player, represents one of the fastest-growing segments of the golf population in the United States. The reasons have largely to do with available time, discretionary dollars and a larger, more active,

Illus 13-7 Three women who hit the ball farther than most men. Joyce Wethered. (from *Rubs of the Green*)

Illus 13-8 "Babe" Didrickson

Illus 13-9 Laura Davies (Photo by Dom Furore)

healthy and long-lived senior-citizen population.

Recognize that as the body ages there is a gradual loss of strength, a greater loss of flexibility, a deterioration in the neuro-muscular system so the body cannot move as quickly, and less vitality. (Illus 13-10) A poorly conditioned person at age 50 may have only one-half the physiological vitality he had as a youth. On the other hand, a well-conditioned individual might hold to a 50% or higher level past age 75. But a senior's energy level is just not as great as when he was younger. There are positions in the swing that a Tour player can reach which are physically impossible for golfers with the senior bodies they bring to the tee. Exercise would probably help those in poor condition, but some modification of technique may also be needed.

ACCOMMODATIONS FOR AGE

Generally, these considerations should be made:

— Try a *more clockwise-positioned grip*, since a senior's ability to get forearm and hand rotation is reduced.
— *Turn the right foot farther out* to allow for more hip turn and backswing length, or close the stance.
— *Place the ball in a more centered position*, if necessary, since a senior's flexibility and, therefore, lateral motion, is reduced.
— *Use equipment that is easier to handle*, such as more lofted woods, offset irons, low flex point and lighter shafts, but not extremely light heads as some head weight is needed for extension in the swing. Lighter golf shoes will help conserve physical energy. Two-piece balls may help increase distance.
— *Exercise* to help maintain or increase flexibility and strength.
— Get the right kind of glasses. (f 13-3) If you need bifocals, make sure the lower portion focuses at the distance to the ball in the setup position.

Illus 13-10 Age deteriorates skill, and no one escapes . . . even the greatest. Gene Sarazen, Sam Snead and Byron Nelson on the first tee at the Masters with Chairman Hord Hardin. (Photo by Stephen Szurlej)

— Soak your hands in warm water before play if arthritis is a problem and see that the club's grip size fits your hands.
— *Practice more on your short game.* As Sam Snead has commented, "You can't make a good body turn if your muscles won't let you, but you can still pluck a lot of chickens with good chipping and putting."
— And when all else fails, "Use more club."

LEFT-HANDED

It is estimated that roughly 10–15% of the people in the United States are left-handed but only 3–6% of our golfers play left-handed. (f13-4, f13-5) One reason the second figure is smaller is that many left-handers are still encouraged

f13-3 *One noted senior player plays in half glasses (only the top portion) so he can judge distances. Then when he looks back to the ball it is in his normal direct-line vision. (See Appendix 9-A)*

f13-4 *In some countries or regions of countries there are larger left-handed golf populations than normal. In Canada, with many hockey players, there are more left-handed golfers. And at Newton–Moor Golf Course in Scotland, 55% of the golfers are left-handed because they play a stick-and-ball game called Shinty from the left side.*

f13-5 *Address for the National Association for Left-handed Golfers:*
NALG
10105 Hamerly
#714
Houston, TX 77080

to play right-handed. Is this a wise decision? One reason frequently offered is that if a left-hander swings right-handed, then the leading arm (the left) in the forward swing will be stronger, which is to his advantage. If that logic is sound, then why don't all natural right-handers play left-handed? The reason is this: how one chooses to swing should be based on a criterion other than a strong leading arm. The choice should always favor the player's natural body rotation strength in swinging an item such as a bat. From which side do you demonstrate the greater strength and coordination of the rotary action of trunk, hips and back, those muscle groups which are used in slinging, throwing, and striking? Find that side and go with that strength.

A SIMPLE TEST

If you are unsure about your handedness (eat and write left-handed, throw right-handed, but bowl left-handed), take this simple test. Take a club, grip and swing it as though it were a baseball bat, first right-handed, then left-handed. Which side makes the most natural and most powerful swing? *Go with that side,* be it left or right. (f 13-6)

If you are equally good (or bad) left and right, check your throwing motion with both hands. Again, if the throw shows equal skill, go with the right hand because that's how instruction

is written and there are few left-handed professional players to model. Instructors see more right-handed students and are generally more comfortable teaching them.

RIGHT-HANDED ADVANTAGE

Bob Charles, the only left-handed golfer ever to win a major golf championship (British Open 1963) has flatly stated that the strategy, technique and physical demands of golf are no different for the left-handed golfer than for the right-handed golfer. (Illus 13-11) (f 13-7) There was a time when left-handed clubs were either scarce or poorly designed. That time has passed.

Illus 13-11 Bob Charles, the premier left-handed golfer in the game's history.

f13-6 *Several PGA Tour players are naturally left-handed but play right-handed. Among them are Johnny Miller and Curtis Strange.*

f13-7 *Other than in games like cricket and golf, requiring two hands, Bob Charles is naturally right-handed.*

There are not as many brands or models to choose from, but the available left-handed clubs are certainly of equal quality to right-handed ones. Older course designs may have encouraged the left-hander to play a weaker tee shot, the fade, since hooking for him on counterclockwise layouts was flirting with out of bounds. Today's courses use a variety in layout which balances any such tendencies. This should no longer constitute a drawback for left-handers.

JUNIOR GOLFERS

PGA Professionals can be proud of the leadership role their association has taken in junior golf. In 1978 the PGA Junior Golf Foundation was founded and in the first ten years raised some $2,750,000. This money has been used for a broad variety of services, programs, booklets and visual aids to stimulate junior golf participation. The scope of the PGA's involvement is far-reaching. They have created a "Clubs for Kids Program," the PGA Junior Golf Academy, the School Development Program, the PGA National Jr. Championship, the Jr. Medalist Teaching Program, publications such as *Rick Tees Off, First Swing* and the *First Swing Curriculum Guide, The Cadet and Caddy Program*, and films on junior instruction, academies and competition. (Illus 13-12, 13-13) One of the directions of future PGA junior activities will be to serve as the leader in coalition efforts to bring the resources from golfing agencies and associations to a Community Golf Program Design.

Much of the present effort of the national organization is directed toward encouraging and supporting the local grass roots program in schools and recreation departments at daily-fee courses, private clubs, military bases, par 3's and executive courses, golf ranges and resorts. Recognizing that our future golfers must come from our youth, the PGA is striving to develop opportunities for youngsters to get interested, exposed and instructed in golf. The PGA, its sections and its members, constitutes *the* major force in promoting junior golf in the United States. (Illus 13-14, 13-15, 13-16)

THE PHYSICALLY CHALLENGED GOLFER

When we speak of handicaps in golf, our thoughts first turn to the system of identifying playing ability (18 handicap, 2 handicap) and its

Illus 13-12 One of the PGA's junior golf promotion programs is Clubs For Kids. The Minnesota PGA gave out over 200 clubs on this day.

Illus 13-13 The PGA National Academy of Golf is conducted by The PGA of America at several sites across the country.

Illus 13-14 Headquarters for the PGA of America, which houses a junior director and department.

Illus 13-16 Getting them started young is PGA professional Mike Dowaliby's theme. (Photo by Jared Howe)

Illus 13-15 The PGA of America has several sections, like the Middle Atlantic, which sponsor junior golf camps. (Photo by Joe Gambatese)

playing golf and enjoying it. Proficiency can be a long-term goal but simply getting out and "doing," regardless of how well one performs, can be an exhilarating experience for the physically challenged person. (Illus 13-17, 13-18)

Illus 13-17 At a disadvantage? These athletes would rather just say physically challenged. (Note left arm and hand prosthesis.) (Photo courtesy of the National Amputee Golf Association)

application to equalizing competition. But there are golfers with other types of handicaps, the disabled, disadvantaged or physically challenged golfer who has a physical or mental impairment: amputees (single, double or multiple), people with congenital birth defects, victims of accidents, stroke victims, paraplegics, mentally retarded, blind, deaf, and those with degenerative or debilitative diseases. One of every seven people in the United States has some form of disability. Most are capable of

Illus 13-18 These players do not let a disability keep them from their golf. (Note left leg prosthesis.) (Photo courtesy of the National Amputee Golf Association)

GOLF—A LIFESAVER

Consider this story. A middle-aged former Air Force test pilot suffered a stroke that left one side of his body nearly useless. From an active outgoing person, he became a recluse on the verge of suicide. Then a PGA Professional in Southern California, John Klein, encouraged him to come back to golf. Klein worked with him to help modify his style. The experience was not without frustration and discouragement for the player. But Klein was optimistic, patient and reliable. Progress was made to where the student began to enjoy golf again, and it gave him something to look forward to. In his own words, "It saved my life." There is a group of loyal professionals in America who have devoted many hours of their teaching time to working with the physically challenged.

A SPECIAL PLACE

The one facility which regularly teaches golf to the full gamut of disabled is the Joe Spoonster Golf School at the Vocational Development Center for the Handicapped in Akron, Ohio. (f13-8)

While this facility specializes in the blind, its program deals with any disability. Joe Spoonster, Jr., the director who has 20 years experience replaced his founder father, says, "One of the most important values of teaching the handicapped comes from them simply being part of the regular population and participating, being included. Helen Keller said it best, 'Blindness is not so terrible. The great tragedy is the isolation it imposes on people.' "

VIDEO HELP FOR THE PHYSICALLY CHALLENGED

Two videos are currently available which deal with helping the physically challenged golfer. PGA professional Peter Longo, with Wilson & Co.'s help, presents a very informative and entertaining video for the blind, paraplegic and wheelchair golfer, the one-armed and one-legged player with and without prosthesis, and the arthritic. Longo also shows the alterations that should be made in equipment for these people. He clearly demonstrates that golf is a game everyone can play. (f 13-9)

f13-8 *Address:*
Ohio Vocational
Development Center
332 S. Main St., Akron, OH 44308
c/o Joe Spoonster, Jr.

f13-9 *Peter Longo's tape "Challenge Golf" is available from:*
Motivation Media, Inc.
Audio Visual Marketing Communications
1245 Milwaukee Avenue
Glenview, IL 60025

f13-10 *Kathy Corbin's*
"Never Say Never"
1309 E. Northern #308
Phoenix, AZ 85020

Another tape, entitled "Never Say Never," features Kathy Corbin. (f 13-10) This PING-sponsored production presents golf instruction for a variety of the physically challenged, such as those previously mentioned plus the deaf (closed-captioned) and stroke victims. Corbin is effective in her enthusiastic and emphatic approach.

PHYSICALLY CHALLENGED STAR PERFORMERS

Even though high-level competence is not the primary concern, the fact is that physically challenged golfers can become quite proficient. PGA Champion Tommy Armour had one eye, Ernest Jones one leg, and Jimmy Nichols, who

played in six U.S. Opens, one arm. (Illus 13-19) (f 13-11)

Dennis Walters, the world's only paraplegic professional golfer, travels the globe performing with his show of unusual shots and trick shots played while sitting in a golf car. Walters can play in the middle to high 70s. (Illus 13-20) Pat Browne, a world blind champion from New Orleans, once shot an incredible 74 at Mission Hills in Palm Springs. In the national amputee championships, players like Corbin Cherry, Frank Cothran, Bill Harding and five-time National Champion Bick Long, have broken par though missing one arm or one leg. There are

f13-11 *The address:*
National Amputee Golf Association
c/o Bob Wilson, Executive Director
P.O. Box 1228
Amherst, NH 03031

Illus 13-19 Former star performer Jimmy Nichols, a one armed player, hammed it up with fellow single arm amputee Ralph Ebling saying, "two hands are better than one."

Illus 13-20 Dennis Walters in his show, which has been called "Golf's Most Inspiring Hour."

many physically challenged people whose lives could be enhanced by golf. They just need someone to help them. (f 13-11, f 13-12, f 13-13)

The PGA of America, through its Teaching and Growth of the Game Committee, assists individuals and organizations that fall under the physically challenged category. They also have a list of PGA Professionals who have experienced working with the disadvantaged or physically challenged.

f13-12   *U.S. Blind Golfers Association*
c/o Pat Browne
300 Carondelet Street at Gravier
New Orleans, LA 70130

f13-13   *PGA of America*
c/o Henry Thrower
Box 109601
Palm Beach Gardens, FL 33410
407-624-8400

CHAPTER 14

PHYSICAL TRAINING FOR GOLF

Playing golf is a physical athletic skill requiring strength, flexibility, neuromuscular coordination and, to a certain degree, cardiovascular and muscular endurance. Players with low levels of muscular strength and a limited range of motion will be severely hampered in their ability to swing, and potential to score.

The golf swing is a mechanical performance. But if the machine (the body) performing the action is underpowered, has poor stability and parts that don't function, the result will be neither efficient nor consistent. Gradually, golfers are coming to realize that better maintenance of their bodies will produce better results on their scorecards.

How fit does one have to be to play golf well? More so than one would think. Physical deterioration or general lack of conditioning is the number-one factor that causes the regular playing adult handicap to go up. If a player's handicap was at one time lower than it is now and he is still playing with the same frequency, look first to body condition for the answer. Loss of strength and flexibility will alter technique. When hands and forearms lose strength or suppleness, and the straight ball returns into a slice, a player automatically starts to make adjustments in aim, grip and swing path. What he might better have checked is the conditioning of his body.

CONDITIONING AND THE TOURS

Don't be fooled by seeing a few potbellies on television golf. Most of the PGA Tour players are pretty fair athletes with a high degree of strength and flexibility related to their sport. Even those wearing a portion of their midsection outside their trousers have strong arms, hands and trunks with greater-than-average flexibility. Far more Tour players are fit than not. (Illus 14-1, 14-2, 14-3) Physical training for golf is slowly being recognized on the Tour as an important factor in maintaining playing ability. The most visible evidence of this state-

Illus 14-1 Tour golfers are athletes who possess greater-than-average strength, flexibility or both, like Jack Nicklaus . . . (Photo by Stephen Szurlej)

Illus 14-2 . . . or Nick Faldo . . . (Photo by Stephen Szurlej)

Illus 14-3 . . . or Paul Azinger. (Photo by Stephen Szurlej)

ment is the presence of fitness trailers on the PGA Tour, Senior PGA Tour and LPGA Tour. Deane Beman, Commissioner of the PGA Tour and a former Tour player himself, recognized the need for improvement in physical training when he said, "Perhaps the single most neglected aspect of a PGA Tour athlete's daily regimen is his attention to physical conditioning and the prevention of injuries, something athletes in most other sports take for granted." But Beman was also able to see that one of the reasons Tour players failed to adopt a solid conditioning program was the difficulty in finding adequate, convenient facilities in a different city each week. Thus was born the idea of a mobile fitness center. Diversified Products (known as DP in the fitness industry) came forward as a sponsor. They funded not only the 45' × 17' mobile units but also research to develop a "best" training program for the world's most skilled golfers. The Centinela Hospital Medical Center was selected as the group to conduct research under the direction of internationally known orthopedist, Dr. Frank Jobe. (Illus 13-4)

In 1985, Tour professionals, club professionals and long-driving champions were tested

Illus 14-4 Fitness trailers are now seen on the PGA Tour, PGA Sr. Tour and LPGA Tour. Here is Dr. Frank Jobe in front of one of the portable units. (Photo by Jeff McBride)

with electromyographical equipment to determine which muscle groups were of particular significance to the skilled player. As a result of that research, the booklet *30 Exercises for Better Golf* (f 14-1) was produced and is used as the basis for the program recommended to players of the regular and senior Tours. This program offers a conservative approach with exercises of low intensity emphasizing prevention and rehabilitation. Thus, it is also quite useful for the amateur golfer who may be poorly conditioned, or a senior facing physical deterioration. The player who is already quite fit and desiring greater strength gains may need to seek additional training references.

The mobile facility is attracting a steady cadre of regulars who sing its praises. (Illus 14-5) Ray Floyd likes "the consistency in care with people who know you and you can trust." John Mahaffey says, "The exercise program goes a

long way toward preventing injuries." And Gary Hallberg observes, "I think this will extend the careers of the older players."

Hallberg's observation is validated by Senior Tour stars Bob Charles and Bruce Crampton. Charles, former British Open Champion and 1988 and 1989 Senior Tour leading money winner says, "The Senior Tour has become so competitive that it's essential that you be in peak physical condition. Someone not in good shape will find out just how important it can be." (Illus 14-6) When preparing originally for his senior debut, Crampton asked the regular Tour physical therapist to formulate a program for him to increase his strength and flexibility. "My strength has increased. I have added flexibility and I'm more relaxed. After a 40-minute workout, I feel great." Crampton won seven times in 1986, at the time setting a Senior Tour winnings record. The potential gains for any

Illus 14-5 The PGA Tour Fitness Trailers are equipped to train and rehabilitate. (PGA Tour professional Gil Morgan on an exercise bike.) (Photo by Jeff McBride)

Illus 14-6 A regular client of the Srs. PGA Fitness Trailer is Bob Charles.

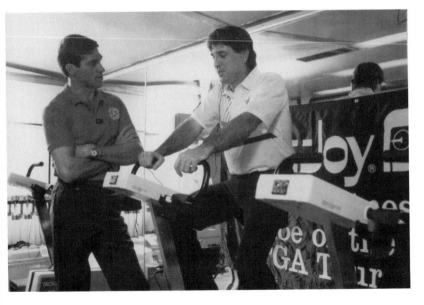

f14-1   *Jobe, Frank W. and Diane Moynes with Bill Bruns, 30 Exercises for Better Golf, Inglewood, Calif., Champion Press (Centinela Hospital Medical Center), 1986.*

player are relative to the present condition of the body. The Tour players are already reasonably fit, because they walk the golf course every day and exercise by hitting many balls. The weekend golfer generally is not fit. For the player in poor physical condition (particularly the amateur senior golfers, both men and women), improvement in performance as a result of proper training could be quite significant.

WHAT'S BEST

No one person or group (even Centinela) has *conclusively* demonstrated that its physical training system is the best for improving golf performance in all body types. Claims by others may be made to this effect, but the fact is that the same prescription does not work for everybody. For example, a senior player may have above-average strength but lack flexibility. (Illus 14-7) Conversely, a female player may

Illus 14-7 The most common physical handicap confronting senior golfers is the loss of flexibility.

> "You'll be able to hit the ball more soundly and efficently if you use the exercises in our book. For the amateur golfer, that means getting better distance and better accuracy."
> —Paul Calloway
> (Physical Therapist
> Tour DP Fitness Van)

possess good flexibility, but lack strength. Each needs a training program geared to his or her weakness(es). Training to improve physical as well as technical deficiencies in the swing will be an important part of a serious golfer's program in the future, but it should be tailored to his or her needs.

WHAT'S AVAILABLE

There are some isolated islands of enlightenment within the private sector that are offering golfers a service matching the Tour players. One such location is "Golfers Fitness and Swing Center" in Jupiter, Florida. This facility is a multifaceted operation which could certainly serve as a model for others in the country. It is directed by Dr. Rolla D. Campbell, Jr., former professor of orthopedic surgery at Cornell University Medical College and brother to internationally famous amateur golfer Bill Campbell of Huntington, West Virginia. The Fitness Swing Center's program includes: a) a physical assessment of all clients by Dr. Campbell, b) computer swing analysis by a staff PGA Golf Professional, c) regular individually supervised training sessions in the sports medicine gym by a fitness professional.

Clients may practice their swings and get feedback with the aid of a Sportek Computer and video equipment plus a host of other learning aids. (Illus 14-8, 14-9) This is in addition to doing their physical training routine which has been selected for them by the clinic staff. In a Florida geographical location where senior citizens abound, it is no surprise that the majority of their clients are experienced golfers looking

Illus 14-8 A view of the physical training equipment from "Golfers Fitness and Swing Center." (Photo courtesy of Dr. Rolla Campbell)

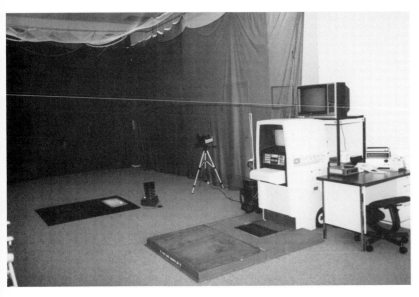

Illus 14-9 Looking at the swing practice center area of the facility, which also has an overhead camera. (Photo courtesy of Dr. Rolla Campbell)

> "That golf is not good exercise is a myth worth debunking . . . It should not be sold short as exercise."
> —Dr. James A. Nicholas

to rejuvenate their games by rejuvenating their bodies—and that's what those participants are doing.

FITNESS ELEMENTS

There are four fitness components which the golfer can develop to improve his golf: 1) strength, 2) flexibility, 3) muscular endurance and 4) cardiovascular endurance. Strength is essential to producing distance, but it must be a specific kind of strength that allows the golfer to swing a golf club with speed. Flexibility is essential in order to allow the body to reach certain positions that can maximize use of the muscular strength available. In golf, strength without flexibility is literally useless. Muscular endurance means that the muscles can still perform with efficiency even after many holes of golf or days of use. Cardiovascular endurance is having the heart and lungs operate efficiently enough to allow the player not to tire easily.

STRENGTH

To develop strength, overload is needed. Overload makes the muscles do more work than that to which they are accustomed. This is accomplished by increasing either the weight of the load lifted or the number of times it is lifted. An example would be to load a barbell with the amount of weight that can be pressed over the head eight times consecutively. Do that on Monday, then nine times on Wednesday, and ten times on Friday. The body needs the in-between days for resting and rebuilding the muscle tissue. On the following Monday, add five pounds and go back to eight repetitions. That's overload.

Intensity of workout is something that must be treated very carefully. A classic mistake is working out too hard before being adequately trained, causing fatigue or injury. *Train, don't strain.* If a person is out of condition and it has taken twenty years to get that way, he or she should not try to reverse that condition in two weeks at the risk of becoming an exercise drop-out. The anticipated feeling of dynamic health will turn into one of fatigue and soreness, the by-products of doing too much, too soon.

Exercising regularly is far more important than achieving big increases in the amount of weight that is lifted. For most of the golf exercises, increases should be undertaken in small increments. There also is a point where increases in weight should stop. That is whenever the weight causes the performer to lose good technique or the workout load produces pain or undue fatigue.

It is estimated that 40–50% of the players on Tour use weight training for physical development. A moderate, safe strength training program for all ages is included in *30 Exercises for Better Golf*. A more aggressive power-building program is suggested in Appendix 10-A.

FLEXIBILITY

Without question, loss of flexibility, which limits the range of motion, is a more common cause of deterioration in the adult male player's swing than is loss of strength. With age and a deteriorating body, men lose the ability to turn, which shortens their swing, decreases their distance and increases their handicap. Women also lose flexibility as they age, but since lack of strength is generally a greater problem (even in younger women) the lower level of strength still remains their most glaring physical golf problem later in life.

Why can a 12-year-old male weighing 110 lbs. hit a drive 20 yards farther than a 55-year-old male weighing 190 lbs.? (After all, the adult could easily pick the boy up and lift him over his head.) The answer is, because the 12-year-old has better technique. The boy is certainly not as strong, but his flexibility allows him to utilize his body fully. (Illus 14-10) The male adult is overweight, cannot turn far enough to use his big muscles and, therefore, slaps at the ball with his hands, arms, shoulders and upper trunk, which weigh about 80 lbs., compared to the boy's 110 lbs. The adult man needs in-

Illus 14-10 Flexibility is certainly more evident in the junior swing. (Photo by John H. Wettermann)

creased flexibility, a program to get him to stretch.

A sensible stretching routine would help not only the adult (male), but many golfers who are unable to make the kind of swing their professional is trying to teach them because their bodies can't do it. Their minds understand, but their bodies won't respond. *Regularly doing the kinds of flexibility exercises suggested in* Appendix 10-B *or those from Dr. Jobe's book would be the greatest single contribution to a male golfer's longevity.*

MUSCULAR ENDURANCE

Muscular endurance is developed by the repetition of light work loads over an extended period of time. It means that your muscles can keep performing at as high a level late in the round as they did earlier. If fatigue sets in, the performance level is impaired. Players who

> Strength gives the ability to control movement . . . once you develop your capacity for relaxed power, your movements take on a new quality of effortlessness, improved reflexes and coordination.
> —Dan Millman

make their living playing golf tend to work more on light weights for muscular endurance than very heavy weights for power.

CARDIOVASCULAR ENDURANCE

Cardiovascular endurance may be the least important of the four fitness items for golf, yet the most important for life. Nonetheless, if a player consistently loses his sharpness on the back nine, or fades out of contention in the last round of a multi-day event, it may be a sign that he or she is in poor cardiovascular condition. If the golfer doesn't swim laps, jog, take vigorous walks, ride a touring or exercise bike or participate in some activity that regularly strengthens his heart and lungs, then he is probably losing his cardiovascular conditioning. *The activity universally considered by the world's leading medical authorities to be the safest, simplest and most beneficial exercise is walking.* (Illus 14-11)

Illus 14-11 Father and son, Jack Nicklaus and Jack Nicklaus, Jr., walking the course as dad serves as the caddy for a change. (Photo by Stephen Szurlej)

A FITNESS EVANGELIST

No golfer in history has practiced and preached the message of fitness as enthusiastically as Masters, U.S. Open, PGA and British Open Champion Gary Player. (Illus 14-12) Not only does he recognize the value of exercise, but he also acknowledges the importance of having the desire to do it. Player makes the following observation, "Most people take stock of their physical condition at some point, whether because of something they read, like this, or something they see in the mirror, and resolve to make themselves physically fit. They cut down their cigarette smoking a little, start jogging, and work out a bit at the local gym. This lasts about three weeks. Then suddenly, the cigarette intake is back up again, the television is more important than the jogging, and the gym is 'too crowded.' It doesn't help you to start something and not finish it. You've got to main-

Illus 14-12 Fitness for Gary Player not only helps his physical performance but also strengthens his confidence and mental attitude. Player demonstrates his strength by giving his caddy a boost to see the flag.

> "I've tried to stay in good condition every day of my life—which is why, at the age of 69 (88 years old at publication), I can still play par golf . . ."
> —Gene Sarazen

tain a consistent exercise program over a long period of time in order for it to be beneficial." So finding the key to exercise habit formation becomes even more critical than knowing exactly what to do and how to do it. Ten such keys are listed in Appendix 10-C.

INJURIES

The most common debilitating injuries to golfers are those of the wrist, back, hand, shoulders and neck. Though they tend to be more chronic than traumatic, their effect on performance can be devastating. There are several examples of top-ten money winners and major tournament champions completely disappearing from contention as a result of a seemingly minor but nagging injury. In one study conducted on PGA Tour players prior to the advent of the fitness trailers, the average loss of time when a player left because of injury was 3 weeks. Of those who came back, 50% were still bothered by the injury.

There are two pieces of advice to help prevent injury. The first is to warm up before play. The second is to have an exercise program which is conducive to developing strength, flexibility and muscular endurance.

LOWER-BACK PROBLEMS

An occupational risk for the frequent golfer is the development of lower-back pain. Tour players like Trevino, Zoeller and Archer, who have had back surgery, can attest to that fact. Others like Snead, Peete, Ballesteros, Boros, Nicklaus, North, Goalby, Player and a score of others have not needed surgery, but all have needed ther-

apy. Drs. McCarrol and Giol found in a 1982 study that 25% of the Tour players had lower-back pain. And that's a fairly young age group.

The most common cause of lower-back problems is improper alignment of the spine. It has been estimated that musculoskeletal weakness is the cause of 80% of all backaches today. Weak abdominal muscles allow the stomach to sag, the hips to rotate toward the rear causing an exaggerated curve in the lower-back region. This curve puts consistent pressure on the vertebrae and discs. When there is a combination of being overweight, lacking muscle tone, and having poor flexibility and bad posture habits, it increases pressure on the vertebrae. Over the course of time this pressure eventually leads to the problems that send golfers to their doctors.

Contributing to the problems that golfers can have with the lower back is a player's technique. The swing requires twisting of the spine and a forceful release of energy, but some styles are much more stressful than others. Golfers who attempt to wind the upper body 90 degrees or more while holding the lower-body rotation to a minimum will put greater stress on the lumbar spine. Also, a player who drives aggressively toward the target with his lower body while keeping his upper body back in a reverse "C" position will be more prone to lower-back injury than a player with a swing in which he finishes more level. (Illus 14-13) A jarring swing into a root, a rock or the turf can also injure the back; therefore, every attempt should be made to take no unnecessary chances when those conditions are present.

One of the best things to do for a healthy back is to stand properly—at all times! Hips should be tucked under and the stomach pulled in. In order to do this one must have strong stomach muscles and flexibility in the ham-

> "I don't do the fitness for golf only. I do it for general health. To me, it's one of the most important things in life."
> —Gary Player

Illus 14-13 A more vertical finish, such as that of two-time U.S. Open champion Curtis Strange, puts less strain on the lower back. (Photo by Stephen Szurlej)

string muscles in the back of the legs. Jack Joseph, director of the Fit-Back Exercise Program, makes these observations, "Common treatment for simple backache includes drugs (muscle relaxers and pain killers), manipulation, ultrasound, bed rest, and perhaps traction. All that is usually needed is to reverse the degenerative processes which are causing the shortened, inflexible and weak muscles of the abdomen, spine and hips. The ideal way to do this is by beginning a regular regimen of exercise especially designed to improve muscular fitness." Correct exercise almost always helps, but when the exercise stops, the problems usually return. A lower-back exercise program which golfers can use to improve muscular strength and flexibility is offered in Appendix 10-D.

All golfers who wish to protect their backs should be made aware of these cautions:

1. When lifting any object, let the legs do the work, not the back.

2. Don't lift heavy objects (like golf bags) from the car trunk. (Illus 14-14)
3. Don't reach over furniture to open and close windows.
4. At work or home, try to sit in a straight chair with a firm back.
5. Any time you can, sit so that your knees are higher than your hips. Adjust your car seat that way if possible.
6. Never sit or ride for prolonged periods of time, like at your desk, on airline flights or in a car; get up and move around.
7. Don't stand in the same position for a prolonged period or stay bent over, such as when practicing putting. If you can't relocate, at least shift from one foot to another, or stand up and stretch, or walk around.
8. In bed, if lying on your back, it's helpful to have pillows under your knees. If on your side, draw one or both knees up toward the chin.
9. Before you hit your first tee shot, be sure

Illus 14-14 One of the most frequent causes of lower-back injury is lifting a heavy object from the wrong postural position, like golf clubs from the trunk of a car.

Illus 14-15 A warm-up routine can help players prevent injury, as Jack Nicklaus demonstrates. (Photo by Stephen Szurlej)

you have warmed up by hitting balls, working up gradually from short irons to full shots. If that's not possible, then do stretching exercises (calisthenics) before making your first full swing. (Illus 14-15)

10. Keep a sweater or jacket in your bag in the event you are sweating, and the weather starts to chill.

11. When doing strength exercises like swinging a heavy club, add "contras," or swings in the opposite direction to your workout. This will provide muscular balance for both strength and flexibility. Balance keeps your body, vertebrae and other bones in correct alignment.

12. Walk whenever you can; it's great medicine for the back.

NUTRITION

Although we seldom consider diet when thinking of golf performance, it can have an effect. Let's start by making a simple observation.

Most halfway-house food at golf courses is neither nutritous nor good for golf. A cola and a hot dog may fill the stomach, but beyond appetite cessation neither the short-term nor long-term effects are beneficial. (Illus 14-16) For the short term, the sugar gives a quick high followed by depression around the 15th hole. If it's a diet soda instead, the sugar rollercoaster may not be experienced, but the caffeine has the potential for making a person less calm, with the possibility of a slight tremor. If you do select soda for your drink choose diet, caffeine-free. The hot dog, nitrates and all, is just plain bad nutrition. Both are hollow foods, full of additives, high in calories and fat, low in nutritional benefit, requiring the body to desire still more food to handle its needs.

One doesn't have to go to the halfway house, baseball park or circus to find nutritionally bad food. A person can shop at any supermarket and by choice, end up with items that are bad for health and, therefore, bad for golf.

Being overweight presents a performance problem. In a country where almost 50% of the people are overweight, it's far too common to

Illus 14-16 The hot dog may be appealing but it's not nutritionally healthy food.

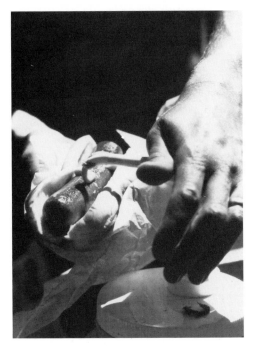

see people hindered in their performance by fat. The truth is, fat people seldom win in competitive golf. In 1987 only one player who won on the men's PGA Tour weighed over 200 lbs.That was 6'4" Andy Bean, and he certainly wouldn't be considered fat. Thirty-eight Tour events were won by players weighing 180 pounds or less. Fat is detrimental to the performance of almost any athlete. In golf, being overweight robs energy and hinders motion. Of course, there are a few exceptions, but they are fighting *heavy odds*. Obesity is a problem with health consequences which can be as serious as those associated with smoking. Also, 10 lbs. of extra fat around one's stomach adds approximately 100 lbs. of extra pressure on the back.

So, to be at one's best, do what is prescribed in any of a dozen magazine articles every month:

1. Consume fewer fats—fatty meat, cream, butter, etc. Choose more lean meat, chicken and fish.
2. Try to eliminate processed foods heavy in additives. Include more fresh vegetables and fruits.
3. Stay away from sugared beverages. If alcohol is consumed, keep it lighter and in small quantities. Drink plenty of water.
4. Ingest low amounts of heavily sugared and salted foods. Choose seasonings that are healthful. For example, substitute fresh lemon juice for salt.
5. Get carbohydrates from whole-grain breads, bran, pasta, cereals. The sweet carbohydrate is the calorie loader.

What should the golfer do between the 9th green and the 10th tee, when the halfway house beckons? (Illus 14-17) Choose water, juice or a sports drink to quench thirst. And either buy or bring from home, fresh fruit, packaged fruit or vegetable snacks. (f 14-1) Suggest to the management of your halfway house or snack bar that they might consider offering selections that are more healthy. There is no rule that one has to indulge oneself at the halfway house at all. Some competitors have found that they per-

Illus 14-17 While sports drinks do contain sweeteners, they are better for one's health than highly sugared sodas. Water is still the best as Masters champion Bernard Langer demonstrates. (Photo by Stephen Szurlej)

form better if they eat nothing in the middle of the round. But the decision would depend largely on the individual's tolerance to blood-sugar depletion.

IS IT WORTH IT?

Life is a series of choices. By choosing to exercise, to watch the diet and to enjoy a sensible lifestyle, we will most certainly enhance and prolong our chances to play our best golf. The benefits have proven to be:

Confidence—Feel good about yourself.
Longevity—Extend your playing years.

f14-1 *On the LPGA tour Nancy Lopez, Pat Bradley, Sally Little and Patty Sheehan, to name but a few, take snacks of apples, sandwiches, cookies, etc., to fight low blood sugar. Several top Senior Tour players do likewise.*

Stamina—Have more cardiovascular and muscular endurance.
Physical Soundness—Prevent injuries.
Distance—Hit the ball farther.
Direction—Have more control of the club.

PRIORITIES

If it's strictly golf improvement you are after and your time is limited, consider the following activities. They are listed in order of priority toward the contribution to golf improvement for most people. All of them contain some degree of exercise.

1. Take instruction and hit balls on the range to improve technique.

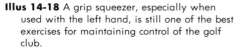

Illus 14-18 A grip squeezer, especially when used with the left hand, is still one of the best exercises for maintaining control of the golf club.

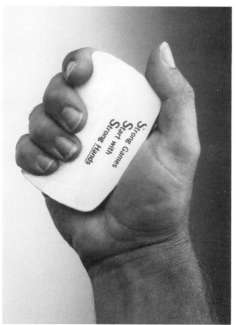

Illus 14-19 This golfer gets his exercise on the way to the course as well as on it. (Photo courtesy of Svensk Golf)

2. Play golf.
3. Practice swinging the club—do drills—visualize and feel the swing.
4. Perform exercises related to golf strength and flexibility: progressive resistance with weights, floor exercises and calisthenics, machines or devices such as Nautilus™, Distance Builder™, Gym-in-a-Bag™, Grip Squeezer, etc. (Illus 14-18)
5. Jog, bicycle, swim, or do built-in exercises for cardiovascular endurance. (Illus 14-19)

If you are in poor physical condition, instruction, hitting balls and playing may be of little help. It's like trying to enjoy skating when one doesn't have enough strength in the ankles and legs to stand up. It can't easily be done. You may need to work on your body if you want to perform well at the game you love, golf.

CHAPTER 15

EQUIPMENT:
Its Role in Performance

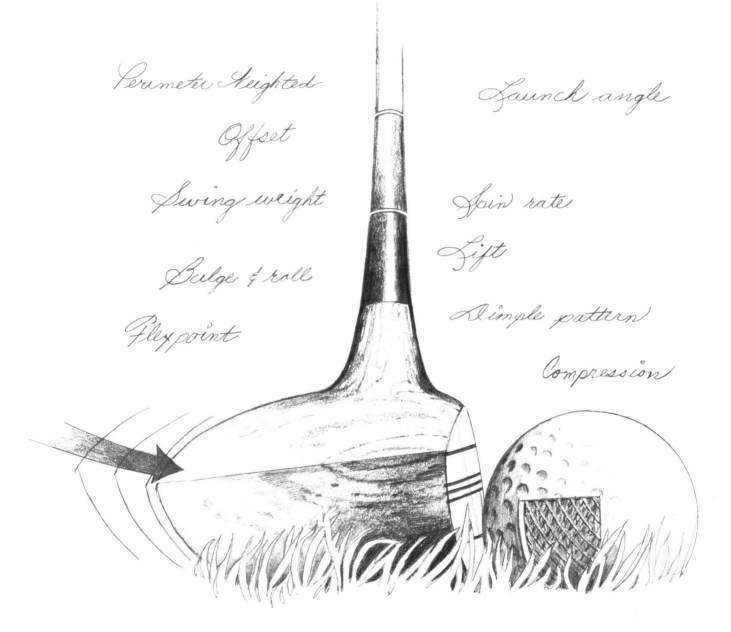

Perimeter Heighted

Offset

Swing weight

Bulge & roll

Flex point

Launch angle

Spin rate

Lift

Dimple pattern

Compression

How much does proper equipment affect your ability to play golf? Do clubs make a difference? Can you improve your ball striking by altering your clubs or changing makes or models? What about your selection of the brand of ball? Are there really some types of balls that are better for certain players than others? The answer to all the questions is decidedly yes, equipment can make a difference and is a topic about which golfers have many questions. While

Illus 15-1 Sir Winston's remark on this plaque would not be appropriate in today's world of hi-tech golf. (Courtesy PGA World Golf Hall of Fame)

Illus 15-2 A person would certainly not buy clothes that didn't fit, nor should one buy golf clubs that don't fit.

equipment alone cannot make a strong player, it is important that the fitting of the equipment be made to the player, rather than the other way around. (Illus 15-1) When one buys clothes, or gloves or shoes, he wouldn't think of buying the wrong size and trying to make them fit. It is the same with golf clubs. A person should have clubs that fit. (Illus 15-2) Why? Because poorly fitted clubs can make golf improvement more difficult.

CLUB FITTING—FIRST A DECISION

Part of the educational process on fitting is to discover the options. Option 1) In many cases a stock club, off the shelf, selected properly, can fit. Sometimes with, sometimes without, minor alterations. Option 2) The professional can order custom clubs from the manufacturer after assessing the player's needs. (Illus 15-3, 15-4) Option 3) The professional who has creditable club fitting skills can buy component parts which he or his staff will assemble after a fitting session with the player. Option 4) The professional can make custom clubs from raw materials after a fitting session, a choice which requires extensive experience and equipment.

In any case, the professional's reputation and service will be enhanced if he is at least prepared to handle adjusting grip size, loft and lie, clubface angle, swing weight, overall weight and length. Much of the decision as to which way to go rests on his interest, skills, market, available time and desires of his customers. The

Illus 15-3 Almost all club manufacturers have custom fitting departments, such as the one shown at Tommy Armour Company where a grip is being applied. (Photo courtesy of Tommy Armour Company)

public will generally ask for those clubs they have seen advertised or written about or have heard being talked up by other players.

THREE IMPORTANT ELEMENTS

Quality, design and *fit* is the major message when considering whether a certain club will improve or hinder your performance. Of these, fit is the most important. There are eleven variables:

1. Clubhead design
2. Club loft
3. Club lie
4. Club length
5. Face angle for woods
6. Swingweight & total weight
7 & 8. Grip size & material
9 & 10. Shaft flex, material and pattern
11. Set makeup

GOLF SHAFTS

The golf shaft is not a producer of power. It can store energy and, if properly matched to the user, deliver the energy at the correct time. Thus, describing it as the timing device in the swing is most appropriate. It is undoubtedly one of the major considerations in fitting.

The consumer is certainly in need of good counsel when considering the best shaft for his game. In addition to the three currently most popular materials of steel, graphite and titanium, there are other exotic or unusual shafts on the market, all of which promise superior performance in their advertising. Steel can offer several choices in weight alone: light weight, extra light, super light, etc. Graphite can have

> "Hickory golf was a game of manipulation and inspiration; steel golf is a game of precision and calculation."
> —Pete Dobereiner

Illus 15-4 And a custom grind on a forged iron. (Photo courtesy of Tommy Armour Company)

an infinite variety of designs, quality, variety of features and construction so that *one graphite is most certainly not like the next.* Once the material is selected, the characteristics of stiffness, flex point, weight, length and torque need to be addressed. So for now we will simply address the two major materials, steel and graphite.

STEEL AND GRAPHITE

A steel shaft was introduced and played as far back as 1891 but it captured little interest. The USGA did not legalize steel shafts until 1924. The R&A delayed approval until 1931. Tempered steel has dominated the market since, despite brief incursions by other materials such as aluminum, fiberglass or stainless steel. Today, the most serious contender to steel is graphite. The flex characteristics of steel are controlled primarily by wall thickness. The thicker the shaft, the stiffer and heavier it will

be and the less torque it will have. Graphite stiffness, flex point and torque are controlled by: 1) the fiber's tensile strength, 2) the amount of fiber, and 3) the pattern in which the fibers are applied. Early graphite had a low torque resistance, which caused a serious control problem for the strong hitter. This has largely been eliminated today because fibers are layered in different directions to create whatever amount of torque and stiffness is desired in that particular part of the shaft. (Illus 15-5) Although graphite shaft prices are coming down, some graphite shafts can cost the manufacturer more than five times that of steel. This is reflected in the price to the professional and his customers. Graphite is generally lighter than steel although the lightness of some graphite can be matched by the super-light steel shafts. So although graphite has some potentially attractive advantages, the two look to be formidable adversaries for some time to come. (f15-1)

f15-1 *While discussing graphite it is worth mentioning that club heads made of this material also have the advantages of perimeter weighting, head size adaptability and feel that is more like wood. Still, graphite has yet to demonstrate any widespread popularity over persimmon or steel as a clubhead material.*

Illus 15-5 Shafts and other club and ball characteristics tested by companies like Tommy Armour. (Photo courtesy of Tommy Armour Company)

Illus 15-6 The ball's evolution: Featherie, smooth gutty, molded gutty and modern wound (Haskell).

GOLF BALLS

In the opening chapter, the evolution of the golf ball was described. (Illus 15-6) Golfers may not be interested in the ball's history, but they are curious about the best ball for their game. There are several points to consider.

BALL DISTANCE

The majority of advertising dollars spent on golf ball sales since 1900 has been devoted to convincing the buyer that the advertised ball would go farther than its competition. This clearly demonstrates the collective judgment of the industry, *that the large majority of golfers seek distance above all else in their selection of a golf ball.*

The distance a ball will travel (assuming a given projected velocity launch angle and spin rate) is affected by dimple design, material of cover and core, size and weight. All balls, to be legal for events played under USGA and R&A rules, must pass a test on initial velocity, size, weight, symmetry of design pattern and an overall distance standard (ODS). (Illus 15-7) When the ball meets these standards it is placed on a list of "conforming balls." (f 15-2) Those not on the list are considered illegal. Control

Illus 15-7 Peter Jacobson, PGA Tour player, checks the dimple pattern which will influence the ball's aerodynamics.

of the ball's distance is essential to maintaining the *essence* of the game. *Nothing would destroy the game of golf faster than to encourage the use of golf balls that travel appreciably farther.* If that were to happen, present-length courses would no longer offer the same challenge. Having to again lengthen courses because of a longer ball would: 1) extend the time of play, 2) require more land for facilities and 3) cost more dollars in maintenance, all of which are problems even with the present length.

WHICH BALL REALLY GOES THE FARTHEST?

How can three different manufacturers claim to have the longest ball? The answer is that each manufacturer designs the test conditions

f15-2 *The USGA's list is published four times a year.*

to maximize the performance of its product. The manufacturer chooses to test with a certain club or combination of clubs, launch the ball at a given trajectory, and hit at a set velocity. It's not false advertising, but it can be interpreted in different ways.

Of the top 20% of balls tested by the U.S.G.A., the difference in distance from first to last was approximately 10 yards. In other words, when comparing *the best balls* on the market, there is not much difference.

What about "super balls"—ones in ads that make claims for "400-yard shots" or "50 extra yards guaranteed"? Such a ball, of course, if it existed, would be illegal and not in the spirit of the game. But more to the point, in tests on driving machines, those kinds of balls, if of the same size and weight of a normal ball, go no farther than any you can buy in the shop. Reputable ball-manufacturing companies spend millions of dollars on research to make a legal optimum ball. No "hype-oriented marketeer" without even a research department is going to put out a better product. They may make a ball smaller or have a nonconforming weight to make up for their ball's composition, but such a ball would certainly not be superior to any major brand.

AERODYNAMICS AND DIMPLES

As was mentioned in Chapter One, the original smooth gutta-percha ball did not fly well until it became nicked. The nicking reduced drag and caused lift by pulling air around the ball, thinning it (lowering the pressure) above and thick-

f15-3 *Interestingly enough there is a raised or bramble pattern back on the market today but not on a regulation ball. The MacGregor "50," a ball originally called the "Cayman Ball," travels roughly 50% the distance of a normal ball and is used in American Modified Golf Association events and on short courses built for this version of the game.*

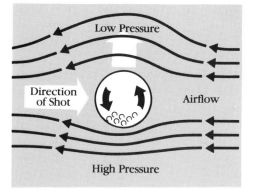

Illus 15-8 Backspin produces lower pressure above the ball causing it to rise.

ening it (increasing the pressure) below. The net pressure difference causes the lift. It is known as the Bernouli Principle. Random patterns of marking developed over the years with little understanding of their influence on the ball's flight. The bramble was the most popular pattern until William Taylor in 1908 came up with the idea of reversing the marking and making concave rather than convex marks—dimples not pimples. Dimples or some form of mesh pattern have been used ever since. (f 15-3)

MODERN PATTERNS

The standard pattern accepted by the industry until the 1970s was the Atti pattern, one which presented circular rows and columns of dimples, an octahedral array. A new arrangement, the icosahedron, was then introduced which grouped the dimples into triangular regions with the advantage of presenting the same dimple pattern to the air no matter in which direction the ball was spinning. Since then, other pattern designs such as the tetraicosahedral, deltahedral and dodecahedral have appeared. claiming improved flight characteristics. These terms simply describe the arrangement of dimples in triangular and pentagonal patterns on the surface of the ball.

Even more popular than the patterning in ball design has been the number of dimples and their shape. Until the 1980s the standard dimple count on a ball was from 324 to 332. With the introduction of a 384-dimple ball in 1983 by Acushnet, the dimple count has become a race of "one-upmanship," with one ball even boasting 500-plus dimples. More, however, does not necessarily mean better. More dimples puts the dimples closer together, which some claim gives the ball a slightly softer feel. It may also cause a higher trajectory, which for some types of ball construction would be better, for others, worse.

Depth and shape of dimples, coupled with their arrangement, has given the aerodynamic scientists the greatest opportunity to demonstrate a contribution to golf. Small and deep dimples tend to make the ball go lower; wider and shallower dimples, higher. Balls which normally would travel higher, such as a three-piece balata-covered ball, may be designed with a smaller or deeper dimple to lower that height. (f15-4) Conversely, a two-piece ball may come with a wide, shallow dimple to help it carry farther.

BALL CONSTRUCTION

Three types of golf balls are sold today: three-, two- and one-piece. The three-piece ball has for its first piece a small rubber core approximately one inch in diamater. It may either be filled with liquid or be solid. Some 30 yards of rubber thread are then stretched up to ten times their normal length and wound symmetrically around the core. This constitutes the second piece. The third piece is the cover which comes in two halves and is molded under great pressure and heated into a single solid cover, most commonly made of balata or a balata blend.

The two-piece ball is made from a synthetic core of varying size (depending on the manufacturer), around which a cover is placed. This

f15-4 *If asked, "What is a truncated dimple?" It is one that's flattened on the bottom.*

is accomplished either by *injection molding* in which the core is centered in a mold by retractable pins and the material is injected around the core, or by *compression molding* in which two cover "preforms" are molded, then assembled around a core and compressed, as in the three-piece ball. In both processes the molding takes place under heat and pressure using a mold made from two halves.

One-piece balls are compression molded and are used primarily for practice ranges. None exist today that are popular for high-level competitive play.

MATERIAL—BALATA AND SURLYN

Balata is the dried green-like substance of the juice from a West Indian or tropical American tree, the "balata," of the sapodilla family. It is related to gutta-percha, the material from which earlier balls were made and which has been used as golf ball cover material since the early 1900s. A shortage of natural balata has resulted in a synthetically produced material which retains the name. In addition, other materials with different names are being substituted for balata. Balata is used primarily on three-piece balls, is softer in feel and cuts more easily than other materials.

Surlyn® (f15-5) is the other most popular golf ball cover material. It is used primarily on two-piece balls, but a few brands also have a three-piece ball with a Surlyn cover. Surlyn is more cut-resistant and has a harder feel. Now several other synthetics have been developed which in the future may challenge Surlyn for its popularity. A Surlyn-covered two-piece ball compared to a three-piece balata ball bounces higher when dropped on a hard surface, putts farther with equal effort, travels at a lower trajectory when struck and rolls farther when it hits the ground. Its distance, when compared to a three-piece balata ball, is influenced by several conditions. Hard fairways would favor the lower trajectory, faster running, two-piece Surlyn ball, as would a headwind or crosswind. The two-

f15-5 *Surlyn® is a registered trade name of the DuPont Company.*

f15-6 *Balata is used as the cover stock on a few two-piece balls.*

f15-7 *It is possible to make a Surlyn-covered two-piece ball which has a higher spin rate and higher trajectory than a balata-covered three-piece ball.*

piece Surlyn ball bores lower in the air and slices or hooks less, since it does not spin as readily. The three-piece balata ball has a greater spin rate; therefore, it has more backspin to hold the greens and a higher trajectory for downwind play. (f15-6, f15-7) Another consideration is temperature. In cold weather the two-piece loses less of its distance-producing properties than the three-piece ball.

Balls are colored (white included) in three ways: 1) by painting after construction, 2) by impregnating the raw material with color before molding, or 3) by combining the two methods. Clear urethane paint is added to the finished ball. Non-white golf balls account for approximately 15% of the market at this time, although when first introduced, climbed to a market share of around 35%.

WHAT IS COMPRESSION?

Compression is the relative hardness of a golf ball. Technically, it is the amount of deflection of a ball when a standard force is applied. The scale runs from 0–200. A ball that does not compress at all from that standard force would rate 200. For every 1,000th of an inch of deflection the rating is reduced by one from the original 200 figure. Therefore a ball that has deflected 100/1,000ths (or 1/10th of an inch) would be a 100-compression ball. Most balls are made to average 90-compression. Those

that exceed 95 are labeled 100, and those that fall below 86 are labeled 80. (f 15-8)

The compression range of 80–100 of the same brand and type of ball does have some but not a significant influence on how far the ball will travel. Feel is the primary difference. The higher-rated ball (100) feels harder and is favored more by the stronger hitter. A fair share of PGA Tour players also use 90 compression. Ball makers run compression checks on their three-piece balls and a few also do so on their two-piece balls. (Illus 15-9) Several manufacturers don't run a a compression test on any of their two-piece products, saying the proper material is the important factor, not the compression.

f15-8 *Compression ratings below 86 relegate the ball primarily to the golf range, "x-outs" or low-end private label balls.*

Illus 15-9 Testing a ball's compression is Wilson's director of research Tom Hardman. (Courtesy *Golf Digest*)

DURABILITY

Without question, the higher handicap player should be using a Surlyn® or similar substance covered two-piece ball. These balls are virtually impossible to cut with a golf club. The balls also have a longer shelf life and stand a chance to last longer than a three-piece ball, even from centerface hits, because there is no core to go "out of round." (For more information on golf balls see Appendix 11-B.)

CONCLUSION

Balls and clubs do make a difference, in feel, in performance and in aesthetics which affect performance. (Illus 15-10)

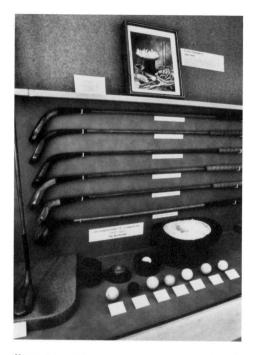

Illus 15-10 To better appreciate the evolution of equipment a player might visit a golf museum such as the PGA World Golf Hall of Fame. (Courtesy PGA World Golf Hall of Fame)

CHAPTER 16

THE PSYCHOLOGY OF PLAYING & COURSE MANAGEMENT

Successful golf requires more than a good swing. One can't overlook the importance of a physically sound body, properly fitted equipment, a solid short game and the ability to adapt to unusual or special conditions. Yet, considering all of the above, one of the most critical factors in determining golf success is still left unmentioned. *Successful golf requires control of your mind and your emotions—successful golf requires psychological strength.* (Illus 16-1) (Appendix 12-A)

Golf is a mental game, but not necessarily an intellectual game. The mental portion grows in importance with the mastery of skills to the

"Hitting a golf ball is an act so precise that there is unlimited room for error. That error begins in the mind and finds expression in the swing."
—Lorne Rubenstein

"The person I fear most in the last two rounds is myself."
—Tom Watson

point where the top players will claim that 70% to 90% of their result depends on their mental performance. They recognize that perfect thinking doesn't always produce perfect results, but flawed thinking does produce flawed results. Without question, the universally agreed upon secret to successful performance is founded on this statement—"*As a man thinketh so shall he be.*" So, whatever one is thinking becomes critical to his results. The philosopher William James said at the beginning of the 20th century, "The greatest discovery of my generation is that human beings can alter their lives by altering their attitudes of mind." The basic principle "Whatever one believes with feeling becomes his reality" has been expanded upon and embellished by popular positive thinkers such as Dale Carnegie, Norman Vincent Peale, W. Clement Stone, Earl Nightingale, Maxwell Maltz, Paul Thomas and Dennis Waitley, all of whom have extolled and taught many of the same principles that are

Illus 16-1 Every player's dream, to compete in a major tournament, might become a stiff test of nerves if it ever happened.

applied to golf psychology today. Before investigating these, let's see where we've been to better understand where we are.

REVIEWING THE LITERATURE

Reference to the mental hazards in golf can be found in the game's very first instruction book, *The Golfer's Manual*, written by H.B. Farnie in 1857. Farnie observes, *"The great stumbling block in the way of all players, veterans and recruits, is excitement."* (What we would identify today as anxiety or nervous tension.) Farnie goes on to note, *"Indecision should be overcome boldly and promptly by the player."* (Today our approach would be "positive mental imagery.") He continues by saying of the player, *"He must have confidence in himself."* (Our present day "positive self-image.") So what's new? What's new is the *HOW TO*! How to not just *recognize*, but *overcome* nervous tension, utilize positive mental imagery, concentrate, relax and create a positive self image. That's the message being offered to today's golfers. (Illus 16-2)

Modern-day golf psychology has been slow to evolve and is far more influenced by the literature and research in psychology than the literature and research in golf. Nonetheless, there has evolved a body of literature on the subject directly pertaining to golf. Here's a chronological list which includes most of the golf books in which the primary subject matter has been the psychology or the mental side of golf:

1908 *The Mystery of Golf*—T.A. Haultain
1922 *Psychology of Golf*—Leslie Schon

Illus 16-2 Facing the posting of a score creates extra tension for most players.

1923 *The Brain and Golf*—Charles W. Bailey
1925 *The Professor on the Golf Links*—Charles W. Bailey
1927 *Mental Handicaps in Golf*—Theodore B. Hyslop
1929 *The Mental Side of Golf*—Charles W. Moore
1930 *Solving the Mental Problem of Golf*—Edwin R. Dillon
1939 The Mental Side of Golf, A Study of the Game as Practiced by Champions—Kenneth R. Thompson
1960 *On Learning Golf*—Percy Boomer
1960 *Golf Is Mental*—Dr. Archie Hovanesian
1961 *The Winning Touch in Golf*—Peter G. Cranford, Ph.D.
1961 *How You can Play Better Golf Using Self-Hypnosis*—Jack Heise
1961 *It's the Damned Ball*—Ike S. Handy
1962 *The Education of a Golfer*—Sam Snead
1972 *Golf in the Kingdom*—Michael Murphy

> "Winners know from experience how they will react to the excitement and pressure of a final-round shootout. They find a way to perform even when their legs and arms go rubbery and their heartbeats make the logos on their shirt jump up and down."
> —Peter Jacobson

1976 *The Missing Links*—David C. Morley, M.D.

1978 *The New Golf Mind*—Gary Wiren, Ph.D., and Richard Coop, Ph.D.

1980 *The Golfing Bodymind*—Sandy Dunlop

1981 *The Inner Game of Golf*—Timothy Gallwey

1981 *Mind Mastery for Winning Golf*—Robert Rotella, Ph.D., and Linda K. Bunker, Ph.D.

1984 *The Golfing Mind*—Vivien Saunders

1986 *Five Days to Golfing Excellence*—Chuck Hogan

There was not much of practical value here that the average golfer could use to his advantage prior to Peter Cranford's *The Winning Touch* in 1961. Most of his material is still quite useful today. The golfing public in the '60s was almost 100% rooted in the golf range "ball-hitting only" mindset for improvement, so despite its usefulness, Cranford's book broke no sales records. Before his book, only a handful of PGA members, like club professional Gene O'Brien from Wichita, Kansas, and Ben Hogan on the PGA Tour, were really into the psychology of golf. Some professionals like Tommy Armour were natural psychologists in their approach to teaching but didn't expound on it much further. It took a plastic surgeon, Dr. Maxwell Maltz, writing a non-golfing book, *Psychocybernetics*, and occasional appearances at seminars by sport psychologists such as Dr. Bruce Ogilive and Dr. Tom Tutko, to create enthusiasm among professionals for increased application of psychological principles to playing and teaching. Maltz promoted the importance of a strong self concept by declaring that "your action, feeling and behavior are always consistent with your self-image." If you think you are a poor putter, you'll be one . . . if you believe you are a choker, you'll choke. Ogilive and Tutko created interesting psychological inventories for athletes, a practice only recently being used for the average golfer.

But the blockbuster book that is still spoken of in reverent tones among golf psychology de-

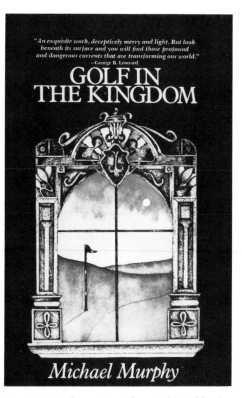

Illus 16-3 Golf's most noted metaphysical book, *Golf in the Kingdom.*

votees is *Golf in the Kingdom.* (Illus 16-3) Golf's premier metaphysical book opened the golfer's eyes to a previously unexplored territory, the world of Eastern mysticism, of Zen and Yin and Yang. Murphy's Eastern "non-thinkers" approach is quite different from the Western "positive thinkers." In *Golf in the Kingdom*, the focus is on the experience, not the outcome. By not trying to make things happen, they do, but only because you let them. It's an approach that has greatly influenced the competitive mind in present-day sports. More on that later.

The first to write a regular column in a major golf magazine that dealt exclusively with the mental aspects of the game was Dr. Michael Morley, whose work appeared in *Golf Digest* from 1971–1974. Since then several publications, even regional golf periodicals, carry the columns of psychologists writing on golf. A non-psychologist, Ed Grant, from Scottsdale, Arizona, brought a new twist to golf psychology by producing an audiocassette program called "Subconscious Golf." Grant studied standard accepted psychological principles and applied them to golf, using examples with which the average player could identify. To those trained in psychology, it may have been "old hat," but to 95% of amateur golfers and an almost equal number of professionals, it was a revelation. For many, it still is.

Tim Gallwey, in his book *The Inner Game of Tennis*, captivated multitudes of tennis buffs with his Self 1 and Self 2, nondirective "bounce/hit" approach to improved performance. His thesis that tennis is overanalyzed and that details are over-taught (much to the detriment of the pupil) fell on some receptive golfers' ears. Transferring his thesis from tennis to golf was relatively simple. After all, what sport is more overanalyzed and details over-taught than golf? So the message changed from "bounce/hit" to "back/hit." That message being, distract the conscious mind by keeping it occupied with a seemingly inane task so the subconscious can take over and perform naturally. The task was repeating "bounce/hit" on each tennis stroke and "back/hit" on a golf shot.

The fact that humans have a two-hemisphere brain structure, each side contributing specific functions related to golf performance, was brought to light in the first left-brain/right-brain sports book written, *The New Golf Mind*, by Dr. Gary Wiren and Dr. Richard Coop. It was an awareness book that set forth a variety of options for the performer to explore and practice to better control his performance on the course.

In *Mind Mastery for Winning Golf*, Dr. Robert Rotella and Dr. Linda Bunker provided a pencil and paper motivational assessment test for the reader, programs for goal-setting, and techniques to help players with their attention control and anxiety reduction.

Coop and Rotella are both full-time university professors in their respective fields of psychology. In addition, they serve extensively as part-time speakers, teachers and consultants on the psychology of golf. (f16-1) Former PGA

f16-1 *Coop and Rotella jointly produced a combination audiocassette tape program and workbook,* Golfing Out Of Your Mind, *1985.*

member Chuck Hogan, president of Sports Enhancement Associates, may be the only individual presently devoting full-time efforts to the study of golf psychology and making a living at it. Hogan, though not a trained psychologist, has authored *Five Days to Golfing Excellence* and conducts his S.E.A. "visualization" programs around the country. His videotape "Nice Shot" is the only major title in the video medium devoted primarily to psychology other than the Sybervision tapes, which utilize "psychological enhancement" along with "modeling" to teach skill technique.

Granted, the first mention of psychology in golf may have been in Farnie's book in 1857, but we are just beginning to get the message.

WHAT, HOW AND HOW MUCH?

There is little doubt that today's better players recognize the importance psychology plays in performance. They have experienced the truth in the statement, "The body won't lie for the brain." But, when it comes to *what to do, how to do it* and *how much to do*, the golfer is still seeking input. The following information should help.

If it were all boiled down into the most simple and useful form, it might look something like this. For a player to perform near his best on the golf course, at a minimum, he would need to develop the following mental/psychological skills:

> "The key to mastering the pressures and adversities of playing golf is complete and constant imperturbability."
> (If the player can say this slowly and clearly he will become poised, confident and in command.)
> —Paul Bertholy

1. The ability to maintain a strong self-image and confidence as a golfer. (Illus 16-4)
2. The ability to concentrate or focus on the task of the moment. (Illus 16-5)
3. The ability to relax and remain mentally and physically composed in stressful situations.
4. The power of creative imagination to produce positive mental pictures and expectations.
5. The desire to be one's best while having the character to maintain perspective and patience. (Illus 16-6)

Let's take a closer look at these five skills.

SELF-CONCEPT AND CONFIDENCE

The message that confidence can be developed and self-concept can be changed is the good news. There is no bad news, unless one expects that change can take place without practice.

Illus 16-5 PGA professional Dave Glenz stays focused in the present.

Illus 16-6 PGA and U.S. Open champion Larry Nelson is a quiet, humble person, known for his mental toughness and strength of character. (Photo by Lanna Swindler)

Illus 16-4 Believing in yourself is one of golf's most important psychological skills. U.S. Open champion Curtis Strange can attest to it.

Golfers perform in a manner consistent with the image or concept they have as a player. One is born without a self-concept; it is developed. Therefore, it can be changed. If, for example, a player feels he just can't play bunker shots, then his self prophecy will be reinforced by his poor performance. But with instruction which gives him a new understanding of bunker principles, with some minor changes in technique and practice, his performance can change dramatically. Experiencing success allows him to alter his self-concept as a bunker player. If the change is strong enough so that he now feels he's a very good bunker player, he probably will be. Among golfers you'll find those who have a split self-concept. Players who think of themselves as a great ball striker most often *are*. If they consider themselves poor putters, they, again, *are*.

SELF-TALK

Imagine you are playing in a two-day pro-am with three other golfers. It's the 16th hole, a par five; the team is 14 under par, right on the cut-line for the next day's championship flight finals. One more birdie and you'll be in for sure. You play first and hook it out-of-bounds. No problem; you have three partners and besides, Charlie with his 26 handicap has two strokes on this hole. The two other partners, Henry and Joe, hit poor tee shots, but Charlie rifles his longest of the day right down the middle. Henry and Joe manage to make about every mistake possible on the way to the hole and, by the time they've reached the green, each has a difficult putt in the 10- to 15-foot range for net bogey. Charlie, however, has hit his career fairway wood to a spot just in front of the green. He has a simple 60-foot pitch over the bunker to the middle of the green, two putts, and his par makes net eagle. A pep talk, "C'mon Charlie, we need this one . . . you can do it," doesn't work, because Charlie chunks it into the bunker. With more words of encouragement from his partners, Charlie is then reminded that all he has to do is to get it out, on the green,

two-putt, and the team still earns a birdie. Charlie leaves it in the bunker—and another thereafter. One more of the same and he hurriedly skulls it across the green into the pond on the far side. The team makes double bogey. On the way to the next tee, should you react to Charlie's failure by saying, "You choker, you klutz! Every time you have a chance to help the team you blow it! Just a simple pitch but you always stick the club in the ground and the ball goes nowhere. Why don't you learn to hit that shot? Your technique is terrible!"

Of course, you would never say that, but Charlie would—to himself. Golfers do it all the time. Charles does it all the time. Does this verbal berating help Charlie do better the next time he faces the same situation, the dreaded pitch shot over the bunker? No, it only reinforces the negative image and compounds the fear. Fear produces tension, which kills the chance of succeeding. Negative self talk, those derogatory little conversations that go on in one's head, can destroy a good self-concept. Words trigger pictures and pictures are the predictors of performance. By expressing negative statements, you conjure up negative pictures and that is tantamount to failure. Words also affect emotions and attitude. Saying, "I hate this course. I can't play it!" makes you lose desire. You create an attitude of wanting more to *get the round over with than play it*.

Golfers should be kinder to themselves, not so critical. The greatest players in the world miss shots, but they try to dismiss the result quickly and focus on the last good one with that club they hit and how it felt. Jack Nicklaus displayed this use of "selective memory" when, after giving an instruction clinic, he was asked a question from the group. "How do you cure a shank?"

"I don't know; I never hit one," laughed Nicklaus.

> "Most golfers prepare for disaster. A good golfer prepares for success."
> —Bob Toski

f16-2 *The player must be realistic and be aware of mistakes made on the course so he can work them out on the practice tee. But he never dwells on previous failures.*

As he turned to handle the next question, his inquisitor persisted, "I saw you hit one." Then, the man from the audience proceeded to identify the year, the course and the hole. The smile left Jack's face. With an icy stare he turned toward the man and replied, "I don't remember. Next question!" That is selective memory in action: recalling the good while erasing the bad. (f16-2) The average player uses negative psycho-feedback, dwelling on past mistakes and errors, resurrecting failures and programming them into his computer. In contrast, it is said that the great Walter Hagen *never* recounted past mistakes. A positive memory practice protects one's golf ego. This is critical, because champion performers in any sport must believe they are the best. (Illus 16-7) According to Dick Aultman's and Ken Bowden's, *The Methods of Golf's Masters*, the one common characteristic

Illus 16-7 Two giants in the realm of confidence, Sarazen and Hagen. One can almost tell by their look. (Photo by Brown Brothers)

of Harry Vardon, Sarazen, Jones, Hagen, Nelson, Hogan, Snead, Palmer, Nicklaus, et al., was not the grip, aim, setup or swing. It wasn't technique at all. *It was the belief that they could beat anybody in the world.*

GAINING A STRONG SELF-CONCEPT

How do you develop a strong self-concept? One way is through performance, by playing well. But, if people always had to wait until they played well to develop this good image, it might never happen. So, you need to first picture yourself as a good player, a good putter, and a good bunker player, which will in turn, with instruction, practice, and continued positive pictures, come true. *Positive affirmation* (saying good things to oneself) will aid this process of enhancing the self-concept. Even though what you are saying may not be totally true, i.e., "I can chip and pitch the ball as well as anyone in the club," by continuing to repeat the statement, repetition transforms a belief into reality. "Whatever the mind of man can conceive and *believe within reality*, it can do."

CONFIDENCE

When golfers feel good about themselves they exude confidence. It's next to impossible to find an outstanding player who isn't confident about his/her ability to play. Some express their confidence openly and may be considered "cocky" or a "hot dog." Others may mask their confidence or hide behind feigned humility—but they still believe strongly in themselves or they couldn't succeed.

A few years back, Tom Watson bunkered his ball on the 17th hole at The Masters on the final day when he was in contention. He went into the bunker and hardly had the cameras picked him up before he played the shot out, close to the hole, subsequently making the putt. When asked later in a press interview why he didn't take more time—wasn't he worried?—he responded, "There were only three

> "... the tournament professional survives by confidence and so must never allow thoughts of his own fallibility to penetrate his consciousness from any source ... he has to believe in his prowess because that faith in himself is his greatest asset."
> —Arnold Palmer

things that were going to happen: (1) I could knock it close and make the putt, (2) I could knock it farther away and make the putt, or (3) I could knock it in. So why did I need to worry?'' That's confidence.

Watson's retort to his caddy at the 17th hole of Pebble Beach in the U.S. Open in 1982 further substantiates this quality. Facing a precarious lie in the rough to a closely cut pin on a lightning-fast green, Watson's reply when his caddy encouraged him to get it close was, "Get it close, hell! We're going to make it!" And, of course, he did. That's confidence! (Illus 16-8)

Remember, confidence won't produce miracles. One can't stand on a ten-story building

Illus 16-8 Tom Watson showed ultimate concentration and confidence at the time in bolting this tricky pitch to win the U.S. Open. (Photo by Lawrence Levy)

and confidently announce, "I can fly; I can fly," then do it. What confidence will do is let the performer do what he/she is capable of doing. It sharpens the focus, energizes the body, and relaxes the proper muscles to enhance performance. Confidence doesn't guarantee a peak performance, but it allows it.

CONCENTRATION

Concentration is the ability to focus sharply on the task at hand. The task at hand is playing the next golf shot. The time this takes from the moment the player arrives at the ball until he/she propels it forward is usually somewhere between 20 and 40 seconds. That's the amount of time a player needs to sustain concentration prior to each shot. But try to focus on something—an object, an idea, a mental image—and sustain it for 40 seconds without allowing any distracting thoughts or sounds to interfere. It is quite difficult. But it can be learned with practice.

Not all players use the same style of concentrating, just as they don't use the same style for relaxing, visualizing, physical training or swinging. Ben Hogan is used as the classic example of the "player in a cocoon" style, one who remained in narrow focus for an entire eighteen holes. This is like driving one's car in first gear across the country, a task requiring a great deal of self-discipline. It's not easy. Lee Trevino is the diametric opposite, 35 minutes of concentration and 3 hours and 25 minutes of gab with whomever will listen. It's a different style of concentration, but it's still concentration.

Golf requires both broad and narrow focus skills. Broad focus is used to gather information on the wind, terrain, ground firmness, lie, hazards, the opponent, the leader board, the whole picture. Narrow focus is used to shut out all unnecessary thoughts and energies on the task at hand.

Before you play a shot, you must broad focus or analyze the situation, make a decision, then narrow focus by clearly visualizing the shot and

Illus 16-9 Clearly picturing (visualizing) the shot definitely helps in producing it.

swing the club with no additional mental interference. (Illus 16-9) Change to broad focus again in evaluating the result, and then go on to enjoy the surroundings, the people, the day, and the game as you proceed to the next shot.

Going from no focus (socializing) to broad focus (analyzing) to narrow focus (the target) takes discipline. If the player does not make the transition, he may find himself still chit-chatting and not notice a wind direction change. Or, he may be ready to start the backswing while he is still thinking about the pot bunker in front of the green. In both cases, his mind is in the wrong place.

Develop a mental routine prior to each shot to integrate with your normal pre-shot routine. For example: 1) All social conversation stops when the bag arrives at the ball. At that point, the serious analyzing begins, although some general information may have been gathered on the way to the ball. 2) Once the club is selected and in hand, narrow focus begins until all concentration is directed toward producing the motion in the body that becomes oneness with the target. An example of narrow focus in playing a lofted iron to the green might be to visualize the ball as though it were controlled by a parabolic "rainbow-colored" ray that starts at ground level, arches upward, then down into the cup. And, 3) Once the image is fixed, feel the sensation in the body that it knows to be

the perfect response and swing the club with the confidence that what was pictured will now happen. (On all U.S. currency, the statement "In God We Trust" appears. Maybe golf manufacturers should stamp on every club, "In Our Swing We Trust.") All this takes but a short time. Call a "30-second moratorium" on unrelated activity before a shot.

RELAXATION

The greatest destroyer of the golf swing is tension, more specifically, an *undue amount* of muscular contraction. Some muscular contraction is needed simply to stand up; a good deal more to make a powerful golf swing. But, while the prime movers (the agonists) are creating motion in the body, their partners (the antagonists) must be relaxing. The ability to do this is called "differential relaxation," which is

> "Letting go is ineffective unless it is preceded by both physical conditioning and mental training. There is no substitute for the hard work and self-discipline that go into athletic training, but without the ability to let go, the discipline invested can actually be counterproductive."
> —Charles Garfield

shortened into a favorite, frequently heard word—"Relax."

There are two fundamental ways to relax: *mechanical and mental.*

Mechanical

1. *Every hour or so in your waking day, close your eyes, take a deep breath, and slowly let it out.* While exhaling, let a wave of relaxation wash over your body as the tension drains out of each muscle group. To make this practice a habit, do it with some routine activity: when you answer the phone, each time you sit down, when the clock sounds the hour or when you see the hour has changed.
2. *Tighten your muscles as tightly as possible, then relax and feel the tension run out your fingertips and toes.*
3. *Practice deep breathing when facing a potentially stressful situation on the golf course.* Take two or three slow, deep breaths, and with each exhalation let the body become more calm.

Mental

1. *Invest in a simple EMG (electromyographical) biofeedback monitoring device to train you in the ability to reduce muscular tension.* In addition, heart rate, peripheral body temperature, EEG brain waves, and blood flow can all be mentally controlled, but the ability to do so is a learned skill requiring mental practice. The electronic monitoring device contains sensitive amplifiers which can detect even the slightest impulse from a muscular contraction. This is converted to an auditory tone or a visual analog or digital readout. This feedback allows you to recognize increases or decreases in muscular tension. With practice, you can learn how to decrease tension by controlling your thoughts. What a useful skill for golf!
2. For centuries, music has been used both to

> "When winning became the most important goal, losing took on added importance as well. It was the fear of losing which was responsible for my poor judgment . . . for overtrying. From this experience I learned for the first time that my will to win was stronger (more effective) if my mind was detached from the consequences."
> —Timothy Gallwey

calm the "savage breast" and to incite the troops to "charge." Researchers have proved that music can keep us awake, put us to sleep, calm us down, or fire us up. But it's not all the same music. Studies show that music with a rhythm of about one beat per second, matching one's natural breathing pattern, is best for relaxing. Touring professional Richard Zokol made history and caused a stir in golf circles when he wore a portable audiocassette player during his rounds in the Milwaukee Open and turned in the best golf of his professional career. Hypertense golfers should have the opportunity to listen to relaxing music on a portable cassette player to see if it helps them to relax.

3. Progressive relaxation was pioneered by Dr. Edmund Jacobson in the 1930s and is still widely used today. It suggests that you find a quiet place away from any potential noise or distraction and sit in a comfortable chair—a recliner is perfect. Close your eyes, count backwards slowly from 10 to one, and with each descending number let the body go deeper and deeper into a relaxed state. You may wish to use the technique of starting at the top of the head, identifying a specific muscle or area one at a time, totally relaxing each group. Work progressively downward until the whole body has been covered. Once in a completely relaxed state, you may wish to suggest positive habit affirmations such as, "I will stroke my putts with a confident, accelerating motion directly to the target." This added element creates a form of self-

> "The one influence most likely to assure the satisfactory progression of the swing is clear visualization in the player's mind of the movement."
> —Bobby Jones

Illus 16-10 Quieting the mind and relaxing the body can be more important before play than hitting balls.

hypnosis with the habit affirmation including a posthypnotic suggestion. After 10 to 20 minutes in this state, you can count slowly from one to five and return to a normal state of alertness. (Illus 16-10)

One of the oversights golfers often make when thinking of relaxation is to think only of muscles when there is just as great a need for the *mind* to be calm. When the mind is in a harried state, the powers of imagery and concentration are severely impaired. By relaxing, the player enhances his ability to visualize. So, calm the mind as well as the muscles.

VISUALIZATION

Visualization, also referred to as "mental imagery" and "mental rehearsal," as well as by

> "The mind's eye is our imagination. In the mind's eye, people 'see' memories of past events, and imagine future situations."
> —Mike Samuels & Nancy Samuels

other terms, is the creation of pictures or vivid thoughts in one's mind. It's a marvelous power made possible by the human brain. In fact, man is the only creature who doesn't have to rely on past performance to control present action. He has an imagination; he can creatively visualize.

Does visualization work? Just prior to the 1980 Winter Olympics, Soviet sports scientists took four groups of world-class athletes and put each of them on a different training regimen: 1) 100 percent physical training, 2) 75 percent physical training and 25 percent mental training (visualization), 3) 50 percent physical training and 50 percent mental training, 4) 25 percent physical training and 75 percent mental training. Group 4 showed the greatest improvement, followed, in order, by groups 3, 2, and 1. These, of course, are world-class athletes whose physical skills are already highly developed. But visualization training can help anyone to perform closer to his/her optimum skill level, whatever it happens to be at that moment.

To further support its immense potential, consider that visualization is the same tool the Yogi uses to increase or decrease heart rate, stop or start the flow of blood, control otherwise automatic reflexes like peristaltic action, regulate the body's temperature, and more. It is the same tool that is used by countless people who have turned the tables on physical ailments as serious as cancer. Dr. Norman Cousins is probably the most widely known individual to have accomplished the task of curing cancer with positive imagery and thoughts. Visualization is used by gymnasts; divers; downhill skiers; weight lifters; track-and-field athletes; professional football, baseball and basketball players; archers and bowlers. Seek the top athletes in any sport and you'll discover that either by for-

> "When I approach the ball I can visualize the shot I want to hit. When I'm taking the club out of the bag I can still see that shot in my mind. When I'm setting up to the ball I see it, and from there it's just a question of going through the movements with my hands, arms and body and what not, to make the shot I see in my mind's eye. If I'm interrupted when I'm in the process of doing this, I very seldom hit a good shot."
> —Sam Snead

mal training or by experience and intuition, they have learned to create successful performance images and to then match them in play.

How do golfers use mental imagery? The applications are numerous. The most commonly discussed are the images one uses to produce a successful shot. They can be realistic like a yellow spray-painted stripe on the putting green running from the ball into the hole, or surre-

Illus 16-11 A player should create a strong image of the target in his mind, then set the clubface and his body to play to that target and sense or feel the swing that will direct the ball to it. (Photo by John David Heckel)

alistic such as a bright red "V"-shaped plastic trough, similar to a long stimpmeter, with little elf-like creatures in Tinker Bell outfits standing on the sides to see that the ball "stays its course." Don't laugh—use *anything* that works. Visualization can tie the target to the swing. (Illus 16-11)

A player has choices. He can picture the ball's flight and final destination, his own perfect swing or that of another model like Al Geilberger from Sybervision; he can form an image of a technique position in the swing, a swing path line on the ground, or the clubshaft riding on a plywood swing plane. The images are limitless. They can be colorized, and the smell of the grass and crowd noises can be added. Dave Stockton recalls how, during the Tuesday practice round for the PGA Championship at Southern Hills in Tulsa, he strode up the 18th fairway and vividly pictured and heard the crowd applauding as they do when the champion is "coming home" on the final day. The fact that it actually happened to him on that Sunday should not be considered a coincidence.

DESIRE, MOTIVATION AND STRENGTH OF CHARACTER

The motivation to *start* a task may be externally influenced, coming from other people or imposed conditions. But, *the motivation to finish it must come from within. Fan the sparks of desire into flames of passion, for passion is the fuel that drives champions.* Jack Nicklaus, as a junior, never had to be told to practice. The young Gary Player was on the range until the sun set because he chose to be there. Arnold Palmer's constant goal was to be on the golf course. In the words of Palmer's father, "Arnold was the worst shop assistant I ever saw, because he was forever locking the door and going to

> "We use imagination to translate theory into feeling."
> —Percy Boomer

> "... good players aren't worried about what anybody else thinks of them. They don't want to **appear** to be mentally tough. They want to **be** mentally tough. And they do that by playing their own game, shot by shot, at their own pace and tempo."
> —Dr. Bob Rotella

the practice tee when he thought nobody was around."

Some might claim that the desire is either there or it's not, that you can't create desire in someone else. (Illus 16-12) But desire is a natural human characteristic; everyone possesses it.

(For information on characteristics of mentally tough performers and a formula for success, both by Dr. James Loehr, see Appendixes 12-B and 12-C.)

CHARACTER

The final element in developing mental strength is character, as expressed by traits: Mental toughness—Perseverance—Honesty—Dedication—Responsibility.

Seve Ballesteros in his book *Natural Golf* with John Andrisani (Atheneum, 1988) makes this marvelous observation on courage, which so typifies Ballesteros' own behavior. "Many good golfers never live up to their full potential because they never learned the secret of developing a courageous on-course attitude. There are the babies who throw clubs, continually cuss themselves out, sulk, or even walk off the course after one too many bad bounces or bad holes. Their problem is that they expect perfection, whereas the complete and intelligent and courageous golfer respects the game's unpredictability, takes it in stride, and gets on with the job as best he possibly can. Even when he's having an absolutely awful day, this player still gives every shot 100 percent concentration. His final score is his absolute best effort for that day, and biting the bullet like this hardens him for future rounds. Thus, in my opinion, courage is not inherited, but developed through a combination of experience, sheer grit, and determination." (Illus 16-13)

Illus 16-13 Great performers are competitively tough people. They have strong character. PGA Hall of Fame star Tom Watson is a classic example. (Photo by Stephen Szurlej)

Illus 16-12 The desire to practice till the sun is gone . . . is it inherent or can it be developed?

"Twenty years ago I was 28 and broke and that's a hell of a difference." (Commenting on his previous performance level and the importance of desire.)
—Arnold Palmer

COURSE MANAGEMENT

Another part of mental-psychological strength for golf is the acquisition of course-management skills. These are separate from the emotions and personality traits just discussed, though one's emotions definitely play a major role in course management execution. Examples of these skills are: perception, judgment, shot selection, special knowledge (related to the weather conditions, the course, rules, equipment), planning, club selection, preparation and pacing. (Illus 16-14)

Best described, course management might just be "playing smart." That's common-sense smart, not intellectual smart. It's what architect/essayist R. Buckminster Fuller calls *Dymaxion*, "getting the most out of the least."

Entire books have been written on this subject so there is a wealth of opinions available.

At the end of this section is a list of course management ideas, plus more in Appendix 12-D, "Strategies for Getting Your Game Under Control," by PGA member Chuck Cook. But one of the most succinct, realistic and useful descriptions of how a player should manage himself in golf competition comes from the book *Maximum Golf* by former PGA Tour winner John Schlee with Swing Meyer (Acorn Sports, 5816 Shakespeare Road, Columbia, SC 29204).

"In golf we mark our progress by something called a score. For 12 years, my score put food on the table, clothes on my back and a roof over my head. Nobody cared how I played. Nobody cared *what I could've shot.* At round's end, they asked me one question, 'What'd you shoot?'

I'll never forget the Houston Open one year. I was on the 18th green, facing a 60-foot putt for birdie. As I started my pre-shot routine, I noticed a group of my fellow competitors stand-

"I don't think I've ever gotten scared on the golf course. After all, what is there to be afraid of? I'm not going to die or lose my family, not even all my money.
It's first a game."
—Ray Floyd

Illus 16-14 How far is it to carry the water? To lay up? Important course management skills. (Photo by Jeff McBride)

ing outside the scorer's tent, watching me intently. I thought to myself, 'This is neat, all those guys watching me.'

"I left the putt hanging on the lip. As I walked up to tap it in, all I saw were 15 or 20 backs headed for the clubhouse. What's the bottom line? Had I three-putted, they all would have made the cut."

A score is. It is posted, then it dies, no matter the number. Here are the rules of the score:

The Rules of the Score

1. Always have a procedure to a specific target.
2. Play each shot, one shot at a time, to the best of your ability at that moment.
3. When the shot does not please you, forgive and forget, then play the next shot to the best of your ability, at that moment.
4. Continue this procedure until all 18 holes are played.
5. Post the score.
6. After the round, applaud your best efforts, then analyze your mistakes, correct them in your mind, and the round is finished.
7. Compare yourself to no one else—only the golfer you know you can be.
8. Repeat the procedure and post a new score, letting yourself get closer to the edge of your ability.

"We share a common love: the game of golf. Through this connection, I can say in all candor that 'I love you.' And along with that love comes boundless forgiveness. Be your best friend. Then, forgive and forget."

DEVELOPING A PROGRAM

There is certainly one commonality between the acquisition of ball-striking skills and mental-performance skills . . . the necessity for practice. To improve psychological performance, one must practice as diligently as one

does when trying to improve his ball striking. Techniques for habit alteration or behavior modification have been successfully employed in psychological circles for some time. A person wishing to change an existing negative habit or behavior pattern while substituting another, practices the new habit a given number of repetitions for a selected number of consecutive days, some claim as quickly as three to four weeks. By this time, the new habit establishes itself as the accepted pattern. Three to four straight weeks of such practice takes real commitment.

A simple program that employs several of the strategies that can enhance psychological performances is labeled *"The Competitive Edge."* (f 16-3) It consists of six segments of information printed on a card which the player keeps handy so that he or she can read it each day. The recommendation is that it be read a minimum of two times per day for a month. By then, the concepts he/she has been reading should be well established with the player. The text of the card is annotated here as are descriptions of the value and purpose of each of the six points.

MENTAL PRACTICE CARD

Picture yourself doing the following . . . I will close my eyes and begin to relax, imagining that I am in a very restful place—the beach, the

> "When you miss a shot, never think of what you did wrong. Come up to the next shot thinking of what you must do right. . . .
> "The average expert player—if he is lucky—hits six, eight or ten real good shots a round. The rest are good misses."
> —Tommy Armour

f16-3 *Originally appearing as "The Carolina Edge," by Gary Wiren.*

> "Golf is like tennis. The game doesn't really start until the serve gets in."
> —Peter Thompson

> "The woods are full of long hitters."
> —Harvey Penick

woods, a mountain, a meadow or a cozy room on a snowy night. I will then visualize the following written material happening in slow motion, I will read it unhurriedly, with several pauses, to allow for the described feelings to establish themselves.

1. MY BODY WILL BECOME VERY RELAXED. / First, my hands and fingers will feel heavy and relaxed. / Then my forearms will become free of tension. / Then my biceps and shoulders will feel relaxed and very heavy. / My neck will relax and my head will feel heavy. / My facial muscles will become very loose. / Then the back of my neck and upper-back muscles will lose their tension and become relaxed. / My chest and stomach will relax. / Then my legs and buttocks, my thighs, knees and calves will feel free of tension and very relaxed. / I will feel that all of the tension is draining out through my feet and toes. / I feel very calm—calm and relaxed, CALM and CONFIDENT!

    Explanation: Progressive relaxation is a widely practiced skill which enhances one's ability to both think and perform. This exercise is a means of quieting your mind and making it more receptive to the suggestions which follow. After reading this first portion through once, go back and slowly work through the suggestions until your body takes on a calm, relaxed feeling. Two key words for the player to remember in competition are CALM and CONFIDENT.

2. I KNOW WHAT MY BEST SWING LOOKS LIKE AND WILL VISUALIZE IT THREE TIMES. / I KNOW WHAT MY BEST SHOTS HAVE FELT LIKE AND I WILL SENSE THAT FEELING THREE TIMES.

    Explanation: Frequently visualizing and feeling your best swing gives you confidence in how it looks and feels when performing well. If these pictures and feelings are clearly established they will carry over into competitive rounds, even under stress.

3. I AM A GOOD PLAYER. I AM A SMART PLAYER. LIKE A PROFESSIONAL, I KNOW WHAT I CAN DO. I DON'T LET THE COURSE, OR SPECTATORS, INFLUENCE ME AND KEEP ME FROM DOING WHAT I KNOW I CAN DO. I AM TOUGH. I DON'T QUIT AND I DON'T NEED EXCUSES.

    Explanation: Self-affirmation technique. "I'm good," "I'm smart," "I'm tough," etc. If a person says, two times a day for thirty days, "I don't quit," when the temptation to quit does arise, chances are very slim that the player would do so.

4. I HAVE A REGULAR ROUTINE THAT I FOLLOW FOR EACH SHOT . . . WOOD CLUB TEE SHOT, FAIRWAY WOOD, FAIRWAY IRON, PITCH, CHIP, BUNKER SHOT AND PUTT. I WILL PRACTICE THAT ROUTINE UNTIL IT BECOMES AUTOMATIC.

    —Assess the lie.
    —Visualize the shot, its shape, trajectory and where it will finish.
    —Make the club selection.
    —Feel the shot—physically, by practice swinging, or mentally, by rehearsing the physical feel.

> "In golf as in life, the attempt to do something in one stroke that needs two is apt to result in taking three."
> —Walter Camp

> "Everyone has his own choking level, a level at which he fails to play his normal golf. As you get more experienced, your choking level rises."
> —Johnny Miller

— Complete the pre-shot routine: grip, aim, setup.
— Focus on a key thought, cue, position, feel or picture—visualize again.
— Swing the club . . . sending the ball to the target.
— Evaluate the response. If it's a good shot, implant it in the brain. If it's bad, make the corrected response and visualize that result. (See Appendix 12-E for information on charting results.)

Explanation: Developing a routine helps occupy the mind, keeping it focused on positive preparation rather than conjuring up pictures of possible negative results. A routine also lends confidence to what you are doing. "If I do this, this and this, I will come up with the correct response."

Do you have a routine? If one doesn't come to mind quickly, you probably don't have one. You needn't adopt the exact routine presented here but may borrow from it to establish your own.

5. COMPETITIVE GOLF IS A GAME OF NUMBERS. I WILL PLAY AS IF I KNOW THAT. I WILL BE PREPARED TO ANSWER THE QUESTION, "WHAT DID YOU SHOOT?"

Explanation: This statement clarifies the objectives of *competitive* golf. (f16-4) It establishes the goal, to shoot a low number. Good form, long drives, and greens hit in regulation all mean nothing if they were not a positive contribution to the score.

6. I AM NOW GOING TO PLAY IN MY MIND A TEE-TO-GREEN ROUND AT THE COURSE ON WHICH I NEXT WILL

PLAY, SEEING ONLY POSITIVE RESULTS. (Illus 16-15)

Explanation: Positive mental rehearsal of the upcoming competition can make visualization on the course in actual competitive play flow more easily.

ADDITIONAL SUGGESTIONS FOR COURSE MANAGEMENT & PSYCHOLOGY

1. When the tee goes in the ground on the first hole, be ready to start the counting machine; otherwise don't swing.
2. A golfer can't always control the conditions, but he can control how he reacts to them. Neither can he always control winning or losing, only whether or not he did his best. (Illus 16-16)
3. Tournament golf is an illusion. The only difference between the friendly round and

> "I never hit a shot, even in practice, without having a very sharp, in-focus picture of it in my head. It's like a color movie. First, I see the ball where I want it to finish, nice white and setting up high on the bright green grass. Then the scene quickly changes and I see the ball going there; its path, trajectory and shape, even its behavior on landing. Then there's a sort of a fadeout and the next scene shows me making the kind of swing that will turn the previous images into reality."
> —Jack Nicklaus
> (from *Golf My Way*)

f16-4 *Remember, this objective applies to competitive golf. Recreational golf may have entirely different objectives, with score only a secondary consideration.*

> "Once you learn how to strike the ball, course management and psychology become the dominant factors in successfully playing the game. If you can't manage yourself and the course, you can't play."
> —Anon

Illus 16-15 Visualize the holes you will be playing the next day and play them over and over in your mind. (Photo by Jeff McBride)

Illus 16-16 Larry Mize couldn't alter the condition, only do his best and he did, holing this shot to win the Masters. (Photo by Stephen Szurlej)

the competitive round is in the mind.

4. When should a competitor take a chance in golf? When he has weighed the worst possible result and accepts the risk.

5. Shutting down the left hemisphere (cognitive) just before and during each shot and releasing the capabilities of the right hemisphere (affective) is an essential part of the accomplished golfer's mental repertoire.

"Learn one basic shot and stick with it, one you can hit under pressure. If you have a good basic shot you'll rarely have to hit a fancy one."
—Harvey Penick

"Consistency in golf will improve when the player sorts out what is important and what isn't. Decide what has to be done, do it, and don't worry about the rest. Then, realize it's not going to be perfect."
—Anon

---

6. Get yardage on the course whenever possible and begin to develop an understanding of how far you actually hit the ball. (Illus 16-17)

7. The most frequent answer given by the one-year touring professional when asked, "What have you learned?" is, "Patience, learning to stick to a game plan and wait for the birdies and breaks to come."

8. One of the best strategies for relieving tension is to reduce the consequences, put it in perspective. Realize that in the big picture of life it's not that important. Relax and let it fly.

9. The greater the pain which accompanies our mistakes the more vivid the impression. This reality hinders the player facing an often-failed, difficult challenge to keep the positive images flowing.

10. Discipline is the secret of all champions. Discipline means giving things up, mostly things we'd rather be doing.

Illus 16-17 Know the pin locations and tee marker positions to get the correct distance on par 3's.

"A five with a slice will always beat a six by Arnold Palmer."
—Jesse Brown

"I never knew what top golf was like until I turned professional—then it was too late."
—Steve Melnyk

11. An opponent is most vulnerable when he's ahead.
12. Playing in the present is a widely recommended but seldom utilized practice.
13. Trying to "cut the corner" on a modest dogleg around trees or water, when a straight shot would give almost the same result, has caused its share of double bogeys. (See Appendix 12-F)

14. Some ABCs of course management might look like this:

   —Find a level spot on which to tee.
   —Tee up on the side of trouble and hit away from it.
   —Use a tee on par 3's.
   —Note pin locations when you pass a hole.
   —When under pressure play the shot in which you have the most confidence.
   —Play more conservatively and within yourself when facing unusual weather or terrain conditions.

And finally, a solid course management tip that comes from the greatest amateur of all time, Bobby Jones, "It is nothing new or original to say that golf is played one stroke at a time. But it took me many years to realize it."

CHAPTER 17

RULES, ETIQUETTE &
THE PLEASURE OF GOLF

There is so much more to playing golf than striking the ball. There is also more to golf than playing the game. Those who seem to appreciate golf the most, and who do so over an entire lifetime, are the ones who not only play but who have also been immersed in the game's lore. Lore could include a lengthy list of subjects; consider: architecture, equipment, history, agronomy, rules, physical training, swing technique, psychology, stories, tournaments, records and feats, players, courses, collectibles and a marvelous literature describing it all. (Illus 16-1) Golf aficionados seem to develop a feeling for the game that transcends the club they hit on hole #8 or what they shot on the back nine last Sunday. "Learning the game" is more than just learning how to play it.

START WITH THE RULES OF THE GAME . . .

A good place to start is with the rules, which must certainly also include the game's etiquette. Golf can be an intimidating experience for new participants. One of the reasons is that they may be aware that there is a procedural format and behavioral code for golf which is unfamiliar. A golfer can hardly be expected to play by the rules or abide by the courtesies of the game if he doesn't know them. Concerning the rules, some astute observer of golf once noted, "The chances of a golfer making a hole-in-one are much greater than the chances he'll ever read the rule book."

Illus 17-1 It is the knowledge of and adherence to *The Rules of Golf* that allows people to play the same game.

The process is simply one of education. It is interesting to note that in The Netherlands a golfer is not allowed on a Dutch Golf Federation member course unless the player has a "license." To earn a license, golfers must pass certain basic skill performance exams as well as a written test on rules and etiquette. One can imagine that The Netherlands is a country that must have polite, knowledgeable golfers. (See Appendix 13-A for a list of golf's first rules.)

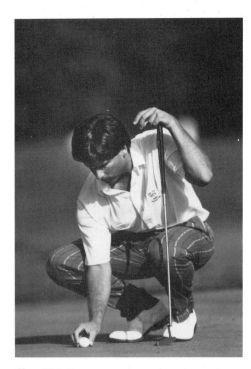

Illus 17-2 Players must know the rules, such as how to mark a ball. (Fred Couples, PGA Tour professional.)

WHY SHOULD I PLAY GOLF?

There are many sources of enjoyment available to a golfer other than "shooting a good round." Here is an edited list of some of golf's joys written by PGA Master Professional John Gerring:

"Why should I play golf? That question is often asked by non-golfers who cannot comprehend why a game has so many participants who love the sport to such a high degree. I feel these nonparticipants do not understand our devotion to a game called GOLF. Maybe these 'reasons' will help you when that question is posed."

A Trip Into Tranquility: Everyone needs a change of scenery. Golf is played on Mother Nature's own turf. For a few brief hours you can change your environment and give your mind a chance to suppress and alleviate all forms of distress. It's better to allow the body's natural protective mechanism to work than to take man-made drugs. (Illus 17-6)

A Change of Pace: It's a game that defies speed and quickened pace. It's four hours with friends all laughing at one another. If four hours is too long, you can always quit at the end of 9 holes and hurry back to the everyday stresses and worries that you were trying to get away from in the beginning.

Builds Character: That it does. You must accept adversity and success within minutes. Not only does the game build character, it also reveals it.

Sociability: One of the few games that allows you to visit and converse with friends as you play.

Illus 17-3 . . . how to drop a ball.

Illus 17-4 . . . what markings on the course mean, such as ground under repair. (Don Smith, PGA of America tournament staff.)

Even-Steven: The handicap system permits everyone to compete on an equal basis. The game embraces *everyone* and lets each player enjoy the competition.

Individualism: Hitting a golf ball does not require any special physique so *everyone is qualified!* "It ain't much . . . but it's all I got . . . I intend to make it work," is the philosophy. The hitting of a golf ball permits a variety of methods, and the only thing that really matters in competition is how one scores.

Decision Making: The game allows each player to make his or her own decisions in a prompt manner. Each correct decision brings on a glow and feeling of satisfaction, and even on a bad day there are a lot of glows *if you look for them.*

It's Close: The golf course is relatively close compared to taking a trip to the beach or mountains to get away. Proximity is one of the game's greatest virtues. (Illus 17-7)

Longevity: "A game of a lifetime." (My father has been a member of the PGA for half a century.) Each year more players are shooting their ages. I have a member who has been playing for 65 years and shot his age at 85, eleven times last year. What a thrill for everyone! (Illus 17-8, 17-9)

Exercise-Calories: Carrying your own bag and walking 18 holes will use up more calories than jogging 3 miles.

Illus 17-6 There are many other rewards in golf if people will only look . . . such as trips into tranquility. Forgetting about life's problems and thinking about golf. (Photo by Jeff McBride)

Illus 17-7 There is probably a beautiful golf course at least within an hour's drive of most people's home.

Illus 17-5 . . . The elation of victory is only one of golf's joys. (Larry Mowry winning the PGA Seniors' Championship. Photo by Richard Dole)

Illus **17-8** You can start when you are young (John Ross, age 16 months) . . . (Photo by Richard Dole)

Illus **17-9** . . . and play for a lifetime like Andrew Carnegie (on the left) and John D. Rockefeller, who shared the mutual love of golf into their 90s.

Competition: At every course there is friendly competition, which can satisfy the competitive urge. There is no lack of competition if you have this type of interest and drive. (Appendixes 13-B and 13-C)

Sportsmanship: The game makes everyone face success and failure with each shot. You must also accept the good breaks with the bad. It gives you the opportunity to exhibit self-discipline in the face of adversity. (Illus 17-10)

Entertainment: Golf is a game! Please don't lose sight of that fact. In this hectic world, we all need to play more games for enjoyment.

Be Yourself: It is one of the few sports you can play alone. You don't need a partner, and if you wish to spend a few hours by yourself, there could not be a better opportunity than a golf course or practice range.

Practice: Many players enjoy the challenge of the golf swing. An hour or two hitting practice balls and working on your technique is a

> "Golf is the only sport where a man (of) sixty can play with the best. That's why golf is such a great game. And no one has ever licked it."
> —Sam Snead

wonderful remedy for tension and distress. There are some players who enjoy practicing even more than playing.

Integrity: One of the few sports that has no referees or umpires. You are on your own, as an honest man or woman. In this way the game allows you to like yourself a lot better if you play by the rules.

"I would like to state that I have seen this great game save a lot of lives from sadness, disaster and even death. All the reasons above will not apply on one given day, but every round of golf can touch lightly on many of them. The game is intoxicating to those who play and, therefore, helps us renew and refresh our outlook towards this complicated world. The game is like a drug, but it's harmless and it's available for everyone to enjoy. It's not just a sport or a game, but a grand way of life."

AN EMOTION THAT DESTROYS

An unfortunate occurrence in golf is a player losing his temper. Getting angry because of what happens on a golf course, no matter what or who caused the anger, is plain nonsense if it destroys what is supposed to be an enjoyable experience. Negative actions by one golfer can

Illus **17-10** A chance to be the sportsman in friendly competition is demonstrated by Lonnie Neilsen and Bob Ford in the finals of the PGA Match Play Championship for club professionals. (Photo by Jeff McBride.)

Illus **17-11** Anger has never been compatible with the essence of golf. (Photo courtesy of U.C. Ferguson)

spoil not only his own pleasure but also damage the fun for the rest of the group. (Illus 17-11)

Dr. Orrin Hunt in his book *The Joy of Golf* suggests seven steps to eliminate temper from the personality while playing. He prefaces them with following comments.

"What are the benefits of eliminating temper? I play better golf; my friends and family have rejoined me and, best of all, I feel *good* about myself. I truly do experience *Joy* when I play golf!"

"If you want to eliminate temper from your personality while playing golf (and, incidentally, enjoy the benefits of that absence that carries over into the rest of your life), do the following:

Step 1—Make a decision right now to commit yourself to the conviction that you are in charge of yourself.

Step 2—Subscribe to the concept that *you* and you alone own your feelings. Nothing outside of yourself can dictate to you how you feel, unless you give it or "them" permission to do so.

Step 3—Temper in all forms, including hostility, irritation, anger at yourself and anger at others (persons, things or circumstances) will be eliminated from your personality.

Step 4—On each round of golf you play from now on, mark a "T" on your personal score card at every hole where you become even slightly perturbed.

Step 5—Temporarily stop playing for scores. Your new game is to play for zero

"The person who enjoys his work as much as he does his hobby is a genius. The golfer who lets frustration destroy the pleasure of the game is a fool."
—Anon

> "All my life I wanted to play golf like Jack Nicklaus, and now I do."
> —Paul Harvey (News commentator after Jack Nicklaus shot an 83 in the British Open)

"T's" on your score card. If you have even one, you lose the round. If you have none, you win!

Step 6—Continue playing for a total absence of "T's" until you accomplish at least three "T"-free rounds. Then resume your usual score-conscious efforts.

Step 7—Never let a "T" occur on your score card again.

All you have to gain is the Joy of Golf in its *real* sense. All you have to lose is your temper."

DEVELOP A REALISTIC EXPECTATION LEVEL

Golf is a simple game: knock a ball from here to there with a stick, and hole it out. Simple, yes; but not easy. It just looks easy, particularly on television when one watches the greatest players in the world hit incredible shots in routine fashion. When the show leaves the air, what happens? The golfing viewers flock to their courses immediately after switching off the set. They have spent two hours watching professionals who have practiced exhaustively since they were in grade school, who have had the finest teachers in the world, who play with the best equipment, who compete three out of every four weeks during the year, and who feel that par is a bad round. In comparison, the TV viewer is lucky to squeeze in two games a week,

> "Golf etiquette is kind of like the second verse of the national anthem—good stuff but read by practically nobody."
> —Herb Graffis

Illus 17-12 Tommy Armour had a sensible philosophy for playing golf.

practices infrequently, takes too much of his instruction from friends, and uses clubs that are not matched to his swing. Yet this golfer somehow expects to perform like those players he saw on TV. How much more healthy and enjoyable it is to have a reasonable level of expectation. The over-competitive mind-set is unrealistic and puts too much pressure on what should be a *more relaxed* experience. No player is ever going to be perfect, so golfers should become familiar with the words of Tommy Armour who said, "Missing simple shots is part of being human." Golfers are going to err so they should be prepared for it. (Illus 17-12) (For an enjoyable discourse on keeping things in perspective, see Appendix 13-D.)

GETTING THE MOST FROM THE EXPERIENCE

Let's put things in perspective. The vast majority of golfers don't play for a living; they play for enjoyment. So the question is, "How are you going to get the most enjoyment from your golf?"

One approach is to put all your eggs in the basket of scoring. Sure, you want to play well, and when you do, you *will* enjoy it more. But if you only have fun when you are playing well, you are going to have fun about 10 percent of the time.

You should look for other elements of the game from which you can derive satisfaction and pleasure other than a low number on a scorecard. Playing with people you enjoy is worth a lot; so is a beautiful day; a break from the routine; a walk among the trees; a bird, a flower, a butterfly, a beautiful setting; appreciating a good shot by an opponent; a laugh, a challenge, a long putt that drops, no matter that it's for a seven. (Appendixes 13-E, 13-F) You should not let the beautiful setting disappear because you've made a double bogey. We as people are not our golf games. How we react to our golf performance, however, may reflect WHAT *we really are.* (f17-1)

ENJOY—IT'S A WINNING ATTITUDE

It is an incontrovertible fact that world-class athletes perform best in a state which may be described as "enjoying the experience" . . . even in the heat of battle. Adding a little Fuzzy Zoeller "walk in the park" approach to the game may not only make it more fun, it may also make it better.

If you aren't getting what you want from your golf, then change . . . Change something. Don't get stuck in a tedious golfing rut. Why not play with people who are fun? Try various forms of competitive play: best ball, scramble,

> "I play for fun, friends, exercise and fresh air."
> —Bill Roland, golf writer

f17-1   *In* Personal Par, *a book written by Barbara Keogh and Carol Smith, a psychological system to enjoy golf more is presented for women, but could apply to anyone.*

> "Golf is the toy department of life. So it should be enjoyable."
> —Herb Graffis

> "Golf is the only game having its etiquette modified in 12 articles of conduct representing several centuries of civilized experience."
> —Anon

Scotch foursome, mixed foursomes, alternate shot, match play rather than always for medal score. Notice and appreciate the beauty of the surroundings. Contrast the relaxed atmosphere to what is found in most working environments. If playing in the middle of the day, riding a golf car in a competitive event with a group you don't really like, at a course that plays too long to post a decent score and isn't enjoyable, then you should change! Next time tee off at 7:30 a.m. or late in the day, walk with one or two friends, play for fun from the senior tees. If that's still not it, try some other combination; but find that special blending of elements so you can answer more often, "I really had a good time."

It's your golf life. Live it the way you want and have fun!

POSTSCRIPT—THE PURPOSE OF IT ALL

What is the purpose of golf? What is the value of this game to an individual—to the world?

The purpose of golf can be included within the answer, "In life, what is the purpose of play?" Human beings have a fundamental desire for play which is as old as man himself. Toys have been found among the ruins of ancient Babylonia, China and Egypt with evidence of various forms of games or contests to match. *Play is what people do for fun or enjoyment.* An adult enjoys it in his leisure away

> "Golf is the Esperanto of sport. All over the world golfers talk the same language . . ."
> —Henry Longhurst

from work, a child as a part of life growing up. Golf is simply one of those play choices.

These are various forms of play:

1. Active motor play such as running, jumping, swimming and sports like golf.
2. Passive intellectual play such as cards, chess and crossword puzzles.
3. Sensory play, or being a spectator of a game or sport.

Not all people enjoy active motor play, therefore participation in sports does not appeal to them. This is something we must acknowledge . . . golf isn't for everyone. Others, who generally do like sports, might find golf not active enough; they prefer more rapid-moving or physically demanding games. But for millions of people around the world golf has a compelling attraction. Some golfers seek the solitude of the game and don't wish to be forced into competition with others; some like the walk; others want "action"—competition to show who is the better performer; some may like golf because it gives them the chance to meet people and socialize; others just like to be outdoors in a beautiful setting. It's the blend of all of these benefits and more which is appealing. However golfers find their joy, whatever it is that creates excitement at the prospect of play, golf is their chosen game. *What a great choice!*

> "Golf is like fishing and hunting. What counts is the companionship and fellowship of friends, not what you catch or shoot."
> —George Archer

PHOTO GALLERY
Pictures of the Game's Greatest Players

PHOTO GALLERY

An outstanding collection of swing pictures is presented in this section. By studying these closely, two conclusions can be made:

1. There are many common positions and movements among golf's great players.
2. There are many variations of standard fundamentals which demonstrate a great deal of individual differences.

So while there are highly desirable preferences there is no one specific swing which fits all or which all must fit.

SELECTION OF PLAYERS

The criteria for selecting players to include in this gallery of photos was:

1. Level of achievement during playing career.
2. Body type—(seeking variety).
3. Exceptional or unique style.
4. Availability of pictures.

We purposefully have excluded any remarks from the picture pages themselves. This is to let readers come to their own conclusions about what they see. The reader may wish to write his/her comments in the book and see if the thoughts correspond with those of others. To start thinking about what to look for it is suggested that certain positions and moves be observed to gain insight into the player's similarities as well as differences. Note the following:

Address

— Position of hands on the grip, how far down, to what degree rotated.
— Ball position relative to the left foot, left shoulder and centerline of the body.
— Hand position at address relative to the ball, clubhead, left arm and left thigh.
— Width of foot placement and angle of left and right foot from perpendicular.
— Apparent lateral weight distribution, separately for lower body and upper body.
— Angle of forward body inclination at hips.
— Distance from a ball and arm extension.
— Amount of knee flex.
— Relationship of right elbow to left (above, beneath, even).
— Head and chin position.
— Body and foot alignment (open, closed, square).

Backswing

— Relationship of club to left arm.
— Point at which wrists begin to cock.
— Angle of club when left arm is horizontal or parallel with the ground.
— Degree of rotation of clubface.
— Sequence of motion.
— Amount of upper and lower body lateral motion.

Top of Swing

— Relation of club to ground for that particular club, iron or wood. (Short of horizontal, past horizontal, or right on horizontal?)
— Left knee pointed ahead, even or behind the ball?

—Head and centerline of upper body behind, even or ahead of the ball?

—Position of right knee?

—Amount of shoulder turn, hip turn and shoulder turn related to hip turn.

Top of Swing (down line view)

—Left wrist cupped, flat or bowed?

—What is the position of the clubface . . . open, square, closed?

—Right leg, more flexed, the same as at address, or straightened?

—Angle of forwarded body inclination increased, decreased or the same as at address?

—Club shaft parallel to target line, or pointed either right or left?

—Swing plane flat, medium or upright? Does it change from the backswing to the forward swing? How?

—Right elbow pointing horizontal, downward or in between?

Forward Swing

—What is the first move in the forward swing?

—At the beginning of the forward swing, is the angle between the left arm and clubshaft increased, decreased or the same?

—How long into the forward swing do the left arm and clubshaft retain at least a 90-degree angle?

—Does the head move?

—Does the body stay relatively level or bow toward the target?

—Does the right heel leave the ground before impact?

Forward Swing (down line view)

—The forward swing plane: is it under, over or the same as the backswing plane?

—Is the swing path from the inside, on line or outside the intended flight line?

—Where is the right elbow?

Impact

—What is the position of the clubface?

—Is the left arm extended or bent?

—Where is the lower body weight in relation to the centerline—the upper body weight?

—What is the position of the head?

—Is the left knee straight or flexed?

—Is the right heel down or in the air?

—How far left have the shoulders turned and the hips rotated?

—Is the upper body level or tilted—how much?

—Has the right arm extended fully yet?

Follow-Through

—When does the right arm go into full extension?

—What does the left arm do when the right is extended?

—At left hip height on the follow-through, what is the position of arms, hands and clubface?

—Where is the player's weight at that point?

—What is the player's head position at that point?

—In the finish position has the grip opened or stayed closed around the club?

—Is the player's body position at the finish more vertical or arched?

—Does the club finish high or move around?

—Is the left wrist still flat or has it cupped?

—Where does the body point?

—What is the position of the feet?

After studying the pictures and these questions, the reader may wish to conjecture on whether or not there has been an evolution in the golf swing, comparing the swings from various eras.

James Braid

George Duncan

H.H. Hilton

Willie Park

J.H. Taylor

Harry Vardon

Cecil Leitch

Lady Margaret Scott

Jim Barnes*

*First American PGA champion, 1916

Bobby Jones

Walter Hagen

Gene Sarazen

Joyce Wethered

Tommy Armour

Ben Hogan

Photos by Chuck Brenkus

Byron Nelson

Photos by Chuck Brenkus

Sam Snead

Helen Hicks

Isao Aoki

Paul Azinger

Seve Ballesteros

Miller Barber

Miller Barber

Mark Calcavecchia

Billy Casper

Photos by Chuck Brenkus

Bob Charles

Photos by Chuck Brenkus

Ben Crenshaw

Nick Faldo

Raymond Floyd

Hale Irwin

Tom Kite

Gene Littler

Photos by Chuck Brenkus

Davis Love III

Jack Nicklaus

Photos by Chuck Brenkus

Greg Norman

Charley Owens*

*Cross-handed grip

Arnold Palmer

Gary Player

Photos by Chuck Brenkus

Craig Stadler

Payne Stewart

Curtis Strange

Lee Trevino

Bob Tway

Bob Tway

Tom Watson

Amy Alcott

Pat Bradley

Beth Daniel

Nancy Lopez

Patty Sheehan

Photos by Dost & Evans

Kathy Whitworth

Mickey Wright

Photos by Chuck Brenkus

BIBLIOGRAPHY

ADAMSON, Alistair B. *Allan Robertson—Golfer, His Life and Times*, Worcestershire: Grant Books, 1985.

ADWICK, Ken. *Dictionary of Golf*, New York: Drake Publishers, Inc., 1974.

ARMOUR, Tommy. *A Round of Golf With Tommy Armour*, New York: Simon & Schuster, 1959.

—. *Tommy Armour's ABC's of Golf*, New York: Simon & Schuster, 1967.

—. *How To Play Your Best Golf All The Time*, New York: Simon & Schuster, 1953.

ARNOLD, A.E. *Putting and Spared Shots*, London: Mathuan and Co., Ltd., 1939.

AULTMAN, Dick, & BOWDEN, Ken. *The Method of Golf's Masters*, New York: Coward, McCann & Geoghegan, Inc., 1975.

—. *The Square-to-Square Golf Swing*, New York: Golf Digest, Inc., 1970.

BAIRD, Archie. *Golf on Gullane Hill.* Edinburgh: MacDonald Printers, Ltd., 1982.

BAILEY, C.W., M.A. *The Brain and Golf*, Boston: Small, Maynard & Co., 1924.

BALLARD, Jimmy. *How to Perfect Your Golf Swing*, Norwalk, CT: Golf Digest/Tennis Inc., 1981.

BALLESTEROS, Seve, with John Andrisani. *Natural Golf*, New York: Atheneum, 1988.

BARNES, James M. *Picture Analysis of Golf Strokes*, Philadelphia: J.B. Lippincott Co., 1919.

BARRETT, David. *Fit to Be Tired*, Golf Magazine, January 1986.

BELDMAN, George W. & Taylor, J.H. *Golf Faults Illustrated*, London: George Newnes, Ltd., 1905.

—. *The World's Champion Golfers*, London: Their Art Disclosed by the Ultra-Rapid Camera, Photochrom Co., 1924.

BELL, Peggy Kirk. *A Woman's Way to Better Golf*, New York: E.P Dutton & Co., Inc., 1966.

BERG, Patty. *Golf for Women Illustrated*, London: Cassell & Co., Ltd., 1951.

BERNARDONI, Gus. *Golf God's Way*, Carol Stream, IL: Creation House, 1978.

BLAKE, Mindy. *The Golf Swing of the Future*, London: Souvenir Press Ltd., 1972.

—. *Golf, the Technique Barrier*, London: The Souvenir Press, Ltd., 1978.

BOOMER, PERCY. *On Learning Golf*, New York: Alfred P. Knopf, 1961.

BOROS, Julius. *How to Play Golf with an Effortless Swing*, Englewood Cliffs, NJ: Doubleday & Co., Inc., 1964.

—. *Swing Easy, Hit Hard*, New York: Harper & Row, 1965.

BRAID, James. *Advanced Golf or Hints and Instruction for Progressive Players*, Philadelphia, PA: George W. Jacobs Co., 1927.

BREWER, Gay. *Gay Brewer Shows You How to Score Better Than You Swing*, Connecticut: Golf Digest, Inc., 1968.

BRISTOL–MYERS. *Sports Injuries, an Aid to Prevention and Treatment*, 1982 booklet.

BROER, Marion R. & ZERNICKE, Ronald F., Ph.D. *Efficiency of Human Movement*, Philadelphia: W. B. Saunders Co., 1979.

BROWNING, Robert H.K. *A History of Golf*, New York: E.P. Dutton & Co., Inc., 1955.

—. *Moments with Golfing Masters*, London: Methuen & Co., Ltd., 1932.

BURKE, Jack. *The Natural Way to Better Golf*, New York: Bantam Books, 1954.

CARROLL, John R., M.D. & GIOE, Terrance, M.D. "Professional Golfers and the Price They Pay," *Physicians and Sports Medicine*, Vol. 10, No. 7, July 1982.

CASPER, Billy. *Golf Shotmaking with Billy Casper*, Garden City, NY: Doubleday & Co., Inc., 1966.

CHAMBERLAIN, Peter. *Good Golf*, Gothenburg, Sweden: Queen Anne Press, 1985.

CHARLES, Bob, with GANEM, Roger P. *Left-Handed Golf*, Englewood Cliffs, NJ: Prentice–Hall, Inc., 1965.

CHIEGER, Bob & SULLIVAN, Pat. *Inside Golf*, New York: Atheneum, 1985.

CLARK, ROBERT, ed. *Golf, A Royal and Ancient Game*, London: MacMillan & Co., 1899.

CLEVELAND, Charles B. *Approaching and Putting*, New York: Thomas Y. Crowell Co., 1953.

COCHRAN, Alastair & STOBBS, John. *The Search for the Perfect Swing*, Philadelphia: J.B. Lippincott Co., 1968.

COTTON, Henry. *My Golfing Album*, London: Country Life, Ltd., 1959.

—. *Study the Game with Henry Cotton*, London: Country Life, Ltd., 1964.

—. *This Game of Golf*, London: Country Life, Ltd., 1984.

CRANFORD, Peter G., Ph.D. *The Winning Touch in Golf*, New York: Bramhall House, 1961.

DANTE, Jim & ELLIOTT, Len. *The Nine Bad Shots of Golf*, New York: McGraw–Hill Book Co., Inc., 1947.

DANTE, Joe & ELLIOTT, Len. *The Four Magic Moves to Winning Golf*, New York: McGraw–Hill, 1962.

DARO, August F. with GRAFFIS, Herb. *The Inside Swing: Key to Better Golf*, New York: Thomas Y. Crowell Co., 1972.

DAVIES, Peter. *Davies' Dictionary of Golfing Terms*, New York: Simon & Schuster, 1980.

DAWKINS, George. *Keys to the Golf Swing*, Englewood Cliffs, NJ: Prentice-Hall, 1976.

DEGARMO, Louis. *Play Golf and Enjoy It*, New York: Greenburg, 1954.

DEMARET, Jimmy; SARAZEN, Gene & SUGGS, Louise. *Golf Magazine's Your Short Game*, New York: Harper & Row, 1962.

DEMARET, Jimmy; SARAZEN, Gene and BELL, Peggy Kirk, eds. *Golf Magazine's Your Long Game*, New York: Harper & Row, 1964.

DEVLIN, Bruce. *Play Like the Devil*, Garden City, New York: Doubleday & Co., 1970.

DOBEREINER, Peter. *The Glorious World of Golf*, New York: McGraw–Hill Book Co., 1973.

DUNN, John Duncan. *Natural Golf*, New York: G.P. Putnam's Sons, 1931.

DUNN, Seymour. *Golf Fundamentals*, Lake Placid, NY: Seymour Dunn, 1922.

EAST, J. Victor. *Better Golf in 5 Minutes*, Englewood Cliffs, NJ: Prentice–Hall, Inc., 1956.

ELLIS, Wes, Jr. *All-Weather Golf*, London: D. Van Nostrand Co., Ltd., 1967.

EVANS, Chick. *Golf For Boys & Girls*, Chicago, IL: Windsor Press, 1954.

EVANS, Webster, comp., *Encyclopedia of Golf*, New York: St. Martin's Press, Inc., 1974.

FINSTERWALD, Dow. *Fundamentals of Golf*, Ronald Sports Library, New York: The Ronald Press Co., 1961.

FISHMAN, Lew, ed. *Shortcuts to Better Golf*, New York: Harper & Row Publishers, Inc., 1979.

FORD, Doug. *Getting Started in Golf*, New York: Sterling Publishing, 1964.

GALLWEY, Timothy W. *The Inner Game of Golf*, New York: Random House, Inc., 1981.

GALVANO, Phil. *Secrets of Accurate Putting & Chipping*, Englewood Cliffs, NJ: Prentice–Hall, Inc., 1957.

—. *Secrets of the Perfect Golf Swing*, Englewood Cliffs, NJ: Prentice–Hall, Inc., 1961.

GEIBERGER, Al with DENNIS, Larry. *Tempo, Golf's Master Key, How to Find It, How to Keep It*, Norwalk, CT: Golf Digest, Inc., 1980.

GIBSON, Nevin H. *The Encyclopedia of Golf*, New York: A.S. Barnes & Co., 1958.

GOLF DIGEST. *Instant Golf Lessons*, Norwalk, CT: 1978.

GOLF DIGEST (compiled by the editors). *How to Solve Your Golf Problems*, Norwalk, CT: Grosset & Dunlap, 1963.

GOLF DIGEST (compiled by the editors). *80 Five-Minute Golf Lessons:* Englewood Cliffs, NJ: Prentice–Hall, Inc., 1968.

GOLF DIGEST, ed., trilogy: SNEAD, Sam, *The Driver Book*; ROSBURG, Bob, *The Putter Book*; FORD, Doug, *The Wedge Book*, South Norwalk, CT: Golf Digest, Inc., 1963.

GOLF MAGAZINE. *Handbook of Putting*, NY: Harper & Row Publishers, 1973.

GOLF WORLD. *Improve Your Golf*, London: Willow Books, 1986.

GRAFFIS, Herb. *World of Golf*, New York: Esquire, Inc., 1965.

—. *The PGA, The Official History of the Professional Golfers' Association of America.* New York: Thomas Y. Crowell & Co., 1975.

GREGSON, Gene. *Hogan, The Man Who Played for Glory*, Englewood Cliffs, NJ: Prentice–Hall, Inc., 1978.

GRIMSLEY, Will. *Golf, Its History, People & Events*, Englewood Cliffs, NJ: Prentice–Hall, Inc., 1966.

GROUT, Jack. *Jack Grout's Golf Clinic*, North Palm Beach, FL: Athletic Institute, 1985.

HAHN, Paul. *Paul Hahn Shows You How to Play Trouble Shots*, New York: David McKay Co., Inc., 1965.

HAMILTON, David. *Early Aberdeen Golf*, London, Glasgow & Oxford, 1985.

—. *Early Golf in Glasgow 1589–1787*, Oxford: Patrick Press, 1985.

HANDY, Ike S. *How to Hit a Golf Ball Straight*, San Francisco: Cameron & Co., 1967.

HANDY, Ike S. *It's the Damned Ball*, Chicago, IL: Twentieth Century Press, 1956.

HARRIS, Robert. *Sixty Years of Golf*, London: Batchworth Press, 1953.

HAULTAIN, Arnold. *The Mystery of Golf*, New York: St. Martins Press, 1979.

HAY, Alex. *The Mechanics of Golf*, New York: St. Martins Press, 1979.

—. *The Handbook of Golf*, Salem, NH: Salem House, 1985.

HAY, James G. & REID, T. Gavin. *Anatomy, Mechanics and Human Motion*, Englewood Cliffs, NJ: Prentice–Hall, 1988.

HEBRON, Michael. *See and Feel the Inside Move the Outside*, Smithtown, NY: Private publication, 1984.

HEISE, Jack. *How You Can Play Better Golf, Using Self-Hypnosis*, Hollywood, CA: Wilshire Book Co., 1963.

HENDERSON, Ian & STIRK, David. *Golf in the Making*, London: Henderson & Stirk, Ltd. 1979.

—, —. *The Complete Golfer*, England: Henderson & Stirk, Ltd., 1982.

HENDRY, W. Garden. *The Dynamic Anatomy of the Golf Swing*, Littleton, MA: PSG Publishing Co., 1985.

HILTON, Harold H. *My Golfing Reminiscences*, London: James Nisbet & Co., Ltd., 1907.

HOGAN, Ben. *Power Golf*, New York: A. S. Barnes & Co., 1948.

—. *Five Lessons: The Modern Fundamentals Of Golf*, New York: A. S. Barnes & Co., 1957.

HOGAN, Charles with DALSEM, Van & DAVIS, Susan. *5 Days to Golfing Excellence*, Lake Oswego, OR: Merl Miller & Associates, Ltd., 1986.

HOWE, Winston and LAMPLEY, Will. *Swing Dynamics*, Denver, CO: Privately published by Dye Designs, 1988.

HUNT, Orrin T., Ph.D. *The Joy of Golf*, Jacksonville, FL: Convention Press, 1977.

HUTCHINSON, Horace G. *The Badminton Library: Golf*, London: Longmans, Green, & Co., 1895.

—. *The British Golf Links*, London: J. S. Virtue & Co., Ltd, 1897.

HYSLOP, Theo B. *Mental Handicaps in Golf*, London: Bailliere, Tindall & Co., 1927.

JACOBS, John. *Practical Golf*, New York: Quadrangle Books, Inc., 1972.

—. *Play Better Golf*, New York: Arco Publishing Co., Inc., 1972.

JOBE, Frank W., M.D. & MOYNES, Diane R. *Thirty Exercises for Better Golf*, Inglewood, CA: Champion Press, 1989.

JONES, Ernest & KEELER, O.B. *Down the Fairway*, New York: Minton, Balch, & Co., 1927.

JONES, Ernest & Keeler, O.B. *Down the Fairway*, New York: Minton, Balch, & Co., 1927.

JONES, Robert Tyre. *Bobby Jones on Golf*, Garden City, NY: Doubleday & Co., Inc., 1966.

A KEEN HAND. *The Golfer's Manual*, New

York: Vantage Press, 1985, originally published in 1857.

KELLEY, Homer. *The Golfing Machine*, Seattle, WA: Star Systems Press, 1971.

KEOGH, Barbara K. & SMITH, Carol E. *Personal Par, a Psychological System of Golf for Women*, Champaign, IL: Human Kinetics Publishers, Inc., 1985.

KING, Leslie. *The Master Key to Success at Golf*, New York: Harper & Row Publishers, Inc., 1963.

KOSTIS, Peter. *The Inside Path to Better Golf*, Norwalk, CT: Golf Digest/Tennis, Inc., 1982.

LOCKE, Bobby. *Bobby Locke on Golf*, New York: Simon & Schuster, 1954.

LOEHR, James E., Ed.D. *Mental Toughness Training for Sports, Achieving Athletic Excellence*, Lexington, MA: The Stephen Greene Press, 1982.

LOHREN, Carl with DENNIS, Larry. *One Move to Better Golf*, Norwalk, CT: Golf Digest, Inc., 1975.

LOW, George with BARKOW, Al. *The Master of Putting*, New York: Atheneum, 1986.

MacDONALD, Bob. *Golf*, Chicago, IL: The Wallace Press, 1927.

MacDONALD, Charles B. *Scotland's Gift, Golf*, New York: Charles Scribner's Sons, 1928.

McCARTHY, Coleman. *The Pleasures of the Game*, New York: The Dial Press, 1977.

McGURN, Robert & WILLIAMS, S.A. *Golf Power in Motion, A Golf Digest Book*, Englewood Cliffs, NJ: Prentice–Hall, Inc., 1967.

MAGILL, Richard A. *Motor Learning: Concepts and Application*, Dubuque, IA: W. C. Brown, 1989.

MARTIN, H.B. *Fifty Years of American Golf*, New York: Argosy–Antiquarian, Ltd., 1936.

—. *Great Golfers in the Making*, New York: Dodd, Mead & Co., 1932.

MARTIN, John Stuart. *The Curious Story of the Golf Ball, Mankind's Most Fascinating Sphere*, New York: Horizon Press, 1968.

MERRINS, Eddie. *Swing the Handle, Not the Clubhead*, Norwalk, CT: Golf Digest, Inc., 1973.

METZ, Richard. *The Graduated Swing Method*, New York: Charles Scribner's Sons, 1981.

MICHAEL, Tom & the Editors of Golf Digest. *Golf's Winning Stroke, Putting*, New York: Coward–McCann, Inc., 1967.

MIDDLECOFF, Cary. *The Golf Swing*, Englewood Cliffs, NJ: Prentice–Hall, Inc., 1974.

MISTER X. *More Golf Lessons with Mister X*, Englewood Cliffs, NJ: Prentice–Hall, Inc., 1972.

MOORE, Charles W. *The Mental Side of Golf*, New York: Horace Liveright, 1929.

MORLEY, David C., M.D. *The Missing Links*, New York: Atheneum/SMI, 1976.

MORRISON, Alex J. *Better Golf Without Practice*, New York: Simon & Schuster, 1940.

—. *A New Way to Better Golf*, New York: Simon & Schuster, 1932.

MORRISON, Ian. *The Hamlyn Encyclopedia of Golf*, London: Hamlyn Publishing Co., 1986.

MURDOCH, Joseph S.F. *The Library of Golf*, Detroit, MI: Gale Research Co., 1968.

MURPHY, Michael. *Golf in the Kingdom*, New York: Dell Publishing Co., Inc., 1972.

NELSON, Byron. *Winning Golf*, New York: A.S. Barnes & Co., 1946.

NETTLETON, Brian. *You're the Coach*, Canberra: Australian Government Publishing Services, 1980.

NIBLICK (pseud.). *Hints to Golfers*, Salem, MA: Salem Press, 1902.

NICHOLS, Bobby. *Never Say Never: The Psychology of Winning Golf*, New York: Fleet Publishing Co., 1965.

NICKLAUS, Jack. *The Full Swing*, Norwalk, CT: Golf Digest/Tennis, Inc., 1984.

—. *My 55 Ways to Lower Your Golf Score*, New York: Simon & Schuster, 1964.

—, with BOWDEN, Ken. *Golf My Way*, New York: Simon & Schuster, 1974.

—, —. *Jack Nicklaus' Lesson Tee*, Norwalk, CT: Golf Digest, Inc., 1977.

NIEPORTE, Tom & SAUERS, Don. *Mind over Golf*, Garden City, NY: Doubleday & Co., Inc., 1968.

NORWOOD, Joe with SMITH, Marilynn & BLICKER, Stanley. *Golf-O-Metrics*, Garden City, NY: Doubleday & Co., Inc., 1978.

NOVAK, Joe. *Golf Can Be an Easy Game*, Englewood Cliffs, NJ: Prentice–Hall, Inc., 1962.

—. *How to Put Power and Direction in Your Golf*, New York: Prentice–Hall, Inc., 1954.

OLMAN, John M. & OLMAN, Morton W. *The Encyclopedia of Golf Collectibles*, Florence, AL: Books Americana, Inc., 1985.

PALMER, Arnold. *My Game and Yours*, New York: Simon & Schuster, 1965.

—, & DOBEREINER, Peter. *Arnold Palmer's Complete Book of Putting*, New York: Atheneum, 1986.

PARK W., Jr. *The Art of Putting*, Edinburgh: J & J Bray & Co., 1920.

—. *The Game of Golf*, London: Longmans, Green & Company, 1896.

PELZ, Dave with MASTRONI, Nick. *Putt Like the Pros*, New York: Harper & Row, 1989.

PEPER, George, ed. *Golf in America: The First Hundred Years*, New York: Harry N. Abrams, Inc., 1987.

—. *Scrambling Golf: How to Get out of Trouble and into the Cup*, Englewood Cliffs, NJ: Prentice–Hall, 1977.

PLAYER, Gary. *Positive Golf*, New York: McGraw–Hill Book Co., 1967.

—. *Gary Player's Golf Secrets*, Englewood Cliffs, NJ: Prentice–Hall, Inc., 1966.

—. "The Physically Fit Will Play Better Golf," *Golf Magazine, February 1974.*

POTTER, Stephen. *Golfmanship*, New York: McGraw–Hill Book Co., 1968.

PRATT, William A., M.D. & JENNISON, Kenneth. *Year-Around Conditioning for Part-Time Golfers*, New York: Atheneum/SMI, 1979.

PRICE, Charles. *The World of Golf*, New York: Random House, 1962.

PUCKETT, Earl. *295 Golf Lessons by Billy Casper*, Northfield, IL: Digest Books, Inc., 1973.

REES, Dai. *Dai Rees on Golf*, New York: A. S. Barnes & Co., Inc., 1960.

REVOLTA, Johnny & CLEVELAND, Charles B. *Johnny Revolta's Short Cuts to Better Golf*, New York: Thomas Y. Crowell Co., 1956.

ROSBURG, Bob. *The Putter Book*, Norwalk, CT: Golf Digest, Inc., 1963.

ROTELLA, Robert J. & BUNKER, Linda K. *Mind Mastery for Winning Golf*, Englewood

Cliffs, NJ: Prentice–Hall, Inc., 1981.

RUNYAN, Paul. *Paul Runyan's Book for Senior Golfers*, New York: Dodd, Mead & Co., 1962.

—, with AULTMAN, Dick. *The Short Way to Lower Scoring*, Norwalk, CT: Golf Digest, Inc., 1979.

SANDERS, Doug. *Compact Golf*, New York: Thomas Y. Crowell, Co., 1964.

SARAZEN, Gene. *Better Golf After Fifty*, New York: Harper & Row, 1967.

SCHLEE, John with MEYER, D. Swing. *Maximum Golf*, Columbia, SC: Acorn Sports, 1986.

SCHON, Leslie. *The Psychology of Golf*, Boston, MA: Small, Maynard & Co., 1923.

SHANKLAND, Craig; SHANKLAND, Dale; LUPO, Dom & BENJAMIN, Roy. *The Golfer's Stroke-Saving Handbook*, Boston/Toronto: Little, Brown & Co., 1978.

SHAPIRO, Mel; WARREN, John & BERGER, Leonard. *Golf: A Turn of the Century Treasury*, Castle: 1956.

SILVEY, Jim. *Golf—How to Learn the Total Game*, Tucson, Arizona: Golf Unlimited, 1982.

SIMEK, Thomas C. & O'BRIEN, Richard M. *Total Golf*, Garden City, NY: Doubleday & Co., Inc., 1981.

SIMPSON, Sir W.G. *The Art of Golf*, Edinburgh: Dave Douglas, 1887.

SMITH, Alex. *Lessons in Golf*, New York: Grannis Press, 1904.

SMITH, Horton & TAYLOR, Dawson. *The Master's Secret of Putting*, San Diego, CA: A.S. Barnes & Co., Inc., 1982.

SNEAD, Sam. *On Golf*, Englewood Cliffs, NJ: Prentice–Hall, Inc., 1961.

—. *Golf Begins At Forty*, New York: Dial Press, 1978.

—, with SHEEHAN, Larry. *Sam Snead Teaches You His Simple "Key" Approach to Golf*, New York: Atheneum, 1975.

SNEAD, Sam, with STUMP, Al. *The Education of a Golfer*, New York: Simon & Schuster, 1962.

SOLEY, Dr. Clyne. *How Well Should You Putt: A Search for a Putting Standard*, Soley Golf Bureau, 1977.

STANLEY, Louis T. *How To Be a Better Woman Golfer*, New York: Thomas Y. Crowell, Co., 1952.

—. *Master Golfers in Action*, London: MacDonald, 1950.

—. *Style Analysis*, London: The Naldrett Press, 1951.

—. *Golf with Your Hands*, New York: Thomas Y. Crowell Co., 1966.

STEEL, Donald. *Golf Facts and Feats*, Enfield, England: Guiness Superlatives, Ltd., 1982.

SUGGS, Louise, et al. *Golf for Women*, New York: Cornerstone Library, 1960.

TEMPLETON, H.A. *Vector Putting: The Art and Science of Reading Greens and Computing Break*, Vector Golf, 1984.

THOMPSON, Kenneth R. *The Mental Side of Golf*, New York: Funk & Wagnalls Co., 1947.

TIMBROOK, Bud. *Golf's Mystique Solved*, Los Angeles, CA: Timbrook–Stone Publishing Co., 1982.

TOSKI, Bob with AULTMAN, Dick. *The Touch System for Better Golf*, Norwalk, CT: Golf Digest, 1971.

—, & FLICK, Jim. *How to Become a Complete Golfer*, New York: Golf Digest, Inc., 1978.

—, & LOVE, Davis, Jr. with CARNEY, Robert. *How to Feel a Real Golf Swing*, Trumbull, CT: Golf Digest, Inc., 1988.

TRAVERS, Jerome D. *Travers Golf Book*, New York: The Macmillan Co., 1913.

TRAVIS, Walter J. *Practical Golf*, New York: Harper & Brothers, 1909.

TUCKER, Jerry & HOLDEN, Bill. *Golf and TLM: Training Log Method*, St. Louis, MO: TLM, Inc., 1986.

TUFTS, Richard S. *The Principles Behind the Rules of Golf*, Pinehurst, NC: 1961.

VAILE, P.A. *Putting Made Easy: The Mark G. Harris Method*, Chicago, IL: Reilly & Lee Co., 1935.

—. *The New Golf*, New York: E.P. Dutton & Co., 1916.

—. *How to Putt and Training Golf*, Thomas E. Wilson & Co., 1919.

VAN HENGEL, Steven J.H. *Early Golf*, privately published in the Netherlands, 1982.

VARDON, Harry. *The Complete Golfer*, New York: McClure & Phillips Co., 1907.

VENTURI, Ken with BARKOW, Al. *The Ken Venturi Analysis*, New York: Atheneum, 1981.

VON NIDA, Norman with MUIR, MacLaren. *Golf Is My Business*, London: Frederick Muller, Ltd., 1956.

WATSON, Tom. *The New Rules of Golf*, New York: Random House, Inc., 1984.

WHITTON, Ivo. *Golf*, Melbourne: Robertson & Mullens, Ltd., 1947.

WILLIAMS, Ambrose. *The Principles of the Golf Swing*, Australian Capital Territory: T. Watt & Co., 1965.

WILLIAMS, David. *The Science of the Golf Swing*, London: Pelham Books, 1969.

WILLIAMS, Evan "Big Cat" with SHEEHAN, Larry. *You Can Hit the Golf Ball Farther*, Norwalk, CT: Golf Digest, Inc., 1979.

WIND, Herbert Warren. *The Complete Golfer*, New York: Simon & Schuster, 1954.

—, ed. *Tips from the Top*, New York: Bramhall House, 1956.

WIREN, Gary. *Planning and Conducting a Junior Golf Program*, Chicago, IL: The National Golf Foundation, 1973.

—. *Golf: Building a Solid Game*, Englewood Cliffs, NJ: Prentice–Hall, Inc., 1987.

—, and COOP, Dick. *The New Golf Mind*, New York: Simon & Schuster, 1978.

—, with TAYLOR, Dawson. *Super Power Golf*, Chicago, IL: Contemporary Books, Inc., 1984.

—, with TAYLOR, Dawson. *Sure Shot*, Chicago, IL: Contemporary, 1987.

WRIGHT, Mickey. *Play Golf the Wright Way*, Garden City, NJ: Doubleday & Co., Inc., 1962.

YOGI, Count. *Five Simple Steps to Perfect Golf*, New York: Simon & Schuster, 1979.

ZAHARIAS, Mildred Didrikson. *Championship Golf*, New York: A. S. Barnes & Co., Inc., 1948.

ZANGER, Jack, ed. *Exercise for Better Golf*, New York: Thomas Nelson & Sons, 1965.

APPENDIXES

GOLF'S INCEPTION A DECEPTION?

by Nick Poppa, originally published in *Ohio Golfer* magazine

Historians concede that the origin of golf is not known conclusively. Researchers tend to divide the history of the game into two phases.

First, there was a centuries-old pastime consisting of the striking of a small, hard object with a stick of sorts toward a designated spot by two or more individuals in an open outdoor area.

Second, there were more formalized recreational and competitive activities with clubs and balls over specific courses with primitively designated tees and greens.

- Roman soldiers in Caesar's time played "Paganica" using curved wooden sticks to hit feather-filled leather balls. The soldiers overran Europe and occupied parts of England and Scotland until the fourth century. It is believed the invaders' game of Paganica was adopted by the natives and later became the pattern for golf in Scotland, England, Belgium, France and Holland.
- Scottish historians generally agree on 1100 as the year their "golf" was born and became their "invention." Robert Browning in his "History of Golf" maintains the "Scots devised [golf's] essential features . . . the combination of hitting for distance with the final nicety of approach to an exiguous mark, and the independent progress of each player with his own ball, free from interference by his adversary . . ."
- A game similar to Paganica was played during the reign of Edward III and was

called "Cambuca." It was banned in 1363 along with all games so that men would have more time to practice archery for military defense.
- France had a game called "jeu de mail" that was also known as "touchstone." It was played in open country within a designated area. The player who took the fewest strokes to reach the target about ½ mile along a road was the winner.
- A print survives showing Araucanos Indians playing "El Sueca" in Chile with clubs and balls back in the 16th century.
- Yet another contention is that golf began in Holland in the 13th century in Loenen where there were four hotels. Dutch artists of the 17th and 18th centuries depicted scenes, both on ice and land, of players hitting balls toward targets in a game they called "het kolven." Dutch "kolf" has often been mentioned in historical references.
- As far back as five centuries ago, golf was popular in Scotland, sometimes too much so. King James II, in 1457, was concerned about the defense of his country. He wanted more time to be spent practicing archery and issued this edict: ". . . that fute-ball and golfe be utterly cryed downe, and not be used . . ." Golf was considered a threat to national security. Compulsory archery practice was being ignored by golfers who had become absorbed in a new pastime.
- The ban continued for about 50 years

when, in 1503, King James IV married a daughter of King Henry VII and signed a treaty of peace with England. Golfers, including King James, were allowed to resume play.

- This union between Scotland and England helped introduce golf to the latter. In 1513, Queen Catherine of Aragon wrote that she "regretted that she would not often be hearing from her husband, King Henry VIII, but that all his subjects be very glad, I thank God, to be busy with Golfe for they take it for a pastime . . ." Almost a century passed before King James VI of Scotland succeeded to the throne of England as King James I and brought serious golf to England.

- Mary Queen of Scots was a golf addict. It spelled her doom. Either because she was seeking solace, or did not care, she was seen playing golf a few days after the murder of her husband in 1567. "A poor view" was taken of her golfing at such a time, according to historians.

- British royalty supported golf. Early House of Stuart monarchs all played. King James VII of Scotland and II of England was often on the links at Leith. King James VI was probably the first real promoter of "junior" golf. He considered golf "great recreation for the young." He encouraged his two sons, Prince Henry and Prince Charles, to golf. The latter, when he had become King Charles I, was in a match at Leith when word reached him of an Irish rebellion. He left immediately. Evidently he was losing at the time and some accused him of leaving in a hurry ". . . to save his half-crown (the bet) rather than his crown." Apparently his last golf round was at Shield Field outside the walls of Newcastle upon Tyne, where he was a prisoner.

- Royal participation in golf trailed off after the passing of the Stuarts, although Bonnie Prince Charlie was seen practicing while exiled in Italy just before the Jacobite Rebellion in 1745. Royal patronage bounced back in 1833 when King William IV be-

stowed the designation "Royal" on the Perth Golfing Society. The next year, he accepted the invitation to be the patron and subsequently designated "The Royal and Ancient Golf Club of St. Andrews."

- It was about this time that golf made the transition from the isolated individual encounters of Phase One to the "club" atmosphere of Phase Two. Take your pick as to where and when the first "golf club" was organized.

- Royal Blackheath, instituted in 1608, lays claim to being the oldest golf club in the world. Evidence is lacking of any such club until well into the 1700s.

- Seniority is claimed by the Honourable Company of Edinburgh Golfers, which boasts of a 1744 start. For a few years prior to that, it was recorded that "gentlemen of honor, skillful in the ancient and healthful exercise of Golf" had been playing on the five-hole links at Leith. To obtain formal recognition, they appealed to the Edinburgh Town Council, who gave them a silver club to use as an annual prize. They formed the Company, kept minutes from that day forward and compiled the oldest continuous record of any golf club in the world. Twenty years later, in 1764, Club rules were enacted, and competition was limited to members only.

- Historians have concluded that most of the early golf clubs were founded by Masons. Records show that the foundation stone for Golf House at St. Andrews was laid by William St. Clair, Grandmaster Mason of Scotland. All members on hand were Masons and full Masonic honors were observed. The Royal Burgess Society of Edinburgh was formed in 1735; however, there were no recorded minutes. Minutes of several other beginnings are missing, which indicates that Masonic affairs were secret and records were destroyed when the societies accepted golfers into their organization even though they were not Masons.

- There were only 10 golf clubs in the late

1700s. In 1818, the Old Manchester Club was founded. It was the oldest golf club outside Scotland, after Blackheath.

- The Calcutta Club was formed in India in 1829 and the Bombay Club in 1842. The Calcutta Club conducted the Amateur Championship of India, which became the oldest national championship outside the British Isles.
- Golf reached the west coast of Scotland at Prestwick in 1851. Earlier, golf was played in Great Britain on linksland along the eastern coasts of Scotland. Links were formed when the sea receded and left wild, undulating wastes of sand. The land had little agricultural use. It was usually remote from towns and provided weather conditions that proved challenging to those who pursed the hardy pastime. As one observer put it, "grass and hazards were already there; the ground had natural movement and fashioning . . . a course needed no great imagination or labor . . . From the beginning, links provided classic settings . . . greatest courses lie on such land . . ." There were bunkers in abundance, many resulting from the digging for shells. Slightly raised areas were suitable for teeing grounds and greens. The Old Course at St. Andrews came about "naturally." Nature was its only architect. Its design did not require the hand of man and this great links golf course has survived the test of centuries except for an occasional alteration as equipment became more sophisticated and efficient.
- At St. Andrews, the Old Course had 22 holes—11 out, 11 back. In 1764, William St. Clair used 121 strokes for a round. It was then decided to convert the first four holes to two. The same fairways and greens were used going out and back and the round thus was cut to 18 holes as is the case with most courses today. At 64 years of age, St. Clair scored a 99 over the 18 holes. Breaking of 100 was an extraordinary accomplishment. In 1767, James Durham won the Silver Club at St. Andrews

with 94—a score that held up for 86 years, probably the longest-standing record of all time. J.C. Stewart broke it in 1853 when he won the King William IV Medal with a 90.

- In 1856, the first golf club on the European continent was formed at Pau, France.
- The oldest seaside course outside Scotland, called the Royal North Devon Course, opened in 1864 at Westward Ho.
- At one time, golf almost disappeared. In Holland, it vanished for more than 300 years. Golf declined in the 1500s. But after years of sporadic warfare, in 1603 the crowns of Scotland and England were united, and King James VI moved his palace to London. Golfing went along and the growth of golf resumed.
- Holland's claim to golf's origination was supported by the discovery of a wooden ball about 2 inches in diameter in the mud of Amsterdam harbor where it was buried under a pile driven into silt to support a building. Metal club heads were uncovered at a city dump.
- Records show that the first clubs intended specifically for golf were made by a bowmaker in Perth for King James IV. The oldest extant clubs are probably those preserved at Troon, Scotland. A set of six wooden clubs and two irons was found in Hull, along with a 1741 Yorkshire news clipping which described them. Clubs were not numbered as now. One of the oldest wooden sets at St. Andrews includes a "play club," "long spoon," "mid-spoon," "short spoon," "baffling spoon," "driving putter" and "putter." Irons developed later and were called "cleeks," "track irons" (for hitting balls out of railway lines), "rut irons" and "play clubs."
- Steel-shafted clubs were tried before World War I but the Royal and Ancient Rules Committee frowned upon them as being too radical a departure from the original wooden shafts. Only after April, 1924, did the USGA permit metal shafts in all its competitions. However, Bobby Jones and

many others continued to use wooden shafts and in 1930 Jones scored his Grand Slam with handmade hickory shafts. In May, 1930, the R & A finally fell in line and approved steel shafts.

- Golf balls have undergone an even more spectacular transition. First there were stones and rocks, then round wooden objects before someone stuffed feathers into leather spheres back in the dark ages of golf. The leather usually was untanned bull's hide stuffed with about a top hatful of feathers. On dry days, a feathery carried upwards to 200 yards but it cut easily. It was the standard golf ball until the 1840s. By 1848, the feathery was doomed by the "gutta-percha"—a rubbery substance, hand molded into a round sphere the size of today's ball. It outdistanced the feathery, cost about a fourth less, rolled more truly on greens, but did not fly as well until dimples were developed.

- A Cleveland man, Coburn Haskell, is credited with revolutionizing the game. He came up with a ball that was made up of thin rubber windings around a solid core. Its popularity soared, mostly because it flew about 25 yards farther and putted more accurately. It sealed the doom of the gutta-percha in 1901 when Walter Travis used the Haskell to win the U.S. Amateur Championship.

- Willie Dunn was the first professional golfer in England at Blackheath in 1851.

- Historical references can be deceptive. Court records at Fort Orange in Albany refer to fines being levied for "playing golf in the streets" as early as 1657. But can you call this street game "golf"?

- During the Revolutionary War, it was reported that Scottish officers played golf in America. Before the end of the 18th century, there were golf clubs in South Carolina and Savannah, Georgia. Historians question the existence of "golf" among members who might have used the name of golf for their dining clubs simply for the sake of tradition.

- In 1888, a Scotsman, John Reid, set up a three-hole golf course in a cow pasture near Yonkers, NY, with several friends. It was called St. Andrews. He was not an enthusiastic pioneer because he opposed moving to a more spacious site and he objected to any increase in club membership. However, in four years membership increased to 13, and the course expanded to six holes and later had to be relocated in a nearby apple orchard, where the golfers became known as the "Apple Tree Gang." In its present location at Mt. Hope it became an 18-hole course.

- It was on Long Island that American golf received its greatest impetus. Fabled Scottish pro Willie Dunn was engaged to build a 12-hole course at Shinnecock Hills.* An imposing clubhouse was designed by noted architect Stanford White. In 1891, Shinnecock became the first U.S. golf club to have a clubhouse, the first to be incorporated, and the first to have a waiting list. And it is reputed to be the first American golf course that actually looked like a golf course.

---

*Note: Subsequent research attributes the design of Shinnecock to Willie Davis, who was the professional at Royal Montreal in 1881, making him the first professional to come to North America.

IMPORTANT DATES

by Ian Morrisson
Adapted from *The Hamlyn Encyclopedia of Golf*
Twickenham, England, 1986

1457 Golf was first mentioned in a Scottish Act of Parliament which discouraged the playing of the sport because of the need for archery practice.

1744 The first golf club came into existence when the Gentlemen Golfers of Edinburgh (later the Honourable Company of Edinburgh Golfers) was formed. They drew up the first set of rules for the game.

1754 The Royal and Ancient Club was established as the Society of St. Andrews Golfers.

1759 Stroke-play first mentioned. Previously all golf had consisted of matches.

1779 Golf is believed to have been first played in the United States, near New York.

1811 The first women's golf tournament was organized at Musselburgh on 9 January for the town's "fishwives."

1818 The Edinburgh Burgess Golfing Society met the Bruntsfield Links Club at Bruntsfield on 4 June in the first inter-club match.

1829 The first golf club outside Britain was founded at Calcutta, India. It later became the Royal Calcutta Club.

1833 Perth became the first golf club to attain "royal" status, when the title was bestowed upon it by William IV.

1834 The Royal and Ancient Club was granted its name.

1848 The gutta-percha (gutty) ball was introduced.

1856 The first European course outside Britain was opened at Pau, France.

1857 H.B. Farnie published *The Golfer's Manual*, the first golfing handbook.

1860 Willie Park won the first British Open, at Prestwick.

1867 The first women's golf club was founded at St. Andrews.

1893 The Ladies' Golf Union was formed. The first Ladies' Amateur Championship, at Lytham, was won by Lady Margaret Scott.

1894 John Taylor won the first British Open to be held in England, at Sandwich.

1894 The United States Golf Association was formed.

1895 The first U.S. Open was won by Horace Rawlins at Newport, Rhode Island.

1895 The first U.S. Amateur Championship, also held at Newport, Rhode Island, was won by Charles Blair MacDonald.

1898 The rubber-cored ball was invented by Coburn Haskell at Cleveland, Ohio.

1899 George F. Grant of Boston, Massachusetts, patented the golf tee.

1901 The Professional Golfers' Association of Britain was founded in London.

1910 Arthur F. Knight of Schenectady, New York, patented the steel-shafted club.

1916 The Professional Golfers' Association of America was founded in New York.

1916 An Englishman, Jim Barnes, won the

first U.S. PGA title at Siwanoy, New York.

1919 Control of the British Open and British Amateur championships was taken over by the Royal and Ancient Club.

1921 The first restrictions on the size of the golf ball were introduced.

1922 The United States won the first Walker Cup, at Long Island, New York.

1927 The United States won the first official Ryder Cup Match, at Worcester, Massachusetts.

1932 The United States won the first Curtis Cup match, at Wentworth, England.

1934 Horton Smith won the first U.S. Masters at Augusta, Georgia.

1937 The European Golf Association was formed in Luxembourg.

1938 On 15 July, BBC television covered its first golf match at Roehampton in Southwest London.

1953 Argentina won the first Canada Cup (later World Cup).

1958 The first World Amateur Team Championship for the Eisenhower Trophy was held at St. Andrews and won by Australia, which beat the United States in a playoff.

1959 The Asian Circuit began in Hong Kong.

1960 The larger American Ball was used in a British tournament (at Wentworth) for the first time.

1964 The Women's World Amateur Team Championship for the Espirito Santo Trophy was inaugurated, in Paris, and won by the host nation.

1974 The use of the larger ball was made compulsory in the British Open for the first time.

1975 The Tournament Players' Division of the British PGA was formed.

1979 European golfers were allowed to take part in the Ryder Cup for the first time.

Editor's note: These dates of importance reflect a British perspective

APPENDIX 1–C

A TRIBUTE TO PATTY BERG

Forward from *Golf for Women Illustrated*, 1951,
written by L.B. Icely, then president of Wilson & Company

It has been my pleasure to be associated with Patty Berg for nearly a decade.

When we first approached Patty with an offer to turn professional, we ran into a somewhat unusual situation. Here was a girl who was not basically interested in how much money she could earn on the job but rather how much could she contribute toward the improvement and encouragement of women's golf.

Since accepting our offer, she has worked tirelessly toward achieving the highest standards possible for her sport.

Travelling an estimated 60,000 miles a year, Patty conducts clinics and plays exhibitions in clubs and colleges of every size and type.

Although she can spare little time to work on her own game, you can always find Patty's name right up among the leaders of the many tournaments in which she participates throughout the United States.

Typical of the real Patty Berg and indicative of her sincere love for women's golf was her promptness in turning the $500 cheque she received for winning the 1948 Women's Western Open over to the Women's Golf Association with the unassuming remark, "please accept this with my best wishes and use it in the manner you think will best promote junior golf among girls."

Editor's note: This is a wonderful statement about a person who has been a tireless contributor to golf. The golf world could use more Patty Bergs.

DEVELOPING A MODEL SWING

At the Grand Cypress Academy of Golf there is a computer model of the ideal golf swing. Biomechanics expert Dr. Ralph Mann filmed and studied the swings of over 50 top PGA professionals (including Jack Nicklaus, Greg Norman and Arnold Palmer) to develop a model that can be adjusted to one's size and body type.

With the computer model, CompuSport also determines the correct lie, length, swingweight and shaft flex of equipment one needs to swing more toward his/her model.

The work by Dr. Mann and PGA member Fred Griffin in conjunction with earlier research by Dr. Jim Suttie has contributed to the following stick figure diagrams and annotations. The thesis of this PGA manual is to allow for individuality under a workable system of principles. This would suggest that one composite golf swing may not be the answer for everyone. This is particularly true when trying to match players of high handicap talent with PGA Tour professionals. The work, however, that has been done by these researchers and professionals on identifying the characteristics of our top players is, and will continue to be, a most useful contribution and source of information. Our thanks to them.

The CompuSport Model for a #5 iron is demonstrated following this text.

CompuSport Model

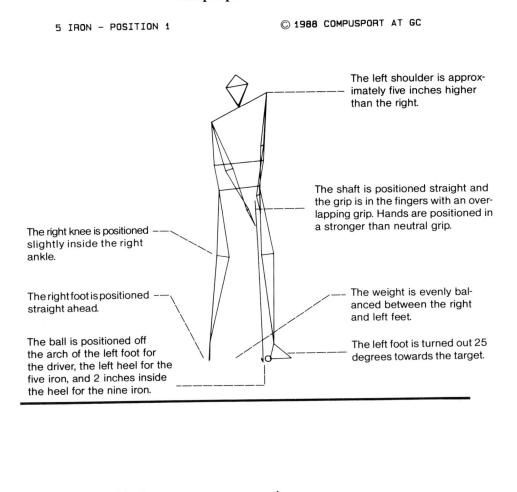

The left shoulder is approximately five inches higher
than the right.

The shaft is positioned straight and
the grip is in the fingers with an overlapping grip. Hands are positioned in
a stronger than neutral grip.

The right knee is positioned
slightly inside the right
ankle.

The right foot is positioned
straight ahead.

The weight is evenly bal-
anced between the right
and left feet.

The ball is positioned off
the arch of the left foot for
the driver, the left heel for the
five iron, and 2 inches inside
the heel for the nine iron.

The left foot is turned out 25
degrees towards the target.

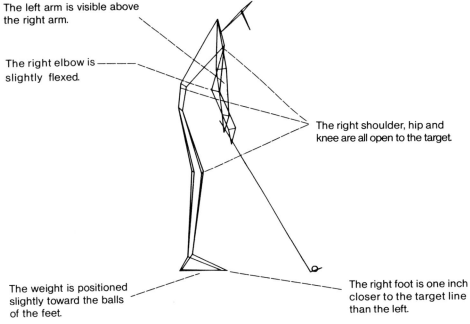

The left arm is visible above
the right arm.

The right elbow is
slightly flexed.

The right shoulder, hip and
knee are all open to the target.

The weight is positioned
slightly toward the balls
of the feet.

The right foot is one inch
closer to the target line
than the left.

5 IRON - POSITION 2   © 1988 COMPUSPORT AT GC

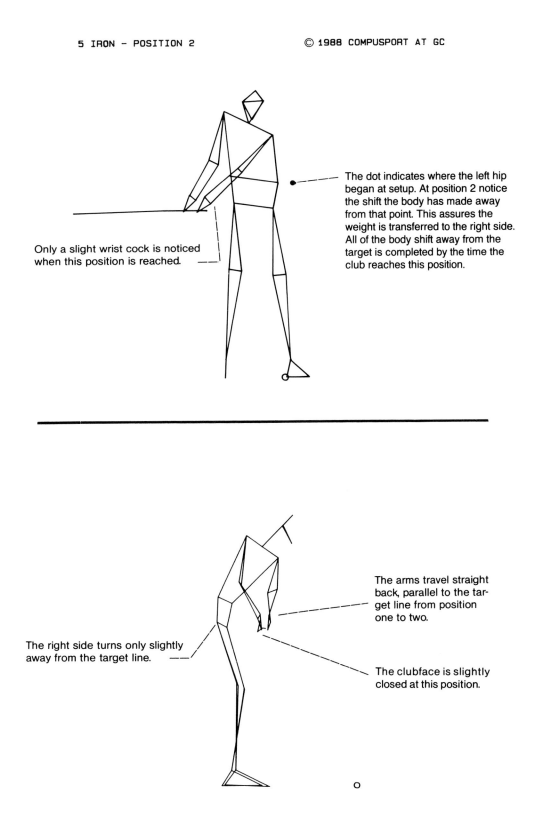

The dot indicates where the left hip began at setup. At position 2 notice the shift the body has made away from that point. This assures the weight is transferred to the right side. All of the body shift away from the target is completed by the time the club reaches this position.

Only a slight wrist cock is noticed when this position is reached.

The arms travel straight back, parallel to the target line from position one to two.

The right side turns only slightly away from the target line.

The clubface is slightly closed at this position.

5 IRON - POSITION 3   © 1988 COMPUSPORT AT GC

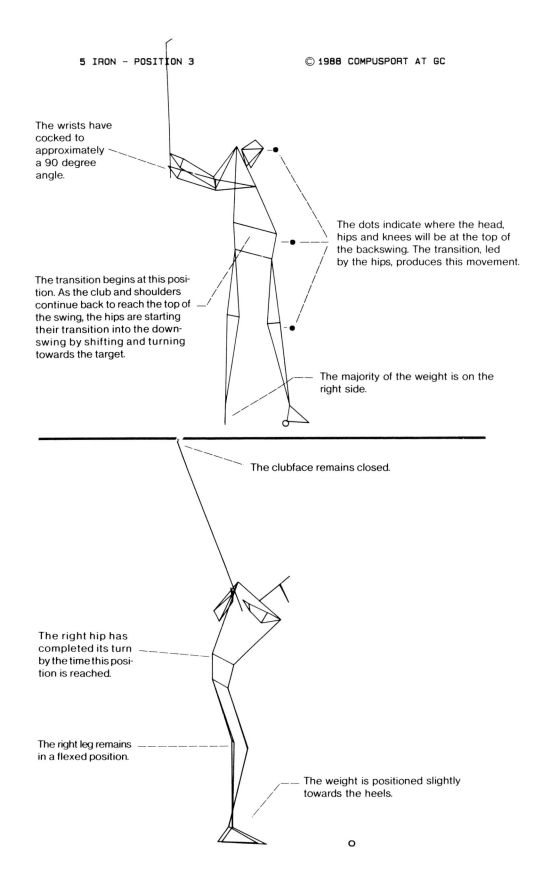

The wrists have cocked to approximately a 90 degree angle.

The dots indicate where the head, hips and knees will be at the top of the backswing. The transition, led by the hips, produces this movement.

The transition begins at this position. As the club and shoulders continue back to reach the top of the swing, the hips are starting their transition into the downswing by shifting and turning towards the target.

The majority of the weight is on the right side.

The clubface remains closed.

The right hip has completed its turn by the time this position is reached.

The right leg remains in a flexed position.

The weight is positioned slightly towards the heels.

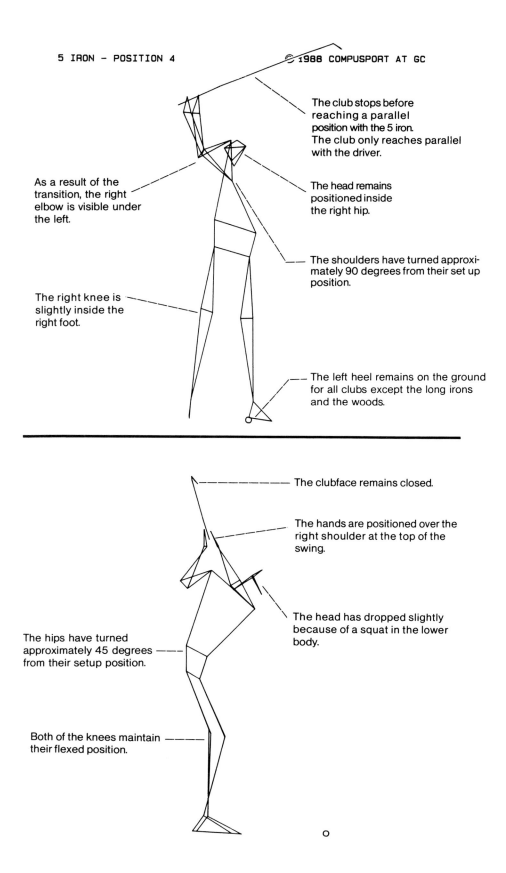

5 IRON - POSITION 4

The club stops before reaching a parallel position with the 5 iron. The club only reaches parallel with the driver.

As a result of the transition, the right elbow is visible under the left.

The head remains positioned inside the right hip.

The shoulders have turned approximately 90 degrees from their set up position.

The right knee is slightly inside the right foot.

The left heel remains on the ground for all clubs except the long irons and the woods.

The clubface remains closed.

The hands are positioned over the right shoulder at the top of the swing.

The hips have turned approximately 45 degrees from their setup position.

The head has dropped slightly because of a squat in the lower body.

Both of the knees maintain their flexed position.

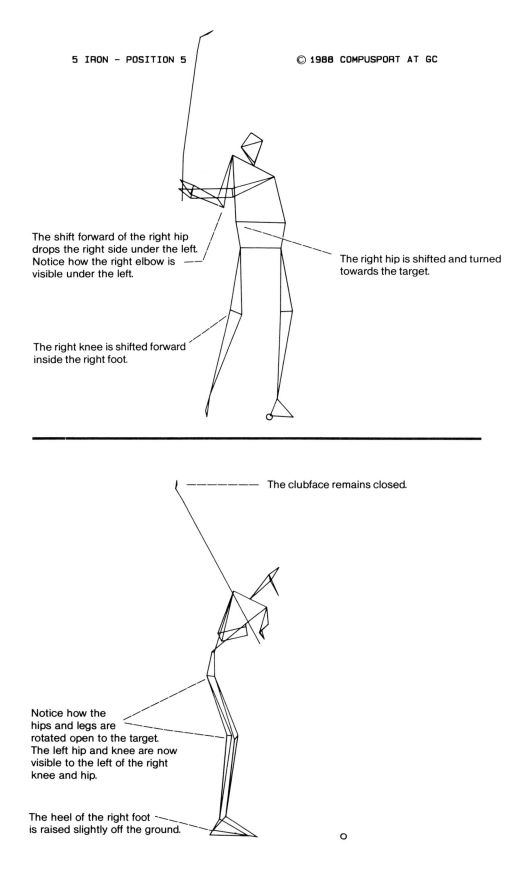

5 IRON — POSITION 5   © 1988 COMPUSPORT AT GC

The shift forward of the right hip drops the right side under the left. Notice how the right elbow is visible under the left.

The right hip is shifted and turned towards the target.

The right knee is shifted forward inside the right foot.

The clubface remains closed.

Notice how the hips and legs are rotated open to the target. The left hip and knee are now visible to the left of the right knee and hip.

The heel of the right foot is raised slightly off the ground.

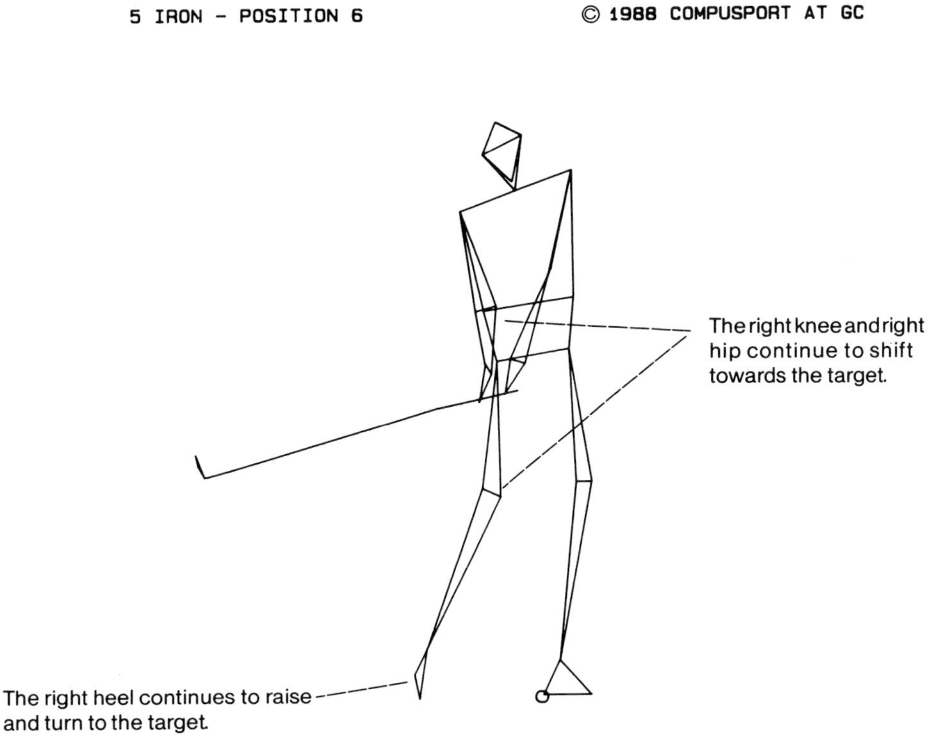

5 IRON - POSITION 6   © 1988 COMPUSPORT AT GC

The right knee and right
hip continue to shift
towards the target.

The right heel continues to raise
and turn to the target.

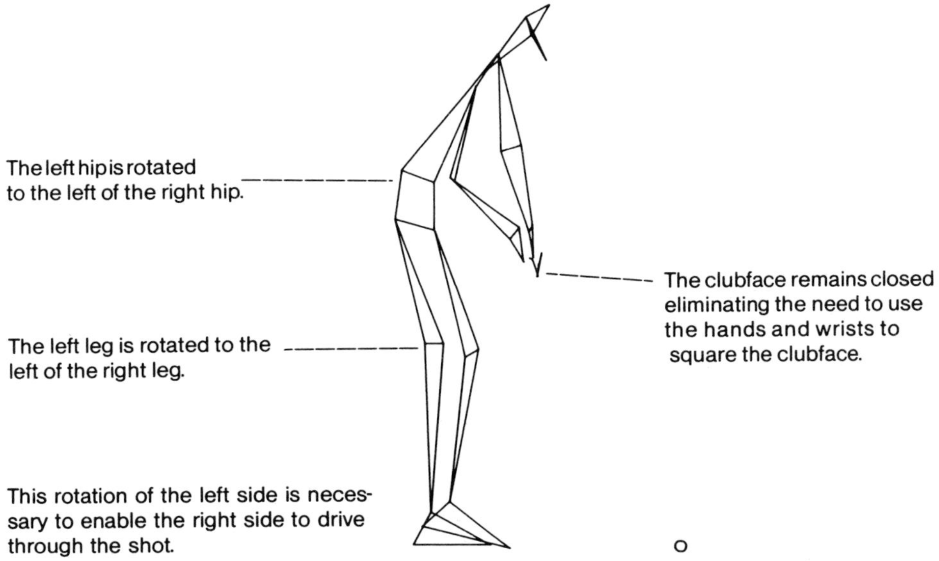

The left hip is rotated
to the left of the right hip.

The clubface remains closed
eliminating the need to use
the hands and wrists to
square the clubface.

The left leg is rotated to the
left of the right leg.

This rotation of the left side is necessary to enable the right side to drive
through the shot.

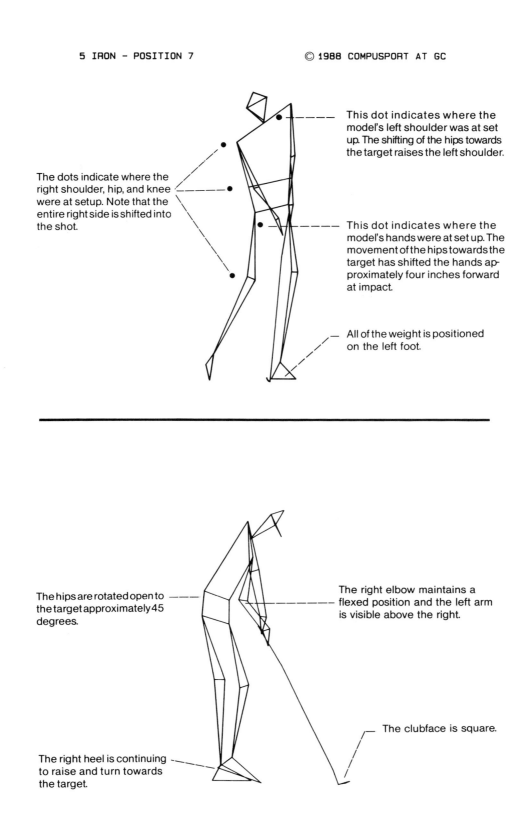

5 IRON – POSITION 7   © 1988 COMPUSPORT AT GC

This dot indicates where the model's left shoulder was at set up. The shifting of the hips towards the target raises the left shoulder.

The dots indicate where the right shoulder, hip, and knee were at setup. Note that the entire right side is shifted into the shot.

This dot indicates where the model's hands were at set up. The movement of the hips towards the target has shifted the hands approximately four inches forward at impact.

All of the weight is positioned on the left foot.

The hips are rotated open to the target approximately 45 degrees.

The right elbow maintains a flexed position and the left arm is visible above the right.

The clubface is square.

The right heel is continuing to raise and turn towards the target.

5 IRON - POSITION 8   © 1988 COMPUSPORT AT GC

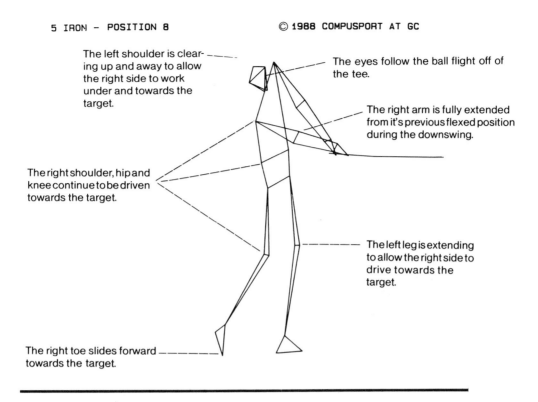

The left shoulder is clearing up and away to allow the right side to work under and towards the target.

The eyes follow the ball flight off of the tee.

The right arm is fully extended from it's previous flexed position during the downswing.

The right shoulder, hip and knee continue to be driven towards the target.

The left leg is extending to allow the right side to drive towards the target.

The right toe slides forward towards the target.

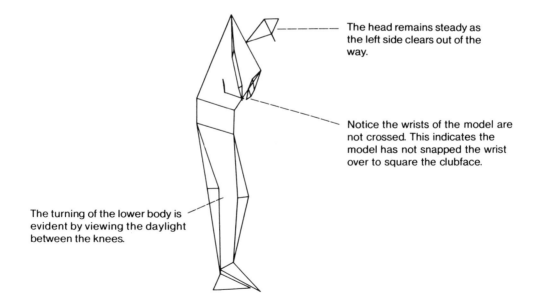

The head remains steady as the left side clears out of the way.

Notice the wrists of the model are not crossed. This indicates the model has not snapped the wrist over to square the clubface.

The turning of the lower body is evident by viewing the daylight between the knees.

5 IRON - POSITION 9   © 1988 COMPUSPORT AT GC

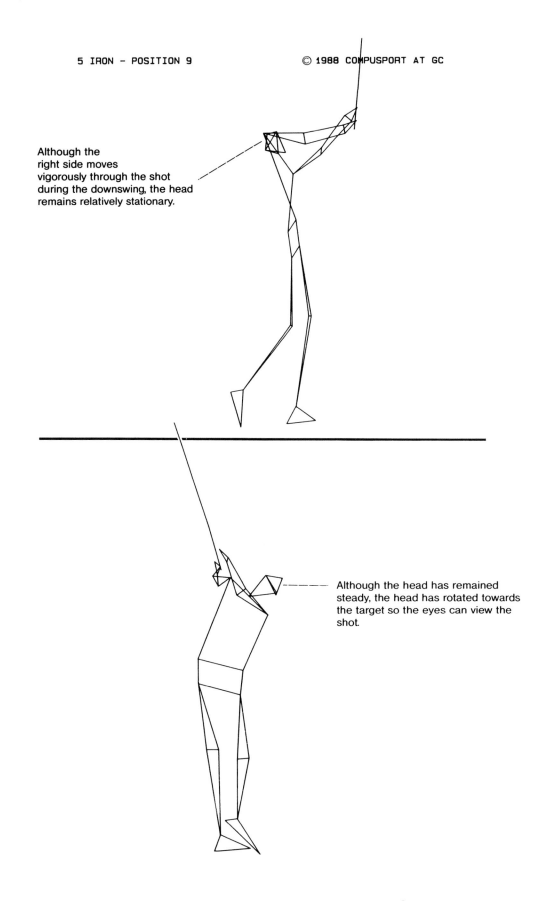

Although the
right side moves
vigorously through the shot
during the downswing, the head
remains relatively stationary.

Although the head has remained
steady, the head has rotated towards
the target so the eyes can view the
shot.

5 IRON – POSITION 10   © 1988 COMPUSPORT AT GC

Notice how the right
shoulder is well ahead of
the left shoulder.

The hips finish the swing ahead
of the shoulders.

The right knee has driven
towards the target to finish
even with the left knee.

The entire body has completed
the turn so it's directly facing the
target.

INFORMATION THAT MIGHT HELP ME SCORE BETTER

Ball Temperature

The temperature of a golf ball affects its ability to rebound from the clubface. The following chart is the approximate influence of temperature on the ball for a shot that would normally carry 220 yards at 75 degree temperature.

Carry in yards	Degrees (Fahrenheit)
226	105
224	95
222	85
220	75
216	65
214	55
205	45
196	35

Since rubber is a poor conductor of heat, placing the ball in your pocket would not be sufficient to warm the ball. Keeping balls in a warm room overnight and interchanging the ball every three holes would be better. It is against the rules, however, to use a handwarmer or similar device for the purpose of heating the ball during a round.

Influence of Wind

Wind can have a great deal of influence on your shots and club selection. Here is a chart with approximate figures on the effect of following and head wind.

Wind (mph)	Carry of Shots (yards)	Total Length (yards)
30	158	162
15	187	208
0	200	232
15	209	255
30	223	268

In a head wind of approximately 30 mph, a ball that is sliced or hooked will curve 5 times greater against the wind than it will downwind.

Off-Center Hits

Clubhead speed is most generally thought of when discussions of distance take place. Another important consideration is squareness of contact in relation to the center of the clubface. Listed below are approximate figures related to off-center hits.

Center Face Hit (driver)	250 yards
¼″ off-center	245 yards
½″ off-center	235 yards
¾″ off-center	215 yards

The above information based on data from *The Search For The Perfect Swing*, Alastair Cochran and John Stobbs, Lippincott, NY, 1968.

APPENDIX 2–C

FLEXIBILITY TEST PROTRACTOR

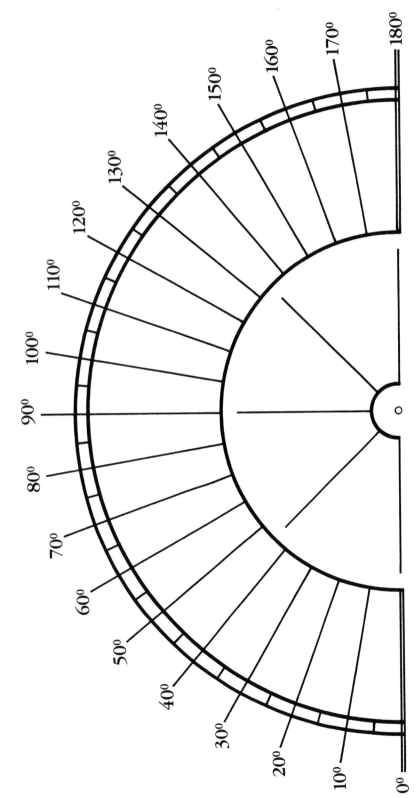

GOLF SWING MISCONCEPTIONS*

by Dr. Jim Suttie, PGA Professional,
Medinah Country Club and
Golf Coach, Northwestern University

In previous articles, I emphasize that the golf swing is primarily a rotational movement of the body in which the big muscles of the shoulders and hips dominate. The small muscles of the hands and arms simply follow this movement and respond to this rotation. As a result, proper weight shift during the golf swing is attained by this body rotation.

In this article, we'll discuss some long-held beliefs about the golf swing and try to explain how some of these beliefs have actually inhibited the learning of a correct golf swing motion. Let's get started:

Misconception 1: Keep the left arm (or lead arm) straight or stiff.
Reasons why this is not true: If the left (lead) arm is kept rigid and stiff throughout the entire swing motion, the arms will work independently of the body. Also, the stiffness in the arm will induce tension and limit the rotation of the left shoulder.

Misconception 2: Keep your head down.
Reasons: If the golfer has his head buried in his chest, he will inevitably lift it up as he comes into impact. The "head down" syndrome limits the ability of the shoulders to turn under the chin. Usually, this head position is a result of poor posture at setup.

Misconception 3: Keep your head still.
Reasons: If the golfer keeps his head absolutely still, he will limit his ability to rotate and get his weight over the back leg. There are very few tour players who can keep their heads absolutely still. Most players allow their heads to move just slightly in order to get an acceptable shoulder turn. Usually the head moves with the upper spine on the backswing until it has moved about two inches from where it started.

Misconception 4: The center of your golf swing is the sternum or the center of your golf swing is the head.
Reasons: If we pivot around a point of our body (the sternum or the head), we will never be able to get the weight shifted over the right leg (for right-handed golfers). Actually, the center of the swing is the posterior lower spine just below the small of the back.

Misconception 5: There is lateral motion away from and toward the target during the swing.
Reasons: Since the golf swing is a circular motion with the club, we must create a rotary motion with our bodies. There is little, if any, lateral motion during the swing. Essentially, what appears to be lateral motion is simply rotation of the body until the right hip is over the right heel on the backswing and the left hip has rotated over the left heel on the forward swing (for right-handed golfers).

Misconception 6: The arms swing and the body simply responds to that motion or the hands and arms move first and then the shoulders and hips follow.
Reasons: If the hands and arms move first in

*Reprinted courtesy of *Chicago Metro Golfer*.

the backswing, the shoulders will turn late in the backswing. As a result, the golfer will lose his extension and create an overly long and loose swing that is likely to come outside and over-the-top on the downswing.

Actually, the first part of the backswing should be a one-piece movement with the hands, arms, clubhead, shoulders and hips all moving away together. This insures a weight shift, arm and club extension and a firm and short swing.

Furthermore, if the swing produces centrifugal force, the center of the swing must move first to create the force. The true center of the swing is located in the posterior lower spine somewhere behind the hips. This part moves first and the hands, arms and clubhead simply respond to this initial movement. The big muscles of the shoulders, back and hips are the slowest moving yet most powerful muscles in the body. These muscles move first and keep the faster moving muscles of the hands and arms under control. Correct movement is always produced from the center of the body outward—never from the clubhead inwards.

Misconception 7: Feel like you are sitting on a bar stool with the weight back on the heels at the start of the swing.
Reasons: If we sit back on the heels at address, we are likely to have the knees over-flexed. With weight on the heels and over-flexed knees, we are not able to rotate the lower body because of abducted hips. Also, when starting with weight on the heels, there's usually no place to move except to the toes.

Misconception 8: The ball position changes for the different clubs in the bag. For example, the ball should be positioned forward for the driver and back toward the center of the stance for the nine iron.
Reasons: What appears to be a change in ball position with the shorter clubs is really only a narrower, more open stance with the weight distributed more on the front leg at the start of the swing. The ball actually looks like it is being played in the center of the stance for a

nine iron and off the left heel for the driver. In reality, the ball position will be approximately the same for both the woods and the irons. It is the open and narrow stance that makes the ball appear back in the stance with the short irons. Essentially, there is only one bottom to your swing arc if you are going to create any consistently struck golf shots.

Misconception 9: The club moves straight away from the ball on the takeaway.
Reasons: The golf swing is a side of the line hitting game. By this, I mean that we are standing to the side of the ball. Because of the way we are set up, we must arc the club inside the target line as we take it back. In addition to this, the hands and the arms follow the body rotation both on the backswing and the downswing. If we follow the principle, then the turning of the shoulders and hips will naturally cause the club to come a little inside the target line on the backswing.

Misconception 10: The weight starts on the right leg (for right-handed golfers) at the start of the swing.
Reasons: If the weight started on the back leg at the address, it would be impossible to make a rotational move with the body. Because of this, the golfer would become a hand and arm player. Also, if the weight is set to the right at address, it is likely to move to the left on the backswing. This is the reverse weight shift that most golfers have in their golf swings.

Actually, the weight shift should start slightly forward on the front leg. From this position, the golfer has somewhere to move—to the right side.

Misconception 11: Restrict your hips on the backswing and coil your shoulders against them.
Reasons: If the golfer restricts his hip turn on the backswing, he will limit the range of motion of the shoulder turn. Only the very flexible and coordinated golfer is able to do this.

In reality, the hips control the shoulders both on the backswing and the downswing. Therefore, if the golfer restricts his hip turn, he will restrict his shoulder turn. With a restricted shoulder turn, the golfer is likely to start the downswing with the shoulders unwinding ahead of the hips. This will produce pulls and pull slices.

Misconception 12: We should return to the address position at impact.

Reasons: At impact, we see pictures of the tour stars that show them with the majority of their weight on their lead leg with hips opened to the target line and shoulders parallel to the target line. In fact, the hips are just slightly forward of the position they started in. The mistake most people make here is they slide their hips too far forward on the downswing, creating weight shift and balance problems at impact.

In reality, the shoulders out-turn the hips on the backswing. This allows the hips to move first on the downswing and to open up and stay ahead of the shoulders at impact.

Misconception 13: The golfer should consciously try to release the club. This definition of release means to pronate and supinate the hands and arms and to consciously try to turn the club over through the impact area.

Reasons: Correct body (shoulder and hip) rotation will automatically create correct hand and arm rotation. Any conscious effort to open or close the clubhead, either on backswing or downswing, will most likely create an inconsistency in your ball striking. Any conscious effort to try to release the clubhead is a compensation for poor body rotation.

If the golf swing is a circular motion in which centrifugal force is produced, the inertia and the weight of the swinging clubhead will automatically create the release.

Misconception 14: The power source in the golf swing comes from the hands, arms and wrists. We should try to snap our wrists as we come into the impact area.

Reasons: Power in the golf swing comes from leverage (swing arc), torsion (body rotation) and weight shift. In order to achieve these three goals, we must rotate our bodies. The real power source in the golf swing is the hips. The faster we move the hips in the downswing, the faster the hands and arms will work. There is no conscious use of the wrists and hands through the impact area. The hands and arms rotate in response to body rotation.

Misconception 15: The golfer should stay behind the ball long after the ball is hit. A corollary to this is that the golfer should keep his head down and right (or left) shoulder back for as long as possible after impact.

Reasons: It is true that the head is behind the ball at the point of contact. But, just after impact, the forceful unwinding of the shoulders should allow the head to rotate with the shoulders and come up out of the shot. Any effort to keep the head and right shoulder back behind the ball after the point of contact will cause the weight to stay on the back leg. This error will cause all kinds of poor shots including pulls, pull hooks and push fades.

In reality, the shoulders turn about 200 degrees on the forward swing. The shoulders actually catch up to and pass the hips just after impact. At the finish of the swing, the right shoulder should be just slightly higher than the left with the chest facing to the left of the target line and the hips facing directly down the target line. This finish position insures that the shoulders have out-turned the hips and a correct weight shift to the left leg has been made.

Misconception 16: The golfer should pull the club down from the top of the swing with the left (or right) hand and arm. Another related movement would ask the golfer to pull the butt of the club at the ball on the downswing.

Reasons: If the golfer pulls the butt of the club down on the downswing or pulls down with the left (or right) hand or arm on the downswing, he creates angles with his arms. In this case, pulling down with the left hand and arm will force the left elbow up to the sky, which will leave the clubface open through impact. Better advice might be "start the downswing with the lower body and try to keep the elbows down throughout the entire swing motion." If the golfer turns his hips through the ball instead of sliding through it, the clubface will naturally close and the left arm will fold downward after impact.

In addition to this, the golf swing is a bilateral motion and shouldn't be dominated by either the right or left side of the body.

Misconception 17: The path of the clubhead on a correct golf swing is inside-outside.
Reasons: Most of us have been taught to swing inside-outside. Unfortunately, this is not correct. If the golfer swings excessively inside-outside, he will push-fade and hook most of his golf shots. It might feel like we are swinging inside-outside, but what really should happen is this: The golf club approaches the ball from inside the target line through impact, and then moves off to the left of the target line after impact. This occurs because the hands and arms follow the body rotation both on the backswing and downswing. It is this "inward—to straight—to inward" club movement that creates a natural release of the clubhead through impact and divots that point slightly left of the target line.

Misconception 18: The weight stays centered throughout the entire swinging motion.
Reasons: If the weight stayed centered throughout the entire swing, the golfer would be unable to make a weight shift. Also, the golf swing is an elliptical arc (egg-shaped). This type of arc is created because the golfer is working out of two shoulder sockets and two hip sockets. On the backswing, the shoulder and hip turn create

a weight shift over the right heel. Finally, on the downswing, the movement of the feet, knees and hips creates a weight shift over the left heel.

Misconception 19: The golfer should try to shift his weight.
Reason: The weight shift is created by shoulder and hip rotation. The shoulders turn and the one-piece takeaway is responsible for most of the weight shift on the backswing while the hip turn is responsible for the weight shift on the downswing. There is a minimal amount, if any, of sliding the hips during the swing.

Misconception 20: The club is swung on a single swing-plane.
Reason: First of all, everybody has their own unique swingplane because of posture, body build, how far they stand away from the ball, and their timing system. But, generally speaking, the downswing plane does come below the backswing plane because the weight is moving to the left pivot point. This movement to the left side abducts the arms (arms get closer) to the body and drops the plane below the way it went back. But each case is very individual as there have been many successful golfers who have come down outside the way they went back. The important thing to remember is that it is impossible to swing on a single plane on both the backswing and downswing. Also, about 24 inches prior to impact, the clubhead is approaching the ball from inside the target line.

TEST ON PUTTING

adapted from the book
How Well Should You Putt?
by Dr. Clyne Soley

Published by
Soley Golf Bureau
5541 Cribari Circle
San Jose, CA 95135

Chapter 1.

a. If a golfer's handicap is 10, how many putts should be taken per round?_____

Chapter 2.

a. Does a golfer average the same number of putts on all length courses?_____

b. Why do women have a lower percentage of putts than men?_____

c. On what length course would a 20 handicap man have his putts equal to 50% of his score?_____

d. On what length course would a 20 handicap woman have her putts equal to 50% of her score?_____

Chapter 3.

a. Why is the number of 2-putt greens almost exactly constant all across the handicap scale?_____

b. How often do the top men professionals 3-putt per round?_____

c. How often do the top men professionals 2-putt per round?_____

d. Some golfers say they never 4-putt; how come?_____

Chapter 4.

a. Why do the top men professionals have less than 31 putts when they shoot about 70 or 71?_____

b. On normal courses, from what distance do the top men professionals sink half of their putts?_____

c. Do the top men professionals ever miss short putts?_____

Chapter 5.

a. What percent of professional women's scores are putts?_____

b. At what handicap level does a man average the same number of total putts per round as the top LPGA players?_____

c. Which members 3-putt more greens, LPGA or PGA?_____
_____

d. If the men actually putt better than their pro counterparts in the LPGA, what are some of the possible reasons?_____
_____
_____

Chapter 6.

a. Do the top professionals take fewer putts in their good rounds than in their average or poor rounds?_____

b. In going from their best scores to their worst ones, the percent of putts in the total score decreases. True or False?_____

c. As their scores increase, do the strokes to get on the greens and number of putts both increase?_____

Chapter 7.

a. Why are more putts missed by top men professionals on greens prepared for important tournaments than on normal greens?
_____

b. How can a skilled professional golfer miss a putt of 6 inches or less?_____

c. Some amateur players claim they have

never missed a putt less than a foot long. How do you explain that?_____

d. If a player concentrates properly, shouldn't all putts of 2 feet or less be holed?_____

Chapter 8.

a. For scratch men golfers (0-handicap), how much easier are 3-foot putts than the 6-footers?_____

b. For the average 18 handicap male, how much easier are the 3-footers than the 6-footers?_____

c. What handicap player would make as many 3-foot putts as the scratch player would make from 6 feet?_____

d. Is there a fairly constant difference between the percent of putts made from 3 and 6 feet as the handicap increases?_____

Chapter 9.

a. For scratch women golfers, how much easier are 3-foot putts than 6-footers?_____

b. For the average woman golfer (handicap 38), how much easier are the 3-footers than those from 6 feet?_____

c. What handicap level woman golfer would make as many 3-footers as the scratch woman player makes from 6 feet?_____

d. How does the difference vary between percent of putts made from 3 feet and 6 feet as the handicap increases?_____

e. How do you convert 9-hole handicaps to 18-hole handicaps?_____

Chapter 10.

a. Why are downhill putts more difficult than uphill ones?_____

b. How can a typical amateur minimize the increased difficulty of downhill putts, especially the danger of 3-putting?_____

Chapter 11.

a. What is the main reason sidehill putts are more difficult than level or straight uphill putts?_____

b. What are some of the reasons that many golfers find right-to-left putts easier than left-to-right ones?_____

Chapter 12.

a. Is it easier to get a putt close to the hole than it is for another type shot, considering they are of equal length?_____

b. Do the best putters get the first putt near the hole?_____

Chapter 13.

a. The average male golfer (handicap 18) takes 34.1 putts per round. The 18 handicap lady takes only 32.8 putts. How come?

_____

b. At a handicap of 10, men and women have the same number of putts. What percent of men have a handicap of 10 or less?_____

c. What percent of women have a handicap of 10 or less?_____

Chapter 14.

a. It has been shown that a crosswind can deflect a short putt. How do good players handle this situation?_____

b. Would wind affect putts more on fast greens or slow ones?_____

Chapter 16.

a. Why was the croquet putter banned?_____

Chapter 20.

a. Why is the 4 to 8 foot range of putts so important?_____

b. Does every golfer at some time or another take more than 3 putts on a green?_____

c. Some top tournament players seem to putt better when they first go on the tour, and then lose their putting touch after their middle 30s. Is that true for all golfers?_____

d. Why are some kids in their teens such good putters?_____

Chapter 21.

a. Is there any rule against putting one-handed?

_____

Editor's note: The original test from Dr. Clyne Soley's *How Well Should You Putt?* does not include any questions for its Chapters 15, 17, 18 or 19.

ANSWERS

adapted from the book
How Well Should You Putt?
by
Dr. Clyne Soley

Chapter 1.
a. 32.1

Chapter 2.
a. Yes
b. For a given score, women require more strokes to reach the greens. For the same score, they have fewer putts.
c. About 3,000 yards.
d. About 1,900 yards.

Chapter 3.
a. Because the number of 1-putt greens is off-set by the number of 3- and 4-putt greens.
b. About once every two rounds.
c. About 11.6 times per round.
d. They always concede themselves the third putt.

Chapter 4.
a. They don't hit all the greens in regulation.
b. From 7 feet.
c. Yes

Chapter 5.
a. 42 %
b. 7
c. LPGA
d. Perhaps men have better hand-eye coordination, and perhaps they are slightly more aggressive on the greens.

Chapter 6.
a. Yes
b. True
c. Yes

Chapter 7.
a. Even short putts are much more difficult on fast greens prepared for important tournaments.

b. Carelessness
c. They always concede them.
d. No

Chapter 8.
a. From 6 feet they miss 48%. From 3 feet only 18%.
b. From 6 feet they miss 60%. From 3 feet only 27%.
c. 36
d. Yes

Chapter 9.
a. From 6 feet they miss 54%. From 3 feet they miss 19%.
b. From 6 feet they miss 65%. From 3 feet they miss 36%.
c. 60
d. The difference decreased as the handicap increased.
e. Multiply by 2 and add 5%.

Chapter 10.
a. Both distance and direction are more easily controlled when putting uphill.
b. Reduce the distance from which you just lag the first putt to the hole.

Chapter 11.
a. Sidehill putts change direction on the way to the hole.
b. Most golfers feel more comfortable with a right-to-left putt. By the action of contacting the ball with the toe of the putter (as many golfers do) more putts will be made in the direction of right-to-left.

Chapter 12.
a. Yes
b. Yes

Chapter 13.
a. Only a small percentage of women have a handicap of 18, while the 18 level for men is midway in the scale.
b. 18
c. 1.3

Chapter 14.
a. They hit the putt a little more firmly.
b. Fast greens.

Chapter 16.
a. The USGA decided it did not look like golf.

Chapter 20.
a. Up to 3 feet, most players make almost all of them anyway, and from 10 feet on up only a small percentage go in. The big difference comes in the 4- to 8-foot range.
b. Yes
c. No
d. Good coordination, good vision and confidence.

Chapter 21.
a. No

HOW TO BECOME A GOLFER

A Message That Every Player of the Game Should Hear
National Golf Foundation ES-3

Golf is a lifetime activity in that participation can be rewarding at any age. Early exposure to the game—in *all* its dimensions—will insure lifelong benefits in return.

In addition to skill, success in golf lies in sportsmanship and fair play. It is a game which revolves around the concept of courtesy and proper conduct. It is a game which requires self-discipline—in the sense of control of individual emotions and also in the sense of integrity, because many of its rules depend upon self-enforcement. The true "golfer" is one who commands respect not only for his or her actions on the course but also for the awareness of correct procedures in the clubhouse. Such respect is an outgrowth of one's self-respect and is nurtured by concern for the following:

1. **Knowledge of and Adherence to the Official Rules of the Game.** Rules make it possible for everyone to play the game on the same basis of fairness and wholesome spirit. Fair-minded, good sportsmen would not knowingly break the rules. **The "Golfer" studies the Rules . . . then develops a sound working knowledge of them.** By observing the "golfer's" adherence to rules, other players will follow his or her example.

2. **Personal Conduct.** The myriad of playing situations which confront the player during a round pose a constant test of personality and character. The GOLFER realizes this and accepts moments of discouragement as part of the game's challenge.

3. **Care of the Course.** The average golf hole requires thousands of dollars to construct, and additional thousands to maintain. In recognition of such costs, acts which reflect concern for course maintenance can be readily observed in the behavior of a GOLFER. Attention to the following matters will require special effort by the beginning player, but will soon become habit comfortably incorporated into the normal sequence of play.

The GOLFER Always:

—Hits from the designated tee area.
—Replaces divots, even if only a small amount of turf has been removed.
—Rakes the sand to smooth footprints and clubmarks following a bunker shot.
—Repairs ball marks on the putting green—oftentimes more than just one's own.
—Refrains from scuffing the green with spikes and does not walk near the edge of the cup.
—Places the bag of clubs *off* the green and nearer the next tee before putting.
—Refrains from pulling a cart across edges of the green.
—Follows designated pathways for the motorized golf car, being careful not to drive over teeing grounds or onto apron areas of the green.
—Discards litter in proper containers.
—Leaves pets at home.

4. **Safety.** The act of compressing a hard ball with a clubface traveling in the range of 100 miles per hour occurs several times during a round. When crowded, the golf course becomes acres of dangerous ground—UNLESS each player is alert.

The GOLFER Always:

—Waits until players ahead are well out of range before hitting, taking extra precaution on "blind" holes.
—Shouts the warning cry "FORE" whenever a shot astray could endanger others.
—Takes practice swings judiciously, where space is clear of obstructions and other players.
—Observes out-of-bounds areas designated within the course premises which prohibit play of a ball on an adjacent fairway.
—Leaves small children at home.

5. **Pace of Play.** The game of golf was designed to be played with continuity of effort. Its challenge calls for sustained concentration combined with the physical ability to execute the swing under scores of playing conditions. The GOLFER determines the pace at which he or she performs best and which is compatible with fellow players.

The GOLFER Always:

—Always is ready to hit in turn.
—Walks to the ball with dispatch. Plans club selection and shot execution while approaching the ball or waiting for others to hit.
—Sets a pace which maintains a comfortable distance between groups ahead and those behind. Should the distance of a hole exist between you and those ahead of you, allow faster players to play through. To avoid congestion on the tee area of par 3 holes where appropriate, upon reaching the green allow those waiting on the tee to hit their shots.
—Learns the habit of following the flight of the ball closely, marking the point where it lands so that excessive time need not be taken to determine its location. If ball is thought to be lost or out-of-bounds, hits a "provisional ball," following USGA rules procedures.
—Is discriminating in the number of practice swings taken. Avoids giving one's self or others a "lesson" while on the course.
—Upon reaching the green, leaves bags, carts or motorized golf cars nearer the next tee—never in front of the green.
—Practices efficient handling of the flagstick to shave seconds from "green-time." Rule of thumb states that the player whose ball lies closest to the hole attends or removes the flagstick; it is the responsibility of the player who first holes out to replace it.
—Leaves the green immediately upon concluding play of that hole. Practice putting is discouraged. Scores should be recorded en route to or at the next tee rather than on the putting green.

By observing these procedures, a round of golf can be shortened as much as one hour—while increasing its enjoyment!

PERSONAL COMPETITIVE GOLF OBJECTIVES

by Gary Wiren, Ph.D.

1. Set a reasonable schedule of practice and training that you can meet and then stick to it. There will be emergencies and situations that cause an occasional miss, but be as regular as possible.

2. Be positive about yourself, your game and what you are doing.

3. Practice with an objective in mind. Since your time is short, make your practice time of the highest quality. Make each shot as though on the course, except when warming up. Fewer balls; more perfect shots.

4. When playing even in a casual round, take enough time to execute properly. As long as you are taking the time to play, even for fun, do it right. Make it a habit.

5. Winners are not always those who have finished first. A winner is someone who gives the most in preparation to reach his potential and makes every effort to perform at his highest level. There will be times when that is accomplished and you still aren't victorious; but you are a winner.

6. No opponent is deserving of either lack of respect or an attitude of awe. In any reasonable match of talent either competitor can win on a given day.

7. You may not have the best talent in a match. But tough competitors often overcome superior talent. Patience and perseverance will pay off in golf.

8. Be consistent in your performance, focusing on the task at hand for the full time you are playing. Don't ease up when ahead or quit when you're behind. You never know what might happen to you or an opponent, so keep your focus.

9. Self-control is a trait that you should strive to achieve. Loss of self-control is harmful to performance as well as to individual growth as a person. It reveals itself in club throwing, displays of temper, offensive language, verbal abuse of spectators or officials, complaining or discrediting the event or facility, etc. *Composure!*

10. Keep your body in good physical shape by observing the following:

    (a) Eat three balanced meals daily avoiding as much as possible fried foods, rich desserts, too much protein, fat and salt. Eat more fresh fruits, vegetables, cereals and grains.
    (b) Get 7–8 hours of sleep a night.
    (c) Limit or abstain from the use of chemicals including alcohol. Moderation is a good guide. Don't train faithfully and then waste yourself in one night.
    (d) Include a mixture of flexibility, cardiovascular and strength work in your physical training program.

11. Be committed but put competing in perspective. There are more important things in life. Putting it in perspective will help you as a competitor to realize *you don't have to win,* only to do your best.

12. Enjoy what you are doing. If it isn't rewarding or enjoyable then reevaluate your program and make it so.

Appreciation is given to St. Olaf hockey coach "Whitey" Aus, who created the model for this set of objectives.

DRILLS

by Gary Wiren, Ph.D.

Law: Speed

Drill: Whoosher Drill

Purpose: To create greater clubhead speed.

Description: Take the driver and turn it upside down so the left-hand grip will be taken on the neck of the club. Swing the club with both arms allowing the right hand to come off just before impact, while the left continues to the finish. Listen for a "whooshing" sound. The louder the sound, the greater the speed. Leave both hands on and try to maintain the same speed level as judged by the sound.

Drill: Sling-It Drill

Purpose: To create greater clubhead speed.

Description: Pick a target like a flagstick, fifty to one hundred yards away. Imagine throwing the club over the flagstick on the fly, as though you were going to wind-up, unwind and sling it—but don't actually let go. Such an action requires a big body coil, back turned fully to the target and then a vigorous unwind of the trunk, accompanied by a light grip pressure, to get the greatest speed. Use the whooshing sound as in the previous drill to test for speed. Apply the same uninhibited "slinging feeling" motion to the ball.

Drill: Baseball Cuts Drill

Purpose: To increase clubhead speed.

Description: Players who can generate speed on a horizontal plane often lose too much of it when they bend forward to make a golf swing, which is more inclined. Make an aggressive horizontal baseball-type swing at waist height. Then gradually lower the height while retaining the speed until the swing touches the ground.

Law: Centeredness

Drill: Center Putt Drill

Purpose: To strike the ball in the center of the putter face.

Description: Tape two tees or matchsticks on the face of a putter about a golf ball's width apart, bracketing the "sweet spot." Putt without hitting the taped-on tees.

Drill: Face Tape Drill

Purpose: To see if the ball is being struck on the center of the clubface.

Description: Put a piece of adhesive, masking, or commercial golf marking tape on the face of a club. Hit a shot and see where the ball is being struck by the mark that is left.

Drill: Divot Drill

Purpose: To deliver the club with enough descent to get the center of the clubface to the ball.

Description: Place a tee in the ground adjacent to the back edge of the ball. Hit the shot with an iron club and take a divot which starts at the tee and continues forward. This assures that the horizontal center axis of the club gets to the ball.

Law: Face

Drill: Impact Drill

Purpose: To deliver the clubface at right angles (square) to the intended flight line.

Description: Take a bag made of strong material and stuff it with cloth material.* Place it on the floor against a heavy chair, or if on the grass, against a tree or golf car tire. Stand so that when impact is made with the bag its position is the same as if a ball were present. Use any club, but make sure that the back of the left hand and wrist are flat when impact is made. Put a club under the bag for a target line to make sure the swing comes from the inside. The bag does not have to be hit hard. Make sure after several swings into the bag, that those are followed by some practice swings to a full finish, as a golf swing is always *through*, not *to*.

Drill: Square Face Check Drill

Purpose: To check and see if the clubface is square at address.

Description: After taking a grip position and before soling the club, push the clubface against any firm object that has a straight edge, like a driving range mat, a two-by-four, a post on a tree, a tee marker, etc. This provides a square face check.

Drill: Right Angles Drill

Purpose: To check and see if the clubface is square at address.

Description: Use any straight line or right angle, i.e., a club layed on the ground, a pattern on a carpet, boards on the floor, linoleum squares, or a seam in the concrete, as a reference to see if the face is at right angles to the line. It may seem simple but correct alignment needs to be regularly confirmed.

Law: Path

Drill: Back and Under Drill

*Available commercially under the trademarked name Impact Bag™.

Purpose: To retrain an outside-to-in swing path pattern to an approach that is from the inside.

Description: Take an appropriate stance with the club of choice (#5 iron, for example) and elevate it so the clubhead is about 1½ feet above the ground. Make a backswing that is not pulled quickly inside. Note the angle of the plane going back. Now make a forward swing in which the plane is under or shallower than the backswing plane. "Back, under—back, under." Lower the club to the ball and repeat a similar pattern.

Drill: Shaft Path Drill

Purpose: To produce the desired swing path.

Description: Push three shafts into the ground at the desired plane angle. Place the shafts in the following manner: The middle shaft at a location just opposite an imaginary ball position; the shaft on the right to control the backswing and path prior to impact; the shaft on the left to control the post-impact swingpath direction. If the desired path is inside-to-out, place the right side shaft so you must swing inside it on the back and forward motion. The left shaft should be located so you must swing outside of it. If an out-to-in motion is desired, locate the shafts so you go outside the right-side shaft on the back and through swings and inside of the shaft on the follow-through. Path can be controlled by selecting the shaft placement and determining whether the swing path is to go inside or outside the shafts placed in the ground.

Drill: Painted Path Lines Drill

Purpose: To develop the desired swing path.

Description: Paint a straight red line pointed to the target. For a straight shot paint a white arc line coming from slightly inside the red target line and contacting it at the ball's location and returning back to the inside. For a draw shot make the arc come from the inside to the out; for a fade, from outside to in.

Law: Angle of Approach

Drill: Sidehill Lies Drill

Purpose: To flatten the angle of approach to the ball.

Description: Create a sidehill lie either by finding a natural sidehill location or create one artificially by using "tall tees" or a slant platform. This inclined stance position automatically causes you to make a shallower swing.

Drill: Stay Under Drill

Purpose: To flatten the angle of approach to the ball.

Description: Take an old shaft and angle it into the ground so the grip end is 1–2 feet off the ground. Swing underneath it on the forward swing to flatten the approach angle. Adjust the angle as needed.

Drill: Clear the Shaft Drill

Purpose: To steepen the angle of approach to the ball for a bunker shot, cut shot or intentional slice.

Description: Place an old shaft vertically in the ground to the right so that the backswing and forward swing must clear it. The approach will be steepened and will be travelling outside-to-in.

Principle: Grip

Drill: Off and On Drill

Purpose: To find the natural positioning of the hands for the grip.

Description: Select a middle iron. A friend should then kneel and hold the shaft so when you let go of the club it remains in the same position. Let your arms hang naturally then swing them onto the grip, release and repeat, until it is evident that a natural arm/body position is quite easy to achieve.

Drill: In the Air Drill

Purpose: To find a natural position for the hands on the grip.

Description: Elevate the club and hold it at face height in the right hand where the shaft meets the grip. Angle the shaft so the clubhead is toward the right side of the face and the grip is in front of the left part of the chest. Now reach out with the left hand and place it on the grip in a position where the last three fingers can exert the strongest pressure and two or three knuckles of the top of the left hand are visible. With the right hand holding the shaft in the channel of the fingers, simply slide the right hand down to abut with the left hand in either a ten-finger, overlapping or interlocking grip.

Drill: Military Grip Drill

Purpose: To establish a consistent, solid, grip position.

Description: Stand at attention with feet close together and both arms hanging at the sides. Position the club outside the left leg so when the left arm hangs naturally the club's grip would find the correct position in the fingers of the left hand. Put the left thumb on the right side of the shaft and grip the club snugly in the last three fingers of the left hand. Elevate the club so the clubhead is pointing to the sky and the left hand is at chin height. Add the right hand grip in the fingers. Check to see if the leading edge is square (vertical), before soling the club.

Principle: Aim

Drill: Parallel Clubs Drill

Purpose: To align the body and clubface square to the target.

Description: Without question the most widely used practice drill for aiming the body is to lay a club on the ground pointing at the target and then place a club parallel to the first. The target club is used to identify the intended line and check the clubface to see if it's at right angles. The second club is to be used to check the aim of the feet, hips and shoulders, to see if they are square.

Drill: Painted Aim Lines Drill

Purpose: To align the body and clubface so they are appropriate for the shot being played.

Description: Using golf course marking paint

to create aim lines in the grass or permanent marks on a mat can be useful for a variety of shots. Parallel lines for full shots, a T-line for putting, open stance lines for chipping, pitching and bunker play.

Drill: Mirror to Aim Drill

Purpose: To check body alignment.

Description: Put reference clubs, tape or lines on the floor which match the desired alignment. Place them pointing toward a mirror so that when the body is set up to the lines the body alignment can be checked in the mirror. Look for square feet, hips and particularly shoulders.

Principle: Setup

Drill: Arms to Chest Drill

Purpose: To help establish the correct distance from the ball.

Description: After the club has been gripped and is being held with the clubhead in the air, wrist cocked and hands at chin height, bring the arms down so they put pressure on the chest. When pressure is felt then bend forward from the hips until the club is only 2–3 inches off the ground, then sit slightly in the knees until the club is soled. The hands will end up about six inches from the left leg and will be inside a line dropped vertically from the eyes.

Drill: Make a Letter T or H Drill

Purpose: To get aligned correctly while finding the correct ball location.

Description: Using clubs or golf course spray paint make either a capital letter H or T on the ground so you can relate to the correct aim and the location of the ball relative to the feet. The vertical baseline of the T gives a ball position reference as does the horizontal bar on the H.

Drill: Make a Stance Drill

Purpose: To be able to find a consistent ball position and width of stance.

Description: Select an iron club (probably a #7, #8 or #9 iron) that is the same length from the lowest portion of the grip to the hosel as is the width of the stance from left toe to right toe in the driver shot. Once that is established when practicing the driver, lay the selected club down and place tees in the ground at the hosel and bottom of the grip locations. That is the correct consistent width for the driver shot for every practice session. Next locate and memorize or mark the number of shaft steps that the feet are closer together for a #2 iron, #6 iron and wedge. Use tees again to put in the ground when practicing with these clubs to get a consistent stance width. Also note a position on the shaft where the ball should be placed between the feet for irons and woods. Again use a tee to mark those locations in the grass. The spot on the shaft can be marked with a dab of paint. Remember, consistency in shots comes from consistency in preparation.

Principle: Arc Length

Drill: Mirror Arc Check Drill

Purpose: To locate a consistent effective length of backswing.

Description: Stand facing a mirror which has a piece of tape running horizontally across the mirror at head height level. Watch to see that the club shaft reaches a position within five degrees (plus or minus) of that line when making a full driver swing.

Drill: Put It on the Shelf Drill

Purpose: To limit the length of the backswing, particularly for players who have too long a backswing.

Description: Find a cabinet, shelf or any flat surface at head height. Stand close to and with your left side facing the shelf or surface. Use the shelf or cabinet top as a barrier to stop the backswing.

Drill: Turn and Hold Drill

Purpose: To increase the amount of turn you can get in the backswing.

Description: Stand with your back to the wall, heels approximately one foot from the base of the wall. Turn first to the right (back-swing) and place the hands (with fingers spread) flat against the wall. Hold for 30 seconds. Then go the other direction and repeat the process. Each day, work the hands slightly farther across the wall, thus creating more stretch and greater trunk flexibility.

Principle: Arc Width

Drill: Pre-Set Width Drill

Purpose: To create sufficient width in the swing radius.

Description: Assume a pre-set position where the wrists are cocked, left arm extended, toe of the club pointing up but the clubhead not quite to hip height. Make a turn to the top of the swing and focus on maintaining an extended left arm as it was at the beginning of the drill.

Drill: Rifle Barrel Drill

Purpose: To develop extension in the impact and throughswing position.

Description: Swing past impact up to hip height in the follow-through. At this point the right arm should be fully extended and the left arm a bit folded, fairly close to the left side. Hold this spot in the toe up club position for thirty seconds, then relax and repeat. This drill is also excellent to get a player to open, close or square the face at impact. Simply turn the clubface down so the back of the left hand faces the ground if a hook is desired, face up to the sky for a slice and toe up for straight. Hold and repeat. Then swing through that practice position while striking a ball.

Drill: Lighten Up Drill

Purpose: To relax the muscles to allow centrifugal force to create expansion and release.

Description: Grip the club as tightly as possible (a 10 level) and try to swing the club. The result is a slower, higher-off-the-ground, reduced swing arc effort. Then try an eight in grip pressure level, a six and a four, each followed by swings simulating those numbers. Notice how the swing arc expands and reaches the ground more easily, taking grass

when the grip pressure decreases. Centrifugal force and gravity are working to help you if you'll allow them to not be squeezed out.

Principle: Lever System

Drill: Pre-Set Drill

Purpose: To create a potentially powerful second lever in the backswing.

Description: Take your grip and stance position with a #5 iron. Then while the arms are still in front, cock the wrists to a position of about 70 degrees from ground level. A second lever has now been created. Swing those two levers to the top of the backswing. Gradually blend in the takeaway as part of the creation of the second lever.

Drill: Half Grip Drill

Purpose: To create a second lever in the backswing.

Description: Take a normal left-hand grip but put the right hand halfway down the shaft. Use the right hand to set the second lever while the left arm remains in an extended position still in front of the body. Tug the left arm to the top with the fingers of the right hand pulling on the shaft. Repeat the drill noting the feeling of the left wrist when fully cocked.

Drill: Early Set Drill

Purpose: To guarantee that you will cock your wrists in the backswing.

Description: After you have taken your address position, immediately cock the wrists (set the angle) in the takeaway. This will ensure that you don't reach the top of the backswing still in a one-lever position.

Principle: Swing Center

Drill: Doorjam Drill

Purpose: To keep the center of rotation in control.

Description: Stand in a doorway facing the doorjam and bend forward at the hips until the body inclination matches that used for a full swing. Let the arms hang fully in front. Touch the hair or top of the forehead lightly against the doorjam and make a limited backswing and throughswing similar to that used for a short-iron shot. The head will rotate slightly in the backswing returning back to the original position on the forward swing, then turning left and moving up as the right shoulder contacts the chin. Some lateral head movement can be allowed as the shot gets longer. In driver swings the lateral movement of the head may be slightly greater although successful swings may also be made with just head rotation and little lateral head movement.

Drill: Don't Spill the Soup Drill

Purpose: To keep the swing center from moving too far back and down.

Description: While the swing center has some degree of movement possible, it can move out of position (too far back and down if there is an attempt by the player to overuse the legs by driving them to the target). This tilts the upper body backward in order to compensate, making the angle of approach less than ideal. Imagine a bowl of soup has been placed on the top of your head and that you are to stay level through the swing so as not to spill it. In fact there is some body tilt forward in the swing but this concept and drill can help level out those who exaggerate.

Drill: Head Control Drill

Purpose: To keep the swing center from raising.

Description: Raising the head up (which elevates the swing center) is usually the result of some other technical error. It is one of the most common mistakes that the novice makes. To eliminate it, bend forward from the hips in a good setup position. A friend should then hold a club so that the grip rests like a low ceiling just above your head. Maintain your forward body tilt and swing center by not allowing the head to raise up and hit this barrier which you imagine to be a ceiling of sharp spikes.

Principle: Timing Drill

Drill: Baaack and Through

Purpose: To develop a well-timed swing with rhythm.

Description: Use the words back and through in this fashion: say BAAACK by stretching it out to create an unhurried backswing fashion. The AND represents the completion of the backswing and transition to the forward swing. THROUGH is said more quickly, representing acceleration.

Drill: By the Numbers Drill

Purpose: To develop timing and rhythm in the swing.

Description: Count 1–2–3—4–5–6 with each swing while hitting balls. Count out loud and try to keep the numbers at an even level of intensity. If too much hitting effort is expended there will be an increase in vocal intensity on the number 4.

Drill: Good Swings by Osmosis Drill

Purpose: To develop timing and rhythm in the swing.

Description: Select a Tour player's swing that you would like to emulate—one that has good timing and rhythm. If possible watch the Tour player repeatedly swinging on video. When you are on the course, visualize your Tour model and swing as closely to that model as you can.

Principle: Release

Drill: Baseball Swing Drill

Purpose: To get forearm rotation for a full release.

Description: Hold the club about 1½ feet above the ground as in swinging at a low pitch in baseball. At this height it is easy to get forearm rotation. Gradually lower the position while maintaining the release.

Drill: Toe Up to Toe Up Drill

Purpose: To return the clubface to square by getting a correct club position on both sides of the ball.

Description: From a position in the backswing where the club is horizontal to the ground at hip height with the toe of the club pointing skyward, clubface vertical, swing to a position in the follow-through with the club shaft again horizontal at hip height, the toe of the club to the sky and the leading edge vertical.

Drill: Shake Hands to Shake Hands Drill

Purpose: To square the clubface at impact by locating the correct position of the right hand prior to and after impact.

Description: Put the right hand out at hip height to the right side as though shaking hands with someone—the right arm should be folded at the elbow and the body should be turned slightly in that direction. Then repeat the shake hands position at hip height on the left side but this time with the right arm more in extension.

Principle: Dynamic Balance

Drill: Gary Player Down the Fairway Drill

Purpose: Get the weight transferred to the left side in the forward swing.

Description: Follow through by taking a step with the right foot down the fairway after the shot, much as Gary Player often does.

Drill: Lift the Leg Drill

Purpose: To make absolutely certain the weight is being transferred correctly on both the back and forward swings.

Description: To make sure that the weight is transferred to the right leg in the backswing, raise the left leg off the ground during the backswing. To make sure the weight is transferred to the left foot in the forward swing, raise the right foot off the ground in the follow-through. Gradually reduce the height of the lifted leg until the foot actually stays in contact with the ground and gradually finds its correct position.

Drill: Right Knee Hits Left Knee Drill

Purpose: To complete the trunk rotation on the throughswing and allow the weight to finish on the left side.

Description: In a stance with the feet not too far apart, see that the right knee actually touches the left knee (right knee pointing to the target) on the follow-through.

Principle: Position

Drill: Pre-Set for Position Drill

Purpose: To establish the correct position at the top of the swing by setting it early enough to observe its position.

Description: After making a good grip, cock the wrists immediately in front to about 70 degrees without swinging the arms back. Check to see that the toe of the club is pointing to the sky (leading edge vertical). This is a square position. Swing the club to the top without any change in the wrist position so that the face will still be square.

Drill: Mirror Image Drill

Purpose: To check the position of the hands, wrists, arms and clubface at the top of the swing.

Description: Stand with the right side of the body facing a mirror. Swing a club to the top of the backswing and look to see if the club is aligned parallel to the target, the clubface is at approximately 45 degrees and is in plane with the left wrist and back of the left forearm. When the correct position is found, put a strip of tape on the mirror to match that angle and to use as a reference.

Drill: Lift, Set and Turn Drill

Purpose: To find the correct position at the top of the backswing.

Description: Take a good grip. Raise the club off the ground by elevating the hands to hip height. Cock the wrists so the left wrist is basically flat and the club is angled over the right shoulder. Bend forward at the waist and then turn the shoulders, allowing the hands to go over the right shoulder but without changing their pre-set alignment. This should represent the correct position at the top.

Principle: Plane

Drill: Flagstick Drill

Purpose: To locate the on-plane position of the

arms and hands in the backswing and forward swing.

Description: Take an old flagstick and grasp it in the middle. Swing to the top and monitor the extended portion from the butt of the left hand. This extension should point through the ball on the downswing and also point to a line extended from the ball (target line) at all times during the swing. This drill can also be done by gripping a driver in the middle of the shaft on the steel.

Drill: Flashlight Drill
Purpose: To identify an on-plane swing.
Description: Attach a pen light (flashlight) to the top of the grip. Choke down below the light and while standing in a partially darkened room which has a baseline strip of tape placed on the floor as the target line, swing, matching the beam of light to the line.

Drill: Plane Imaging Drill
Purpose: To put the club on-plane during the swing.
Description: Visualize standing in the center hole of a large sheet of plywood which has been tilted so the baseline is resting on the ground and the opposite side lifted, creating an angle of some 55 to 65 degrees. Feel as though the arms are swinging back and through, allowing the club shaft to simply ride on the plywood plane while the club goes from toe up to toe up.

Principle: Impact (see Face)

Principle: Connection

Drill: Head Mitts Drill
Purpose: To maintain the upper body parts in their correct relationship during the swing.
Description: Take two head covers, preferably the large soft material type, and put them under each armpit. Hit wedge shots maintaining the head covers in this underarm position. Sense this same relationship of arms to body when playing, although the swing will have more freedom.

Drill: Strap Drill
Purpose: To maintain the upper body parts in their correct relationship during the swing.
Description: Put an elastic strap (homemade or commercial) around the arms, or arms and chest to restrain the right elbow from lifting in the backswing and the left arm from separating too widely from the left side in the throughswing. Swing and hit balls.

Drill: Club Attached Drill
Purpose: To maintain the upper body parts in their correct relationship during the swing.
Description: Hold the club with both hands on the steel just at the bottom of the grip and place the butt of the club against the stomach so the club is horizontal. Turn back and through as though making a golf swing and note the feeling of how the hands, forearms and body stay in the same relationship.

Skill: Chip and Pitch

Drill: Extender Drill
Purpose: To keep the clubhead from passing the hands prior to impact.
Description: Cut the top portion of the grip from the butt end of a chipping or pitching club. Run an old shaft taken from a driver down inside the top so that it extends to make the iron club much longer. If you attempt to scoop the ball and break down the left wrist, the extended portion will bump you in the side of the ribs.

Drill: Grass Ahead Drill
Purpose: To keep the clubhead from passing the hands prior to impact.
Description: Step a few inches away from the ball and make a practice swing in which you brush the grass ahead, to the left of the ball. You will not be able to do so if the left wrist breaks prematurely.

Drill: Wrist Flat Drill
Purpose: To keep the clubhead from passing the hands prior to impact.
Description: Keeping the left wrist flat is a

great protection against letting the clubhead release prematurely. Some of the ways to accomplish this position are: a) use a tongue depressor or any smooth flat stick under the back of the glove that resists the hinging of the back of the left wrist toward the top of the forearm; b) put a tee in the top of the grip and never let the tee point toward the body; c) establish a reverse letter Y position in the set-up with the club being the leg of the Y and maintain the Y to the finish of the stroke; d) try and decrease the loft of the clubface from address position to contact rather than increase it; e) apply pressure on the left thumb with the butt of the right hand and feel the butt of the right hand leading the stroke.

Skill: Bunker

Drill: Line Drill

Purpose: To develop a consistent entry point in the sand in correct relation to the ball position.

Description: Draw a straight line 10 feet long in the sand with the butt end of the club or rake handle. Straddle the line so it is slightly left of center in your stance. Make swings so you splash sand forward with the entry point starting on the line. Travel down the line repeating the drill until the entry point is consistent. Then add a ball some three inches ahead of the line and repeat.

Drill: Rocks Drill

Purpose: To reduce the anxiety in playing bunker shots.

Description: In a practice bunker that is close to the edge of the green make a full bunker swing and splash sand out onto the green. The grains of sand are like miniature golf balls and playing a ball out is no more difficult. Find some small pebbles or rocks and place them on top of the sand so they can be splashed out like the sand, only as bigger grains. Then place a ball, like the rocks, on top of the sand and splash sand again onto the green, only now there is a big white rock

(the ball) which will go with the sand.

Drill: Board Drill

Purpose: To achieve the proper bounce that should come from the sole of the sand iron.

Description: Get a piece of firm board like a 1×4 or 2×4 and bury it in the sand slightly below the surface. Put a ½ inch layer of sand on the board and play the shot utilizing the bounce of the board against the flat portion of the sole of the sand iron.

Drill: Overlap Release Drill

Purpose: To encourage you to finish the swing rather than decelerating and stopping.

Description: Place your right-hand grip totally over the left hand so the right hand cannot squeeze, and in doing so apply too much pressure on the shaft causing it to slow down. Hit balls with this grip. The momentum will carry the swing to a good finish.

Skill: Putting

Drill: Push Putt Drill

Purpose: To make the putter blade go to the target following through rather than stopping at the ball.

Description: From a very short distance (1–2 feet) place the ball on a level portion of the green. Set the putter face against the ball with the blade at right angles to the target. Vigorously push the putter blade toward the center of the cup with enough acceleration so the ball leaves the face.

Drill: Pace Drill

Purpose: To develop a stroke which can produce a consistent pace for various distances.

Description: Place three balls on the putting green. Putt one ball to no particular target, but closely monitor the effort it took to get there. Putt each of the other two balls so they finish the same distance as the first.

Drill: One Arm Putting

Purpose: To eliminate wrist breakdown in putting.

Description: Grip the putter with the right hand alone so the wrist is slightly extended (back of the hand toward the top of the forearm). Putt using no wrist action. Switch to the left hand alone (may need to go lower on the grip for control) and with the back of the left hand solid, do likewise. Then putt some with both hands mimicking the action practiced when using the hands separately.

Contests and Games

Putting

1. **Ten-in-a-Row:** Put tees at one-foot increments starting two feet from the hole. Putt progressively from each location trying to make ten in a row. When there is a miss, return to the beginning.

2. **Around the World:** Place four balls around the cup in each direction, N–S–E–W, at a distance of two feet. Make them all, then move to 3, 4, 5 and 6 feet, see how many successful putts can be recorded out of 20.

3. **Twenty-one:** Play 21 against one or more competitors. Each plays one, two or three balls depending upon the number of players; three balls with two players, two with three or four, one with more than four. The closest balls to the hole with two players score one point each, closest of three balls each score a point when more than two players are involved. A sink is worth three points; a sink on top of another cancels the first and gets three. Three-putting subtracts two points. Player must hit 21 exactly or lose. Player who previously scored points putts first.

4. **Horse:** Play horse, like in the basketball game. As many players as desired can play. The first player selects a putt and if he/she makes it, the person following must do likewise from the same location or get a horse. If the second player makes the putt, the third player must do so as well or receive a horse. If the second player fails to make the putt, the next player may choose a new location. Play to three or five points before out, depending on the number of players.

5. **Contract Bridge:** Player selects a location longer than three feet and bids the number of strokes it will take him/her to hole out three balls. His opponent may bid lower, accept the contract or double the bid. If the original bidder makes his contract or fewer, he gets three points. Should he fail by one stroke he loses three, if he fails by two, he loses six, and three or more, he loses nine. For every stroke fewer than the contract, he receives two points per stroke bonus. If he is doubled, he may re-double. The game is to 30 points.

6. **Pull Back:** Players putt against each other in clock golf fashion from different lengths. If the putt is not holed on the first stroke, it must be pulled back from its location one additional putter length. If the second putt is missed, it must be pulled back as well, continuing until the putt is holed. (This also may be played as double pull back or two putter lengths.)

Pitch & Chip

1. **Up and Down:** Take six balls and challenge yourself or someone else to an up and down contest from six different locations.

2. **In the Circle:** Make a circle with a radius of a putter length marked with tees. See how many the player can get into the circle from different locations.

3. **Trajectory:** String two cords or tape one foot apart between two shafts stuck in the ground. Chip or pitch under, through and over to learn trajectory. Score points.

4. **Pitch to Win:** Spray two ten-foot lines twenty-five yards apart that run parallel . . . one a starting line, one a finish line. Make a third parallel line five feet long and five yards from the starting line; it will be the opening line. From back of the starting line pitch a ball with a sand wedge that lands in the air beyond the opening line. Then pitch a second ball to

land past the opening line and finish beyond the first ball. Continue, always pitching the next shot past the opening line and always finishing past the previous shot. See how many balls can be hit in succession before exceeding the finish line. Once a ball has finished short of the previous ball, the game is over and the number of successful shots is the score. The contestant is allowed three tries to get the first shot past the opening line. As soon as one is passed the game begins. After three successive short misses, one point is deducted from the final score for each additional short opening shot.

Bunker Contests

1. **Bunker Challenge:** With three players in the bunker, rotate the order of playing first and selecting the type of shot to be played and its location. Closest to the hole for the three is worth two points, one for next closest, none for farthest. A hole out is worth double the closest points, or in this case four. If five players play points go 4–3–2–1 and 8 for a hole out. Game is to 21 points.
2. **Bunker Up and Down:** Set up a six-hole course playing from various locations in the bunker to designated pin locations. Make two of the shots buried lies. Play up and down for total score.

3. **Get Them Out—Get Them Close:** Depending upon your level, see how many consecutive balls you can, a) get out of the bunker, b) get on the green, c) get inside a seven-foot radius (one flagstick). Set your record then try and improve it.

Full Swing Contests

1. **Direction Challenge:** With two competitors select a wedge and play to a target approximately 100 yards in the distance. The ball that comes closest on-line with the target (providing it is not a mishit) is awarded a point. Play to five points and go to a #8 iron, five more points then a #6, etc. Each club is a new game. If three competitors play, score two points for closest and one for next closest; the game is to seven points.
2. **Greens in Regulation:** Play tee to green rounds imagining the course you plan to play next. If the first hole is a par five, start with the driver, picture the hole and make the shot. Depending on the result, select the club for the second shot and play accordingly. Then the appropriate iron to a target on the range. Estimate how many fairways and greens were hit in regulation.

APPENDIX 7

LIGHTNING

What you should know about golf's killer hazard
by Dorothy Geisler*

True or False?

1. Rubber tires don't protect you from the force of a lightning bolt.
2. Lightning does not have to hit you directly in order for you to be seriously injured.
3. Water attracts lightning.
4. If stranded in a forest, it is best to stand under a group of shorter trees.
5. An "apparently dead" lightning victim can sometimes be revived.
6. Lightning carries many times the charge of an electrical power line.
7. It is safe to touch a lightning victim almost immediately following the injury.
8. Lightning always takes the path of least resistance.
9. Your hair may stand on end just before lightning is ready to strike.
10. Lightning kills more people each year than tornadoes do.

The answer for each of these 10 statements is *true*. Here's why golfers should take lightning more seriously than they do:

Lightning seems as much attracted to golf courses as golfers are. The mixture of trees, open spaces, high and low spots, water, metal shoe spikes, metal clubs, wet grass, golf cars, sprinkler systems and a golfer's determination not to be defeated by the elements all add up to a most likely target for lightning statistics.

*Adapted from *Golf Digest* article, June 1982.

Lightning First Aid**

"You should first check to see if the victim is breathing and if his heart is still beating. If there is no heartbeat, Cardiopulmonary Resuscitation (CPR) should be started immediately. If the victim's heart is still beating, but he is not breathing, mouth-to-mouth resuscitation is needed." CPR is a combination of mouth-to-mouth resuscitation and external cardiac compression, and treatment should be administered only by persons with proper training. About eight hours of classroom instruction are needed to learn CPR. It is offered by the American Heart Association and the American Red Cross.

The Red Cross advises that immediate first aid to restore breathing is necessary to prevent irrevocable brain damage and must begin within the first four to six minutes. Mouth-to-mouth resuscitation once every five seconds is necessary for adults.

"Once breathing and a heartbeat are established you should check for burn areas," says Tod Turriff of the National Safety Council. "There will usually be a point where the lightning entered and a point where it exited. These will be second- or third-degree burns. They should be covered with a clean cloth. Other burn marks may appear around jewelry—watches, rings and belt buckles. The victim is

****From Tod Turiff, National Safety Council, *Golf Digest*, June 1983.

likely to be in shock and should be treated for this."

To treat for shock, keep the victim lying down. Cover the body enough to maintain body temperature and get medical attention promptly. Even someone without apparent injuries can still die from shock alone.

The victim who has a heartbeat and is breathing will probably recover spontaneously, but should receive burn and shock attention as soon as possible.

Preventive measures and myths.

Check the latest weather forecast before beginning any outdoor activity. It is not advisable to begin a round of golf if there are severe weather watches or warnings posted. There are signs to watch for that indicate an electrical storm is approaching and may indicate an immediate need to seek shelter. Don't ignore very dark clouds, thunderheads and occasional flashes of lightning in the distance—they all signal an approaching storm.

Generally, if you take heed you will have ample time to find shelter. Your best protection is inside a large building or an all-metal vehicle. Contrary to popular opinion, a golf car is *not* a safe place to be. The rubber tires will not protect you. However, when lightning strikes an enclosed car you are protected by the vehicle's shell, which diverts the charge of the bolt along the metal skin of the vehicle before it jumps to the ground. Likewise, rubber-soled shoes offer little protection from lightning.

Small, isolated sheds in open areas will attract lightning and will not offer the protection you need. Any object that projects above the rest of the landscape could draw a lightning bolt. Because lightning follows the path of least resistance, it is drawn to the tallest object. That may be a large tree, or even a person standing on an elevated area, such as a green or tee.

To minimize your chance of being struck, find a low spot away from water and metal objects. "Waiting out a thunderstorm under a tall tree on the golf course is like standing in the middle of a freeway at rush hour," says Mike Mogil, a severe-storm expert with the National Weather Service. "You may not be hit, but you're taking a dangerous and unnecessary risk."

If you are in a wooded area, seek shelter in a low place under a thick growth of small trees. The larger trees are most likely to be struck first. You may receive residual lightning, but that's better than a direct hit.

The most ominous warning signal occurs when your hair literally stands on end, caused by highly charged air. If this happens, get away from any metal object and drop to your hands and knees immediately. The danger of your body acting as a conductor will be minimized.

Too many golfers' attitudes about lightning are reflected in the comments of a lightning strike victim, who fortunately survived. "We had no fear of lightning or a storm," he says. "Our main concern was that we wanted to finish our round. Too many people just don't think getting struck by lightning can happen. Believe me, it can."

A PARTIAL LIST OF
GOLF SCHOOLS IN THE UNITED STATES

The Academy of Golf at the Hills of Lakeway
& Dave Pelz Short Game
One World of Tennis Square
Austin, TX 78738

Arnold Palmer Golf School
9000 Bay Hill Boulevard
Orlando, FL 32910

Ben Sutton's Golf School
P.O. Box 9199
Canton, OH 44711

Berkshire School of Golf
Cranwell Resort
55 Lee Road
Lenox, MA 01240

Bertholy Method Golf School
Foxfire Village
Jackson Springs, NC 27281

Bill Skelley's Schools of Golf
Miami Lakes Inn & Golf Resort
Miami Lakes, FL 33014

Craft-Zavichas Golf School
600 Dittmer Avenue
Pueblo, CO 81005

The Florida Golf Academy
720 Goodlette Road, Suite 303
Naples, FL 33940

The Florida Golf School
Rolling Hills Resort
3501 W. Rolling Hills Circle
Ft. Lauderdale, FL 33328

Golf Digest Instruction School
5520 Park Ave., Box 395
Trumbull, CT 06611

The Golf School
Plantation Golf Resort
P.O. Box 1116
Crystal River, FL 32629

The Golf School
Mount Snow Resort
Mount Snow, VT 05356

The Golf School at Pebble Beach
P.O. Box M
Carmel, CA 93921

Golf University of the Midwest
Lodge of the Four Seasons
Lake Ozark, MO 65409

The Golf University at San Diego
2001 Old Hwy. 395
Fallbrook, CA 92028

Grand Cypress School of Golf
Grand Cypress Resort
1 North Jacaranda
Orlando, FL 32819

The Illinois Golf School at
Eagle Ridge Inn & Resort
U.S. Route 20, Box 777
Galena, IL 61036

Innisbrook Golf Institute
P.O. Drawer 1088
Tarpon Springs, FL 34688-1088

Jeri Reid's Golf School
2059 Southwest 15th Street
Deerfield Beach, FL 33442

Jimmy Ballard Golf Workshop
Doral Country Club
4400 NW 87th Avenue
Miami, FL 33178

John Jacobs' Practical Golf School
7127 East Sahuaro, Suite 101
Scottsdale, AZ 85254

John Schlee's Maximum Golf School
4923 Avila Avenue
Carlsbad, CA 92008

La Costa Golf School
La Costa Hotel and Spa
Carlsbad, CA 92008

Margo Walden Golf School
Seabrook Island Resort
P.O. Box 32099
Charleston, SC 29417

National Academy of Golf
490 Fourth Avenue South
Naples, FL 33940

Paul Tessler's Westgate Golf Center
3781 State Rt. 5
Newton Falls, OH 44444

Performance Golf Schools
Orange Tree Golf Resort
Phoenix, AZ 85254

PGA National Golf School
1000 Avenue of the Champions
Palm Beach Gardens, FL 33418

Pinehurst Golf Advantage
Golf Advantage Teaching Center
P.O. Box 4000
Pinehurst Country Club
Pinehurst, NC 28374

Pine Needles Golf Camps
Pine Needles Lodge & C.C.
Box 88
Southern Pines, NC 28387

Roland Stafford Golf School
Kass Inn
Route 30
Margaretville, NY 12455

The Sebring Golf School
281 U.S. 27 North
Sebring, FL 33870

Sports Enhancement Associates (SEA)
P.O. Box 2788
Sedona, AZ 86336

The Stratton Golf School
The Stratton/Scottsdale Corporation
Stratton Mountain, VT 05155

Swing's The Thing Golf School
P.O. Box 200
Shawnee-On-Delaware, PA 18356

SyberVision Golf School
11 Maiden Lane, Suite 400
San Francisco, CA 94108

U.S. Golf Academy
5203 Plymouth LaPorte Terrace
Plymouth, IN 46563

Vintage Golf Schools
Port Royal Resort
P.O. Box 5045
Hilton Head, SC 29938

GLASSES AND VISION PROBLEMS FOR GOLFERS

by Dr. Curtis D. Benton*

How many senior golfers wear glasses for golf? At least one per foursome. If you're that one, you ought to consider special glasses for golf. But, what kind?

Up to their mid-forties, those wearing glasses probably need only single-vision lenses, that is, lenses that have no bifocal. There is no problem for them looking down, up or sideways; the focus is all the same. That rule holds true unless you get into rather strong prescriptions where the element of distortion creeps into the picture. Golfers who need such prescriptions often wear contact lenses. They correct vision as near normal in every way as is possible to do and are ideal for golf. But not everybody has the desire or the ability to wear contacts successfully.

Getting Fitted

Back to the glasses. If you need glasses for clear distance vision, your best golf glasses are single-vision lenses. There is no bifocal to get in your way and cause you to see two balls where one should be.

Perhaps you can't see the scorecard well enough to read the yardage or mark the scores and thus, prefer bifocals. If so, have the segments set very low in the lenses or even shifted a bit to the right of center (if you are a right-handed golfer). That way the bifocal area will

*Adapted from *Senior Golfer* Magazine.

not interfere with play but will be present for use in seeing the scorecard.

If your distance vision is satisfactory without glasses but you can't see up close, take along a pair of reading glasses to slip on easily when you want to read the rules sheet or the scorecard.

In selecting frames for your golf glasses, choose ear pieces that curve enough around your ears to hold the glasses nicely in place when you bend your head over to putt. Some golfers even use an elastic strap around the back of the head to hold the glasses firmly in place. The old "wrap around" ear pieces that now are hard to find work best of any.

There's a flurry of interest these days in ultraviolet light, with the suggestion that it is part of the cause of cataracts and other eye problems. While it is true that cataracts are much more common in the world's sun belt, there appear to be other factors such as heredity and nutrition. The final vote isn't in yet, but certainly there is no reason to panic. If you do wear tinted glasses for golf, and you want to fully protect yourself from ultraviolet light, ask for the new filter that effectively blocks all wavelengths shorter than 400 nms.

Nearsighted or Farsighted

Watch the next couple of foursomes approach the tee at your home course. Most of the players are about the same height, usually considered as average, but a few are decidedly taller and some are somewhat shorter. Eyes come in somewhat the same distribution. Some are longsighted, most are medium (normal) and some are shortsighted.

To understand farsightedness think of the last time a grandchild came running up to you and thrust his or her newest work of crayon art a putter head distance from your sunburned nose. Your sight is only clear far beyond that distance.

Now shift the scene to the first tee. A farsighted person, if only slightly or moderately farsighted, can see the green and the flag but possibly can't read the name printed on the golf ball as he addresses his drive. If a person is severely farsighted, the green is too close to be seen clearly and he or she must wear magnifying glasses to bring it into clear focus. But even with normal eyes you'd need a magnifying glass to see your grandchild's masterpiece near the tip of your nose or to see a tiny splinter in your finger. On the other hand, the nearsighted golfer's eyes are too strong. They have their own built-in magnifying glass, as it were. From the first tee they can't even see the fairway bunker, much less the green, without glasses that reverse the magnifying effect. If a normal-eyed person looks through a nearsighted person's glasses, objects look smaller than they really are.

Astigmatism

To complicate matters, there's a condition called astigmatism. This is due to the shape of the eyeball when it is out of round, rather like a golf ball when it leaves the clubface. Hold up a clear, smooth, straight glass of water. We call its shape a cylinder. Look at someone's face through the glass of water and see how it is stretched out like a chipmunk with a golf ball in each cheek pouch. Now if you tilt your glass sideways, right or left, the distortion shifts accordingly.

Golfers with uncorrected astigmatism (an as-

tigmatism can be present along with farsighted, nearsighted or otherwise normal-sighted eyes) see things fatter, thinner or on a slant.

Astigmatism is corrected by glasses shaped like cylinders which slant objects in the opposite direction, resulting in a proper squaring up of the landscape.

An excellent senior golfer, holder of several titles, came to me a couple of years ago complaining that he couldn't read the breaks of the greens with his new glasses. He had been given a correction for farsightedness and astigmatism, but the cylinder was tilted several degrees the wrong way. When I prescribed proper glasses his putting improved dramatically.

Other Problems

Golfers who are seniors by some years also may develop eye diseases characteristic of aging. I'll mention only cataracts and macular degeneration. With cataracts there is a gradual dimming and blurring of vision. With macular degeneration there is a fading of the central portion of the total span of vision, called the visual field.

Typically, golfers with either of these conditions lose sight of the golf ball as it leaves the tee or the ground and have to ask where it went. Sometimes they spy a ball in flight or when it hits the ground and bounces, for motion is perceived more easily.

If one eye goes bad or out of line with the other, there is a loss of judgment of depth. It is amazing, however, how well that defect can be overcome.

One of the best senior golfers with whom I play has only one eye. When he is uncertain as to the smoothness of the ground where his ball lies he looks at it from two directions. He also pays close attention to yardage markers instead of relying on eyeball judgment of distance. He's a tough competitor and can beat most of his two-eyed opponents.

Your problems in judging distances may not always have to do with your eyesight. Even with normal eyesight, geographic and atmospheric conditions can affect a golfer's visual perception.

When playing at the foot of steep mountains, such as Palm Desert or Colorado Springs, huge mountains dwarf the foreground. This makes the course look smaller than it really is and you tend to hit short. Flat courses also cause underclubbing at first. When I first moved to Florida from Atlanta, Georgia, I had to relearn judging distance, at first being one or two clubs short because of a lack of ground contours. You

will find that hillocks and elevated greens help you to make more accurate distance judgments. Also, low gray clouds tend to shorten perspective whereas brilliant sunshine stretches the distances out a bit.

All of which has to do with the eyes and the game of golf. And let me urge you, in the interest of getting the most out of your game, to have your eyes checked annually by an ophthalmologist. If you can find one who plays golf, all the better. He'll understand your frustrations.

PHYSICAL TRAINING FOR GOLF*

by Gary Wiren, Ph.D.

Golfers can use weight training to increase strength, flexibility and muscular endurance. It helps develop balance for golfers with weak leg muscles and allows the athlete to assume advantageous biomechanical positions.

A golfer's technique reflects the natural selection process of determining one's own assets and finding a style to fit them. Depending on the selected technique, golfers will vary in their strength emphasis. Generally, hands, forearms, trunk rotators, back, abdomen and legs are the most important areas of emphasis.

Strength in golf is of little use without flexibility. Most men with whom I work need more flexibility than strength. The opposite is generally true for women, they need more strength.

*Reprinted from *Getting Stronger* by Bill Pearl and Gary T. Moran, Ph.D. © 1986 Shelter Publications, Inc., Bolinas, Calif. Distributed in bookstores by Random House. Reprinted by permission.

Golf is a rotary activity, so exercise emphasizing the rotary movements of the trunk are extremely important.

Other effective techniques for increasing strength for golf could include a program of calisthenics and the swinging of a weighted club (both for strength and flexibility).

Golf is not a leader in the world of weight training for improvement in performance. The acceptance of improving strength and flexibility through weight training is relatively new to the sport, and is an important breakthrough.

The training programs that follow are rigorous off-season, pre-season and in-season workouts. They are for the golfer athlete who is interested in competition. These exercises are strenuous and should not be attempted without a doctor's consultation. *Train Don't Strain.* Following the programs are more complete descriptions of each exercise pictured from the program—note the reference in the lower left hand corner.

GOLF OFF-SEASON PROGRAM

Aims:

The off-season program is designed to strengthen all major muscle groups to provide proper muscle balance.

Days per week:

Three days, with one day rest between workouts.

Exercises	Sets	Reps	Exercises	Sets	Reps
1 Lying Leg Crossover See A-9	1	15 to 25 each side	**4** Rear Deltoid Raise See S-1	2	10-10
Optional Leg Pull-In See A-6	1	10 to 25	**5** Tricep Press Down See Tr-2	2	10-10
2 Seated Barbell Twist See A-5	1	20 to 50 each side	**6** Palms-Up Wrist Curl See F-1	1-2	15 to 20 per set
Optional Barbell Side Bend See A-2	1	15 to 30 each side	**7** Palms-Down Wrist Curl See F-2	1-2	15 to 20 per set
Optional Incline Back Kick See A-10	1	25 to 50 each leg	**8** Leg Press See Th-1	2	15-15 per set
3 Hyperextension See B-2	2	8 to 15 per set			

GOLF PRE-SEASON PROGRAM

Aims:

The pre-season program is similar to the off-season program, but with different exercises for certain body parts. During this time, more time is spent golfing and working on specific golfing skills. Always remember to include some form of cardiovascular training.

Days per week:

Two days, with one-two days rest between workouts.

Exercises	Sets	Reps	Exercises	Sets	Reps
1 Hip Roll *See A-7*	1	15 to 25	**4 Rear Deltoid Raise** *See S-3*	2	10-10 each arm
2 Dumbbell Side Bend *See A-3*	1	20 to 30 each side	**5 Tricep Curl** *See Tr-1*	2	10-10 each arm
Optional Twisting Bend *See A-4*	1	10 to 20	**6 Stand-Ups** *See Th-2*	1-2	10 to 15 per set each leg
3 Hyperextension *See B-2*	1	10 to 20 each side	**7 Palms-Up Wrist Curl** *See F-1*	1-2	15 to 20 per set
Optional Side Leg Raise *See A-8*	1	25 to 50 each leg	**8 Palms-Down Wrist Curl** *See F-2*	1-2	15 to 20 per set
Optional Leg Crossover *See A-9*	1	15 to 30 each leg			

GOLF IN-SEASON PROGRAM

Aims:

The in-season program is designed to maintain levels achieved during the off- and pre-season programs. In season, hip, wrist and forearm work can be optional.

Days per week:

Two days, with one-two days rest between workouts, and two days rest before competitions. Some golfers are more relaxed and swing more smoothly if they have a weight workout on a golfing day, or one day prior to golfing. Others need more time off before golfing. Find the schedule that works best for you.

Exercises	Sets	Reps	Exercises	Sets	Reps
1 Hyperextension See B-2	1-2	5 to 10 per set	**4 Rear Lat Pull Down** See B-1	2	10-10
2 Bent-Knee Sit-Up See A-1	1	10 to 20	**Optional Incline Lateral** See C-1	1-2	10 (10)
3 Seated Barbell Twist See A-5	1	15 to 30 each side	**5 Tricep Extension** See Tr-2	2	10-10
Optional Freehand Side Lunge See Th-3	1-2	10 per set per side	**6 Roller Wrist Curl** See F-3	1-2	Floor to top
Optional Side Lateral Raise See S-2	1-2	10 (10)			

Exercise Options:

1. Circuit training
2. Nautilus, pulleys or cable exercises
3. Weighted club exercises
4. Sport-specific resistance exercises that copy swing

Problem Areas:

1. A year-round flexibility program is very important.

2. Pay attention to individual strengths or weaknesses when devising programs.
3. Some type of cardiovascular conditioning should be done year-round: biking, swimming, aerobics, circuit training, running.

Additional Exercises:

1. Machines may be substituted
2. Dumbbells may be substituted
3. Leg extensions
4. Step-ups with weights
5. Lunges with weights
6. Shoulder shrugs
7. Lateral dumbbell raises
8. Medicine ball exercises

ABDOMINALS

A-1 Bent-Knee Sit-Up

Upper Abdominals

- Hook feet under strap of sit-up board.
- Keep knees bent 45°.
- Put hands behind head, chin on chest.
- Lie back until lower back touches.
- Return to starting position.
- Inhale down, exhale up.
- To make harder, adjust bench to higher angle.

A-2 Barbell Side Bend

Obliques

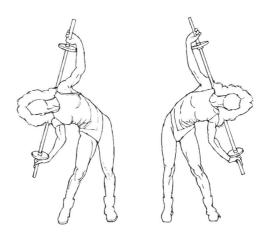

- Stand erect, feet 16″ apart.
- Place light barbell on shoulders.
- Keep back straight, head up.
- Bend to right as far as possible, then bend to left as far as possible.
- Bend at waist only, not at hips or knees.
- This exercise can also be done seated.
- Inhale to right, exhale to left.

A-3 Dumbbell Side Bend

Obliques

- Stand erect, feet 16″ apart.
- Hold dumbbell in right hand, palms in.
- Place left hand on waist.
- Keep back straight.
- Bend to right as far as possible, then bend to left as far as possible.
- Change weight to left hand and repeat movement.
- Bend at waist only, not at hips or knees.
- Inhale to right, exhale to left.
- Can be done with free hand on side of head.

A-4 Alternated Twisting Dumbbell Bend to Opposite Foot

Obliques and Lower Back

- Stand erect, feet 16″ apart.
- Hold dumbbells, palms in.
- Keep back straight, head up, hips and knees locked.
- Inhale and twist torso to right, then bend, holding twist until dumbbells nearly touch right foot.
- Return to starting position and exhale.
- Repeat movement to left side.
- A movement to the right and left equals one rep.

A-5 Seated Barbell Twist

Obliques

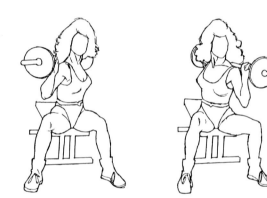

- Place light barbell on shoulders.
- Sit at end of bench, feet firmly on floor.
- Twist torso to right, then to left by twisting at waist only.
- Do not move head from side to side.
- Keep back straight, head up.
- Inhale to right, exhale to left.
- Can also be done standing.
- Can also be done holding dumbbell next to chest.

A-6 Leg Pull-In

Lower Abdominals

- Lie on floor with hands under buttocks, palms down, legs extended.
- Bend knees, pulling upper thighs into mid-section.
- Return to starting position.
- Concentrate on lower abdominals.
- Inhale up, exhale down.
- To make harder, hold light dumbbell between feet.

A-7 Hip Roll

Obliques

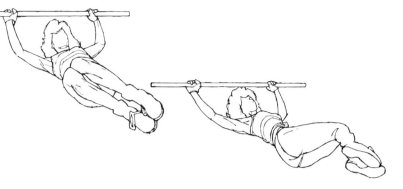

- Lie on your back.
- Hold an object behind your head for support or place hands under buttocks, palms down.
- Bend knees, feet firmly on floor.
- Lower legs to right side until upper thigh touches floor.
- Return to starting position, then repeat to left side.
- Do all bending at waist.
- Do not let shoulders come off floor.
- Inhale to right, exhale to left.

A-8 Lying Side Leg Raise

Hips

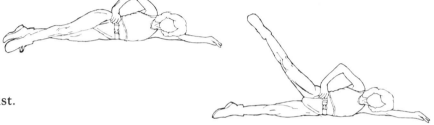

- Lie on left side.
- Tilt body slightly forward.
- Raise right leg as far as possible.
- Keep leg straight, do not bend at waist.
- Return leg to starting position.
- Lie on right side and repeat with left leg.
- Inhale up, exhale down.
- Can also be done on standing incline bench.

A-9 Lying Leg Crossover

Hips and Obliques

- Lie on back.
- Hold an object behind head with a wider-than-shoulder grip.
- Keep shoulders on floor.
- Swing right leg over left leg, as far to the side as possible until it is nearly as high as your head.
- Keep leg close to floor.
- Return to starting position, then repeat movement with left leg.
- Keep knees locked, legs as straight as possible.
- Inhale as you swing leg, exhale as you lower it.

A-10 Incline Back-Kick

Hips

- Lie face down on incline bench.
- Raise right leg straight back.
- Return leg to starting position.
- Keep leg as straight as possible.
- Repeat with left leg.
- Inhale up, exhale down.
- Can also be done lying on floor.

B-1 Wide-Grip Rear Lat Pull-Down

Upper Lats

- Hold lat bar with hands about 36" apart.
- Kneel down far enough to support weights with arms extended overhead.
- Pull bar straight down until it touches back of neck just above shoulders.
- Return to starting position.
- Inhale down, exhale up.
- Can also be done with medium grip.

B-2 Hyperextension

Lower Back

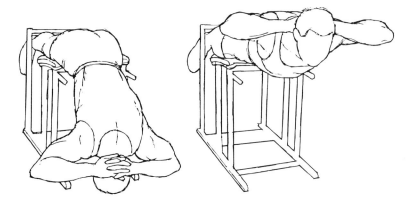

- Extend upper body over end of high bench.
- Lock legs under support.
- End of bench should be at hips.
- Bend down at waist so upper body is vertical to floor.
- Place hands behind head.
- Raise torso straight up until slightly past parallel.
- Return to starting position.
- Inhale up, exhale down.
- Can also be done with weight behind neck to increase resistance.

FOREARMS

The value of forearm exercises in golf has been overrated. Do not overdo them. Hand and finger strength is more important, especially in the left hand.

F-1 Seated Palms-Up Barbell Wrist Curl

Outside Forearms

- Hold barbell with both hands, palms up, hands 16" apart.
- Sit at end of bench, feet on floor about 20" apart.
- Lean forward, place forearms on upper thighs.
- Place backs of wrists over knees.
- Lower bar as far as possible, keeping tight grip.
- Curl bar as high as possible.
- Do not let forearms raise up.
- Inhale up, exhale down.

F-2 Seated Palms-Down Barbell Wrist Curl

Inside Forearms

- Hold barbell with both hands, palms down, hands 16" apart.
- Sit at end of bench, feet on floor about 20" apart.
- Lean forward, place forearms on upper thighs.
- Place wrists over knees.
- Lower bar as far as possible, keeping tight grip.
- Curl bar as high as possible.
- Do not let forearms raise up.
- Inhale up, exhale down.

F-3 Standing Arms-Extended Wrist-Roller Wrist Curl

Outside Forearms

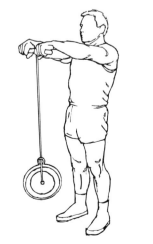

- Place light weight on end of rope of wrist roller.
- Stand erect, back straight, head up.
- Hold wrist roller with both hands, palms down.
- Extend arms straight out.
- Roll weight up by curling right hand over and down, then left hand over and down.
- Keep arms parallel to floor.
- Continue curling right to left hand until weight touches bar.
- Lower weight to starting position by reversing movement.

SHOULDERS

Shoulder exercises should also be done in moderation.

S-1 Lying Rear Deltoid Raise

Rear Deltoids

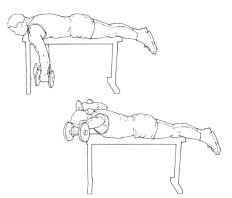

- Lie face down on fairly tall flat bench.
- Hold dumbbells, palms facing, arms hanging down.
- Keep elbows locked, arms straight.
- Raise dumbbells in semicircular motion to shoulder height, in line with ears at top of lift.
- Lower to starting position using same path.
- Inhale up, exhale down.

S-2 Seated Side Lateral Raise

Front and Outer Deltoids

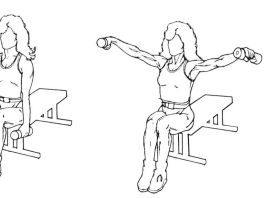

- Sit at end of bench, feet firmly on floor.
- Hold dumbbells, palms in, arms straight down at sides.
- Raise dumbbells in semicircular motion a little above shoulder height.
- Pause, then lower to starting position using same path.
- Keep arms straight.
- Inhale up, exhale down.
- Can also be done standing.

S-3 Lying Floor Low-Pulley Across Body Rear Deltoid Raise

Rear Deltoids

- Lie on left side in front of wall pulley.
- Hold low handle with right hand.
- Lie far enough from pulley to have full range of motion.
- With right arm in front of you, in line with shoulders, raise arm in semicircular motion until vertical above right shoulder.
- Keep arm straight, in line with shoulder.
- Inhale up, exhale down.
- Reverse position and repeat with left arm.

Th-1 Medium-Stance Top-Pad Leg Press on Universal Machine

Upper Thighs

- Adjust seat so upper thighs are nearly vertical to floor in contracted position.
- Hold hand rails under buttocks.
- Place feet on top pads.
- Press out until thighs are straight, knees locked.
- Let weight stack down until it nearly touches remaining plates.
- Keep knees slightly out.
- Inhale down, exhale up.

Th-2 Step-Ups with Barbell

Upper Thighs

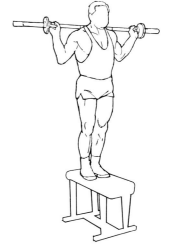

- Place barbell on shoulders.
- Step up with left leg onto flat bench.
- Step up with right leg.
- Step down with left leg first, then right leg.
- Repeat, starting with right leg.
- Inhale down, exhale up.

Th-3 Freehand Side Lunge

Inner Thighs and Hamstrings

- Stand erect with hands on hips.
- Back straight, head up, feet close together.
- Step to side as far as possible with left leg until upper thigh is almost parallel to floor.
- Keep right leg as straight as possible.
- Step back to starting position.
- Inhale out, exhale back.
- Repeat with right leg.

TRICEPS

Tr-1 Standing One-Arm Dumbbell Triceps Curl

Triceps (Do double on left arm)

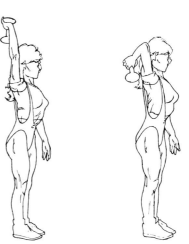

- Hold dumbbell in right hand and raise overhead to arm's length.
- Stand erect, head up, feet 16" apart.
- Keep upper arm close to head.
- Lower dumbbell in semicircular motion behind head until forearm touches biceps.
- Return to starting position.
- Inhale down, exhale up.
- Repeat with left arm.
- Can also be done seated.

Tr-2 Standing Close-Grip Triceps Press-Down on Lat Machine

Outer Triceps

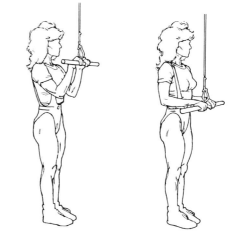

- Stand erect, head up, feet 16" apart, in front of machine.
- Hold bar with hands 8" apart, palms down.
- Bring upper arms to sides and keep them there.
- Start with forearms and biceps touching.
- Press bar down in semicircular motion to arms' length.
- Return to starting position.
- Inhale down, exhale up.
- Can also be done with medium or reverse grip.

Tr-3 Kneeling Head-Supported Close-Grip Triceps Extension on High Pulley
Triceps

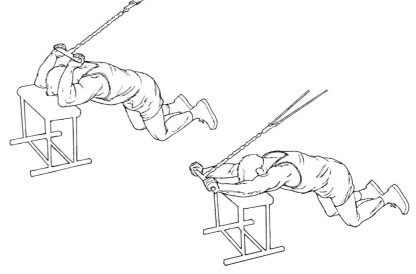

- Place bench sideways in front of high pulley.
- Hold bar with hands 6" apart, palms down.
- Face away from machine and kneel.
- Place head and front of upper arms on bench.
- Keep upper arms close to head.
- Start with forearms and biceps touching.
- Press cable out in semicircular motion until elbows are locked, arms parallel to floor.
- Return cable to starting position.
- Inhale out, exhale back.
- Can also be done with medium grip.

GOLF FLEXIBILITY EXERCISES

Do stretching gently and hold the position, *no bouncing, abrupt forcing or jerking.* Warm-up before stretching with some light jogging-in-place or jumping jacks.

1. *Lace fingers and extend hands upwards; 15 seconds. (Hands, fingers and shoulders).*

2. *Hands and arms behind head, 15 seconds each side.*

3. *With golf club or towel stretch back; 15 seconds. (Shoulders)*

4. *Feet flat on the floor, twist and place hands on the wall; 30 seconds each side. (Hips and obliques)*

5. *Keep the heel of the rear leg on the floor; 30 seconds each leg. (Lower leg)*

6. *Grab foot with opposing hand, pull toward buttocks till stretch is felt and hold; 15 seconds each leg. (Quadriceps)*

7. *Put elbow behind the head and gently pull toward center of back until stretch is felt and hold; 15 seconds each arm. (Shoulders)*

8. *Form a tight ball position and rock back and forth; about 8 to 10 times. (Back)*

9. *Keeping shoulders flat, swing knee to floor till stretch is felt and hold; 15 seconds each leg. (Iliotibial band)*

10. *Sitting upright, place feet together and push gently down on knees until stretch is felt and hold; 30 seconds. (Groin)*

11. *Grab ankle or shin and hold; 30 seconds each leg. (Hamstrings)*

12. *Sit backward toward heels till stretch is felt and hold; 20 seconds (Wrists)*

TEN KEYS TO EXERCISE HABIT FORMATION

It is not too difficult to get *started* exercising; keeping it going is another matter . . . Why? . . . That's a hard question to answer, for invariably, the "exercise dropout" admits to the many benefits he experienced when he was exercising. But for various reasons, some valid and some weak, these people begin to be absent from their activity sessions. The absences become more frequent, then they quit altogether. When this happens "the dropout" usually feels a sense of guilt and failure. Hey, we're all going to fail! Make no mistake about it, no one, NO ONE, accomplishes the task of getting to every exercise session he has planned to make. We all will fail sometimes, *temporarily*—the key is not to fail *permanently*. If you have missed or dropped out for a time, then drop back in. It may be a little discouraging at first to see the ground you have lost but the rewards will come quickly . . . Now to some keys to exercise habit formation.

Key 1 Desire

The single most important factor to any undertaking is the intensity of the desire to take part in that activity, or to achieve the rewards that the activity will produce. Whatever it is, you must want it badly enough to give it some priority and to commit time and effort to complete the activity successfully.

Key 2 Progressive Goal Setting

Having desire to accomplish something without actually knowing where it is you are going leads to aimless wasted effort. Know precisely what it is you are seeking, when you plan to achieve it and then set a goal to do just that. If the goal is far in the future, set intermediate goals to reach on the way. Every journey of a thousand miles begins with the first step.

Key 3 Measurement

There must be a way to measure whether or not you are progressing toward your goal successfully. Keeping records and charts before— during—and after activity is the way in which measurement can provide you with essential feedback to sustain your motivation.

Key 4 Activity Selection

Having decided what it is you want and when you plan to get it, then marshall whatever resources are available to achieve your goal. If it is a better swing or longer shots, select those activities which best lead to that goal, the place, time and facility you need to realize the successful experience of that activity, and acquire the equipment you need to help you continue over a long period of time. Choose something that is FUN if possible. Also try to steer away from anything that will become monotonous. A variety of activities by season may be necessary to avoid this pitfall (monotony) which is a motivation killer.

Key 5 Regularity

A moderate amount of activity over a long period of time (like five days per week) is far more desirable than a lot of activity all at once like on a weekend. Set a schedule that includes exercising or engaging in activity at a regular time each day. That is what a habit is, something done consistently on a regular basis.

Key 6 Frequency and Duration

The benefits of activity are directly related to "how often" and "how long" as well as "how intense." As a rule, the greater effort you expend, the greater will be your physiological reward, as long as the stress is not so great as to harass or overwhelm you.

Key 7 Patience

A person who has been in good physical condition does not lose it in a matter of days as a rule. More common is the "creeping up on you" syndrome which takes several years to take its toll. Though it may have taken years to lose your fitness, you can regain it in a comparatively short period of time, like in several weeks

or months. But don't be impatient and expect that state to return in a few days.

Key 8 Plateauing

The law of diminishing returns will eventually set in during fitness progression. As a person gets nearer a high state of physical fitness he will find the improvements over previous performances less noticeable. This leveling off or plateauing is to be expected and is the point (if at your goal) where you should institute a maintenance program to hold that level.

Key 9 Perseverance from Interruption

Try not to let schedule changes and other activities cause you to miss your workout. Have an alternate plan, rainy day or otherwise. If guests visit, include them. If you are traveling, take your hotel-motel workout routine. When sickness or emergency does interrupt, and it probably will, gradually work back to your regular routine, but don't expect to perform at your top level for a couple of weeks.

Key 10 Cause and Effect

Nothing positive will happen to you in the fitness world to improve your golf unless you cause it to happen. For certain, we know this about fitness: You can't buy it, borrow it or steal it, and once you have it you can't even store it. You must earn it, and you will, if you make it become a habit, a part of your everyday life.

EXERCISES FOR THE LOWER BACK

1. Partial Curl Up

Tilt pelvis to flatten back. Grasp hands behind head supporting neck. Raise upper body until shoulder blades clear the floor. Hold 5 seconds. Gradually increase repetitions.

2. Upper Body Extension With Chin Tuck

Place a pillow under your abdomen. Clasp hands behind you. First pull shoulders back pinching shoulder blades. Secondly, raise head and shoulders off the table with chin tucked during exercise. Hold 5 seconds, relax. Gradually increase repetitions.

3. Four Point Hip Extension

Keep neck in a neutral position as you raise one leg up behind you. Knee is kept slightly flexed. Do not arch your back. Hold 5 seconds. Relax. Gradually increase repetitions.

4. Four Point Upper Back Extension

Keep neck in a neutral position as you raise one arm out in front of you. Keep back flat as you do so. Hold for 5 seconds. Relax. Gradually increase repetitions.

5. Prone Push Up

Push up with your arms lifting upper body. Keep hips in contact with the floor. Gradually increase repetitions.

6. Mad Cat

Hands directly under shoulders, knees under hips. Tuck chin and tighten your abdominals to arch your back. Hold for 5 seconds. Relax. Gradually increase repetitions.

7. Double Knee To Chest

Pull both knees up to chest to feel a comfortable stretch in low back and buttocks. Gradually increase repetitions.

8. Single Knee To Chest

Pull one knee up to chest to feel a comfortable stretch in low back and buttocks. Do the same with the opposite knee. Gradually increase repetitions.

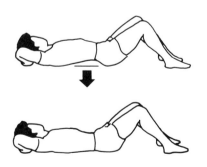

9. Pelvic Tilt

Flatten your back by tightening the muscles of your stomach and buttocks. Gradually increase repetitions.

STANDARD CLUB SPECIFICATIONS

from CPGA Teaching Manual, Chapter 2

STANDARD WOOD SPECIFICATIONS

#	Lengths (inches)	Lofts (degrees)	Lies (degrees)	H.W.* (grams)
1	43	11	55	203.5
3	42	16	57	213.5
4	41.5	19	58	218.5

STANDARD IRON SPECIFICATIONS

#	Lengths (inches)	Lofts (degrees)	Lies (degrees)	H.W.* (grams)
2	39	21	59	242
3	38.5	25	60	249
4	38	29	61	256
5	37.5	33	62	263
6	37	37	63	270
7	36.5	41	64	277
8	36	45	65	284
9	35.5	49	66	291
P	35	53	67	298
S	35	57	67	305

*H.W.   =   Head Weights.

APPENDIX 11–B

YOUR GOLF BALL

by Frank Hannigan*

For the minority who are prepared to swallow the truth, an understanding of the five standards applied to golf balls is essential:

1. Weight—The ball can't be heavier than 1.62 ounces. A ball a little heavier would probably travel a little longer.
2. Size—The ball can't be smaller than 1.68 inches in diameter. A smaller ball might be advantageous—especially when played into the wind. The test used in the USGA lab calls for balls to be tested at 75 degrees Fahrenheit after preparation in an incubator. It's such a sensitive test that a five-degree drop in temperature can make the difference between pass and fail because the ball contracts as it cools.
3. Initial Velocity—The standard is expressed as 250 feet per second, with a 2% tolerance, on the USGA apparatus, which features a metal flywheel as a striker. The tolerance is a scientific message saying that the device might fluctuate by as much as five feet per second. Manufacturers are confident that the performance is much better than the 2% tolerance indicates. Many tend to build right up to 255 feet per second—the standard plus the tolerance. Occasionally a brand will fall over the line—ever so slightly—and is stricken from the USGA list.
4. Spherical Symmetry—This test was introduced in 1983 following development of a

*Adapted from the 1987 U.S. Open Program.

ball with an asymmetrical dimpling arrangement advertised as being a preventer of extreme hooks and slices. A symmetrical ball will do what it's supposed to do—swerve off line when struck improperly. It was on this principle and to introduce the symmetry standard that the USGA prevailed.

5. Overall Distance—Introduced in 1976, this vital test is performed by robot—the celebrated Iron Byron—which hits balls into a fairway outside the USGA Research and Test Center. Iron Byron used a conventional wooden driver with a loft angle of 11 degrees. At the instant of impact this club is travelling 109 miles per hour, about the speed of a long-hitting touring pro. A calibration ball is launched at nine degrees. The clubhead is laminated, not persimmon, because it simply doesn't matter—in terms of distance. About every 4,000 hits a shaft snaps, which makes for a lively few seconds in the Test Center as the clubhead ricochets off a wall or ceiling.

For a ball to flunk the overall distance test, it would have to travel 296.8 yards—carry plus roll—under controlled conditions. This is stated in the specifications as a maximum of 280 yards plus a tolerance of 6%. When the Overall Distance Standard was established in 1976 it was with the understanding that no ball then in existence or in the pipeline of research would fail. Thus, manufacturers were given a kind of innovative tolerance amounting to an improvement on the order of 4%. That gap has just about been closed.

In other words, the USGA now takes the position that golf balls, when struck by a mechanical golfer designed to replicate what happens in real life, are never to go more than a few yards longer than to-day's balls. It's a shame the USGA couldn't have said that 30 or 50 years ago, but it's useful to be able to say it today.

Note that there is a modifier in the US-GA's level of confidence. It applies to drivers. A variety of factors, including dimpling configuration and weight distribution, causes balls to perform differently at different launch angles.

APPENDIX 12–A

GOLF: THE 25% THEORY*

Think of GOLF as being divided into FOUR primary areas:

I. BALL STRIKING—25%
   A. Area Where Golf Teachers Focus
   B. Players Think Most Improvement Takes Place Here
   C. Yet—It Is Only 25% Of The Game
      1. More important factor for beginners and intermediates
      2. Less important factor for accomplished players
II. SHORT GAME—25% / Chipping, Pitching and Putting
   A. Area Where Most Golfers Can Lower Their Scores *First*
   B. Difficult Area To Teach

*Material Provided by PGA Member Jim McLean.

   1. Tends to be boring
   2. Golfers do not understand relationship to scoring
III. MENTAL SIDE—25% / Deal With The Emotions
   A. How Does Player's Game Hold Up Player Pressure?
   B. How Good A Competitor Is The Player? (Heart?)
   C. How Much Desire Does Player Have? (Motivation?)
   This Area Not Often Taught By Teachers / Sports Psychology
IV. MANAGEMENT—25%
   A. Playing the Game / Non-Mechanics
   B. Maximizing Individual Talents Minimizing Individual Weaknesses
   C. Playing Smart Golf
   D. Understanding Limitations

CHARACTERISTICS OF MENTALLY TOUGH COMPETITORS*

by Dr. James Loehr

The world's greatest athletes give testimony to the reality of mental toughness every time they perform. All the great artists of sports have exemplified this special kind of inner strength that goes well beyond the limits of their natural talent and skill. It is the thin line which separates the few who make it from the thousands who don't. The deciding factor is always the same: your INNER STRENGTH makes the ultimate difference (all of these skills can be learned).

Self-Motivated And Self-Directed

He doesn't need to be pushed, shoved or forced from the outside. His direction comes from within. He's involved because he wants to be, because it's his thing, not somebody else's.

Positive But Realistic

He's not a complainer, a criticizer or a faultfinder. He's a builder, not a destroyer. His trademark is a blend of realism and optimism. His eye is always fixed on success, on what can happen, and on what is possible—not on their opposites.

In Control Of His Emotions

Every player or competitor understands all too well the unfortunate performance consequences of poor emotional control. Bad refereeing, stupid mistakes, obnoxious opponents, poor playing conditions, etc., represent powerful triggers of negative emotion. Anger, frustration, and fear must be controlled, or they most certainly will control you. The tough competitor has tamed the lion inside.

Calm And Relaxed Under Fire

He doesn't avoid pressure; he's challenged by it. He's at his best when the pressure is on and the odds against him. Being put to the test is not a threat. It's another opportunity to explore the outer limits of his potential.

Highly Energetic And Ready for Action

He is capable of getting himself pumped up and energized for playing his best, no matter how he feels or how bad or meaningless the situation. He is his own igniter and can, in spite of fatigue, overcome personal problems or bad luck.

*From: *Mental Toughness Training for Sports—Achieving Athletic Excellence*, by Dr. James Loehr: Stephen Green Press, Lexington, MA, 1986.

Determined

His sheer force of will to succeed in what he has started is beyond comprehension for those who do not share the same vision. He is relentless in his pursuit of his goals. Setbacks are taken in stride as he inches his way further forward.

Mentally Alert And Focused

He is capable of long and intensive periods of total concentration. He is capable of tuning in what's important and tuning out what's not, whether there is no pressure or great pressure. In short, he has attentional control.

Doggedly Self-Confident

He displays a nearly unshatterable sense of confidence and belief in himself and in his ability to perform well. He rarely falls victim to his own or others' self-defeating thoughts and ideas. As a consequence, he is not easily intimidated. On the contrary, because of his confident appearance, he often becomes the intimidator.

Fully Responsible

He takes full responsibility for his own actions. There are no excuses. He either did or he didn't. Ultimately, everything begins and ends with him, and he is comfortable with that. He is fully aware that his destiny as an athlete is in his own hands. His future is his own.

A FORMULA FOR SUCCESS*

by Dr. James Loehr

The following four-step formula evolved from interviews and discussions with top performing athletes conducted over a period of nearly ten years.

Step 1: Self-discipline. Everything worthwhile begins at this level. It simply means doing whatever you have to do and making whatever sacrifices are necessary to get the job done the best you know how. It's hard work; it's giving up things you like in order to achieve a higher goal.

Step 2: Self-control. Self-discipline leads directly to self-control. As you discipline yourself, you experience steady increases in self-

*From *Mental Toughness Training for Sports—Achieving Athletic Excellence*, by Dr. James Loehr: Stephen Green Press, Lexington, MA, 1986.

control—control of what you do, what you think, and how you react. Without self-control, being the best you can be as an athlete is nothing more than a fantasy.

Step 3: Self-confidence. Self-control leads directly to self-confidence. What tracks are to a train, self-confidence is to the athlete—without it, he can go nowhere. Self-confidence, that unshatterable belief in yourself, comes from knowing that you are in control.

Step 4: Self-realization. Self-realization is simply becoming the best you can be, the manifestation of your talent and skill as an athlete. It is the fulfillment and the ecstasy of sport. Self-realization follows directly from self-confidence. Once you believe in yourself and feel good about yourself, you are opening doors to your fullest potential.

STRATEGIES FOR GETTING YOUR GAME UNDER CONTROL*

by Chuck Cook, PGA Professional

RULE ONE—DO NOT TRY TO DO WHAT YOU CANNOT DO

You see beginning players trying to use clubs they can't use, intermediate players trying to play shots they can't hit and advanced players playing to targets that are totally unreasonable.

For instance, in research we've conducted, we've found that in order to hit a medium-size green half the time from a perfect lie from 150 yards out, your handicap must be less than 10. Yet, too many club players play shots from this far out (or farther) without giving any regard to the consequences of missing the green—what kind of trouble they might be in and how difficult the recovery shot might be.

In other testing, we've found that unless you can create clubhead speed of at least 85 miles per hour, you can hit a three-wood farther in the air than a driver. Yet most players feel a compulsion to hit a driver whenever possible.

For advanced players, we've found that it's almost as difficult to make a putt just outside of 12 feet as it is to make one of almost 40 feet. Therefore, if you are an advanced player, check yourself to find out how many putts you have inside 12 feet. You should not expect to hole a lot of putts if you don't have a lot of chances inside that distance. We often hear good players say, "I'm hitting a lot of greens, but I can't

*Adapted from "Do Not Try What You Cannot Do," *The Golf Club Magazine.*

putt." Quite often the problem is not with the putting. As Ben Hogan once said, "Hit it closer."

At the Academy, we have established general guidelines that say a beginner is a player whose handicap is higher than 24, an intermediate player is 12 to 24 and an advanced player is one with a handicap under 12. Of course, there are individual ability levels within those ranges.

Beginning players (handicap over 24) should apply Rule One by learning to hit a driving club (normally a five-wood) and a playing club (normally a five-iron) and learning a short-game system (usually involving a seven-iron, sand wedge and putter). As you advance, you can add clubs to all three areas. However, advancement is based on the ability to hit more difficult clubs on the range before you take them to the course. In other words, make your clubs earn their way to the course.

Intermediate players (handicap 12–24) should learn one basic shot, then use it all the way around the course. Don't try any fancy stuff—hooks and slices, high and low shots. Just become consistent with one swing and one shot. As your skills improve, you can add shots (proven in practice) to your inventory.

Advanced players (handicap 12 & under) must learn the fundamentals of shotmaking, the ability to hit shots of different shapes and trajectories, the knowledge that will let them play from all situations. My system for them then becomes, "Practice the shots you don't like and play with the shots you do like."

Play to Your Strengths

In keeping with Rule One, play to your strengths whenever you can. If you can't, then be judicious about pitting yourself against the hole's strengths. The order of priorities are:

1. Player's strength versus hole's weakness

As you plan your round, look for the holes where you should be most aggressive. For instance, beginning players should look for holes (and/or courses) that are relatively trouble-free with forced carries. Intermediate players should look for holes (and/or courses) that have big target areas with several options for playing the hole. Advanced players should look for holes (and/or courses) that favor their "natural" shots.

2. Player's strength versus hole's strength

Whenever possible, play with your natural ball flight. Try to fit your shot to the hole. If you can't do that, these holes (and/or courses) should be approached with caution and should be played for your par (with your handicap).

3. Player's weakness versus hole's weakness

There are times when a player has to play away from what is most comfortable for him. (And that's really what golf is all about.) For instance, a beginner has to carry a pond, or an advanced player has to play away from his natural shot or aim at trouble. Playing away from your natural shot is better than aiming at trouble. When encountering this situation, you should be looking for the best place to miss the shot. The beginning player trying to carry water might look for the shortest carry. The intermediate player might look to avoid bunkers or the advanced player might look to the long side of the green.

4. Player's weakness versus hole's strength

This is a situation to be avoided . . . always. It almost always invites disaster. There is no reason ever to encounter this matchup.

RULE TWO—DO NOT AIM WHERE A STRAIGHT SHOT WILL HURT YOU

By testing, we've found that substantially more penalty shots are incurred from poor starting direction than from curve, by a ratio of almost 12 to 1. (For our testing, we assumed that a 10-yard curve had to be allowed. Therefore, any ball hit into a penalty situation with more curve than that was attributed to curve. With any less curve than that, the problem was starting direction.) Thus, aiming at or near trouble is virtually assuring that you will get there.

If you are a beginning player, then play to a spot where you can putt it. Most beginning players have an abnormal amount of mishits (tops, fats, toed shots, etc.) that will leave the ball on the ground. Therefore, playing toward "run ways" of the hole is the way to avoid disaster.

Intermediate players should use the "scattergun" approach, assuming that most of them play with shots that scatter as opposed to shots that hit the target with rifle-like precision. Pick the biggest target for each shot and shade it to the side away from the most trouble.

For advanced players, the task is simple. Aim away from trouble and curve the ball toward trouble.

Strategies To Fit The Shots

There are too many specific strategies for each course and for each hole to cover here. But following are my general recommendations for shots you will encounter:

For the tee shot—Your strategy for this important shot is to be less aggressive off the tee than for the other shots. Your rule of thumb should be that the closer to the hole you are, the more aggressive you should be. On the tee shot, the objective is to put the ball in position to use the easier shots. We have our players test themselves to identify the longest club they can hit and reasonably expect to hit the fairway half the time. For most players, this is rarely more than a three-wood.

For the advancement shot—An advancement shot is one that cannot reach the green after the tee shot. The strategy here is to make your next shot as easy as possible. So many players will use the longest wood in the bag without any regard for how hard the club is to hit or what will happen if it is not hit well. We test players to determine the longest club they can hit from the fairway onto the fairway at least half the time. For most players, this is rarely more than a four- or five-wood.

For the target shot—A target shot is one with which you can expect to hit the green. The key word here is expect. Everyone has a different zone or distance from which that occurs. A beginning player's target zone might be 50 yards from the green and in. The zone for most intermediate players extends only to about 100 to 125 yards, and an advanced player's target zone rarely exceeds 150 to 175 yards from the green. What that means is that from whatever distance you can expect to hit the green at least half the time, you are qualified to play a target shot rather than another advancement shot. That qualification zone is increased by either of two factors—improved target play or an accomplished short game. If you have a good short game, you can attempt more target shots from your given distance and beyond. Just be honest with yourself in making this assessment.

For the partial shots—These are all the less-than-full shots around the green, including putts, chips, pitches and bunker shots. Your priorities on shots from off the green should be, in order, on first, close second, hole out third. On the green, the closer to the hole you are, the more aggressive you should be, while the farther away you are, the more cautious you should be. This doesn't necessarily mean you

should "charge" the short putts and "lag" the long putts, rather, you should establish a mental expectancy of success on short putts and a judgmental satisfaction on long putts laid close enough to two-putt. Too often, players react in the opposite manner—they are timid on short putts and too bold on long putts.

For the trouble shots—These are shots that crop up when you have placed your ball where you don't want it. The philosophy here is, "Don't follow a bad shot with a bad decision." In other words, first put the ball back in play, gambling only when you are reasonably sure of success and the gamble will save at least half a shot. If you are satisfied that the shot you are about to attempt can net you a score of four and not worse than a five, go for it. If a miss will cost you a six or worse, get the ball into play and proceed from there.

To achieve your best results, you should always follow the same procedure:

Plan your round—Decide which holes best suit your game and make a mental note to be aggressive on those holes, knowing that your normal tendencies will be in your favor. Also note which holes do not suit your game and remind yourself to proceed with caution here. Visualize and plan where to aim on all tee shots. Most of you have done this through trial and error, because you play the same course all the time. But if you are playing a course that is not familiar to you, here are a couple of thoughts that will help. First, identify the trouble, which should be obvious enough if you take the time to look. Second, locate the yardage markers so you have a feel for the distance to the green on each hole.

Warm up—When possible, you should schedule a warm-up session after arriving at the course. This session should satisfy three goals:

1. Loosen the muscles to enhance play and discourage injury.
2. Determine which swings are available that day.
3. Identify ball-flight tendencies that might change your planning.

Work your plan—Stay with your plan, even if things don't work out exactly as you expected. If you have problems, don't try to "catch up" or push your game beyond your capabilities. The purpose of planning is to prepare for the best way to shoot a low score. Changing the plan under the heat of play can only mean taking a route that you decided beforehand was not the best way. If you do that, a couple of lost strokes can balloon to a dozen or more.

To get in the proper frame of mind, follow this procedure:

1. Select a swing

No one feels the same from day to day for any number of reasons—health (sick, hung over), diet (had lots of salt the night before and hands feel puffy), recent history (haven't been playing a lot or have been playing a lot) and so forth. Consequently, to expect the body to achieve the same degree of efficiency every day is unrealistic. Some days your swing feels stiff and choppy. The nice thing about playing golf is that you have 14 "tools" to help you. It's just that a tool that fits the freewheeling, loose days needs to be changed for one that fits the tight, stiff days. However, your target can be reached both days. So, the first consideration is to select a swing that can be used effectively given the conditions of your body.

2. Select a target

Once you have selected a swing, you'll know which targets are available. On days when your swing feels great, more options are available. On the days when you feel out of sorts, your targets are limited.

3. Select a club

The next step in the process is choosing the right tool. That's easy—Comfortable Swing + Comfortable Target = Proper Club Selection.

4. Drive a familiar road

The more often you do something, the more familiar it becomes. The more familiar you are with something, the more comfortable you feel. The first time you drive down a dark, winding road at night, your driving is cautious, filled with quick stops and starts.

After taking the same road for several nights, you can almost drive it subconsciously. Your learning to hit golf shots should follow the same pattern. Develop a consistent pre-shot approach and use it in practice and on the course.

By doing this, you soon will be "driving that familiar road" to better shots and lower scores.

THE WIREN—COOP CHARTING SYSTEM

The top card shows how a golfer might jot down mental or mechanical miscues during a round or immediately after. The bottom card shows a highly detailed profile of the same round, exclusively in terms of mechanics. Golfers need not keep track of every aspect of play, as is done here, to benefit from such an appraisal. Symbols for the charting system are listed in the box at right. Putts are charted with the same symbols. The first putt is described in the upper left corner of the "putts" box. Total putts are recorded in the lower right corner. On one-putt holes, distance in feet is noted in the lower left corner. Thus, on the second hole, Tom bogeyed by driving straight, pushing his second shot short, just missing the green in three and taking two putts for a 5.

From *The New Golf Mind* by Gary Wiren and Dick Coop, Simon & Schuster, NY, 1978.

TOM	5	5	3	7	4	5	4	3	4	40
HOLE	1	2	3	4	5	6	7	8	9	OUT
BLUE	400	415	340	490	184	485	416	166	404	3300
MEN'S PAR	4	4	4	5	3	5	4	3	4	36

DATE _____ SCORER _____

4	4	6	4	5	4	5	4	5	41	40	81
HOLE	10	11	12	13	14	15	16	17	18	IN	OUT	TOTAL
BLUE	375	200	470	330	495	350	355	180	500	3255	3300	6555
MEN'S PAR	4	3	4	4	5	4	4	3	5	36	36	72

ATTEST _____

HOLE	1	2	3	4	5	6	7	8	9	OUT
BLUE	400	415	340	490	184	485	416	166	404	3300
MEN'S PAR	4	4	4	5	3	5	4	3	4	36
TOM	5	5	3	7	4	5	4	3	4	40
DRIVE										
2ND SHOT										
3RD SHOT										
PUTTS										

HOLE	10	11	12	13	14	15	16	17	18	IN	OUT	TOTAL
BLUE	375	200	470	330	495	350	355	180	500	3255	3300	6555
MEN'S PAR	4	3	4	4	5	4	4	3	5	36	36	72
	4	4	6	4	5	4	5	4	5	41	40	81
DRIVE												
2ND SHOT												
3RD SHOT												
PUTTS												

Symbols

|	Straight shot	T	Short
\	Pull	↑	Long
/	Push	s	Sand
⟍	Hook	w	Water
⟋	Slice	o	Out-of-bounds

425

STROKE-SAVER SYSTEM FOR COURSE MANAGEMENT

1. I will use enough club to comfortably get to the flag.
2. I will use a routine for every shot and play in pictures.
3. I will not leave a makeable putt short.
4. Into the wind, uphill to an elevated green, I will use a more straight-bladed club; with the opposite conditions, a more lofted club.
5. I will not hit a shot with a negative thought in my mind.
6. I will never swing with more effort than that needed to produce my E.S.S. (effective swing speed).

FIRST RULES OF GOLF—1744

1. You must tee your ball within one club's length of hole.
2. Your tee must be on the ground.
3. You are not to change the ball you strike off the tee.
4. You are not to remove Stones, Bones or any Break Club, for sake of playing your ball, except upon the Fair Green and that only within a club's length of your ball.
5. If your Ball come among watter or any wattery filth, you are at liberty to take out your Ball and, bringing it behind the hazard and teeing it, you may play it with any club and allow your Adversary a Stroke, for so getting out your ball.
6. If your balls be found anywhere touching one another you are to lift the first ball, till you play the last.
7. At Holing, you are to play your Ball honestly for the Hole, and not play upon your Adversary's Ball, not lying in your way to the Hole.
8. If you should lose your Ball, by its being taken up, or any other way you are to go back to the Spot, where you struck last, and drop another Ball, and allow your adversary a stroke for the misfortune.
9. No man at Holing his Ball is to be allowed, to mark his way to the Hole with his club or anything else.
10. If a Ball be stopp'd by any person, Horse, Dog or anything else, the Ball so stopp'd must be played where it lyes.
11. If you draw your Club, in order to Strike and proceed so far in the Stroke, as to be bringing down your Club: If then your Club shall break, in any way, it is to be Accounted a Stroke.
12. He whose Ball lyes farthest from the Hole is obliged to play first.
13. Neither Trench, Ditch or Dyke, made for the presentation of the Links, nor the Scholar's Holes or the Soldier's Lines, Shall be accounted a Hazard. But the ball is to be taken out and tee'd and play'd with any iron club.

(No penalties for violations were contained in the 13 original rules. They were for match, not medal, play.)

COMPARATIVE SCORE RECORD

Here is a useful tool for the golfer who likes detail.

My home course rating is _____. My average score for the year at my home course was _____. For all courses _____.

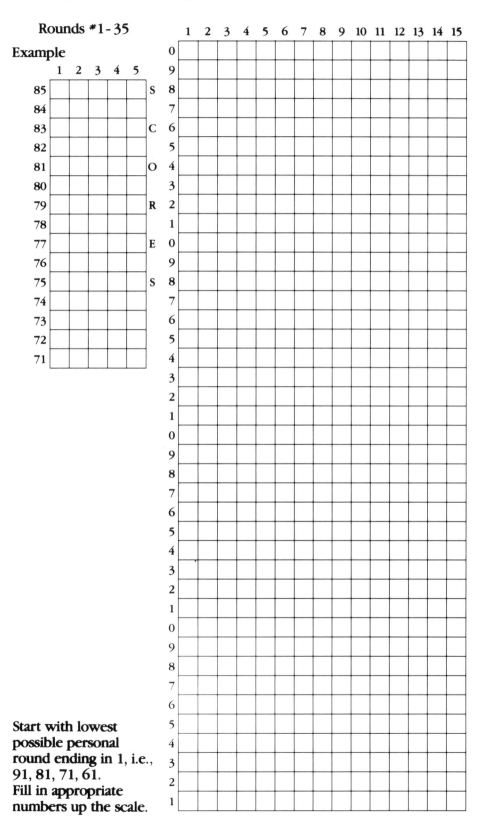

Rounds #1-35

Example

	1	2	3	4	5	
85						S
84						
83						C
82						
81						O
80						
79						R
78						
77						E
76						
75						S
74						
73						
72						
71						

Start with lowest possible personal round ending in 1, i.e., 91, 81, 71, 61. Fill in appropriate numbers up the scale.

Rounds #36–70—Use different color. If over
70 rounds, use third or fourth color if necessary.

16 17 18 19 20 21 22 23 24 25 26 27 28 29 30 31 32 33 34 35

Take this opportunity to plot your scores so
you can have a visual picture of your progress.
Place a dot recording your round on the appropriate score line and connect the dots to make
a graph.

Put a circle around any score shot at a facility
other than your home course, and write in the
course rating.

For 9-hole rounds take number of strokes
over par, double it, and add that to the 18-hole
par and enter the figure.

RINGER SCORE RECORD

A Ringer Score is your best gross figure* for each hole on the course, considering every round you shoot. It's an enjoyable statistic to keep—particularly if you play at one course over a long period of time.

One of the all-time great Ringer Scores was recorded by the late Freddie McLeod, 1908 U.S. Open Champion. Here is his Ringer over a period of 59 years at Columbia Country Club, Chevy Chase, Md., where he served as professional for that period of time.

Fred McLeod's Ringer Score

Hole	1	2	3	4	5	6	7	8	9	Out
Score	2	2	2	2	3	3	2	2	3	21
Yards	338	304	338	170	524	437	322	175	401	3009
Par	4	4	4	3	5	4	4	3	4	35

	10	11	12	13	14	15	16	17	18	In
Score	2	3	2	1	2	2	1	2	3	18
Yards	416	413	511	158	359	358	126	234	395	2970
Par	4	4	5	3	4	4	3	3	4	34

18 Hole Total 39
Par 69

May we suggest for more enjoyment that you keep an annual Ringer Score Record at your home and compare it from one year to the next, as well as an all-time best Ringer Score record. It will make golf more fun.

*A Net Ringer Score with your handicap may also be kept.

GOLF IS FOR FUN

by Gary Wiren, Ph.D.

"Golf is a game and as such is meant to be enjoyed." That is the opening line of my first golf instruction book, and no truer words about this game have ever been spoken. To tell the truth, we all would like to play better. If we only have fun when we play well, we're going to enjoy golf about 10% of the time. We should be having a good time with golf all of the time and, if we're not, we should find out why and do something about it.

Why do you play golf?

☐ Enjoy it   ☐ Competition
☐ To get exercise   ☐ Reduce stress &
☐ The challenge   tension
☐ Social contacts   ☐ Be with spouse/
☐ Business relations   family
☐ Being out-of-doors   ☐ To make money

How could you enjoy it more?

1. Know basically why you play and see that your objective is met.
2. Have a realistic appraisal of the level of your game based on how much you've practiced, how you've been playing, the course and the competition.
3. Find some fun people to play with.
4. Learn to appreciate the surroundings, the people, and the game itself and how people react to it.
5. Read more about the game's history to help you appreciate what we have today.
6. Remember that no one has or will master the game. No matter how much you improve, the game will always humble you on occasion. Accept it, and remember—there's always a tomorrow for golfers.
7. Get a good teacher; set a goal; practice; and play better golf.
8. Try to improve, but after a bad day you may wish to use the philosophical approach:

"If the pleasure of golf is in striking a ball and seven a hole you do, I who had fourteen in all have had twice as much fun as you."—*Sutphen Van Tassel*

U.S. OPEN WINNERS QUIZ

You can have fun with golf not only when playing it, but also when discussing it. Use the following clues to discover the names of former U.S. Open champions. Some are clues for the given name, some for the family name.

1. Wine for three
   _____

2. Hors d'oeuvres
   _____

3. Protective accoutrement
   _____

4. December 25th
   _____

5. Poet and Admiral
   _____

6. Card cheat
   _____

7. "Et tu Brute"
   _____

8. Sheriff's offspring
   _____

9. scotch with a small "s"
   _____

10. "Keep up with the _____."
    _____

11. Kindergarten snacking delight
    _____

12. Blue-yellow
    _____

13. Admiral Byrd
    _____

14. Personality trait
    _____

15. Ghostly figure
    _____

16. Lightning
    _____

17. City official
    _____

18. Median
    _____

19. Size comparison
    _____

20. "The conquering hero"
    _____

21. "Nilly"—"Andy"
    _____

22. Noisy bird
    _____

23. Famous W.C. Fields endearment
    _____

24. Talking mule
    _____

25. Principle of physics
    _____

26. A cigarette and competitor
    _____

27. And recreation department
    _____

28. Sleuth's sidekick
    _____

Adapted from original material by Dick Haskell, Massachusetts Golf Association.

29. Large timepiece

30. Farm building

31. They give you a sunburn

32. Grain for bread

USGA WOMEN'S OPEN WINNERS QUIZ

1. Little Women

2. Famous General (WWII)

3. Arnold

4. Alligator

5. Cake mix (last name)

6. Christmas decoration

7. Waltzing Matilda

8. Makes bread

9. Christmas song

10. Disney World character

11. A Vanderbilt

12. American flag

13. Downed the Titanic

14. Infant

15. Chicago gangster

Answers
U.S. Open Winners Quiz

1. Lee *Trevino*
2. Jerry *Pate*
3. Tommy *Armour*
4. Jack *Nicklaus* (St.)
5. Byron or Larry *Nelson*
6. Arnold *Palmer*
7. *Julius* Boros
8. *Lawson* Little
9. Walter *Hagen* (Haig & Haig)
10. Bobby *Jones* (Joneses)
11. Lou *Graham* (cracker)
12. Hubert *Green*
13. Andy *North* (Pole)
14. Orville *Moody*
15. Billy *Casper* (the ghost)
16. Tommy *Bolt*
17. Dick *Mayer*
18. Cary *Middle*coff
19. Gene *Littler*
20. *Hale* Irwin (hail)
21. *Willie Anderson*
22. *Jay* Hebert
23. *Chick* Evans ("chickadee")
24. *Francis* Ouimet
25. Ken *Venturi*
26. Gary *Player*
27. Sam *Parks*
28. Tom *Watson* (Holmes)
29. *Ben* Hogan (Big)
30. Jim *Barnes*
31. *Ray* Floyd (rays) or Ted *Ray*
32. Johnny *Miller*

Answers
USGA Women's Open Winners Quiz

1. Amy *Alcott*
2. Pat *Bradley*
3. Sandra *Palmer*
4. Catherine *La Coste*
5. Fay *Crocker*
6. *Hollis* Stacy
7. Jan *Stephenson*
8. Kathy *Baker*
9. *Carol* Mann
10. *Mickey* Wright
11. Kathy *Cornelius*
12. *Betsy* Rawls
13. Patty *Berg*
14. *"Babe"* Zaharias
15. Donna *Caponi*

PUTTING IT IN PERSPECTIVE

Golfers with a high degree of skill and success can develop an overblown sense of their own importance.

Helping put a golfer's achievements in perspective is this essay written in 1978 by Patrick Caton, *10 years of age*, from Bermuda.

"Dimples"

I was feeling rather embarrassed. Here I was, an adventurous golf ball sitting in a shop window with everyone staring at me. I would rather be knocked about a golf course than sit here doing nothing.

It was nearing my third day in the shop window when I was bought. I thought I would finally see a golf course. The buyer took me to his house and put me in a golf bag. I found another golf ball who told me that there was a golf tournament the next day. I then fell into contented sleep thinking that at last I would see a golf course.

At the tournament I was taken out of the bag and teed off with a mighty "Whack." I sailed down the fairway and landed with a thump on the grass. My owner came up and sailed me away again and again.

After the first few holes I was feeling sore. I was dirty and exhausted from those mighty "Whacks and Thumps." I wanted to rest but my owner wouldn't allow me. I just had to score hole after hole. As I neared the eighteenth hole, I felt that I was going to fall apart. I was not used to this rough treatment. With a last "Whack"—I landed within two inches from a ten-foot putt. My owner putted me into the hole and took me out again. The spectators cheered wildly, whistled and stomped their feet. When I looked around and saw this, I muttered slowly to myself, "I do all the work and he gets all the credit."

Editor's Note: So, if any of us happens to temporarily master the game, remember—"Nothing is ever accomplished alone." Enjoy your golf.

INDEX